Intimate Commerce

INTIMATE COMMERCE

*Exchange, Gender, and Subjectivity
in Greek Tragedy*

VICTORIA WOHL

UNIVERSITY OF TEXAS PRESS

AUSTIN

Library of Congress Cataloging-in-Publication Data

Wohl, Victoria, 1966–
Intimate commerce : exchange, gender, and subjectivity in Greek
tragedy / by Victoria Wohl.
p.   cm.
Includes bibliographical references and index.
ISBN 978-0-292-79114-5
— ISBN 0-292-79114-3 (pbk. : alk. paper)
1. Greek drama (Tragedy)—History and criticism.   2. Femininity
(Psychology) in literature.   3. Man-woman relationships in
literature.   4. Literature and society—Greece.   5. Women and
literature—Greece.   6. Ceremonial exchange—Greece.
7. Subjectivity in literature.   8. Sex role in literature.   9. Women
in literature.   10. Sophocles. Trachiniae.   11. Aeschylus.
Agamemnon.   12. Euripides.   I. Title.
PA3136.W64   1998
882'.0109352042—dc21   97-9872

For my parents

CONTENTS

CONTENTS

ACKNOWLEDGMENTS

In a book so much about gifts and debts, I would like to begin by expressing my gratitude to those who have helped in its completion. I am particularly indebted to my dissertation advisors, Leslie Kurke and Mark Griffith. The project first took shape under the guidance of Leslie Kurke: she started me thinking about exchange and gender, and encouraged me to pursue these topics. Throughout the process, she has been generous with her ideas; her criticism has been invaluable, and her own scholarship, with its blend of complexity and clarity, has been a standard to which I have aspired. Mark Griffith has exemplified *kharis*, the grace of a favor freely given: his comments on countless drafts of the manuscript have been both perceptive and prolific, and have left their clear imprint upon the final version; his unstinting generosity with his time and advice has left a mark less visible, but no less important. Further thanks are due to those who have read the manuscript along the way: Daniel Melia provided a sympathetic nonclassical perspective; audiences at the University of California–Berkeley, University of Oregon, University of California–Los Angeles, and University of Texas–Austin heard various parts presented as talks and offered useful criticism. Conversations with Roger Travis and other members of the object-relations seminar at Berkeley (led by Janet Adelman and Nancy Chodorow) clarified my understanding of psychoanalytic theory and its application to literature. Ali Hossaini at The University of Texas Press has been both encouraging and efficient, and comments from the Press's readers and the copyeditor, Sherry Wert, were immensely helpful in the final revisions. Much of the book was written with financial assistance from the Andrew W. Mellon Fellowship in the Humanities, the Chancellor's Fellowship at the University of California–Berkeley, and a Faculty Research Grant from The University of Texas–San Antonio. Finally, I owe an inexpressible debt of gratitude to my family for their unflagging interest and support, and to Erik Gunderson, who has been the sine qua non of this project.

✖

INTRODUCTION

Exchange, Gender, and Subjectivity

✖

*In human society, it is the men who
exchange the women, and not vice versa.*

— CLAUDE LÉVI-STRAUSS, STRUCTURAL ANTHROPOLOGY

THE TRAGIC EXCHANGE

In the second choral ode of Sophocles' *Trachiniae*, the chorus sings of the matched contest between the hero Heracles and the river-god Achelous for the hand of the princess Deianira. The two heroes wrestle in the dust, the language of the ode vividly evoking the male world of athletic contests and war. Meanwhile, Deianira, the prize for which they fight, "sat on a distant hill, waiting for the man who would be her husband. . . . And suddenly she is gone from her mother, like a calf abandoned" (*Trachiniae* 523–30).

This scene is paradigmatic of a structure termed by anthropologists "the exchange of women." In the broadest sense, the term refers to the movement of a woman from one man to another as a bride, a gift, or, as here, a prize. Whether the exchange is amicable (as in a marriage) or hostile (as in this contest), the transfer of a woman between two men constitutes the social world, generating bonds between the men and defining their social identities. So, in this scene, the competition for Deianira brings the two heroes together in a wrestling match so intimate as to be almost erotic. Their relation of antagonistic equality gives way to a relation of domination as Heracles emerges victorious over Achelous. The woman is the suture between the two men. The competition over this woman also defines the men as social subjects: as heroes and mighty competitors, as winner and loser, as subjects of action. At the same time, it positions the woman, Deianira, as the object of their action, silently awaiting its outcome.[1] This contest illustrates with particular clarity the dynamic that forms the focus of this book: a woman is passed as an object between men, her movement generating and defining an entire social order.

Greek tragedy dramatizes the exchange of women with almost obsessive regularity: imported as brides, captured as war-booty, given as gifts, won in competitions, stolen through rape, hoarded as treasures, bequeathed as inheritances, even offered as sacrifices to the gods, women become objects of a transaction that provides a focal point for tragedy's exploration of social and economic relations, gender, and the nature of the self. Sometimes tragedy seems to present the exchange of women as a socially constructive system; more often than not, however, something goes wrong: the woman refuses to go from one man to another, or goes with vociferous complaint, or tries to exchange others rather than be exchanged herself. The result of these failed transfers is catastrophe: the relationships between men that should be cemented are instead sundered; the men who should be declared virile and heroic subjects are emasculated and eviscerated; the social order that should be instituted is more often left in ruins. By the end of each play this havoc is contained; the male self and his world are rebuilt and resecured, but upon a foundation that has been shown to be essentially unstable.

The tragic exchange of women, I shall argue, calls into question the social world it calls into being. As a generative structure, the exchange reveals tragedy in the process of constructing its normative social hierarchies, gender relations, and subjects. But the tragic exchange is, by nature, a system ever in crisis and always prone to failure, and it opens to interrogation the world and subjects it structures, exposing their fault lines, constitutive exclusions, and foreclosed alternatives. The exchange of women allows tragedy to expose the genealogy of its own social world, in order not only to justify and reinaugurate that world, but also to examine and reimagine it, and to reproduce it precisely as a world open to and under debate.

This commerce in women lies at the dense intersection between the material and the psychological, and extends simultaneously in both directions. On the one hand, exchanging women is a marked example of a more general system of gift exchange; as such it mediates between different economic levels, between competition and cooperation, and between elitism and egalitarianism, all mediations central to fifth-century Athens as it debates the nature and extent of its democracy. On the other hand, this transaction opens insistently onto questions of subjectivity. The exchange is built around a distinction between the male giver and the female gift, but this distinction collapses once the woman refuses her role as object. In dramatizing the woman's attempt to position herself as a subject, tragedy reveals the ways in which a subject is constructed, the material factors by which it is determined, the social hierarchies within which it is articulated, the relation of self to other and to ideology. The study of the tragic exchange, then, will enter into debates on both Athenian economic and social formations and the ancient conception of the gendered self.

This book examines three tragedies structured around exchanges of women: Sophocles' *Trachiniae*, Aeschylus's *Agamemnon*, and Euripides' *Alcestis*. There are, to be sure, other tragedies and even other genres in which the movement of women between men features prominently and to which the approach I propose here could be fruitfully applied. But since I believe that the individual transactions can only be understood within the context of their plays and, conversely, that they can illuminate the entire play, I here limit myself to these three dramas rather than undertake a broad survey. Even so, I do not pretend to exhaust these three plays, aiming to supplement rather than to supplant the excellent work already done on them.

In *Trachiniae*, Deianira, won by Heracles in the contest against Achelous, is driven to desperate measures by Heracles' introduction into the house of the slave-girl Iole, his war-booty and concubine. Having been an object of exchange in her past, Deianira tries to position herself as its subject: in return for the "gift" of Iole, she gives Heracles a robe smeared with what she thinks is a love charm. But the love charm is in fact poison, and in Heracles' agonizing demise we see the fatal effects of a woman's gifts. At the same time, unable to define herself successfully in male terms (as a gift-giver, as a hero, as an aristocrat), Deianira is found, in a central scene of the play, seeking other modes of subject-formation, and constructing herself as a subject by imagining a subjectivity for the silent and passive Iole, a subjectivity not compromised, as hers had been, by misogynist stereotypes. This fantasy of a free female subject is harshly foreclosed with Deianira's death (in a suicide that both transgresses and resecures gender categories); nonetheless, the possibility of a female subject, once raised, refuses to evaporate, and it returns to interrupt the play's final scene, in which a dying Heracles bequeaths his authority and property to his son along with his concubine Iole.

Two exchanges, the theft of Helen and the sacrifice of Iphigeneia, lie behind Aeschylus's *Agamemnon*. A war is fought for Helen, but was this obscure object worth the price: the life of Iphigeneia, sacrificed by her father so that the ships might sail; the lives of countless Greek soldiers; the life, ultimately, of the king Agamemnon, who returns from Troy only to be murdered by his adulterous wife Clytemnestra, and with him his prize of war, Cassandra? The trade in women reaps no benefits in this play, but exacts a heavy toll: the social bonds that should be created dissolve in impious war; the men who should be declared subjects are instead turned into objects, as Greek soldiers return as dust in urns and Agamemnon himself is reduced to a corpse. The agent of this destruction is Clytemnestra, who avenges the female victims of exchange, her daughter Iphigeneia and her sister Helen. But whereas Clytemnestra punishes the violence wrought over women, Cassandra offers forgiveness; and while Clytemnestra's overdetermined transgressions justify the exchange's gender hierarchy, Cassandra's forgiveness redeems the male subject and repairs the psychic damage that has been shown to be the true return on a traffic in women.

Euripides' *Alcestis* dramatizes a literal exchange: Alcestis offers to die in the place of her husband Admetus, graciously giving herself to buy him life. But the life he receives is not worth living, as he discovers, for though Alcestis's self-sacrifice wins her praise and fame, it brands Admetus as a coward. Even in the supreme act of uxorial devotion, a woman would seem to be a dangerous gift-giver, as Admetus loses not only his reputation, but also his masculinity and legitimacy. These losses are recouped by his relationship with Heracles, a relation sealed in the last scene of the play by the exchange of a mysterious woman who turns out to be Alcestis herself, returned from the dead. No longer the brave and heroic subject of her own fate, Alcestis is returned as a gift, silent and veiled. This final episode would seem to reaffirm the objectification and circulation of women as the foundation of male social relations, but Alcestis's silence, her reduction to a deathlike state, reminds us of the violence behind this economics and injects a profound sense of discomfort into this ostensibly happy reunion.

The position of women in classical Athens was severely circumscribed, as a number of recent studies have detailed.[2] Women were not citizens in the democracy (although citizenship passed through them to their sons), and they had no political rights. They lived in a state of life-long minority, always subject to a male *kurios* ("owner," "lord," or "guardian"), first their father, then their husband; they could own little if any property and could make few economic decisions independent of this male guardian. In a city in which glory and power were won and wielded only in the public arena—the marketplace, assembly, law-courts, and battlefield—women were relegated to the domestic space of the *oikos*, the house (indeed, to the women's quarters of the house), and upper-class women, at least, were rarely seen or mentioned by men to whom they were not related. Although the extent to which these bare facts represent the lived experience of Athenian women is much debated (and this is a debate into which I cannot enter here),[3] one might imagine that in a culture in which women had only limited rights to themselves, in which barely pubescent girls were given in marriage (one Greek term for marriage is *ekdosis*, a "giving away") from father-guardian to husband-guardian, the contrast in exchange between active men and passive women would be particularly stark.[4]

Tragedy's representation of the circulation of women reflects this state of affairs and also, without doubt, reproduces it: it reaffirms the integrity and mastery of the male givers in contrast to the object status of the female gift; it valorizes the necessary exclusion of women from positions of social dominance by dramatizing the catastrophe that results when they attain such positions; it dismantles any foundations upon which a valid female subject or an equal relation between male and female could be raised. But even as it reproduces a familiar and unequal gender organization, in the process of this very reproduction it exposes its constructed, arbitrary, and contingent nature. This is key, for what is shown to be constructed is open to reconstruction, rearticulation, reimagination. Tragedy thus encourages us to ask after the genesis and history of such concepts as woman, gender difference, male domination, the individual subject, social and economic hierarchy, the state. Not only is this anti-essentialism fundamental to feminist critique, but it is also, I believe, one of the boons offered us by the study of an alien culture, as ancient

Athens in many ways is. In exposing the historical contingency and ideological investment of another culture's social arrangements, we may come
to question the necessity, inevitability, or even desirability of our own.

REAFFIRMATION, RESISTANCE, NEGOTIATION

Taking the exchange of women as a point of entry into a culture is hardly
a new approach. The topic was opened by Lévi-Strauss, for whom the
circulation of women in marriage is the "elementary structure of kinship."[5] As the practical instantiation of the incest taboo, the trading
of women comprises the basic social cement, creating lasting affinities
between different men, families, and communities. Lévi-Strauss built a
(male) society upon this trade; Freud had laid the same foundation for
the (male) subject. The Oedipal complex, the most critical moment in
male psychological development (according to the Freudian model), is in
essence an exchange of women: the little boy renounces his desire for his
mother, "giving" her to his father; in compensation he receives paternal
approval and the tacit promise of a woman of his own. For Freud and
Lévi-Strauss, then, the exchange of women is the foundation for an entire
social and subjective order.

Given the times in which they wrote and their individual projects, it is
no surprise that these founding fathers should have viewed this commerce in a positive light, emphasizing the benefits of the structure for a
society that is always for them (explicitly or implicitly) male-dominated
and male-oriented. But, more recently, feminist theorists have been quick
to point out how these boons for the male givers are won at the expense
of the female gift. Gayle Rubin, in her ground-breaking 1975 article
"The Traffic in Women: Notes on the 'Political Economy' of Sex," argues
forcefully that the exchange of women is predicated upon and reproduces
a system of gender inequity:

If women are the gifts, then it is men who are the exchange partners. And it is the
partners, not the presents, upon whom reciprocal exchange confers its quasi-
mystical power of social linkage. The relations of such a system are such that
women are in no position to realize the benefits of their own circulation. As long
as the relations specify that men exchange women, it is men who are the bene-
ficiaries of the product of such exchanges—social organization.[6]

Not only a cultural organizing structure, "the exchange of women is a profound perception of a system in which women do not have full rights to themselves."[7] The "exchange of women" thus becomes for feminists a theoretical shorthand for a psychological and social order founded upon, productive of, and complicit in the objectification and oppression of women.

If we return, by way of example, to the passage from *Trachiniae* that opened this chapter, at the risk of great oversimplification we might see the Freudian and Lévi-Straussian approach emphasizing the positive social results of Deianira's exchange: Heracles' victory over the monstrous Achelous (and, by extension, the victory of the "civilization hero" over all the forces of barbarity), the marriage of the hero and the princess, the emergence of culture out of nature. For Rubin and those feminists who have followed in her footsteps, this exchange might bear a very different valence; they might focus not on the glorious fray, but rather on its prize, Deianira, objectified, marginalized, reduced to a terrified and bereft calf. More is at stake here than a simple choice between two readings; the question is one of finding a way to read tragedy—or any text—in a manner that recognizes the more oppressive aspects of its ideology without condoning them, or, conversely, that uncovers resistance within the text or culture to such oppressions without the anachronistic retrojection of modern politics.

Nancy Sorkin Rabinowitz, in her recent study of the exchange of women in Euripides, offers a nuanced and provocative approach to this problem.[8] Focusing on the exchange as a means of reproducing normative (unequal) gender relations, Rabinowitz provides a sophisticated and insightful reading of Euripidean tragedy, uncovering a bedrock of male anxiety and a compensatory dynamic of containment of female sexuality and subjectivity. She stresses the "ideological work" these plays did in encouraging the audience's compliance with the cultural practice of marriage exchange, as well as in the passivity and constraint of women it entailed; thus her reading of Euripides is also a critique of the misogynist culture of ancient Athens. Facing tragedy's prevalent oppression as both a feminist and a classicist, she seeks a "third position" between complicity in an ideology of gender asymmetry and a resistance that reinscribes women as victims, a balance between "read[ing] the text with the ideology, as the author would have us do," and "read[ing] against that position in various ways" (1993: 23). She argues that Euripides tacitly—

"almost despite himself" (ibid.: 27)—acknowledges the female strength he works to control, and she imagines an ancient female audience who watched subversively and found positive models of empowerment in a genre designed for their suppression.[9] In this audience she finds hope for the "misfiring" of tragedy's patriarchal ideology (ibid.: 12).

While there is little argument that Athenian culture in general and tragedy in particular are male-oriented, and while most feminist readers of tragedy must sympathize with Rabinowitz's refusal to condone their misogyny, nonetheless, this sort of critique runs the risk of oversimplification: of the role of female characters, who fall into categories of praise or blame; of tragedy, which becomes an instrument of oppression; and of ideology itself, which is pictured as repressive, monolithic, and masculine.[10] The genders become radically polarized in this scenario by a system of exchange (and a state-produced genre) that is always good for men and bad for women.[11] It is perhaps this conviction of tragedy's repressive agenda that leads Rabinowitz to seek resistance largely outside of tragedy, in the female audience. This is problematic, however, not only because the evidence for women's presence at the dramatic festival is far from conclusive,[12] but also because it is essentializing and dangerous to assume that women watched in a radically different way from men.[13] Presumably audience reactions (whether that audience was all male or mixed in gender, as it was in status, age, occupation, nationality, etc.) were diverse; if that is true, it is not because tragedy failed to control all its possible valences and interpretations, but rather because it actively encouraged multiple readings, both complicit and subversive.

Like Rabinowitz, I look for a "third position," a middle ground between tragedy as "misogynist" and tragedy as "feminist," and between the classic approach to the exchange, which highlights its benefits for male society, and the feminist critique, which emphasizes its oppression of women. I do not seek this position in a dialectic between male text and female reader, however; rather, I see these two hermeneutics as coexisting within the text itself—indeed, within the very structure of the exchange of women.[14] The tragic exchange, in my view, is generative, not merely repressive: it creates social relations and subjects, male and female. Much of this creative energy, as Rabinowitz so rightly notes, is in the service of a reproduction of various relations of domination, especially those oppressive of women. But, I think, if we imagine the tragic exchange as constructing social relations as well as imposing and reinforcing them, then there is room for hope that alongside the more oppressive mechanisms will also be generated less oppressive alternatives.[15]

The exchange rests upon and perpetuates a distinction between male subject and female object, but tragedy, by giving this object a voice, shows up the essential speciousness of the dichotomy. Tragedy's dramatization of the transaction raises insistently the possibility of a female subject, whether the woman tries to participate actively in exchange (as the heroines do in the three plays examined here) or merely offers her subjective (and often critical) view upon it. This female subject is, of course, a male fantasy: I take it as a given that tragedy was produced by men for men, and that the subject at issue in the tragedies is male. Moreover, this fantasied space is one that is always, with varying degrees of panic, foreclosed: the female subject is always shown to be invalid, subjected, dangerous, or impossible. Nonetheless, this foreclosed female subject offers a site of potential resistance built into the very structure of the exchange. When the exchange is reinscribed within the plays (two of the three plays here conclude with transfers of women, as if this brings resolution), so too is the woman, whose presence disrupts even as it enables a smooth and easy reciprocity. It is in the ambiguous status of the woman as a space of resistance institutionalized within the exchange that I see the plays themselves taking up the "third position" that Rabinowitz advocates.

Returning once more to my example from *Trachiniae*, rather than focus exclusively on either the glorious struggle of the male heroes or the lonely plight of the female prize, I would emphasize the way the ode juxtaposes the two, casting the pall of the latter over the epinician splendor of the former. This scene of heroic contest is filtered through—maybe even witnessed by—its female victim, and the ode's sympathy for her draws under suspicion not only the contest but the heroic identities and society built upon it. Deianira watches from afar, unhappily, critically, maybe even subversively. As the prize of this contest, she constitutes its fulcrum, but also an instability right at its core, an instability the contest generates as surely as it does the stable male subject. Thus resistance, as Foucault says, is not opposed to power, but is everywhere within it, its product, and contributory to its dominion.[16]

This necessary imbrication of power and resistance in tragedy—of reinscribing the exchange and challenging it—is not merely structural, however, but active, practical, and political. In their work on radical democracy, Laclau and Mouffe suggest that every social or ideological institution is a site of hegemonic negotiation, a site of ongoing struggle over the temporary and variable articulation of the terms of discourse and the relation between different discursive or political spheres. Inherent in these continuous struggles are potential subversions as well as oppressions, potentials that are actualized or suppressed in the course of political debate.[17] The exchange of women, I propose, is precisely such a nodal point of hegemonic negotiation in tragedy. It is a site at which power is articulated through a condensation of certain class relations, gender relations, and subject positions. But because this articulation is contingent and provisional (not essential or inevitable), it contains the possibility of endless rearticulations. The exchange thus can be oppressive and hegemonic, reconfirming gender inequality and a world owned and ruled by male subjects; but at the same time it is potentially subversive, constantly calling attention to its own exclusions and violences, and laying open to critique the society and subjectivities founded upon it.

Once we view the exchange as a site of constant, active negotiation between the hegemonic and the counterhegemonic, we can escape the false and reductive polarity between a repressive, misogynist tragedy and a revolutionary, protofeminist tragedy. The "third position" Rabinowitz and others have sought between these two extremes is precisely this site of contestation, and the ambivalence of the audience is firmly rooted in the ambiguities of the text. To say this is not, however, to revert to a New Critical or Deconstructionist fetishization of the free play of poetic ambiguities. The ambiguities at issue here are less poetic than political: the possibilities raised in discursive negotiation are stances that could be taken up in practice. Women were exchanged in practice in Athens—in marriage, concubinage, slavery, prostitution—and the plays thus have their half-life in the lived experience of individual men and women. While it is difficult to be much more specific about this relationship, we can see tragedy as constituting a discursive framework, a set of problems, issues, and alternatives, that could then be taken up in different modalities and with varying effects in practice. Thus, discourse and practice form a continuum, as the business begun in the theater of Dionysus is finished in the household, the marketplace, the law-courts, and the assembly.

Not all of the possibilities tragedy raises were equally viable in practice, of course, within the specific political regime of fifth-century Athens.[18] Negotiation is not the same as neutrality, and if the counter-hegemonic shares a platform with the hegemonic in tragedy, in practice it is generally either subsumed or ostracized (indeed, that is the nature of hegemony). Nor is there neutrality within tragedy itself.[19] Tragedy may question the trade in women, but it ultimately reinscribes both the system and its attendant hierarchies and oppressions. Often the woman's very critique of the exchange justifies her subjection and serves in the end to bolster the elite male subject her critique had threatened. And yet, if the questions raised receive all too familiar answers, if alternatives are eliminated and radical potentialities barred from political actualization, that does not obviate the advantages of raising the questions and posing the alternatives. Our reading of tragedy, then, must take notice of both the multiplicity of options the plays offer, and the dynamics by which they make some of those options viable and others not.

Implicit in this conceptualization of the exchange as a site of hegemonic negotiation within tragedy is an analogous understanding of the role of tragedy itself within the Athenian democracy. Just as the tragic world is under debate within the tragic exchange, challenged even as it is reconfirmed, so Athenian ideology is contested within tragedy. Most readings that see tragedy as either enforcing or opposing "Athenian ideology" assume an ideology that is monolithic, univocal, and repressive. In this context Althusser is often invoked and tragedy declared an Ideological State Apparatus, the hand that wields the hammer of Athenian "state ideology."[20] Of course, in some sense, this is accurate: tragedy was sponsored by the democratic state for the education as well as the entertainment of its citizens. The plays themselves were only a part of the annual festival, the City Dionysia, which also included sacrifices, a parade of those young men raised by the state who had reached adulthood, the presentation of tribute by Athens's subject nations, and the crowning of victorious generals.[21] So it is with much justice that tragedy has often been seen as a sort of initiation into Athenian citizenship and a celebration of civic ideology.[22] However, even to speak of the state and its ideology in these terms is to reify what I think is really a dynamic and open-ended process. That is to say, if tragedy is in some way an "apparatus" of Athenian ideology, that ideology is as complex and contested as the tragedies it produced. Tragedy, then, neither imposes nor opposes "ideology"; rather, it is engaged in an ongoing and contentious process of formulating, reformulating, articulating, and interrogating an ideology that itself, like tragedy, contains the possibility of its own critique.

THE SOCIAL ECONOMY OF EXCHANGE

If the exchange of women is a particularly fertile site for negotiation in tragedy, that is in part because it opens simultaneously onto two of tragedy's central concerns: social relations and the gendered self. As a social transaction, the trade of women is rooted in the materiality of tragedy's social world:[23] the relations of a woman's exchange (both gender and class relations) are a condensation of tragedy's broader social and power relations. At the same time, as a structure that generates subjects, the exchange is a window onto the tragic subject and what we might call tragedy's psychic economy. These two areas—the material and the psychological—are inseparable: material relations are the sediment of individual strategies and the determinant for further strategies; subjectivities are formulated within and by material relations. The transferral of a woman lies at the point of intersection between these two areas, and their necessary overlap and interpenetration around the transaction is a central focus of this study.

In order to reach this intersection between the social and the subjective, I have found it profitable to approach the exchange of women through two different methodologies at the same time. In discussing the economic and social issues that surround the exchange—the economic level it occupies, the relations of exchange it reproduces, its costs and profits (economic or symbolic), the social interests it reveals or conceals—I use key concepts borrowed from Karl Marx and Pierre Bourdieu. From these theorists I take a belief in the primacy of social and economic relations, the concept of class interest (however loosely we define class: see below, note 32), a conviction of the ideological function of literature (that is, its implication in the reproduction of social relations), and the observation that economic relations are often obscured by ideological enchantment. For a precise conception and terminology of "the subject," on the other hand, I turn to psychoanalytic theory (primarily in the forms associated with Jacques Lacan and Melanie Klein), which affords a concept of the self and a theory of gender, a vocabulary in which to speak of complex internal processes, and a mechanics for the individual's psychic investment in objects and people external to himself or herself.

Again, I shall insist throughout upon the total imbrication of these two sets of concerns around the transfer of women; hence I have resisted methodological homogenization in the chapters that follow, allowing economic and psychoanalytic concerns and theories to coexist, to illuminate and complicate one another.[24] That is not to suggest that either the economic or the psychoanalytic theories I use are incomplete in their own terms, but rather to take seriously the location of the exchange between the two and to take advantage of the doubled theoretical wealth that location affords.[25] I realize, further, that in choosing this combined approach rather than working within a single theoretical framework, I run the risk of oversimplification or of mixing water and oil.[26] But I am not trying to reconcile these two theoretical approaches across the board, but hope instead to let them supplement and complement one another around the specific issue of exchange, materialism elucidating the social underpinnings of the transfer of the woman, psychoanalysis pursuing its psychological effects. By approaching both economic and psychoanalytic theories with a set of questions that are strictly tangential to these theories' broader aims, I hope to avoid the fraught issues of orthodoxy surrounding each methodology.

Finally, it may seem a peculiar oversight that a project with the word "gender" in the title should make no mention of feminism as a theoretical model. I do not mean to marginalize the female, which is so central to the project as a whole; however, I consider it one of the strengths of feminism that it can work with other, more formal methodologies.[27] Though feminism's relationship with both Marxism[28] and psychoanalysis[29] has historically been tense, I am not trying to redeem or appropriate these methodologies for feminism so much as to allow the concerns and terms of feminism to complicate both economic and psychoanalytic theory, and to theorize the implication of gender in other social relations. My focus, therefore, like that of most recent feminist work, falls on what Rubin calls the "sex/gender system," rather than on "women" as such: the tragic exchange, I argue, serves not so much to oppress or manipulate a preconstituted and clearly defined group, "women," as actually to constitute that group.[30] The "women" thus constituted are, of course, a male construct: on the most literal level, each female character is at heart a male actor. We must not confuse females on the stage, then, with "real women," ancient or modern, nor conceive of "women" as a universal or essential category; instead we must approach the tragic woman as a fantasy—fictional and ideologically invested—through which the male subject thinks about himself and his place in the world.

Exchange, at its most basic level, is about social relations, about equality between partners and hierarchy within that equality; it is about social norms and how they can be manipulated by the socially adept; it is about different sorts of capital (symbolic, political, financial) and the ways in which they can be evaluated, invested, and interconverted. All of these issues are central to a tension in fifth-century Athenian society between elitism and egalitarianism, a tension played out and mediated in part through the City Dionysia.[31]

Athenian society was structured simultaneously by an ideology of equality and an unspoken elitism.[32] *Isonomia*, the equality before the law on which the Athenians prided themselves, was not only an ideal, but to a large extent a practical reality as well: most civil positions were filled by lot with strict term limitations and accountability, and the vote of the *dēmos*, the people, whether in the courts or the assembly, was final. Within that ideology of *isonomia*, however, there remained inequalities based on wealth, birth, education, or access (afforded by leisure or geographical proximity) to the centers of power. Such advantages were manifested not only in greater de facto political power (for example, the powerful generals tended to come from a few old families), but also in an implicit—if largely unarticulated—valorization of the idea of a hierarchy within a society of equals.[33] Josiah Ober has argued that this tension between "mass" and "elite" was rife throughout the fifth and fourth centuries and that the outbreak of overt civil conflict during this time was prevented largely by its continual negotiation within such institutional arenas as drama and legal and political rhetoric.[34] This negotiation between equality and hierarchy is central to Greek tragedy. Indeed, J.-P. Vernant has suggested that the conflict between the civic group and the heroic individual is built into the very structure of tragedy in the opposition between the protagonist and the chorus.[35]

One way in which the tension between equality and elitism is played out in tragedy is through the theme of exchange, whether the medium of exchange be words, blows, goods, or women. In the most general terms, exchange relates the two participants simultaneously in a relationship of equality and of hierarchy.[36] On the one hand, the very act of exchange—especially on a public occasion such as a marriage—declares a certain basic equality between the two exchangers, or creates one where it did not already exist. On the other hand, if the exchange is subjected to closer scrutiny, it usually also suggests an inequality between the partners, setting up a debt relationship that subordinates (if only temporarily) one partner to the other.[37]

Thus exchange is simultaneously cooperative and competitive; at one pole lies *xenia*, "guest-friendship," an amicable relation between equals often institutionalized through the reciprocal exchange of gifts; at the other, the *agōn*, competition, be it a wrestling match, a lawsuit, or a war.[38] But these two poles collapse constantly into one another: the *agōn* contains a seed of homoeroticism; *xenia*, a latent hostility. The two especially tend to collapse when the object of exchange is a woman. Eve Kosofsky Sedgwick, in her important book *Between Men: English Literature and Male Homosocial Desire*, studies the role of women (and especially their exchange) in the negotiation of "male homosocial desire," the term she uses to describe a continuum of relations between men that ranges from aggression to homoeroticism. She shows how in the exchange of women, heterosexual eros—the desire for the woman that at first glance seems to motivate her transfer—often functions as a blind for a more profound homosocial impulse, a desire for relations between men.[39] In tragedy, as in much of the English literature Sedgwick studies, the homosociality at the core of the exchange is both erotic and agonistic. Erotic desire, as in Athenian homosexual practice, is hierarchical, not reciprocal, and sexual lust slides easily into the lust for domination. As for the woman, fetishized as object of desire, she at once both obscures the more complex desires beneath the exchange and bears the brunt of the violence into which these desires erupt.

The relations of domination latent within even the most amicable exchanges have a corollary in the economic register. Much excellent work has been done on the economy of gift exchange in ancient Greece.[40] Following Marcel Mauss's famous *Essai sur le don*, scholars have identified gift exchange as a symbolic transaction, spontaneous and reciprocal, aimed not at financial profit but at social union.[41] In contrast to the base exchanges of goods and money between strangers in the marketplace, gift exchange was the preserve of an elite class, those who could afford, whether by economic or "symbolic" capital, to deal in such intangibles.

The economic distinction between the symbolic exchange of gifts and the commercial exchange of commodities, then, is the basis of a social distinction, and a prop of elitism.[42]

The separation of these two economic (and hence social) tiers is not ontological, however; instead, it is the result of a self-interested mystification of the relations of exchange. Marx writes of the process of fetishization in which the relations of exchange—socially embedded power relations—come to be reified in and occluded by the movement of objects.[43] Bourdieu expands upon this, arguing that this fetishization is fundamental to the reproduction of a social elite: when economic wealth is misrepresented or misrecognized ("euphemized" or "enchanted") as symbolic wealth, the material basis of social differences is in turn obscured, so that the power of the elite, like the value of the gifts they exchange, comes to appear inherent and unalienable.[44] To "disenchant" the symbolic gift exchange, then, to expose it as no more than an idealized form of commodity exchange and to lay bare the power relations that lie concealed beneath it, is to challenge the social prerogatives built upon it.

In tragedy, this labor of disenchantment often falls to the woman. The exchange of women is part of the elite economy of gift exchange. Women are ideal gifts within this economy,[45] for their value is inherently mystified, that is, it appears to resist the precise accountancy of the marketplace. Their exchange, too, is easily mystified, as the financial negotiations of the betrothal are overshadowed by the wedding ceremony, with its fertility symbolism, mythic precedents, and cosmic implications. Beneath this symbolic exchange, however, always lurks the economic: women are bartered for a profit, whether it is measured in money, prestige, social alliances, the favor of the gods, or other women. When the heroines in these plays try to engage actively in the exchange, they reveal the unsavory economics behind it: in their mouths, gifts become crass commodities and the trade in women a form of prostitution.

By subjecting the exchange of women to a strict accountancy, the heroines of these plays expose to critique the mystified social relations that underpin this business and the elite male subject predicated upon it. This critique, however, does not ultimately undermine the elite economy. Tragedy disenchants the elite economy and elite subject in order to reexamine the bases of elitism, which is shown to rest not on wealth or birth alone, but also on morality or behavior. Thus elitism and the elite subject can be reinscribed in a form with which each individual in the audience, regardless of his actual status and with varying degrees of idealization and wish fulfillment, could identify.[46] Elitism and elite values are reaffirmed in the complementary fantasies of the democratic nobleman and the noble *dēmos*. But even while it enables this productive convergence, the woman's disenchantment of gift exchange is an act of bad faith[47] that declares her failure as an aristocrat (and, indeed, a fundamental incompatibility of status and gender for women) and justifies her exclusion from active participation in the elite economy that traffics in women. Thus the hierarchy of man over woman is yoked to the hierarchy of elite over masses (aristocrat over nonaristocrat, gift exchanger over commodity exchanger), and the subject who emerges supreme from the exchange is both a man and a gentleman.[48]

The desire that drives the exchange, the nexus of homoeroticism and aggression at its core, the investment of objects with psychic significance, the enchantment and disenchantment of economic relations: these material issues gesture always toward the psychological.[49] The social and economic relations of exchange find their telos in the lived experience of individuals; subjects carry their entire social world within them, reproducing it even as it produces them. Thus a study of the social economy of trading women directs us toward an investigation of this trade's psychic effects.

THE SUBJECT OF EXCHANGE

Exchange generates subjects. Structured around the opposition between male givers and female gift, the tragic exchange opens always onto questions of gender and subjectivity. The movement of the female object defines the two men oppositionally as subjects—as agents of action, giver and receiver, father-in-law and son-in-law, or winner and loser. While the men's subject status comes into question generally only when the exchange fails, the woman's subjectivity is inherently problematic.[50] Structurally, the woman functions as an object, but though her object status may be an enabling fiction, it is a fiction nonetheless; Lévi-Strauss himself recognizes this when he concedes that the woman in exchange "could never become just a sign and nothing more, since even in a man's world she is still a person, and since in so far as she is defined as a sign she must be recognized as a generator of signs."[51] On the one hand, the woman is not as obvious or secure a subject as the man; on the other, she is not a complete object, a point that is brought out clearly in all three of the plays studied here by the presence of a silent woman who is the pure and passive object of male activity. Between these two poles—the full male subject and the full female object—the plays' heroines try to define a subjectivity for themselves, in the process exposing the components and modalities of the tragic subject.

J.-P. Vernant, in his essay "The Tragic Subject,"[52] proposes that tragedy in effect creates a new discourse of the subject:

The invention of Greek tragedy, in fifth-century Athens, amounted to more than just the production of the literary works themselves, objects for spiritual consumption designed for the citizens and adapted to them; through the spectacle, reading, imitation, and establishment of a literary tradition, it also involved the creation of a "subject," a tragic consciousness, the introduction of tragic man. Similarly, the works of the Athenian dramatists express and elaborate a tragic vision, a new way for man to understand himself and take up his position in relation to the world, the gods, other people, himself, and his own actions.[53]

He argues that tragedy presents the individual as a problem, "the subject of a debate and interrogation that, through his person, implicates the fifth-century spectator, the citizen of democratic Athens" (1988: 242). Vernant's formulation suggests the appropriateness of this new tragic consciousness for an audience of men growing ever more accustomed to treating every issue as a topic of debate. The tragic subject is embedded not only within its dramatic world but also in the social relations and material conditions—the "moment," as Vernant puts it—of fifth-century Athens. We must be careful, then, as John Jones most forcefully reminds us, not to retroject the quiescent, reflective, and fully realized subject of modern drama onto the masked characters of ancient theater, nor to apply uncritically to the latter methodologies designed to explain the former.[54] Bearing this warning in mind, and aiming again at that space between the material and the psychological where the exchange is located, we need to define a subject that is both psychologically complex and historically specific; a model for such a subject is offered by Louis Althusser, a post-Marxist philosopher strongly influenced by Lacanian psychoanalysis, in his famous essay, "Ideology and Ideological State Apparatuses (Notes towards an Investigation)" (Althusser 1971: 1–60).

As Althusser defines it, the subject is a socially constructed being that reflects upon itself in terms given by the material conditions of its existence. How does this work? Ideology constitutes the subject by "hailing" or "interpellating" the individual. Althusser imagines a scenario in which an individual is stopped on the street by someone (say a policeman) calling, "Hey, you there!" In this moment of recognition ("by this mere one-hundred-and-eighty-degree physical conversion"), the individual becomes a subject within ideology, becomes the person who was called, and accepts that appellation as its own.[55] That the subject is constructed in and through ideology does not diminish its psychological integrity, though. It is part of the effect of ideological interpellation that it interpellates "concrete, individual, distinguishable and (naturally) irreplaceable subjects" (ibid.: 47), that is, subjects who misrecognize their ideologically constructed basis: "The 'obviousness' that you and I are subjects—and that that does not cause any problems—is an ideological effect, the elementary ideological effect" (ibid.: 46).

The notion of interpellation is seminal in theorizing a historical subject, a subject fully constructed in and through its material conditions. Following to its end the logic of Althusser's interpellation means accepting the total interconvertibility of the material and the psychological; the relations of production and power become, in a very real sense, a part (in fact, for Althusser, the basis) of the subject's interior relation to itself and its world.[56] The tragic subject, then, is a wholly social phenomenon, hailed into being by ideological institutions such as exchange.[57] Althusser thus provides a precise theoretical tool for excavating the subjects of exchange, allowing us to move freely between social issues and subjective, economic theory and psychoanalytic, and to understand the mutually productive relations between the two realms. And by rooting the subject in its historical conditions, Althusser will help us to avoid the pitfall of retrojecting a post-Romantic subject into the premodern era, and thus (it is to be hoped) to escape the just criticism of those who argue against the unquestioning presupposition of a transhistorical category of the subject.[58]

The theory also suggests a mode of power that is generative, that creates subjects, rather than one that simply manipulates or represses preexistent subjects. Such a flexible model of power is necessary, as I argued above, if we are to do justice to tragedy's ambiguity. Althusser does, however, open himself to more reductive readings.[59] The very fact that Althusser imagines the interpellating agent in the first instance as a policeman, a representative of the law, implies a repressive model in which the subject is hailed as subjected to the law and subjectivization necessarily entails subjection. Indeed, his own application of the model at the end of the essay, the hailing of Peter by God, seems to attribute an inexorable, irresistible, and unilateral authority to the interpellating "deity." [60] Tragedy itself belies such a monolithic and repressive system. Both men and women are variously and often contradictorily hailed in an ongoing process, so that the tragic subject seems more a collocation of different interpellations than a unitary and stable self.[61] Moreover, tragedy often dramatizes characters—male and (more often) female—rejecting their interpellations, negotiating with the interpellating agent, themselves hailing others, or simply refusing to turn around when called.

In order to reap the full potential of Althusser's extremely useful mechanics of the self, then, we must open him up and read him as flexibly as his text allows. Judith Butler, reading Althusser through her (Derridean) notion of iterability, suggests an illuminating reformulation:[62] power, she argues, is reproduced through the citation of its own authority; each citation is simultaneously a stabilization of the law and the potential for miscitation, deconstruction, or subversion. Thus, in her view, every interpellation is a moment of crisis, not only for the individual hailed but also for the hailing power. There is always the possibility, in her reading, that instead of turning at the policeman's "Hey, you there!" the individual will challenge the authority of the law that hails him. Thus, rather than being constructed from above by a unidirectional and irresistible interpellation (as Peter is hailed by God in Althusser's example), the subject is constructed through a dialogue between the self and the law, and ideology is ever at stake when we speak of the subject. This dialogue between the subject-in-formation and ideology-under-negotiation is precisely what I see happening in tragedy's exchanges. The exchange interpellates subjects (and reproduces itself through these interpellations), but each hailing is also a potential crisis and the reproduction of a potential challenge.

Thus we can return to the idea of hegemonic negotiation, able to see, via Althusser and Butler, the tragic subject himself or herself as a site as well as an object of contestation. The subjects, male and female, hailed by the exchange are contested creatures, subjects in process, constantly under construction and reconstruction, not hailed into being once and for all, but constantly hailed and hailed again by different interpellations, some of which they accept, some of which they reject, some of which reaffirm the power of the interpellating authority, some of which undermine it. Moreover, if we accept the analogy I have been implying between

the tragic exchange and tragedy itself, it is a similarly complex, heterogeneous, variably complicit and resistant subject that tragedy interpellates in its audience: that is to say, tragedy interpellates its audience as
Athenian citizens.

Althusser's theory of interpellation offers an indispensable model for understanding the interrelation between the social and the subjective. His
"Notes towards an Investigation" were not intended to be exhaustive,
however, and require supplementing on each side. Althusser himself recognizes this need in his incorporation of economic Marxism on the one
hand, and Lacanian psychoanalysis on the other. The latter is a particularly salutary supplement, as Althusser's model alone does not elaborate
the affective experience of interpellation, nor can it account specifically
for gender.[63] One of the main contentions of this book is that the interpellating ideologies at work in the exchange of women are simultaneously class and gender ideologies, hailing subjects into a dense matrix of
class and gender hierarchies. To understand the ways in which these various interpellations permeate the subject and determine his or her psychic
relation to the world, we must cross the bridge that Althusser builds between his own psychology and Lacan's.

For Lacan, the individual subject exists within the "symbolic order,"
the order of language, law, and ideology. He imagines a scene in which
a child first sees himself in a mirror; in the moment of self-recognition,
the child becomes a subject. The dynamics of the scene thus far replay
those of Althusser's interpellation, with the important distinction that for
Lacan, the "obviousness" of the subject in ideology is never complete,
but becomes the focus of intense psychic manipulations. When the child
recognizes himself in the mirror, he mistakes for his genuine self the mediated, alienated mirror image: the self-recognition is thus a misrecognition, and the subject within the symbolic crystallizes around an essential
dehiscence.[64]

This subject, for Lacan as for most post-Freudian psychoanalysis, is
implicitly male. Further, the symbolic itself is, as Lacan admits, "androcentric," ontologically grounded by a transcendental masculine figure,
the Name of the Father.[65] It is only under the auspices of this symbolic
Father (through a necessarily imperfect and misrecognized identification) that the boy can become a subject, an existential filiation enacted
through the Oedipal complex, in which the boy relinquishes his mother
in obedience to the paternal law. In exchange for her, the boy receives the

phallus, emblem of his prerogative and paternity within this symbolic order and "the symbolic token which can later be exchanged for a woman."[66]

Where does this leave the woman? She is a fantasied "other" who vouchsafes for the man his subject status:[67] not only does the mother as object of exchange guarantee the Oedipal identification with the father, but it is the mother in the first instance who functions as a mirror for the boy.[68] Moreover, the division and loss of self-presence that the man accepts with entry into the symbolic (the splitting of the "real" self and the mirror self, of signified and signifier) is disavowed by being projected onto the woman. A wounded, lacking subject, subjected within the phallocentric symbolic,[69] she is "the site at which the male subject deposits his lack,"[70] and his tragedy of loss is played out on her "castrated" body.[71]

The world Lacan describes is familiar in its outlines to students of classical Athens, an androcentric universe governed by a transcendental king and father, Zeus. The phallocentrism of the culture has often been noted:[72] from the herms, the ithyphallic statues that stood at roadsides and in front of private homes, to the disembodied "penis birds" that ornament pottery, the equation of penis with phallus and the naturalization of male authority was virtually unchallenged. The Athenian family, to be sure, was very different in its structure from the modern Western bourgeois family that rears the psychoanalytic subject; nonetheless, they share the element most essential to Freudian and post-Freudian psychoanalysis, the overwhelming emphasis on the father-son bond.[73] The numerous institutionalized means in Athens toward securing the identification of son with father (initiation rituals, citizenship and inheritance laws, homoerotic pedagogy, not to mention tragedy itself) insert the individual subject into this paternal symbolic.

And of course the subject thus hailed, in Athens as in Lacan, is male. There were, strictly speaking, no female Athenians,[74] and the woman is relegated to the role of cultural other. Just as the Lacanian male subject is reassured of his authority and authenticity in contrast to the lacking woman, the Athenian citizenry was constructed in contrast to a variety of others—slaves, barbarians, but especially women.[75] The exclusionary logic of the Athenian democracy was replicated on the tragic stage, where the female subject, as Froma Zeitlin says in her important article "Playing the Other: Theater, Theatricality, and the Feminine in Greek Drama," is "designed primarily for exploring the male project of self-

hood in the larger world" (1990: 69).[76] Tragedy, she argues, allows its
male characters, male actors, and male audience to experience what the
culture defines as feminine, "for the purpose of imagining a fuller model
for the masculine self" (Zeitlin 1990: 85), but also in order to explore his
constitutive exclusions—weakness, madness, pathos, corporeality, deceit, in short femininity—and, I would add, by eliminating those exclusions under the name of woman, to resecure himself and his world.[77]

This securing of the male self, however, is always incomplete, tenuous,
and, at base, impossible. For Lacan, the imagined lack of the female
other guarantees for the male subject a conviction of his own plenitude
and self-presence, but one that is essentially false; as a disavowal of his
lack, she always declares as well as denies that lack.[78] This is what Lacan
means when he says, notoriously, that "The woman does not exist": even
as a fantasy, she cannot secure him.[79] The opposition between lacking female other and sovereign male self is thus always liable to failure and in
need of constant, compulsive psychic maintenance.

The exchange of women is a nodal point in tragedy for this fragile alterity. Built upon the structural opposition between male self and female
other (and their radical polarization as subject and object), the exchange
seems to authenticate the male subject. The fact that the female object
can be exchanged defines the men, minimally, as those who cannot be exchanged; thus the male subject (on the stage and in the audience) is guaranteed as "free, autonomous, and inviolable."[80] Yet, as I have suggested,
the exchange obsessively raises the specter of the female subject, filling in
what should be a site of absence. When the heroines in tragedy refuse
their role as objectified other and claim the position of self, not only do
they interrupt the social mechanism of the exchange, but they also jeop-
ardize the male subjects who are predicated upon their supposed lack:
the corollary in tragedy to a female subject is a male object—a corpse.

The disastrous results of female subjectivity within the exchange ne-
cessitate an immediate foreclosure upon that subjectivity. The female
subject is always, in the end, shown to be illegitimate or impossible. For
the heroines of the three plays discussed here, subjectification is subjection, and their failed subjectivity is a testament to the power of the
symbolic law and its legitimate sons. Yet in the very effort of disenfranchisement is revealed the artificiality of the Lacanian schema;[81] the tragedies, by suggesting the possibility of a female subject only to delegiti-
mize it, reveal the process by which woman is constructed as lacking, as
other, as object, and by which man, correspondingly, is guaranteed as

self-present subject. Naturalizing ontology is disrupted, and within this genealogy of the male self and female other can be imagined alternatives: a valid female subject, a male other, a relation between self and other not predicated on lack, a symbolic in which men are not divided or women abjected.

In order to discuss these alternatives in a positive way (rather than as disasters and psychic failures), it will be necessary to leave Lacan and turn to another psychoanalytic theorist, Melanie Klein. In Klein's model (1984), the distinction between self and other (paradigmatically the child and the mother) is not stable, nor is it predicated on lack. The relationship between them is so fluid, so muddled by projections and introjections, that the object seems to exist within the subject and the subject within the object. Psychic development, in this model, is a process of separating self from other; the telos, however, is not the disavowal of the other as lacking, but rather the acceptance of the plenitude and autonomy of the other. A relationship of alterity like the one Klein imagines would mean a radical rearrangement of tragedy's gender organization, one in which the exchange of women would be impossible. But though the plays do acknowledge the intimate interconnection between male subject and female object, this psychic economy is ultimately abandoned in favor of the Lacanian, and the female other is not accepted in the end, but is murdered so that her body may seal the Oedipal pact between father and son.

And yet, if this alternative is repressed, it is not eliminated altogether, but rather is incorporated at the very heart of the exchange, embodied in the figure of the silent virgin, a female other ontologically different from and radically inaccessible to the male self. The virgin is a fantasy of pure *physis:* in her virginity she seems to exist prior to the penetration of ideological interpellation; by her silence she seems to stand beyond the linguistic mediation of the symbolic, and standing thus outside the symbolic ("ek-static," as the French feminists put it), she offers a dream of a genuine and unmediated self, a self beyond ideology or gender.[82] This is, of course, only a dream, and one that the plays themselves ultimately dispel, for as soon as the virgin speaks, she, too, is subjected to the overdetermined logic of the paternal symbolic. But if this space of radical alterity is ultimately foreclosed and shown to be impossible, nonetheless it persists as a potential site of resistance and change, a vantage point from which to examine the symbolic order, and from which it seems no longer unbounded, universal, or inevitable.

Thus when we look at an exchange like that which opens this chapter, we must recognize the complexity of the relations between the male competitors and their female prize. The lonely calf who waits on a hillside, Deianira is the victim of this transaction—oppressed within its social and psychic economy—but also a potential challenge to it. In her dual position—simultaneously at the center of the exchange and beyond it— the woman both reaffirms and destabilizes the exchange, as well as the social relations from which it emerges and which it reproduces, and the elite male subject who enjoys its rewards. The traffic in women shows us in microcosm tragedy's world under negotiation; it reproduces that world, with all its oppressions and hegemonic exclusions; it also reproduces alternatives, instabilities, and resistances. The chapters that follow record these ambiguous returns on tragedy's intimate commerce between the sexes.

SOVEREIGN FATHER AND FEMALE SUBJECT IN SOPHOCLES' *Trachiniae*

⚬

ONE

"THE NOBLEST LAW"
The Paternal Symbolic and Its Reluctant Subject

⚬

THE FINAL EXCHANGE

Sophocles' *Trachiniae* ends with a crisis of succession. Heracles is about to die, poisoned unintentionally by his wife, Deianira. In the agony of his disease, he lays his final commands upon his son, Hyllus, commands that will test the boy's worthiness to inherit the name and glory of his father and to head the clan of his descendants, the Heracleidae. In this episode, which comprises the last third of the play, the two men's identities as heroes are defined and reaffirmed: Heracles, despite the debilitation of pain, wields absolute authority; Hyllus, despite his youth and inexperience, shows himself worthy to carry on his father's legacy. At the same time, the bond between them is cemented, and the dynasty secured. A whole social order, guaranteed at the highest level by Zeus, is reconsecrated in this final scene and handed down to the next generation.

This inaugural moment is celebrated, consolidated, and symbolized by the exchange of a woman.[1] Heracles forces Hyllus to take his concubine, Iole, the booty of his final expedition:

> Τοσοῦτον δή σ' ἐπισκήπτω, τέκνον·
> ταύτην, ἐμοῦ θανόντος, εἴπερ εὐσεβεῖν
> βούλῃ, πατρῴων ὁρκίων μεμνημένος,
> προσθοῦ δάμαρτα, μηδ' ἀπιστήσῃς πατρί.[2]
>
> (1221–24)

This is my command to you, son. When I am
dead, if you wish to be pious and mindful of

your oaths to your father, make this girl your
wife; do not disobey your father.

As part of Heracles' property, Iole is a material bequest from the dying
father to his son. But she also represents a more intangible legacy: won in
Heracles' last military expedition, she stands as a symbol of his heroic
valor; as his bedmate, she memorializes his legendary virility. With her,
Heracles transmits these qualities to his son. As the object of their exchange, Iole defines Heracles and Hyllus as subjects: as giver and recipient, as heroes and as men. She herself, however, if she is onstage at all
during this scene, remains silent.[3]

The moment is Oedipal. In the Oedipal Complex, the male child renounces his desire for his mother in exchange for identification with his
father, for it is only through such an identification that the boy can become a full citizen within the republic of male subjects. By handing over
his mother, the son abandons any rivalry with his father, submitting to
him in the present in exchange for the promise that he will some day occupy the father's position, a coming of age that will be represented by the
boy's taking a wife of his own. So here Hyllus must drop his defense of
his mother (whom he knows to be innocent in his father's death), and is
rewarded by Heracles' declaration of his legitimacy; this identification
between father and son is marked by Heracles' gift to Hyllus of Iole.

This Oedipal pact is signed into law. When Hyllus shrinks from obey-
ing his father's dying commands, Heracles exhorts him by invoking the
kallistos nomos, the "most noble law," the law of paternal authority:

> Ταῦτ' οὖν ἐπειδὴ λαμπρὰ συμβαίνει, τέκνον,
> δεῖ σ' αὖ γενέσθαι τῷδε τἀνδρὶ σύμμαχον,
> καὶ μὴ 'πιμεῖναι τοὐμὸν ὀξῦναι στόμα,
> ἀλλ' αὐτὸν εἰκαθόντα συμπράσσειν, νόμον
> κάλλιστον ἐξευρόντα, πειθαρχεῖν πατρί.
>
> (1174–78)

> Since these oracles are coming true, child, you
> must be my ally; do not wait to provoke my anger;
> you must yield and cooperate, having discovered
> the most noble law: obedience to your father.

This *kallistos nomos* organizes a social and psychic order that is patriarchal, patrilineal, and aristocratic. The law asserts the rule of the father—

patriarchy in its root sense; its power is transmitted patrilineally, as his accession to his father's authority will guarantee Hyllus's own future leadership of the Heracleidae; this "noblest" law establishes a "noble" society, cementing the power of an aristocratic dynasty by validating the legitimacy and nobility of its origins. This psychological and social order, moreover, is founded upon and sealed by exchanges of women, Hyllus's abandonment of his mother's defense and his acceptance of Iole as his father's gift. Thus the *kallistos nomos* that grounds *Trachiniae*'s social order also legislates the circulation of women; the exchange is an enactment of and a monument to the paternal law.

The final transfer of Iole is represented as a resolution to the problems of male society and identity that have troubled *Trachiniae* (problems caused in part by other exchanges of women), and the play would thus seem to end with a strong reaffirmation of a male social and subjective order built upon the traffic in women, and the bequeathal of this order to the next generation.[4] Any positive resolution we might seek in this scene, however, is compromised by reluctance, uncertainty, threats, and coercion. Hyllus attains his patrimony, but only by acceding under duress to terms he considers repugnant and impious. He can assume his legitimate identity only under the *kallistos nomos*, but his reluctance to obey calls into question the validity of this law, even as his eventual obedience ultimately reaffirms it. The law will falter, moreover, precisely at the point where it should be most secure: the exchange of the woman. The transaction that seems at first glance to guarantee a whole symbolic order becomes instead a moment of crisis in which that order is called into doubt, its genealogy exposed, its founding law laid open to interrogation.

That interrogation is the focus of this chapter and the following two. The unease of this final scene has its origin, I argue, in the tragedy of Deianira, whose life and death dominate the first thousand lines of the play. In Chapters 2 and 3, I show how her story undermines the distinction between male subject and female object that the exchange of women requires, first in Deianira's insistence on her own subject status (Chapter 2), and then in her dissolving of the categories of self and other (Chapter 3). In Deianira we see both a critical relation of subject to symbolic and the imagination of alternate psychic (and hence social) organizations. The lessons of Deianira's life will interrupt, if only for a moment, the transition of power in the final scene, making Hyllus hesitate just long enough to call into doubt the world he is about to inherit. But in order to understand what Hyllus risks in this hesitation, we must first examine the power of the paternal law, the society and subjects it governs, and the rewards it offers its obedient sons.

HERACLES: SUBJECT UNDER SIEGE

Heracles in *Trachiniae* is a subject under siege. The disease strikes right at the heart of Heracles' identity as a hero, his physical strength. Throughout his mythology, Heracles is primarily a hero of the body, his heroic identity virtually indistinguishable from his corporeal strength, as in the Homeric periphrasis *biē Heraklēeiē* ("might of Heracles").[5] When we see him writhing in agony on stage, we are witnessing the decomposition both of his integrity as a subject and of his masculinity. Notorious for his virility and his sexual appetite, Heracles is effeminized by pain and sickness, until finally he "finds himself a woman" (1075). The disease also threatens his social status, both as a free man and as a king,[6] his torturous death assimilating him to a slave. At stake in the final exchange of Iole will be the reclamation and restoration of Heracles' integrity as a subject, his physical supremacy, royal status, and masculinity.

It is apt that it should be the transfer of a woman that reaffirms Heracles' shaken identity, since that identity has been negotiated throughout the play through such exchanges, first in the contest with Achelous, from which he emerges victorious with Deianira as his prize, and then in the improper acquisition of Iole, whom he steals violently from her father and gives to Deianira with tragic results. Heracles' first appearance in the play comes in Deianira's narrative of the contest in which he won her.[7] She introduces Heracles as the famed son of Zeus and Alcmene (19); from this first mention, his *kleos* ("fame," "glory") as a hero (ὁ κλεινὸς, "the famous one," 19) is linked to his royal and divine birth. The victory that follows not only proves his physical strength, but also announces his virility: his prize is Deianira, his "chosen bedmate" (λέχος . . . Ἡρακλεῖ κριτόν, 27). This struggle is the first arena for Heracles' heroism and the only example actually narrated in the play from a lifetime of victories over beasts and monsters; his whole career, in this synoptic view, is epitomized by this one contest.

This heroism in competition for a woman is repeated, but more ambiguously, in the story of Heracles' sack of Oechalia and capture of Iole. The play offers two different versions and interpretations of this campaign, one illustrating Heracles' righteous avenging of a wrong against both himself and the code of heroic conduct, the other symbolizing nothing but his violence and uncontrollable lust.[8] In the first version, narrated by Lichas, his loyal retainer, the attack on Oechalia is Heracles' revenge for a transgression of heroic etiquette by Iole's father, Eury-tus. In this account (248–90), Heracles had come, as "a guest-friend of long-standing, to [Eurytus's] house and hearth" (ὃς αὐτὸν ἐλθόντ' ἐς δόμους ἐφέστιον. / ξένον παλαιὸν ὄντα, 262–63), but Eurytus had breached the established norms of *xenia*, guest-friendship, and after in-sulting him, had thrown him out of his house.[9] Heracles, in retaliation, killed his son Iphitus. This murder, according to Lichas's narrative, was a just return (ξὺν δίκῃ χειρουμένῳ, 279) for Eurytus's violation of *xenia*, and would have been condoned by Zeus had Heracles not acted by stealth (275–79). But Heracles, like Eurytus, transgresses the norms of heroic behavior. He kills by deceit (δόλῳ, 277), traditionally the mode of women; fittingly, he suffers a womanly punishment: he himself becomes an object of exchange, sold to the Lydian queen, Omphale.

The Omphale episode is usually considered a low point in Heracles' heroic career: sold to a barbarian queen, Heracles becomes effeminate and a slave, in some versions dressed in a woman's clothes and assigned womanly chores.[10] In Lichas's narrative, however, it becomes part of a story that ultimately proves Heracles' valor.[11] His servitude to Omphale is an inversion of Heracles' normal heroic persona—a free man becomes an effeminate slave—but the inversion is only temporary and serves to reaffirm rather than to undermine the norm.[12] Just as the murder of Iphi-tus is a momentary lapse in Heracles' usually high standard of warfare (Lichas is sure to point out that this was the only time Heracles had ever killed by deceit, 277–78[13]), his punishment is the temporary reversal of his heroic persona. This inversion Heracles redeems with his attack on Eurytus, the author of this insult, and with the destruction of his city (256–57). Heracles proves that he is not a slave by enslaving Eurytus and his family; he proves that he is not a woman by taking the city's women captive. In Lichas's narrative, then, the attack on Oechalia re-deems Heracles' masculinity and his nobility. The story becomes a simple tale of *hubris* punished (280–83) and shows Heracles as the champion of his father's justice. Iole and the captive women, in this version, symbolize Heracles' return to his normal heroic status (281–85); their slavery to him undoes his temporary slavery to Omphale, and declares his suprem-acy and virility as a hero.

The sack of Oechalia bears a different significance in the Messenger's account, however. According to the Messenger, Heracles attacked Oechalia because of his uncontrollable desire for Iole (352–57, 431–33, 476–78). Instead of upholding the laws of *xenia*, Heracles in this version is seduced by Eros into initiating the unprovoked and unjustified attack on Eurytus (351–65).[14] Instead of redeeming his temporary servitude to Omphale, the capture of Iole evokes and repeats that episode; Iole herself becomes a second Omphale. The sack of Oechalia becomes not a heroic victory, but a shameful defeat, in which the hero "who in all other things prevails in strength has been defeated utterly by his passion for this woman" (ὡς τἄλλ᾽ ἐκεῖνος πάντ᾽ ἀριστεύων χεροῖν / τοῦ τῆσδ᾽ ἔρωτος εἰς ἅπανθ᾽ ἥσσων ἔφυ, 488–89).

The play thus tells two versions of the exchange of Iole, one reaffirming Heracles' valor as a champion of justice, the other showing him driven to violent injustice by his lust for a girl. The latter narrative proves to be the more accurate, and Lichas eventually admits his deceit.[15] Defeated by his desire for Iole, Heracles is assimilated to a slave, this servitude to Eros recalling his shameful and emasculating sale to Omphale.[16] He becomes the passive victim of Eros (368, 463, 476), fallen prey to a passion that afflicts him like a disease (445, 544), a premonition of the literal disease that will destroy him.[17] The captive Iole, who should stand as an emblem of his victory and supremacy, instead presages his defeat, slavery, and incipient decrepitude. At issue, then, in the final exchange of Iole will be Heracles' ability to remove the stain cast upon his heroic *kleos*, to control the significance of Iole, and to make her signify not his servitude but his mastery.

Heracles had been enslaved by Omphale and Iole in the past; he is defeated by his wife, Deianira, in the play's present.[18] The central action of the play is an exchange of a woman between husband and wife: Heracles sends Iole to Deianira, and in return for this "gift" (ἀντὶ δώρων δῶρα, 494) receives the robe that will kill him. If the exchange of a woman between two men is, ideally, a socially constructive transaction (and one of the bases of Heracles' subject status in this play, as I have suggested), exchange *with* a woman (at least in tragedy) is generally fatal. Not only are the products of a woman's labor generally suspect in tragedy, but Deianira's gift has a more specific derogatory association: the robe she gives Heracles evokes the robe in which Clytemnestra kills Agamemnon in Aeschylus's *Agamemnon*.[19] I shall return to the problem of Deianira's gift and mode of giving in Chapter 2; for the moment, though, we should note the drastic results of this exchange between husband and wife.

Deianira's gift kills Heracles; he whom no hero or monster could kill, as he says, is destroyed by a woman: "A woman, female and unmanly in nature, she alone destroyed me without a sword" (γυνὴ δέ, θῆλυς οὖσα κἄνανδρος φύσιν, / μόνη με δὴ καθεῖλε φασγάνου δίχα, 1062–63: the pleonasm marks the anomaly). Defeated by a woman, Heracles dies an emasculating death, killed not in combat (φασγάνου δίχα, 1063), but by a love potion, while wrapped in a *peplos*—a woman's robe, and moreover his wife's gift and handiwork[20]—making his death more akin to a female suicide by hanging than to a manly death by the sword.[21]

In the agony caused by the robe, all the elements of Heracles' identity—his physical strength, his social status, and his masculinity—are eroded. The disease disintegrates his body, the famous *biē Heraklēeiē*, before our eyes as Heracles traces the course of the disease with a litany of body parts (hands and back, 1047; shoulders, 1051; sides, flesh, lungs, blood, 1053–55; body, 1056), the same body parts that formerly defeated monstrous foes (1089–91). By the time of his death, Heracles will identify himself completely with his destroyed body as he instructs Hyllus how to dispose of him, that is, of his body (1194, 1197, 1210).

The loss of corporeal integrity is, simultaneously, a loss of status. One of the factors that differentiated a free man in Athens from a slave was his immunity from physical assault.[22] Torture was generally associated with servile deaths, and such treatment of a free man—not to mention a nobleman, as Heracles is—would be a severe compromise to his status. So, Heracles calls his disease an insult (λώβαν, 996; λωβᾶται, 1031). A king himself (1045), and a son of the king Zeus (1087–88, 1106) and a noble mother (1105), he has become, under the torture of his death, "strengthless" and "ragged" (1103), a "mere nothing" (1107).[23]

In his agony, Heracles is also feminized:

> ῏Ιθ᾿, ὦ τέκνον, τόλμησον· οἴκτιρόν τέ με
> πολλοῖσιν οἰκτρόν, ὅστις ὥστε παρθένος
> βέβρυχα κλαίων· καὶ τόδ᾿ οὐδ᾿ ἂν εἷς ποτε
> τόνδ᾿ ἄνδρα φαίη πρόσθ᾿ ἰδεῖν δεδρακότα.
> ἀλλ᾿ ἀστένακτος αἰὲν εἰχόμην κακοῖς.
> νῦν δ᾿ ἐκ τοιούτου θῆλυς ηὕρημαι τάλας.
>
> (1070–75)

Come, child, take heart and pity me, since I
seem pitiable to many, groaning and crying like

9

> a girl, and no one can ever say he saw me doing
> that before, but amidst evils I was always un-
> complaining. But now from such a man, alas,
> I am discovered a woman.

Froma Zeitlin has argued for an association in tragedy between the female and the body, particularly the body in pain.[24] Here the pain of Heracles' disease is assimilated to the pain of childbirth (πόνος, ὀδύνη, 777, 959, 985–86, 1021), and his tears are those of a girl (1071–72).[25] When Heracles reveals his body to public viewing (1078–80), the action that should visually reaffirm his physical maleness bespeaks a ruined masculinity.[26] Showing himself from behind his wrappings (ἐκ καλυμμάτων, 1078), like a bride pulling back her veils in the *anakaluptēria* (the unveiling that formed the centerpiece of the Athenian marriage ceremony),[27] Heracles reveals himself as nothing more than a body in pain: "Come, all of you, look upon my miserable body, see the ill-fortuned man, how pitiable I am" (ἰδού. θεᾶσθε πάντες ἄθλιον δέμας, / ὁρᾶτε τὸν δύστηνον. ὡς οἰκτρῶς ἔχω, 1079–80).[28]

Heracles' besieged identity is shored up in his final exchange with Hyllus, the exchange of Iole. The losses of a bad exchange with Deianira are recouped by a good exchange—in fact, the optimal exchange, the Oedipal exchange—with his son. Though the weakness of disease made Heracles a "girl," his ability to dispose as he wishes of a real girl proves him quite clearly a man. By showing himself in possession of Iole, he obliterates the memory of his own damning possession by her and, before her, Omphale. His ostensible reason for wanting Hyllus to take Iole is so that no other man may lie beside a woman who has lain at his side (1226–28). The reminder of his sexual relationship with Iole recalls, at this moment of physical and sexual weakness, Heracles' mythic virility; indeed, the care Heracles takes with Iole, because she has lain beside him, totemizes Heracles' sexuality as something so precious that whatever comes into contact with it deserves special, almost ritual, treatment. Iole, formerly an ambivalent testament to Heracles' victory over Eurytus but defeat by Eros, becomes in this final exchange an emblem of Heracles' fetishized masculinity.

With this reversal, Heracles regains not only his masculinity, but also his status: once her slave, he is now clearly Iole's master. More importantly, he is also Hyllus's master, and Hyllus's reluctance to accept his father's gift emphasizes the authority Heracles regains by offering it, for his ability to force Hyllus to accept Iole reaffirms Heracles' status as representative of the *kallistos nomos*, the paternal law.[29] This authority, more-over, places an emphasis on legitimacy and lineage that is characteristi-cally aristocratic: the bequest creates and reinforces a direct genealogical line from Zeus, through Heracles, to Hyllus. This final exchange, then, reaffirms Heracles' masculinity and sexual prowess, his position as patri-arch and head of the dynasty, in short, his status as a male subject.[30] And though the exchange cannot restore Heracles' ruined body, it does the next best thing: it replaces his body with that of his son. Iole, an ambigu-ous symbol of Heracles' heroic career, is made finally to signify Heracles' heroism, authority, and virility, and through her, this potent legacy is handed down to Hyllus.

Hyllus: The Reluctant Ephebe

The transfer of Iole not only reestablishes Heracles' status as a male subject; it also secures and defines Hyllus's, for his identity is also at stake, although it is an identity in formation, rather than one in jeopardy. Hyllus is an ephebe, a boy just on the point of entry into the community of adult men; this tragedy, like many others, dramatizes that initiation.[31] His ephebic mission is to seek out and learn about his father (65–66), to discover and bring home his father's *kleos*.[32] His own *kleos* will depend upon this mission and upon his ultimate Oedipal identification with his father, and his identity as a hero will be formulated during his ap-prenticeship as comrade and ally (ξυνέρξων, 83; σύμμαχον, 1175; cf. μαστήρ, 733) to his father.[33]

As he forges a bond with his father, Hyllus must sever his bond with his mother.[34] At the beginning of the play, his bond with his mother is strong and seemingly positive:[35] it is she who urges him to embark upon his initiatory journey to find and help his father. But as it turns out, being an ally to his father will require being an enemy to his mother. This choice between his father and his mother will be Hyllus's first test of le-gitimacy, as Heracles makes clear:

> Ὦ παῖ, γενοῦ μοι παῖς ἐτήτυμος γεγώς,
> καὶ μὴ τὸ μητρὸς ὄνομα πρεσβεύσῃς πλέον.
> (1064–65)

> Oh son, be a true-born son to me and do not give
> more honor to your mother's name.

Heracles demands that Hyllus prove his loyalty—and hence his legitimacy (ἐτήτυμος)—by handing over his mother for punishment. Heracles sets before Hyllus two pitiable spectacles, his mother's death at his
father's hands and his father's death at hers; Hyllus must adjudicate
in this competition of pathos between Deianira and Heracles, and will
himself be judged on his verdict (1066–69).[36] If he chooses wrongly,
pitying his mother's plight over his father's, he will lose his claim to legitimacy. So, later, when he presses his defense of Deianira's innocence, he is
charged with sophistry (1121) and "baseness" (1124, 1129, 1137), a
charge that impugns both nobility and legitimacy. He cannot be his father's "true-born son" if he gives preference to his "mother's name."

This would seem to be a choice that Hyllus had already made: the
"mother's name" (τὸ μητρὸς ὄνομα) he is asked to reject at 1065 he
had already denied at 815–20. There he accuses Deianira of the murder
of his father, condemning her harshly and summarily, wishing her disowned, different, or dead (734–37), and sentencing her to the same
agony she had inflicted on Heracles (819–20). His condemnation culmi-
nates in his denial of her right to bear the name of mother: "But why
should she cherish in vain the dignity of the name of mother when she
does not act at all like a mother?" (ὄγκον γὰρ ἄλλως ὀνόματος τί δεῖ
τρέφειν / μητρῷον, ἥτις μηδὲν ὡς τεκοῦσα δρᾷ; 817–18). In this
initial accusation, Hyllus expresses no doubt that Deianira intentionally
caused Heracles' death (739–40, 773–76, 807–12).[37] At the same time
as he drives her to her suicide, he glorifies his father as "the best of all
men on earth" (πάντων ἄριστον ἄνδρα τῶν ἐπὶ χθονὶ, 811), his
vilification of Deianira proportional to his canonization of Heracles.

Thus Hyllus makes the choice Heracles poses for him, rejecting his
"mother's name" and declaring himself Heracles' "true-born son." The
stakes in this decision are high and the rewards great. It is only under
Heracles' auspices that Hyllus can attain adult male subject-status, a fact
Heracles is sure to emphasize: "Hear, then, your task. You have come
to the moment when you will show what kind of man you are who
are called my son" (Σὺ δ' οὖν ἄκουε τοὔργον· ἐξήκεις δ' ἵνα / φανεὶς
ὁποῖος ὢν ἀνὴρ ἐμὸς καλῇ, 1157–58). Legitimacy is identity for Hyllus—hence the urgency of the repeated exhortations to him to be "a true
son" (1064, 1129, 1157–58, 1175, 1200–1201, 1204–5, 1250–51).
The identity he earns through proof of his legitimacy is that of a nobleman; not only is the whole preoccupation with legitimacy and genealogy elitist by nature, but Hyllus's particular lineage will make him

the son of a king, a grandson of Zeus, and a king in his own right. If Hyllus passes his tests of legitimacy, he will be *kalos*, "noble," with all its social and moral connotations;[38] if he does not, he will be *kakos* ("base," 1129), *kakistos* ("most base," 1137), and *pankakistos* ("entirely base," 1124).

Hyllus agrees to the terms set by his father and reaps the rewards of this pact. The final exchange of Iole is at once a test, a proof, and a reward of his newly acquired subject status. Iole is a symbol of his legitimate paternity, a material bequest from his father, representative of the wealth of the household he stands to inherit. She is also a symbol of his masculinity: he will take the place of his hypervirile father in her bed. The adult masculinity Hyllus assumes along with her will in turn subtend his political status as patriarch of the huge clan of Heracles' offspring. In short, Iole symbolizes all the prerogatives, social and psychological, of male subject-status guaranteed under the *kallistos nomos* of paternal authority.

Hyllus's decision would seem to mark a successful completion of the Oedipal transition: mother is exchanged for wife, maternal cathexis yields to paternal identification, and the boy takes his place as a subject in the world of men. At the same time, however, this scene also suggests the archetypal repressed Oedipal dream of killing the father and marrying the mother: not only will Hyllus identify with his father, but he will in fact replace him, all but setting his body upon the pyre himself. This murder (as Hyllus sees it, 1206–7) is permitted—indeed, commanded—by his father. Following Heracles' command, Hyllus will replace his father as sacrificer to Zeus (1192–1202; cf. 238, 245, 287–89, 608–13, 750–66), even to the extent of performing his task tearlessly (1200), just as Heracles had his own heroic labors (1074). Identification becomes identity as son replaces father. So, too, the son is allowed—again, commanded—to marry his father's woman (and thus a mother figure, if not literally his mother);[39] by complying with his father's order, Hyllus will replace Heracles as Iole's husband.[40] The final exchange, then, allows Hyllus to have it both ways: he gets both the Oedipal fantasy (to kill his father and marry his mother) and the successful Oedipal resolution (to trade his mother for another woman and bond with his father). He is allowed both to keep his mother and to replace her through sublimation, both to identify with his father and to kill him. And all of this is sanctioned and even demanded by the person who ought to prevent and punish it, his father.

This fantasy of total prerogative under the rule of the father is vouchsafed by Hyllus's obedience to the *kallistos nomos* of paternal authority, as if absolute compliance carried with it unlimited privilege—actual and fantasied—for the male subject. The final exchange of Iole, even as it guarantees male subjectivity, also recements the law upon which such subjectivity is grounded, and the social and symbolic order that law governs. The *kallistos nomos* legitimizes patriarchy, as Heracles reaffirms his paternal authority and Hyllus receives his identity only by acceding to that authority;[41] it likewise guarantees patriliny, enshrining the bond between father and son as the most productive social bond (the word "father" and cognates occur twenty-three times in the last 307 lines) and making subjectivities—both father's and son's—dependent upon it.[42] This patriline is, moreover, royal, stretching from the mythic, heroic past to the historic kings of Sparta.[43]

This whole world is guaranteed in the final scene to Hyllus, if only he will swear obedience to his father. And yet Hyllus balks. The inaugural moment is darkened by a marked emphasis on resistance, reluctance, compulsion, and coerced submission.[44] Hyllus is afraid to swear blind obedience to his father's oath (1179–80); he hesitates at Heracles' command that he light the pyre (1203, 1206–7), fearing to become his father's murderer; he refuses to marry Iole, regarding this command as a sacrilege, a *dussebeia*, and a symptom of Heracles' diseased mind (1230–31, 1233–37, 1241, 1243, 1245, 1247). His reluctance is met each time by injunctions to obey the law and the oath, by paternal curses and the threat of disinheritance. In order to reap the benefits of the *kallistos nomos*—legitimacy, identity, masculinity, authority—Hyllus must abase himself before it, must swear blind obedience to it, even though it seems to him a *dussebeia*.

This drama of resistance and compulsion crystallizes around the exchange of Iole. The transaction that should cement and symbolize this moment of reinauguration becomes itself the point of rupture. Given the wealth of prerogatives she represents, why is Hyllus so reluctant to take Iole? Various explanations have been posed for Hyllus's hesitation: Oedipal anxieties,[45] the legal problem of a prince's marriage to a concubine,[46] the peremptory and insensitive manner in which Heracles transacts this exchange,[47] or even the straightforward reason Hyllus himself gives: he holds Iole "solely responsible" (μόνη μεταίτιος, 1233–34) for his parents' deaths. But I suggest that Hyllus's objection is not so much to the modality or manner of the exchange as to the exchange itself and to the psychic economy of the Oedipal bargain, in which the female object is the price paid for the male subject and symbolic. I argue in Chapters 2 and 3 that precisely this schema of male subject and female object—indeed, the very distinction between subject and object—is dissolved in the first part of the play, and that this dissolution haunts the final episode in the figure of Iole, who embodies and represents—re-presents to the audience—the tragedy of Deianira.

Deianira's life offers a wisdom, a psychic model different from that of Heracles. Hyllus's ephebic education, I suggested above, requires that he learn about and identify with his father. But alongside this education is another, which involves learning from his mother. This alternate education is evoked in Hyllus's first line of the play: "Teach me, mother, if it may be taught to me" (δίδαξον, μῆτερ, εἰ διδακτά μοι, 64). While what he learns from his father will make him Heracles' legitimate heir,[48] his *anagnōrisis*, his tragic recognition, will not be insight into his father's heroism, but rather the discovery, too late of course, of his mother's true character and intentions ("Learning too late from those in the house that she did these deeds unwillingly, because of the beast," ὄψ' ἐκδιδα-χθεὶς τῶν κατ' οἶκον οὕνεκα / ἄκουσα πρὸς τοῦ θηρὸς ἔρξειεν τάδε, 934–35).

In this play preoccupied with knowledge, knowledge of another becomes the prototype for epistemological uncertainty in general: the play opens with an ancient warning against judging the life of another, and the sentiment becomes something of a leitmotiv in the play. I shall suggest that Hyllus's *anagnōrisis*, his recognition of his mother's innocence, makes impossible the simple exchange of women that the final scene requires, because it recognizes the wholeness and autonomy—the subjectivity—of the female other. Once Hyllus has recognized Deianira as a subject, can he simply trade her for an objectified Iole? If he does, he risks reproducing in his own generation the tragic events of his father's life.

The traumatic accession to subjectivity of the male hero is built upon the object status of the woman, but *Trachiniae*, by staging Deianira's struggle for subject status, questions this necessary drama of male subjectivity. The woman in *Trachiniae* is the legitimating other, the object that guarantees the male subject, but also a site of potential resistance. The exploration of Deianira's character in the first two-thirds of the play undermines the foundations of *Trachiniae*'s symbolic order, the distinction between self and other and between subject and object, the social economy that exchanges women, and the subjectivities structured by that economy. Deianira's memory is repressed, the very question of her guilt or innocence forgotten. But the repressed returns, and the presence of the female in the final scene unsettles, even as it enables, the paternal symbolic. Hyllus's reluctance to take Iole—a moment's hesitation that calls under suspicion the *kallistos nomos* itself—is the symptom of that uneasy but fertile repression.

The final exchange in *Trachiniae* is paradigmatic of the exchanges of women we shall see in all three tragedies examined in this book. The oppression of women generates a resistance in the text toward the very system that oppresses them. That these two aspects—oppression and resistance—can coexist is manifest in Hyllus's reluctant compliance, his simultaneous exposure and reaffirmation of the *kallistos nomos*. I shall return to this critical moment at the end of Chapter 3, after exploring Deianira's life and legacy, a legacy, I argue, that undermines the stability of the final exchange in a positive way. Hyllus's *anagnōrisis* and the moment of hesitation it precipitates offer a point of resistance that, though it does not in the end hold up against the suasion of the paternal law, nonetheless opens a space for interrogation, critique, and the imagination of alternatives. In Hyllus's ambivalent acceptance of Iole, the power and prerogative that he inherits from his father are reexamined, questioned, and challenged, if only momentarily, by the knowledge and insight that are his mother's bequest.

TWO

THE FORECLOSED FEMALE SUBJECT

W hen we speak of the woman as an object of exchange, what do we really mean? How can a living individual be an object? To call a woman an object is to speak metaphorically, grammatically, structurally. The terms of discussion shift radically when we ask what it is like to occupy that position of object.[1] This is precisely the question I think *Trachiniae* asks. Deianira had been an object of exchange, just like Iole; but unlike Iole, Deianira speaks, narrating her own past objectification and struggling to position herself as a subject. This struggle will ultimately fail, delegitimizing Deianira as a subject and reaffirming the system that has objectified her; Deianira, after disabling any complacent assumption of the female object, ends up finding foreclosed any real possibility of a valid female subject. At the same time, however, her attempt to participate actively in the world of male subjects will pose a critique of that world, elucidating the categories within which the subject—male or female—is constructed and uncovering the simultaneously inescapable and arbitrary nature of this construction.

IOLE, DEIANIRA, AND THE TRIANGLE OF EXCHANGE

I suggested in the last chapter that in Hyllus's reluctance to accept Iole is encapsulated the entire tragedy of Deianira. Iole is in the play's present what Deianira was in the past. Just as in the Oedipal scenario a wife eventually replaces the lost mother, so Iole replaces and represents

Deianira, returning her to the stage in posthumous form. The sublimation of Deianira as Iole is facilitated by the many parallels between the two women.[2] Iole, like Deianira, is a stranger in Trachis (39, 240–41, 299–300), taken from her parents into a new and unhappy existence. Iole will become a second wife to Heracles, sharing Deianira's marriage. Deianira herself openly identifies with the girl, pitying her because her beauty, like Deianira's own, has brought her misery.[3]

Like Iole, moreover, Deianira had been the object of an exchange between men: she is "the much fought-for Deianira" (τὰν ἀμφινεικῆ Δηϊάνειραν, 104; cf. 527). Deianira had been won by Heracles in a wrestling match against the river-god Achelous; the contest is narrated in Deianira's opening speech, and later recounted in more detail by the chorus in the First Stasimon. The play thus opens with the exchange of Deianira just as it closes with the exchange of Iole: the contest for Deianira founds the heroic world that is transmitted with Iole in the final scene. Further, the dynamics we saw in the final exchange are present and even clearer in the first exchange. The transfers of Deianira and Iole both emerge at a point on the spectrum of male homosocial relations where aggression and eroticism intersect: the relations generated by these exchanges are driven simultaneously by a desire for domination and a homoerotic desire.[4] As for the women themselves, as Eve Sedgwick (1985) has shown, they are both central to this bonding between men—constituting their relationship, but also concealing its nature—and at the same time radically excluded from it. Reading Deianira's exchange against Iole's reveals this unspoken homosocial dynamic. It also warns us what is at stake in the final exchange: will that marriage be as tragic as the first? Will Iole be another Deianira and Hyllus another Heracles?

A wrestling match may seem at first sight incomparable to a paternal bequest, but the two transactions are in fact isomorphic. In both the *agōn* (competition) and the bequeathal, the movement of a woman defines a relationship between the two men, and affirms the subject status of each, both vis-à-vis one another and in opposition to the female object. The difference is modal, not structural, the *agōn* emphasizing more the hierarchical relation between the competitors, while the amicable exchange announces their equality and reciprocity. But even the difference of modality is not stable: the amicable exchange of Iole, as we have seen, conceals coercion and structures a deeper inequality; conversely, the competition over Deianira masks an intimate, even erotic, bond between the antagonists.

The competition for Deianira is recounted in the First Stasimon (the second choral ode), which comes just after Deianira has first learned of Heracles' love for Iole. The Stasimon, which begins as an epinician, a victory ode, to Kypris (Aphrodite),[5] would seem to celebrate the goddess's victory over Heracles by recalling a prior victory: Eros now drives him to sack Oechalia for Iole even as it once made him wrestle Achelous for Deianira. As the ode progresses, however, both the directionality and the object of desire become increasingly unclear.

The center of the poem (503–22), as we might expect in an epinician, is devoted to the *agōn*, with vivid descriptions of the sights and sounds of the struggle. The contest is described in the technical terminology of epinician athletic contest: the contestants "enter the ring" (κατέβαν, 504), they "come into the center" (ἵσαν ἐς μέσον, 514) and engage in the "violent and dusty struggle of the contest" (πάμπληκτα παγκό-νιτά τ' ἐξ-/ῆλθον ἄεθλ' ἀγώνων, 505–6), and the "interwoven grap-plings" of wrestling (ἀμφίπλεκτοι κλίμακες, 520); Aphrodite herself is their umpire (ῥαβδονόμει, 516).[6] The agonistic terminology is strongly marked, the aristocratic and high-literary connotations of epinician, not to mention the divinity of the contestants, elevating this *agōn* to heroic grandeur.[7]

But alongside the overt agonistic diction is erotic diction, which may at first sight seem out of place in this violent setting and, more remark-ably, seems to connect Heracles and Achelous, rather than either hero with his ostensible love-object, Deianira.

> οἳ τότ' ἀολλεῖς
> ἵσαν ἐς μέσον ἱέμενοι λεχέων·
> μόνα δ' εὔλεκτρος ἐν μέσῳ Κύπρις
> ῥαβδονόμει ξυνοῦσα.
>
> (513–16)

> Then they came together into the
> center, desiring the marriage bed.
> There in the middle with them, Kypris
> who blesses marriage is their only
> umpire.

The general sexual aura of Aphrodite's presence, as well as the more specific sexual connotations of ξυνοῦσα ("being with"),[8] make the referent of ἱέμενοι λεχέων ("desiring the marriage bed") ambiguous. Modeled on such Homeric phrases as ἱέμενοι μάχης ("desiring battle"), the phrase here seems to locate the focus of erotic desire in the contest itself. The very physical intimacy of the two heroes in their struggle is tinged with eroticism.

How are we to explain the homoerotics of this *agōn*? Is it simply a general and diffused eroticism emanating from the presence of Aphrodite? Sophocles is too careful with his words for this to be a sufficient explanation. Is it an importation of desire for Deianira into the ring? After all, in literal terms, hers is the bed they both desire. But she herself has barely been mentioned, and the position of these erotic words, surrounding the two heroes as they come together, suggests there is more to it. Instead, I would suggest, there is a shift of erotic focus through this ode, away from Deianira and onto the *agōn* itself. If we were to map the erotic trajectory of the ode and its shifting triangulations,[9] we would see a movement from the heterosexual (with each man vying individually for the woman) to the homoerotic (with the bond between the two heroes mediated through the woman).

But there is one final step. In the last strophe, the woman is removed from the arena entirely. Already marginal in the *agōn*, in these last lines Deianira is removed both spatially and emotionally; she cannot even bear to watch. Deianira is replaced as an erotic object and as mediator between the two men by another female, Kypris. She, unlike Deianira, is actively involved in the fray, its object (she is "in the middle," where in Homer the prizes are placed[10]), but also its judge (ῥαβδονόμει); she both joins with the men and joins them one to the other. Therefore the final configuration of this erotic triangle would represent the pure homoerotics of the *agōn*. The desire that suffuses the *agōn*, then, is shown to unite the two male competitors, rather than either competitor with the female object. The competition that should differentiate the two as winner and loser leaves them inseparably entwined (ἀνάμιγδα, "intermixed," 519; ἀμφίπλεκτοι, "interwoven," 520).[11] With Aphrodite as umpire, the *agōn* itself, the very struggle for victory, is eroticized.

A similar homoerotics suffuses the final exchange of Iole. The identification between father and son that the transfer cements is libidinized, and again this homosocial cathexis replaces a heterosexual one. The "delight" (*terpsis*) that should exist between husband and wife is absent in this play, both in the relationship between Heracles and Deianira (whose only *terpsis* is reciprocal murder, 819–20) and in that between Hyllus and Iole (as evinced by Hyllus's total lack of sexual interest in her in the final scene [12]). Instead, *terpsis* inheres within the bond between Hyllus and Heracles (1246). So it is Hyllus, not Deianira, who will spread out the bed for his sick father (901–2, traditionally the wife's task).[13] Heracles even calls on Hyllus to "die with" him (συνθανεῖν, 798), a self-sacrifice usually undertaken by the wife, and one that Deianira claims for herself at 720.[14] The erotic cathexis between father and son elevates this bond above both that between husband and wife and that between mother and son.[15] The effect is a conflation of the biological bond with the homosexual pedagogical bond between *erastēs* and *erōmenos*, lover and beloved, a conflation that legitimates the father as both the social and the natural parent, excluding the mother from this progenitive relationship.[16] And this homosocial bond, like that in the First Stasimon, is also a relation of domination: the relationship depends upon Hyllus's submission; it is that which is Heracles' "delight" at 1246.

At the heart of the exchange of women, then, is a male homosociality in which agonism and desire are thoroughly intermeshed. The desire for a woman that ostensibly motivates the exchange is inseparable from the homosocial desire that unites the two men, and this desire is at base a desire for domination. The relation of domination finds an easy analog in the hierarchy that structures Athenian male homosexuality (with its clear opposition between the active and the passive partner [17]), so that homosocial desire—the desire that drives the exchange—is at once erotic and agonistic. This eroticism of domination within homosocial relations is legitimated by the presence of the woman, who provides an ostensible object for both desire and aggression. In the exchange of a woman, heterosexual "love" is made to conceal homosocial aggression and the desire for a woman to conceal the desire for domination. This is not to deny the *erōs* between men and women—Heracles' love for Iole or Deianira's for Heracles—that is so central to the action of the play, but rather to suggest that this simple (if powerful) passion is only the most explicit aspect of a more complex structure of power and desire that, first and foremost, unites men.

Where does this leave the woman?

> ῾Α δ᾽ εὐῶπις ἁβρὰ
> τηλαυγεῖ παρ᾽ ὄχθῳ

ἧστο τὸν ὃν προσμένουσ᾽ ἀκοίταν.

. . . .

τὸ δ᾽ ἀμφινείκητον ὄμμα νύμφας
ἐλεινὸν ἀμμένει ⟨τέλος⟩·
κἀπὸ ματρὸς ἄφαρ βέβαχ᾽.
ὥστε πόρτις ἐρήμα.

(523–25, 527–30)

But the delicate beauty sat on a distant
hill, waiting for the man who would be
her husband. . . . The fair bride who is
the prize of the strife[18] piteously awaits
the outcome. And suddenly she is gone
from her mother, like a calf abandoned.

The First Stasimon positions the woman not only as an object of the competition, but as an irrelevant object, marginal to the homosocial negotiations that, I have proposed, are the true business of the exchange. Silenced, exiled—a lonely calf—Deianira becomes in this strophe the pure object of exchange that Iole is in the final episode. Like Iole, Deianira is not even present to witness, much less influence, the outcome.

But from this position of total objectification and marginalization Deianira speaks, declaring herself a subject. She opens the play with a strong claim to her subject status: "There is an ancient proverb current among men that you cannot know the life of a mortal before he dies, whether it was good or bad. But I know my own life even before I have gone to Hades, that it is ill-fortuned and sorrowful" (1–3).[19] In this opening sentence, Deianira introduces herself as subject of her own narrative, possessor of that elusive Delphic wisdom that all Sophoclean heroes seek. The proof Deianira offers of this claim to self-knowledge is the narrative of her exchange in the wrestling match between Heracles and Achelous (9–27): her present subject status is forged from her past objectification.[20] Thus while the First Stasimon provides the play's deepest insight into a structure of male relations to which women are truly marginal, it offers the woman, even in that position of marginality, a space for subjectivization. I return to that space in the next chapter, after witnessing what happens when the woman tries to leave the hillside and herself enter into the "violent and dusty struggle of the contest."

Anti dōrōn dōra: Deianira's Gift-Giving

How does a woman position herself as a subject in a world that requires her to be an object? Deianira begins, logically enough, with those institutions through which men define themselves: she tries to participate actively in the *agōn* and gift exchange. She imagines herself in an *agōn* with Iole, a competition for the prize of Heracles. She uses the love potion in the hope that it will allow her to defeat Iole (ὑπερβαλώμεθα, 584–85), lest Iole be a disease, rather than a prize that she may win for herself (ἐξαρούμεθα, 491).[21] Deianira also presents herself, although in negative terms, as a boxer against Eros (441–44, 492); even as she admits the futility of fighting against the gods, Deianira enters into the fray, thus laying claim to a place in the erotic-agonistic triangle.[22]

That Deianira's attempt to situate herself actively within the *agōn* must ultimately fail is emphasized by the placement of the First Stasimon:[23] Deianira's imaginations of herself as an antagonist against Iole cluster immediately before (490–96) and after (531–87) the First Stasimon, the most eloquent elimination of the woman from the heroic arena. The urgency of this elimination was glimpsed in the last chapter: when Deianira is an antagonist, Heracles becomes her prize, feminized, corporealized, objectified. Yet if Deianira is inevitably barred from victory—even from competing—nevertheless, the mere attempt to participate is significant. Deianira's use of agonistic terminology in the first person indicates that the text is aware of the structures that bar her from power, and suggests a desire, however slight and unattainable, to loosen their grip. It is also significant, however, that rather than disavowing the agonistic structure entirely, Deianira hopes merely to occupy one of its positions of power. Thus she becomes a willing participant in the very structures that oppress her.

The result is the same when Deianira tries to participate actively in a gift exchange. The central action of this tragedy is an exchange between husband and wife: Heracles "gives" Deianira Iole; Deianira gives in exchange the poisoned robe that will cause both his death and her own:

> Ἀλλ' εἴσω στέγης
> χωρῶμεν. ὡς λόγων τ' ἐπιστολὰς φέρῃς.
> ἅ τ' ἀντὶ δώρων δῶρα χρὴ προσαρμόσαι.

καὶ ταῦτ᾽ ἄγῃς. Κενὸν γὰρ οὐ δίκαιά σε
χωρεῖν προσελθόνθ᾽ ὧδε σὺν πολλῷ στόλῳ.

(492–96)

But let's go inside so that you may carry the man-
date of my words, and since it is fitting that gifts
be given in exchange for gifts, take these also.
For it is not just that you should go back empty-
handed when you came so well provided.

By accepting Iole as a gift and offering gifts in exchange, Deianira proclaims herself a subject in the exchange and an equal partner with Heracles. The very formulation of the phrase—*anti dōrōn dōra*, gifts in exchange for gifts—emphasizes the reciprocity and equality to which she
lays claim with her "fitting" and "just" (χρή, δίκαιά) return.

The gift she gives, however, immediately disqualifies this claim; for
Deianira's gift is fatal, and instead of uniting her and Heracles, it destroys
them both; instead of affirming her status as a genteel exchanger, it
justifies her exclusion from the exchange. Even in this first formulation,
the lethal nature of Deianira's *dōron* is hinted at: προσαρμόσαι, the verb
used of Deianira's preparation of the gift at 494, anticipates the fasten-
ing of the deadly robe on Heracles at 1051.[24] The robe and poison are
described as Deianira's *tekhnē* ("craft") and *mēkhanē* ("contrivance,"
534, 586, 774), terms that tap into a deep-lying suspicion, manifest
throughout Greek literature, toward the products of women's labor.[25]
Ann Bergren has traced the connection between women's work, especially weaving, and the cultural associations of women with deceit,
dolos.[26] Thus, even in the case of the paradigmatically good and loyal
woman, Penelope, her weaving is a *dolos*; a sign of her domestic produc-
tivity and loyalty, it is also a trick, aimed at the suitors but (they argue,
Od. 2.125ff.) potentially destructive of the wealth of Odysseus's household. So, too, Deianira's *tekhnē* is planned in secret (534, 556, 596,
606–9) inside the house and has connotations of magic:[27] it is a "pain
that brings deliverance" (λυτήριον λύπημα, 554),[28] an "enticement"
(κηλητήριον, 575), a "philter" (φίλτροις, 584), a "charm" (θέλ-
κτροισι, 585), and comes with detailed ritual prescriptions (603–13).
Deianira's deed turns out to be an "evil act" (κακὸν μέγ᾽ ἐκπράξασ᾽,
667), a "terrible deed" (ἔργον δεινὸν, 706), and a crime committed in
innocence is presumed to be a deception (808, 1050).

24

Women's work has generally negative connotations in Greek literature, but Deianira's robe has a more specifically damning association: it
is linked verbally to the robe in which Clytemnestra kills her husband
in Aeschylus's *Agamemnon*. Heracles calls the robe a "woven net of the
Furies" ('Ερινύων / ὑφαντὸν ἀμφίβληστρον, 1051–52), a phrase that
clearly evokes the net in which Clytemnestra entraps and kills Agamemnon (ἄπειρον ἀμφίβληστρον, *Ag.* 1382; ὑφαντοῖς ἐν πέπλοις
'Ερινύων, *Ag.* 1580).[29] Despite very real differences between the intentions and characterizations of the two heroines, Deianira's gift evokes
the most negative stereotype of feminine activity, Clytemnestra.[30] When
Deianira tries to define herself as an active subject in the exchange, she is
instead trapped by a structure that seems to allow her no middle ground
between passive object and dangerous, destructive subject.[31]

Not only is Deianira's gift fatal, but the manner in which she gives it,
and indeed the way in which she conceives the whole exchange, is extremely problematic. The transaction into which Deianira enters with
her *anti dōrōn dōra* is no commonplace trade, but rather a gift exchange,
a prestigious reciprocal exchange between two equal and generally elite
individuals.[32] In gift exchange, as opposed to commodity exchange, the
object given has a primarily symbolic value, reflecting the value of the
bond, the occasion, and the exchangers: the transaction is represented
as a symbolic gesture of goodwill between equals, in contrast to the
self-interested, profit-motivated transactions between strangers in the
marketplace.[33] The quintessential object of gift exchange is the *agalma*,
an object of inestimable value and prestige,[34] the possession of which
marks the exchangers as themselves valuable and prestigious, which is to
say aristocratic.

It is this genteel world of prestigious gifts and elite exchangers that
Deianira enters with her formula *anti dōrōn dōra*. Both gifts in this exchange are *agalmata*. A woman—a bride—is among the most valuable
gifts in the economy of gift exchange, cementing the most important
bonds. Iole, the symbol of Heracles' victory and a bride of high birth, is a
particularly precious *agalma*. Similarly, the robe, despite its disastrous effects, has many qualities of an *agalma*: beautiful, valuable, and magical,
it is carefully preserved, and when it is revealed, the moment is vaguely
epiphanic (604–13).[35] Not only are the gifts prestigious, but the occasion of the exchange is as well: it celebrates Heracles' victory over
Eurytus and the fulfillment of the prophecy that (or so they think) por-
tends Heracles' freedom from labor.

Thus Deianira defines herself as an aristocratic subject by categorizing her dealings with Heracles as an elite gift exchange. Elsewhere, however, she refers to the transaction in terms that debase both the exchange and herself.

Κόρην γάρ. οἶμαι δ' οὐκέτ'. ἀλλ' ἐζευγμένην.
παρεσδέδεγμαι, φόρτον ὥστε ναυτίλος.
λωβητὸν ἐμπόλημα τῆς ἐμῆς φρενός.
καὶ νῦν δύ' οὖσαι μίμνομεν μιᾶς ὑπὸ
χλαίνης ὑπαγκάλισμα. τοιάδ' Ἡρακλῆς.
ὁ πιστὸς ἡμῖν κἀγαθὸς καλούμενος.
οἰκούρι' ἀντέπεμψε τοῦ μακροῦ χρόνου.

(536–42)

I have taken in a maiden—no, a maiden no
longer, I think, but a married woman—like a
sailor taking on cargo, merchandise baneful to
my heart. And now, two women under one blan-
ket, we await his embrace. Such wages for housekeeping has Heracles sent, a man called faithful
and noble, in repayment for his long absence.

By calling Iole "cargo" (φόρτον, ἐμπόλημα), Deianira transforms the aristocratic gift exchange into a base commodity exchange. No longer a priceless *agalma*, Iole becomes unspecified freight.[36] The relationship between Deianira and Heracles is no longer one between aristocratic equals, but one between purveyor and transporter of goods. Likewise, at 542, Deianira calls Iole an οἰκούρια, a *hapax* meaning "payment for housekeeping": she transforms a valuable gift into the payment of wages for domestic services. Heracles sends Iole to Deianira as part of an aris-tocratic reciprocal exchange (ἀντέπεμψε, 542), but she receives her as a payment for service rendered. Her disenchantment of the elite econ-omy is also a demystification of the subjects grounded upon it. If a gift exchange marks the giver an aristocrat, this exchange calls Heracles' status into question: he is ἀγαθὸς καλούμενος (541), a "so-called aristocrat."

In Deianira's mouth, Heracles' entire heroic career is subject to a profit-and-loss accountancy.[37] Heracles' temporary and anomalous slav-ery to Omphale Deianira generalizes to his labors in their entirety: "Such a fate always sends my husband to the house and away again, in servitude to someone" (τοιοῦτος αἰὼν εἰς δόμους τε κἀκ δόμων / ἀεὶ τὸν ἄνδρ' ἔπεμπε λατρεύοντά τῳ, 34–35).[38] So, too, his success is a financial boon: "For even for one who comes later, success buys profit (*kerdos*), whenever one hears of it" (καὶ γὰρ ὑστέρῳ, τό γ' εὖ / πράσσειν ἐπεὶ πύθοιτο, κέρδος ἐμπολᾷ, 92–93).[39] *Kerdos* is one of the most suspect terms for wealth; unlike many other more metaphorical and euphemistic terms, its connotations are almost always crassly material.[40] Ἐμπολᾷ ("buys," 93) not only makes explicit the bartering in Heracles' own history (250), but also foreshadows the ἐμπόλημα ("merchandise") Iole at 538. The hero becomes a trafficker in heroism.

Deianira's mercantile diction thus poses an implicit critique of the entire economy of heroism—an economy built, as we saw in the last chapter, on the circulation of women. The exchange of women, especially in marriage, occupies the highest tier of gift exchange: it is the most prestigious, most idealized form of an already prestigious and idealized transaction. The bride is an *agalma*, precious and priceless, and her exchange symbolic of a lasting bond between two houses. But from another perspective, this exchange is merely a financial transaction between father-in-law and son-in-law, in which the bride herself is part of a dowry given in return for wooing-gifts.[41] When Deianira disenchants her exchange with Heracles, she lays bare a crude economics underlying the romanticized exchange of women: the financial bartering, the dowry and wooing-gifts, the flow of money and goods subtending a transaction that purports to be purely symbolic. Conflating gift exchange and the business of the agora, Deianira locates marriage in the brothel: the traffic in women becomes in her mouth not a glorious, civilization-building structure, but just a bad deal, and those who trade in it, like Heracles, ὁ ἀγαθὸς καλούμενος noble in name alone. It is no coincidence that Deianira's most virulent attacks on the economy of gift exchange fall immediately before (490–96) and after (531–87) the First Stasimon: her critique should be seen in the context of her own past objectification and exchange within this economy.

Imagine the female subject that could be predicated upon such a critique. For a brief moment we are offered the possibility of a counterhegemonic position, of a resistant, critical, even subversive female subject. But that possibility is immediately foreclosed, for when she demystifies the exchange of women, Deianira debases herself. If Iole becomes, in her words, "cargo," she herself becomes a mere sailor, a man of subordinate position and one who, though he may take on cargo, does not have the authority to dispose of it.[42] So, too, if Iole is just an οἰκούρια, payment for housekeeping, as she says at 542, this makes Deianira nothing more than a wage-laborer in Heracles' house. And what looks from one perspective like a conscious critique appears from another to be a simple misunderstanding of the rules of elite exchange or an inability to play by them. Whether cynical critique or tactical failure, Deianira's debased economic language justifies her exclusion from active participation in the economy of gifts.[43]

Moreover, we should note that to the extent that Deianira is in fact able to occupy a legitimate position in the aristocratic gift exchange, it is only by constructing Iole as the object of exchange. We saw in the last chapter that Iole-as-object allows Heracles and Hyllus to define themselves as subjects in the final transaction of the play. Deianira, too, buys her own subjectivity at the price of Iole's, thus reaffirming a system that, in the First Stasimon, had objectified her as well.

Deianira's attempt to engage in the exchange reveals a dynamic that will become all too familiar throughout the course of this book: a dynamic of critique foreclosed. Possibilities are raised only to be proved impossible; potentially subversive alternatives are introduced only to be immediately banished. The woman's failed attempt to participate in the system that oppresses her achieves a multiple purpose: first, it reaffirms the system, which is posited as the only valid forum for subject formation; second, it allows for an institutionalized (and therefore contained) form of resistance to the system, a critique that questions without undermining the basic structure; and third, while allowing that critique to be voiced, it delegitimizes anyone who voices it, thus reinscribing the repressed status of the critique and the hegemonic status of the system and its legitimate participants. This dynamic of critique foreclosed is in part, I suggest, what makes the female subject so useful a construct in tragedy.

In the end, Deianira's very attempt is forgotten and her critique eliminated. Deianira's gift reactivates the prior gift from Nessus, enacting onstage the original conflict between the hero and the centaur. If this reenactment makes her the subject (however abjected or dangerous) of her own exchange, it also makes her actions merely instrumental in the larger conflict between Nessus and Heracles. Just as in the First Stasimon the woman is the medium of a male power struggle, so, too, in the play overall, the woman can be seen as no more than an intermediary in the contest between heroes. Throughout most of the play, Deianira's actions and intentions are at issue; but once Heracles discovers the source of the poison (1114–45), Deianira's involvement is immediately forgotten. Hyllus's belated defense of his mother's innocence is ultimately neither refuted nor accepted, it is simply ignored, and Deianira's agency is subsumed within a larger structure of exchange. She is not mentioned again in the play.

STATUS AND GENDER

We have seen that Deianira tries to participate in the specifically aristocratic world of gift exchange; as the daughter and wife of kings she has some right to consider herself an aristocrat.[44] Her interactions with characters of lower social status, however, show that there is a subtle interplay between the advantages of status and the disadvantages of gender. With the women of lower status—the Nurse[45] and the captive women[46]—Deianira has a relatively unproblematic mistress-slave relationship. Only Iole threatens her authority as Heracles' wife and head of his *oikos*: a princess herself, and innately and manifestly noble (308–9, 313), Iole is introduced into the house not as a slave (367) but as a wife (428). More than Heracles' love (which, as she acknowledges at 460, she has shared before), Deianira resents sharing her marriage and her position as his wife.[47] Status is pitted against gender as Deianira worries that Heracles will be her husband, but the younger woman's "man" (ταῦτ' οὖν φοβοῦμαι μὴ πόσις μὲν Ἡρακλῆς / ἐμὸς καλῆται, τῆς νεωτέρας δ' ἀνήρ, 550–51).

The conflict between status and gender is clearer in Deianira's relationship to the male heralds, men belonging to a lower social echelon.[48] In their first encounter (229–334), Lichas pays no particular deference to Queen Deianira. Addressing her, when he does, only as "lady" (γύναι, 230, 251),[49] Lichas makes no overt recognition of her status, and her (presumed) authority over him; contrast the chorus's vocative ἄνασσα, "queen" (291), and the addresses of the more deferential Messenger (γύναι at 366, but δέσποινα, "mistress," at 370). In the confrontation that follows the revelation of the Messenger, Deianira's social status becomes a focal issue in the attempt to force the truth from Lichas. Deianira's first attempts to confront Lichas fail (398–401), her questions receiving no more truthful or courteous responses than in their first meeting. At that point the investigation is preempted by the Messenger.[50]

It is he who reminds Lichas of his inferior status and the deference he owes Deianira:

ΑΓ. οὗτος, βλέφ' ὧδε. πρὸς τίν' ἐννέπειν δοκεῖς;
. . . .
ΛΙ. πρὸς τὴν κρατοῦσαν Δηάνειραν, Οἰνέως
κόρην, δάμαρτά θ' Ἡρακλέους, εἰ μὴ κυρῶ
λεύσσων μάταια, δεσπότιν τε τὴν ἐμήν.

(402, 405–7)

MESSENGER: Look here, you. Who do you think
you're talking to?
LICHAS: To the queen Deianira, daughter of Oeneus,
wife of Heracles, if my eyes don't deceive me, and my
mistress.

Why doesn't Deianira herself use her status to force Lichas into submission? Why must she wait for recognition from an even more marginal man, the Messenger? Although Deianira's status is an important factor in her power relation with the herald (from that point on, Lichas does refer to her as δέσποινα, 430, 434), she is unable or unwilling to use it to her advantage. Perhaps she is caught between two conflicting sets of rules: those of status and those of femininity. As a queen, she might assert her status over the herald, but as a woman, and especially as a woman speaking publicly with men, she concedes her social advantage.[51]

The Messenger coopts for his own the advantage that Deianira fails to use for herself. As he takes over the questioning, it appears that the evocation of her royalty was merely a rhetorical ploy to put Lichas on the defensive. Deianira now becomes a silent jury in the Messenger's case against the herald. The Messenger may not have legitimate access to the rhetoric of aristocratic evaluation, but he does have use of the democratic Athenian discourse of the law-courts. The diction becomes markedly juridical, with four uses of *dikē* ("justice," "court case") in as many lines (409–12), as does the argument, which is based upon witnesses (422–23) and sworn testimony (427).[52] This is the rhetoric of the Athenian citizen, a rhetoric that, as a woman, Deianira cannot effectively use.

To the juridical discourse of the Messenger, Deianira answers with the aristocratic discourse allowed by her status. With her long speech, loaded with terms of aristocratic evaluation (436–69), Deianira not only regains control of the debate, but actually wins it, forcing Lichas into submission (472–74). She begins the speech by calling attention to her *sōphrosunē*, her wisdom and moderation (438–48), and to her status, not only as queen but as an aristocrat (οὐ . . . γυναικὶ . . . κακῇ, 438). When she turns on Lichas (449–58), she combines aristocratic evaluative terminology (*kalos/kakos*, 450, 452, 454, 457) with the slave-free hierarchy (ἐλευθέρῳ, 453) to force Lichas to tell her the truth by reminding him of the source of her authority over him.[53]

Lichas is defeated: he apologizes and agrees to tell Deianira the truth, "since I know that you think as mortals should and not ignobly" ('Αλλ', ὦ φίλη δέσποιν', ἐπεί σε μανθάνω / θνητὴν φρονοῦσαν θνητὰ κοὐκ ἀγνώμονα, 472–73). The diction is aristocratic, suggesting Lichas's recognition of the basis for Deianira's authority.[54] It is also, significantly, gender-neutral. When Deianira speaks as an aristocrat, she surmounts the limitations of her femininity and wins attention, recognition, and praise.[55]

Deianira does eventually prevail over Lichas, but only as an aristocrat and only to the extent that she can suppress her gender. The scene shows clearly the categories within which the self is constructed and constrained. Ironically, too, the information Deianira obtains in this scene by virtue of being an aristocrat—that Heracles loves Iole—will destroy her as a woman: not only do status and gender work against one another in defining her public persona and her relations with others, they also divide her and make her work against herself.

A WOMAN'S *kleos*

So far, all of Deianira's attempts to define herself as an active subject have been in terms of male heroics. Is there any basis on which a woman can claim any positive social evaluation—*kleos* ("glory") or *aretē* ("excellence")—in her own right, as a woman?[56] Thucydides' (or Pericles') famous pronouncement on women, that their *kleos* is to have nothing said of them for good or ill (2.46), seems to deny them any positive *kleos* whatsoever, and even to locate their *kleos* in their abdication of *kleos*. But tragedy allows women to want glory even if they don't often get it, and thus invites us to imagine what a woman's *kleos* might be.[57]

One possibility is motherhood. Nicole Loraux has shown that there was an extensive crossover of terminology between the male realm of war and the female realm of childbirth, so that a woman's labor in childbirth could be represented as a comparable act of courage and patriotism to a man's labor in war.[58] One might expect to find this theme in *Trachiniae*, where the analogy between the *ponoi* ("labors") of Heracles, away committing acts of heroism, and the *ponoi* of Deianira, raising the children at home alone, would easily lend itself to such an equation. Though there is some parallelism between the labors of the husband and of the wife, Deianira's *ponoi* never refer to childbirth or child-rearing; rather, the *ponos* she dwells on is her loneliness in Heracles' absence (30).[59] Thus for her, *ponos* is stripped of its heroic connotations and implies only suffering. Likewise, at 42, her pains (ὠδῖνας, a word properly referring to birth-pangs) are caused by Heracles' departure. Indeed, in this opening speech, maternal images are fraught with anxiety for Deianira; instead of raising children, she nurtures fear (ἐκ φόβου φόβον τρέφω, 28; δεῖμα τρέφουσαν, 108). She imagines herself as a far-flung field that a farmer visits only rarely to sow and reap (31–33),[60] this traditional metaphor for reproduction signifying not her fertility, but instead her passivity, isolation, and marginality.[61]

Maternity has unpleasant connotations not only for Deianira, but also in the text overall. Night in the Parodos is a mother who has been despoiled (ἐναριζομένα, 94: a violent Homeric word). And night in itself is violent and destructive as well as procreative: it is αἰόλα, "glistening" (94), the same word used to describe Achelous as a serpent (11); it gives birth to the sun, but also "puts him to sleep" (κατευνάζει, 95; cf. εὐνάζειν of Deianira in 106). The dangerous Cretan sea, too, is a mother in this ode, if the difficulties of the text in the second strophe can be adequately untangled. If we keep the manuscripts' τρέφει ("nourishes") in line 117 (as do many recent editors[62]), then the sea, like night, like Deianira, is a destructive mother. And if these are mothers, the child is Heracles.[63]

That Deianira can be represented as a mother in the same ode in which her husband is represented as a child points to another problem with maternity in the play, especially as a basis for a valid female subjectivity. Deianira's maternity is inseparable from her sexual relation to her husband, a sexuality that must, as one cause of Heracles' death, be extremely suspect: *erōs* in *Trachiniae* is represented as a profoundly destructive force, one that is inimical to the stability of the *oikos*.[64] David Halperin has argued in reference to Plato's *Symposium* that one misogynist Greek stereotype of female sexuality saw it as essentially directed toward procreation, and only secondarily toward the husband who would enable procreation.⁶⁵ Ideally, in this view, female sexuality is redeemed by its "natural" orientation toward the positive, socially constructive end of producing male heirs. Although Deianira here seems to fit this stereotype of female sexuality (in that her erotic and maternal loyalties are mutually reinforcing, not conflicting), instead of the positive nature of reproduction redeeming an inherently suspect sexuality, the opposite is the case: maternity, too, becomes tainted by the destructive force of *erōs*.

In *Trachiniae*, Deianira always links maternity and sexuality, and views both with dread. Again in the Parodos, the description of the grieving Deianira shows her in both of these aspects (104–11): nourishing fear, but also lying on the bed (an ambiguous image at best), unable "to put to sleep her desire" (εὐνάζειν . . . πόθον, 106–7).⁶⁶ Deianira herself elsewhere conflates maternity and sexuality as equal causes of suffering: at 150, she includes among the woes of married life fear "either for husband or children" (ἤτοι πρὸς ἀνδρὸς ἢ τέκνων φοβουμένη, 150, the either-or construction marking the parallelism of child and husband). Indeed, she is "pregnant" with these worries (κακοῖσιν οἷς ἐγὼ βαρύνομαι, 152). Similarly, at 308, she presents Iole's mysterious identity in terms of two alternatives: she is either husbandless or a mother. Marriage implies children, and the two are inseparable in Deianira's mind. *Erōs* and childbirth converge with Deianira's death on the marriage bed. According to the logic of the medical writers, whereas strangling or hanging was associated with premenarchal virginity, a woman's blood evoked parturition.⁶⁷ Her death is simultaneously a reenactment of birth, bloody and painful (and potentially fatal), and a sexual act, penetration by the sword on the marriage bed.⁶⁸

This unhappy nexus of maternity and sexuality also surrounds Iole, a woman who has failed to make the transition between *parthenos* (virginal and unmarried) and *gunē* (married and a mother).⁶⁹ If, ideally, sexual experience and maternity are collapsed so that all women are simultaneously deflowered and impregnated,⁷⁰ Iole is caught somewhere in between: she has lain beside Heracles and is therefore in one sense no longer a *parthenos*, but she has not yet borne a child and thus is not yet fully a *gunē*. The text alternates between the two terms when referring to her,⁷¹ and the nuptial associations that surround her heighten this sense of her liminality (428, 857, 894). What maternal imagery is used in reference to Iole is ill-omened: pregnant with disaster and crying in her birth-pangs (325–26), she will bring forth a Fury (893–95).

The sinister connotations of maternity are part of a larger breakdown of the economy of maternity and reproduction in the play. Ideally, the household reproductive economy should produce more than it consumes; that is, one mother and one father should produce a number of children. Here, however, the ratio of wives to children is fatally skewed. Simply put, the house has too many wives. Although Iole may technically be a concubine, Sophocles makes no effort to distinguish this at the level of diction.[72] Heracles' "chosen bed" (27) and his "secret bed" (360) are conflated, and Deianira imagines the two of them sharing one marriage and one embrace (539–40, 545–46, 550–51).

This excess of wives may explain all the faulty two-for-one accountancy in the play: two wives (δύ' οὖσαι) await Heracles under one cloak (539); Heracles, a single man (ἀνὴρ εἷς), has married many women (460); Hyllus will lose two parents at once (εἷς δυοῖν . . . ὠρφανισμένος, 941–42). This bad economy implicates both Deianira and Heracles and is one of the few things that unites them, even if only syntactically: Iole is to be their "common joy" (κείνου τε καὶ σὴν ἐξ ἴσου κοινὴν χάριν, 485), as is the thanks Lichas receives from both Deianira and Heracles for conveying the robe (ἡ χάρις . . . ἐξ ἁπλῆς διπλῆ, 618–20). But, of course, the *terpsis* that they give and receive from each other is only death (819–20).

It is perhaps not surprising that in a family with too many wives there should also be a problem with the production of children. Deianira, we are told, is "full" with children (54; cf. 31), yet only Hyllus is around. The rest of the children are staying with Alcmene (1151–54); the family production has turned in on itself, so that Heracles' children become the children of his mother (1153). Deianira's children are conspicuously absent from her deathbed speech, except perhaps for the textual conundrum of line 911. If this line is sound (reading the codices' οὐσίας), then Deianira seems to lament her "property" left childless for the future.[73] In what sense can the house be said to be left childless at Deianira's death? Again, although there are said to be many children from this union, they are all, with the exception of Hyllus, discounted from the reckoning.

This collapsed economy is ostensibly restored with Heracles' second command to Hyllus, to take Iole as his wife.[74] Now Iole, previously an illegitimate spouse (according to any legal grounds[75]), will become a legitimate wife (1224), the *lekhos* (1227), which is at once the wife, the marriage, and the bed, a symbol of the raw material for reproductive prosperity. This final act would seem to restore the healthy family as a patrilineal family, in which one man marries one woman and produces many children. But this union, as I argued in the last chapter, is fraught with problems, and in the end not just maternity but paternity as well is left in doubt.

Throughout the play we seem to be offered as a potential counterbalance to the negative maternal images a positive paternal model in the figure of Zeus.[76] The Parodos, which revolves obsessively around doomed maternity, ends with a tentative expression of hope: "For who has known Zeus so unmindful of his children?" (ἐπεὶ τίς ὧδε / τέκνοισι Ζῆν᾽ ἄβουλον εἶδεν; 139–40). The question is reiterated with greater pessimism at the end of the tragedy, as Hyllus, carrying his father to the pyre, bemoans the "great cruelty of the gods, who give us birth and are called our fathers, yet can look upon such suffering" (μεγάλην δὲ θεῶν ἀγνωμοσύνην / εἰδότες ἔργων τῶν πρασσομένων, / οἳ φύσαντες καὶ κληζόμενοι / πατέρες τοιαῦτ᾽ ἐφορῶσι πάθη, 1266–69). The certainty of apotheosis, which might prove Zeus's paternal beneficence, is withheld,[77] and the play's final line—"None of this is not Zeus"—eludes closure.[78] We are not, finally, offered any secure positive model of paternity to counterweigh the negative images of maternity, and the parent-child bond remains extremely fraught on every level, from its inextricability from the destructive forces of *erōs*, to its ramifications of cosmic indifference.

Maternity, then, can only be at best an ambivalent and dangerous source of *kleos* for Deianira. Besides childbirth, the only other "heroic" action in a normal Greek woman's life was death.[79] Nicole Loraux has studied in detail the syntax of women's deaths in tragedy.[80] She identifies the most common form of death for a woman in tragedy as suicide in response to her husband's death; thus Deianira, the wife who has never lived with her husband, resolves to die with him (719–20). Like a good wife, Deianira dies on the marriage bed, reconfirming the importance of her marriage in her final words; like a woman, Deianira dies inside, in secrecy, unwitnessed and by her own hand.[81]

But in equally many ways, Deianira's death is anomalous and markedly unfeminine. Deianira is one of only three women in extant tragedy who die by the sword, traditionally the suicide method of heroes. Most tragic women die by hanging, in an act that evokes at once the adornments around a woman's neck (an erotic part of her body), the webs of deceit she traditionally weaves, and a yoke with which she is finally tamed in death.[82] Deianira, on the other hand, kills herself in a Homeric way, with a Homeric weapon (a "double-edged sword," ἀμφιπλῆγι φασγάνῳ, 930),[83] and in a Homeric place, under the liver (ὑφ᾽ ἧπαρ καὶ φρένας, 931).[84] But at the same time this male death is confused by female elements: as Loraux points out, Deianira stabs herself in the left flank (traditionally the female side) rather than the right, where, anatomically, she would hit the liver (926). Furthermore, while the liver is a "heroic" body part for a male hero, for a woman, the part of the body below the belt is generally associated with the womb.[85]

How are we to explain this transgendered death? If we accept Loraux's initial hypothesis that death is a moment of self-mastery and self-definition for tragic women,[86] what sort of identity does Deianira claim by this act, and what sort does she receive? Does she attain in death the perfect balance of masculinity and femininity that she was denied in life? Does this blend of the feminine and the masculine signify some genderless state at the extremes of one's life, just as Heracles shows signs of feminization at his death? If so, what does it mean that this state is achieved only in death? Or, on the other hand, is Deianira trapped by her gender in death as in life, her heroic suicide compromised by the reminders of her sex?

Rather than try to reduce this ambiguous and polyvalent episode, I only suggest that the scene reinforces the impossibility of forming a dominant female subjectivity through male models.[87] If a woman's only access to self-creation is through the means and metaphors used by men, then, I think, she is doomed to failure. After all, Deianira's suicide is an act of self-penetration; she acts upon herself as a man would, objectifying herself, violating herself. In death, she is both a failed man and a failed woman, unable in the end to escape the constraints of gender.

Deianira's struggle for subject status thus both questions and ultimately reaffirms the categories within which the self is formulated. It reasserts the hegemony of the aristocratic and male; Deianira can be a valid subject only to the degree to which she can approximate these qualities, and, as her death shows, she can never approximate them fully. Her attempt to enter into the arenas of male subject-formation—gift exchange, competition, even a heroic death—valorizes the same structures that reproduce her subjection. If, in the process, the inevitability of these structures and categories of self is challenged and alternatives are imagined, this critique is ultimately foreclosed and, along with it, the female subject that might have been built upon such a critique.

But if within the structures of male society the woman's subjectivization is necessarily a subjugation, are there other modes of self-definition available to her? When Deianira tries to enter the dusty fray, she is doomed to failure, but is there another position—far off on a hillside?—from which she can watch with a perspective that is resistant, critical, and yet not foreclosed, perhaps because it is not seen?

THREE

ALTERITY AND INTERSUBJECTIVITY

We have seen in the preceding two chapters how the male self guarantees his own subject status in opposition to an objectified female other. Heracles and Hyllus lay claim to the prerogatives of subjectivity by trading Iole as an object. Deianira, too, uses Iole as an object, receiving her as a gift and thus positioning herself as a subject, albeit a weak one, in a gift exchange. But Deianira can also conceive of Iole as a subject in her own right; in this relation—which we might call intersubjective—Deianira explores her own subjectivity by imagining a subjectivity for Iole. Whereas the objectifying model rigidifies the boundaries between self and other, positioning the other as an object to be used by the self, the intersubjective relation blurs the distinction between self and other; while Deianira creates Iole in her own image and as a means to her own self-definition, she also imagines the other as a unique and autonomous subject, radically separate from and essentially inaccessible to the self. It is in this pure and unknowable other that *Trachiniae* locates the possibility for an unmediated female subject, a possibility that, embodied in Iole, will haunt the play's final episode.

INTERPELLATION OF THE OTHER, CREATION OF THE SELF

The central scenes of *Trachiniae* focus on an investigation of the identity of Iole. The motivation for this investigation is first Deianira's identification with and sympathy for the girl, and later the Messenger's insinuation that Iole is not who she seems. This lengthy and one-sided interview between Deianira and Iole is all the more remarkable in that Iole's identity, motives, and thoughts are properly only tangential to the debate, which should be about Heracles' motives and thoughts. Why, when Deianira is informed that Heracles attacked Oechalia for love of Iole, does she then investigate the identity of Iole, rather than address the many other questions that more naturally spring to mind? In other words, since Iole only bears upon Deianira in her relationship to Heracles, why does Deianira focus on Iole's identity independent of Heracles? Why is it a ξυμφορά, a misfortune (321), for her not to know who Iole is? The question of Iole's identity receives a strange emphasis that foregrounds the dynamic of self and other. This claim is perhaps supported by the structural similarity, often noted, between these scenes and the central scenes of *Oedipus Tyrannus*.[1] In *Oedipus Tyrannus*, the shepherds are questioned about the identity of a child who will turn out to be Oedipus; here the messengers are questioned as to the identity of a woman who will shed light on the identity of Deianira. This parallel suggests that the identification of the other is a central project for the formation of the Sophoclean self, regardless of gender.

It is important to remember that throughout *Trachiniae*, Iole is pure exterior: she does not speak, she has no interiority, no identity of her own at all. In uncovering Iole's identity, then, Deianira is really inventing this identity; her *interpellation* is more properly an *interpolation*. In this process, Deianira functions like the playwright himself, who creates characters by projecting motives and thoughts into the blank space behind the actors' masks.[2]

It is desire in the first instance that Deianira interpolates for Iole, thus interpellating her as a desiring subject. While refusing to condemn— or indeed, even to speculate on—Heracles' motives in sending Iole to Trachis (439–40, 445–46), Deianira ascribes an active motivation to Iole in the affair. The Messenger's revelation of Heracles' passion for Iole (351–68), though to some extent presenting Heracles as a victim of Eros (354–55), had nowhere suggested that Iole had an active role in the events: she is, in the Messenger's account, no more than the object of Heracles' desire. In Deianira's reaction to this revelation (436–69), however, she attributes to Iole an active desire for Heracles. She starts off with the generalization: Love conquers whom it will, herself included. But then, instead of the logical conclusion ("And therefore Heracles, too, can be forgiven for his passion"), she moves in an unexpected direction:

οὗτος γὰρ ἄρχει καὶ θεῶν ὅπως θέλει.
κἀμοῦ γε· πῶς δ᾽ οὐ χἀτέρας οἵας γ᾽ ἐμοῦ·

(443–44)

For Eros rules even the gods as he pleases,
and he rules me, too—why not other women
like me?

Instead of forgiving Heracles for his love, as we might have expected, Deianira forgives Iole for hers, thereby transforming the silent object of the Messenger's account into a subject of desire.

The critical reaction to line 444 is revelatory. Davies (1991) supports the rejection of the line by Wunder and Reeve, criticizing it as "pointlessly distracting, whether it be referred to a generalizing plurality of women or more specifically to Iole herself (whose feelings for Heracles are quite beside the point, dramatically irrelevant to plot and theme alike in the austere and selective world of Greek tragedy)." What Davies is reacting so strongly against, I think, is precisely this unexpected attribution of desire to Iole. Strictly speaking, Iole's desire *is* irrelevant to the plot and theme; this irrelevance, however, only makes Deianira's introduction of Iole's desire here all the more striking and locates the source of Iole's subjectivity all the more firmly in the mind and words of Deianira.

The same critical perplexity marks a similar issue at 462–63; Heracles has loved many women, Deianira explains, and none of them has received injustice from her, nor will Iole, "even if (s)he should be melting with love" (ἥδε τ᾽ οὐδ᾽ ἂν εἰ / κάρτ᾽ ἐντακείη τῷ φιλεῖν). The question here is the subject of ἐντακείη, "melts." Lloyd-Jones and Wilson sum up the problem: "Surely Campbell is right in thinking that, though it would be easier grammatically to take Iole to be the subject, the subject must be Heracles: Deianira does not care what Iole feels about Heracles, but she does care what Heracles feels about Iole."[3] They are right: logically and psychologically Deianira might more naturally be concerned with the desires of Heracles here, but the text suggests otherwise. We can take Iole as the logical, as well as the grammatical, subject of ἐντακείη, and see this desire (which is, as the critics say, irrelevant) as Deianira's own imagination; Deianira transforms this object into a subject, blurring the boundaries, grammatical and psychological, between herself, Heracles, and Iole.

What possible motive can Deianira have in attributing desire to Iole, especially when, as all the commentators point out, she should more properly be concerned with Heracles' desires? Perhaps her motivation is to exonerate herself by exonerating Iole.[4] Deianira, too, has been prey to Eros (104–11, 444); if Iole is forgiven for her desire (the desire Deianira identifies in her), Deianira can be pardoned for her own violent (and ultimately destructive) love. Her claims of Iole's innocence will resonate later when Deianira's own passion and innocence become an issue.

But if Deianira constructs Iole as a desiring subject primarily to exonerate herself, this attribution of desire nonetheless provides a misogynist foothold, and ends up trapping both Deianira and Iole. We have seen the negative connotations and disastrous consequences of female desire in this play. In attributing desire to Iole, Deianira plants the suggestion that Iole is potentially, if not actually, guilty of all that happened. It is because Deianira denies (but suggests) that she is guilty here (τῇ μεταιτίᾳ, 447) that at the end of the play Hyllus can condemn her as solely guilty (μόνη μεταίτιος, 1233–34) of the deaths of his parents. Deianira's interpellation of Iole is overdetermined by Deianira's own interpellation within a misogynist ideology, and subjectivity thus becomes another noose in which women hang themselves.

SPATIAL MODELS OF SELF AND OTHER: PANDORA AND *kalokagathia*

Iole's silence throughout Deianira's investigation makes this interview an exercise in hermeneutics, in reading the interior—motives, feelings, "nature" (*physis*), and "character" (*ēthos*)—from the testimony of the exterior. But as the investigation progresses, it becomes clear that the relationship between interior and exterior is neither self-evident nor seamless, but rather follows a complex and contradictory set of laws.

The identity that Deianira creates for Iole is based initially on two qualities that Deianira sees in her appearance, nobility and virginity: "From her *physis*, she is inexperienced in all these matters and nobly born" (πρὸς μὲν γὰρ φύσιν / πάντων ἄπειρος τῶνδε, γενναία δέ τις, 308–9). All the commentators agree that *physis* here must refer to Iole's physical appearance, although they disagree on how exactly Iole distinguishes herself. "All that is universally agreed," writes Easterling, "is that she 'looks noble.'"[5] Extrapolating thus from her "noble" appearance (however that manifested itself), Deianira assumes a noble *ēthos* for the silent girl, judging the internal from the external. It turns out after further investigation that Iole is in fact a king's daughter; nobility seems, in this case at least, to be more than skin deep, and to create an uninterrupted continuum between external and internal *physis*. The same continuum does not seem to apply, however, to Iole's sexual status. Again judging from her external appearance, Deianira determines that Iole is a virgin (308–9). The cognitive operation is the same, but the results are different, for although Iole looks like a virgin, we already know what Deianira will soon find out, that Iole is in fact Heracles' mistress. Far from being "inexperienced" (ἄπειρος, 309) or "a maiden" (τίς . . . νεανίδων, 307), Iole is to be Heracles' "wife" (γυνή, 400, 447, 486; δάμαρτα, 428), his "hidden bedmate" (κρύφιον . . . λέχος, 360).

That two different dynamics apply in the case of Iole's sexual status and her social status is clear from Deianira's response when she learns of Heracles' love for Iole:

> τίν' ἐσδέδεγμαι πημονὴν ὑπόστεγον
> λαθραῖον; ὦ δύστηνος· ἆρ' ἀνώνυμος
> πέφυκεν, ὥσπερ οὑπάγων διώμνυτο,
> ἡ κάρτα λαμπρὰ καὶ κατ' ὄμμα καὶ φύσιν;[6]
> (376–79)

> O wretched me, what secret pain have I wel-
> comed into my house? For surely she was not
> born nameless, as her escort swore, a girl so
> illustrious in her appearance and nature?

While her nobility shines bright on her face and within her nature, her sexual status is secret and hidden, masked by her virginal appearance. Thus in her interpellation of Iole, Deianira reproduces the tension between status and gender that we saw constrain her in her dealings with the herald; the creation of a new female subject seems to be an opportunity for the rearticulation of familiar oppressive paradigms. But Deianira's investigation of Iole not only replicates the woman's conflict between aristocracy and femininity, but also suggests that these two factors structure different sorts of subject and, more specifically, govern different relations—both gendered and class-coded—between interior and exterior.[7]

I would like to suggest that the imagined relationship between the interior and the exterior of the individual is different for men and women in tragedy. For male characters, the model for this relationship is the aristocratic ideal of *kalokagathia*, "nobility and goodness." This ideal, which governed all areas of archaic aristocratic evaluation, from the aesthetic to the moral, assumed a total congruence in aristocratic men between the external (appearance, strength, reputation, or social status) and the internal (moral virtue, wisdom, "innate nobility"). In Homer, heroes are all attractive;[8] characters who are physically unattractive, like Thersites, are also morally repugnant and socially inferior.[9]

This heroic aesthetic is adopted by tragedy, though not, of course, without problems. Here the paradigm is Aeschylus's description in *Seven against Thebes* of Amphiaraus, whose *kleos* is merely the externalization of his inner nobility: he wants not to seem but to be the best (*Septem* 592). Ideally, there should be a smooth, unbroken continuum between a hero's exterior and his interior. Though this ideal is not always met (one need think only of Euripides' notorious kings in rags), the failures are marked as such, and reaffirm the ideal even as they challenge it.[10] Because tragedy is necessarily located at the site of the visible (the body or the *prosōpon*, the face or mask), this model implies that, at least in theory, the interior male subject may be extrapolated with a certain amount of confidence from his external appearance (*prosōpon*), physical actions (*praxis*), and public reputation (*kleos*).

This imagination of the body is essentially class-coded for men. *Kalokagathia* is an aristocratic ideal, which gets played out in different ways when applied to men of lower social status.[11] The model for women, on the other hand, is status-blind and applies across the board to the "race of women." The paradigm for the relationship between interior and exterior in women, I suggest, is Pandora; beautiful in appearance, Pandora has "wily ways and the mind of a bitch" (κύνεόν τε νόον καὶ ἐπίκλοπον ἦθος, Hes. *Erga* 67).[12] For her and the race of women descended from her, the exterior is largely a smoke screen to obfuscate the interior. So Iole, who looks like a virgin, turns out to be Heracles' concubine. To the extent that Iole's exterior does reflect her interior, it is because she is an aristocrat, but even this relationship is generally unstable for women: one need think only of Clytemnestra, whose royal status makes her ignoble deeds all the more horrible. Rather than a clear mirror reflecting the interior state, a woman's physical appearance, *kleos*, and status serve as a false front for her interior, which is always at least potentially suspect.[13]

It is this relation of inside to outside more than anything else that leaves female subjectivity such a blank page for Greek tragedians. If the exterior does not represent the interior, then the subject must be explored or colonized, excavated or invented. What the Pandora model does, first and foremost, is problematize the female subject, open up the female interior as an area for speculation. It focuses attention on the mysterious interior, as opposed to the model of *kalokagathia*, which concentrates on the exterior and closes off interest in an interior that is ideally only an extension of what is visible to the eye. This is not to say that the male subject is never problematic; it is rather to claim that the female subject is always, inherently, problematic.

These two models are rigidly polarized in *Trachiniae* between the two protagonists.[14] While Heracles struggles to maintain his masculine, heroic self when his body is under siege (that is, to preserve *kalokagathia*), Deianira struggles to bring her exterior (*kleos*) in line with her interior (intention). Throughout the play, her action is distinguished from her intention, and while the former is suspect from its inception and horrific in its results, the latter is essentially noble.[15] Rejecting the "wicked daring" of "daring women" (582–83), Deianira fears lest she "will soon be shown to have committed a great evil from a noble hope" (ἀθυμῶ δ᾽ εἰ φανήσομαι τάχα / κακὸν μέγ᾽ ἐκπράξασ᾽ ἀπ᾽ ἐλπίδος καλῆς, 666–67) and resolves, if her fears are realized, to die, "for to live with a base reputation is unbearable for one who prides herself on not being base by nature" (ζῆν γὰρ κακῶς κλύουσαν οὐκ ἀνασχετόν. / ἥτις προτιμᾷ μὴ κακὴ πεφυκέναι, 721–22). Her death, then, is an attempt to bring *kleos* into line with *physis*, in accordance with the male and aristocratic model of *kalokagathia*.[16] But even as she aspires to *kalokagathia*, she is made to betray the "bitch" mind of a Pandora: as she decides to use the poison, she takes hope in the thought that "when you commit vices in the dark, you never fall into shame" (ὡς σκότῳ / κἂν αἰσχρὰ πράσσῃς, οὔποτ᾽ αἰσχύνη πεσῇ, 596–97). This statement contradicts all of Deianira's aspirations toward the male ideal, and aligns her rather with Pandora, who conceals an evil interior within a noble exterior.[17]

This spatial model of the self is reinforced by a practical experience of space, both on the stage and in the world outside the theater.[18] In Athenian spatial ideology, the woman "belongs" in the interior of the *oikos*, while the man "belongs" outside; the *locus classicus* is Xenophon's *Oeconomicus* (7.22ff.), where God, nature, and law combine to enforce this arrangement, which it is "shameful" and "against nature" to transgress (αἴσχιον, παρ᾽ ἃ ὁ θεὸς ἔφυσε, 7.30). This spatial separation is rigidly maintained in *Trachiniae*, where Deianira and Heracles never meet, and the female and male spaces barely overlap.[19] Heracles is away from the house, and never enters it even to die. Deianira comes out of the house only to reveal what she has done inside,[20] and in her "secret exit" from the house (θυραῖος ἦλθον λάθρᾳ, 533) are juxtaposed the sinister secrecy of the inside and the male space of the outside.

Movement is gendered, too, following this same division.[21] Heracles' movement in the play is centrifugal, circling always around the house, with only a few returns to it.[22] To Deianira, his labors are no more than movements to and from the house (εἰς δόμους τε κἀκ δόμων / ἀεί, 34–35); when she likens him to a farmer who returns only occasionally to his outlying fields (at 31–33), the metaphor is indicative of Heracles' sense of space in that it locates the *oikos* at the margins rather than the center of Heracles' trajectory. His entire heroic project as he sums it up on his deathbed was a matter of calculated movement: approaching unapproachable places, meeting unmeetable beasts (ἄπλατον . . . κἀ-προσήγορον, 1093; ἄμεικτον, 1095; ἀπρόσμαχον, 1098). But it is he himself who is unapproachable from Deianira's point of view; he only once invites her to approach (προσμόλοι, 1109), and this so he can take revenge.[23]

If Heracles' motion is centrifugal, Deianira's is centripetal, when in fact she does move. For the most part Deianira stays in one place: in the narrative she only moves under pressure, when relocated by her husband (39) or father (563). Her only self-chosen movement is her death. This is represented as a journey (875, cf. 880), though one by which she gets nowhere.[24] Significantly, the first verb of motion Deianira uses for herself is οἰχόμεσθα in its metaphorical sense, "we are destroyed" (85).

And spatially as well as metaphorically, Deianira's death is a journey, a journey from the outside of the house to the inside.[25] Deianira leaves the stage in silence (813–16) and enters the house (900); she passes through the *aulos*, the outer hall, the external (male) part of the house, and enters the women's quarters, "having hidden herself where no one would see her" (κρύψασ᾽ ἑαυτὴν ἔνθα μή τις εἰσίδοι, 903). From there she penetrates deeper to the *thalamos*, the bedchamber (913), and finally, at the very focal point of the house, the *lekhos*, the bed. What is remarkable about this journey is that although Deianira moves deeper and deeper into the feminine space of the house, at the very center she reaches not the most female part, but the bedroom and bed of Heracles (τὸν Ἡράκλειον θάλαμον, 913; δεμνίοις τοῖς Ἡρακλείοις, 915–16).

This is a stark reminder of the practical relations behind the Xenophontic division of domestic space. The inside may be the domain of the woman, but it is the property of the man.[26] Just as in Xenophon the wife is set to arranging and tidying provisions that are not hers by ownership, so Deianira retreats into the feminine only to discover that the innermost place is owned by the man.

I would like to read Deianira's death journey as one metaphor for female subjectivity in this tragedy, a female space owned, at its very core, by the man. The metaphor asserts a total right of male possession of female interiority and denies the woman control over a space that it ostensibly designates as her own. This metaphor is the play's strongest assertion both of the male subject's proprietary power and of tragedy's own epistemological reach: at both levels, the other is fully accessible, knowable, and controllable. The model of interior and exterior, then, while ostensibly establishing two separate but equal realms, as in the cheerful division of Xenophon's house, merely serves to mask the fact that both inside and outside are owned by the man.

Deianira's search for subjectivity, as we saw in the last chapter, is an inscription of the male inside the female. Trying to participate actively in such structures as the *agōn* and gift exchange, Deianira reproduces these structures inside herself, structures within which she can only be a subjected subject. As an other, she reflects and reaffirms the hegemonic self; her potential critique, as we have seen, is foreclosed, built into and subsumed by the dominant ideology. This female other thus not only mirrors the male subject to himself, but also reassures him of the extent of his authority. It is a fantasy of psychic and epistemological imperialism: within every female house there is a male bed, just as within every female character there is a male actor, and any real distinction between self and other collapses.[27]

THE VIRGIN IN THE GARDEN

If Deianira, as a woman who tries (and fails) to define herself within male terms, is like the female house concealing a male bed, she imagines in Iole a different type of alterity, an other beyond the ideological structures that determine the self, a fantasy of a radically pure and free female subject.

πεπυσμένη μέν, ὡς ἀπεικάσαι, πάρει
πάθημα τοὐμόν· ὡς δ' ἐγὼ θυμοφθορῶ
μήτ' ἐκμάθοις παθοῦσα, νῦν δ' ἄπειρος εἶ.
τὸ γὰρ νεάζον ἐν τοιοῖσδε βόσκεται
χώροισιν αὑτοῦ, καί νιν οὐ θάλπος θεοῦ,
οὐδ' ὄμβρος, οὐδὲ πνευμάτων οὐδὲν κλονεῖ,
ἀλλ' ἡδοναῖς ἄμοχθον ἐξαίρει βίον
ἐς τοῦθ', ἕως τις ἀντὶ παρθένου γυνὴ
κληθῇ, λάβῃ τ' ἐν νυκτὶ φροντίδων μέρος,
ἤτοι πρὸς ἀνδρὸς ἢ τέκνων φοβουμένη.
τότ' ἄν τις εἰσίδοιτο, τὴν αὑτοῦ σκοπῶν
πρᾶξιν, κακοῖσιν οἷς ἐγὼ βαρύνομαι.[28]

(141–52)

I suppose that you are here because you have
learned of my suffering. But may you never learn
by your own experience how heartbroken I am:
now you are ignorant. For a young thing is nur-
tured in such places of her own, and neither the
god's heat, nor the rainstorm, nor any wind
bothers her, but in pleasure and untroubled
she grows, until that time when she is called a
woman instead of a maiden, and takes on her
share of worries in the night, fearful for her husband or children. Only then might someone
understand, considering her own experience,
the troubles by which I am weighed down.

Deianira presents an idyllic vision of life before experience. This garden,
the *locus amoenus* of lyric poetry, is a refuge, a nostalgic utopia where a
girl can grow freely like a plant. It is imagined as a wholly feminine place,
where gender is unimportant: the young woman is ungendered (τὸ νεάζον, 144) until she reaches the age of maturity and becomes a *gunē*. It
is a place untouched by the vicissitudes of the real world, a fantasy of a
female *physis* beyond or before the rule of the paternal *nomos*.

The garden of virgins offers an alternate understanding of the relation
of self and other to the metaphor of the male bed in the female house. It
posits an other inaccessible to and unknowable by the self. If a *gunē* on

her husband's bed is a figure for the other owned by the self, the figure for this pure and unpossessible other is a virgin. The silent virgin, I suggest, represents throughout tragedy a site of absolute difference, a fantasy of radical otherness beyond the ideological reach of the text and its characters. I designate the virginal other a fantasy in order to indicate not only the fictionality of the construct (for there is no beyond of ideology) but also the psychic investment of the text in it as a locus of stable, if unrecoverable, truth. In *Trachiniae*, this radical alterity is embodied in Iole: silent, inscrutable, unreachable, Iole represents the other in the purest sense.

But this purity is impossible to maintain, for to imagine the garden is to breach its walls. One of tragedy's essential dynamics is the tension between trying to maintain the walls between self and other (to preserve the alterity of the other) and trying to breach the walls (to colonize or appropriate the other). Iole again personifies this dynamic: in her ambiguous status between *parthenos* and *gunē*, Iole is simultaneously in the garden and on the bed. Like the garden that Deianira imagines, Iole occupies a space beyond the play's grasp; she can never be made to speak and remains a cipher to the end. But while her silence places her in the garden of virgins, the text's obsessive investigation of her identity moves her to the *Herakleios thalamos*—metaphorically, as the other is subjected to the paradigms of the self (as Iole is interpellated in the mold of Pandora), but also literally, as the girl who was thought to be a *parthenos* is found to be a *gunē*. Transforming Iole thus from virgin to mistress, the investigation enacts a sort of defloration.[29] When the other is figured as a virgin, knowledge of the other becomes a penetration. Ironically, in this investigation, Deianira herself is the despoiler: the position of the self is a masculine position. At the same time, we should remember that Deianira's only access to *herself* at the moment of her death is also through violent penetration.

Indeed, Deianira's death scene exemplifies the tension between bed and garden, between appropriating the other and preserving its purity. This death is simultaneously public and private, narrated and unwitnessed. When Deianira goes into the house to die, she is followed by the Nurse, who then provides a narrative account of the suicide, but only up to the moment before the actual death. As Deianira removes her robe, the Nurse runs off to get Hyllus; at the crucial moment, Deianira is alone. In the time it takes for the Nurse to return with Hyllus, Deianira is already dead, her suicide presented in the perfect participle as a fait accompli (929–31).[30] Her body—eroticized at the moment of death—is suggested but not shown.[31] We don't even get to see her corpse; instead, her private demise is followed by the public display of Heracles' dying body.[32]

We have looked at Deianira's death as an example of the impossibility of an uncompromised female subject. In her mode of suicide—penetration by the Homeric sword—she showed herself both a failed man and a failed woman, constrained until the end by gender; dying on her husband's bed, she illustrated the male self's proprietorship over the female other. Yet at the same time, by hiding her body and death from the gaze of the audience and characters, the text does perhaps preserve a space for the female, allowing Deianira, even as she dies on Heracles' bed, the privacy of the garden. In a sense we both do and do not see Deianira's death: the narrative gives us enough to know everything, although no one actually sees the moment. Here again is the impossible tension between what tragedy cannot show and what it obsessively tries to show. Deianira's death is in one sense an act of pure, unwitnessed privacy. Yet at the same time, it is already violated on every level: by the penetration of the sword, by the heroic ideology, even by the male actor playing the part.[33] We are invited at every stage to imagine what lies behind the garden walls, yet our (hegemonic) imagination can only show us a reflection of the dominant, male culture. We cannot both look at the other and preserve its alterity.

We might contrast to Deianira's oblique death the spectacle of Heracles' death, which has all the trappings of theater. In his agony, he is a *thauma*, a wondrous sight (1003; cf. θέαμα, 961), a word derived from the verb for theatrical spectation, *theaomai*. Everything he does has an audience: the chorus watches his *agōn* against Achelous (526); his donning of the robe is witnessed by the citizens of Malis (783–84) and takes place in a sort of natural theater, where the rocks on all sides echo back his cries (787–88). At 1079, when he invites Hyllus and the rest to witness and pity his suffering, Heracles reveals his body to view in diction that proposes himself, his body in pain, as theater: "Come, all of you, look upon (*theasthe*) my miserable body" (ἰδού, θεᾶσθε πάντες ἄθλιον δέμας). The play ends with an invitation to all present to come watch Heracles' death on the pyre.

The woman makes for a more ambiguous spectacle. Whether it is the silence and inscrutability of Iole or the interplay of revelation and concealment in Deianira's death, the woman occupies an oblique position in relation to the gaze of the audience. This position—the privacy of the garden—is one that Deianira chooses for herself. She opens the play by setting herself beyond the reach of tragic wisdom.

Λόγος μὲν ἔστ' ἀρχαῖος ἀνθρώπων φανείς
ὡς οὐκ ἂν αἰῶν' ἐκμάθοις βροτῶν, πρὶν ἂν
θάνῃ τις, οὔτ' εἰ χρηστὸς οὔτ' εἴ τῳ κακός·
ἐγὼ δὲ τὸν ἐμόν, καὶ πρὶν εἰς Ἅιδου μολεῖν,
ἔξοιδ' ἔχουσα δυστυχῆ τε καὶ βαρύν.

(1–5)

There is an ancient proverb current among men
that you cannot know the life of a mortal before
he dies, whether it was good or bad. But I know
my own life even before I have gone to Hades,
that it is ill-fortuned and sorrowful.

Scholars, starting with the scholiasts, have attributed this proverb to Solon,[34] but we need not look so far; closer at hand, this utterance suggests the sort of gnomic wisdom with which the chorus typically closes a Sophoclean tragedy.[35] The *men . . . de* construction of this opening passage sets Deianira's knowledge of her own life against the tragic *logos*. Deianira posits knowledge of the other as a central epistemological project for tragedy, but one that always fails.[36] She locates herself in the position of that other who cannot be known, and from that position declares her subjectivity: she knows herself.

This paradoxical narrative of a life declared unnarratable creates a sort of epistemological closure in the play, removing Deianira from the text's scrutiny. It has often been noted (mostly with condemnation[37]) that no knowledge is gained through the action of the play. The gnomic revelation provoked by Deianira's death (943–46) so closely resembles the opening *logos* of the play that it sets up a circularity that serves to close off Deianira's life from interpretive speculation.[38] Thus Deianira's death only reconfirms a tragic wisdom that was, as she herself said, insufficient to understand her life: the tragic *logos* can no more understand or explain her after her death than it could at the opening of the play.[39] By removing herself from tragedy's *logos*, Deianira positions herself in the garden, the place of an alterity that is both known and unknowable.

In this context, it is significant that Deianira's *locus amoenus* of sexual innocence is a specifically lyric image. It recalls the beautiful, erotically charged settings of Sappho and Ibycus, into which the violence of passion enters only by force.[40] This lyric moment, especially in its Sapphic connotations, seems to offer Deianira a female community and a potential locus for a female subjectivity. As Winkler writes of the gardens in Sappho, "They encircle an area of meaning for which there have not been faithful words in the phallocentric tradition. . . . The real secret . . . is women's sexuality and consciousness in general, which men do not know as women know."[41] It is as if tragedy has to look outside of itself for a language in which to express this female space.[42]

But lyric not only allows Deianira the momentary respite of a return to innocence; it also enables her to imagine herself with impunity as a desiring subject. I have already discussed how Deianira uses the image of herself as a boxer against *erōs* to position herself actively as an agonist (441–42). This is a lyric image for desire.[43] Against the male homosocial triangles of desire set up in the First Stasimon (two men mediated by a woman), Deianira counterpoises a lyric triangle of erotics: lover and beloved mediated only by *erōs* itself. The dynamics of this erotic triangle are most clearly seen in Sappho 31, where there is total fluidity between the three points of the triangle, with lover and beloved constantly merging, and the intermediary, the rival, always reseparating them, denying total satiety.[44] Erotic triangles are always in danger of collapsing into dyads as the two lovers unite, but whereas in the homosocial triangle this means the exclusion of the woman, in (Sapphic) lyric desire it means the total equality of the two lovers, and hence, the total valorization of female desire.

In this lyric space, knowledge of the other is likewise a merging with the other. When Iole's identity is discovered, she is transformed into a *gunē*, so that knowledge of the other becomes a form of defloration. Between Deianira and the chorus, however, the model for cognitive interaction is not penetrative but sympathetic. In its first lines, the chorus explains its presence: "For I have learned with a heart full of longing that Deianira . . . never puts to sleep the longing of her eyes nor ends her tears" (103–7).[45] The chorus comes to learn (*punthanomai*) of Deianira's suffering with *pothoumenāi phreni*, a heart full of longing. Learning is connected with desire, and in this desire, subject and object are confused: commentators point out that the sense of the word *pothoumenāi*, which is grammatically medio-passive, must be purely active, and read it as referring to Deianira, although the word order might also suggest taking it with the chorus.[46] But it is in the nature of *pothos*, a desire that is never fulfilled, that it blurs boundaries between the lover and the beloved, between the one who desires and the object of desire.[47] Both the subject and the object of this strophe is a woman's *pothos:* through *pothos*, self and other are merged.[48]

This is the dynamic into which Deianira imagines herself with these appeals to lyric: the innocence of the garden, the fluidity and equality of the lyric triangle. But like everything else in tragedy, lyric, too, can be used against the woman. Just following Deianira's evocation of the lyric boxer (441–42), the First Stasimon shifts the terms, collapsing the erotic triangle into the male agonistic triangle and marginalizing the woman. This leaves Deianira isolated at the end, and her isolation is described with a lyric simile: the young animal bereft of its parent is a traditional lyric image for a girl right at the point of marriage.[49] Whereas Deianira uses lyric to define herself as an active, desiring subject and as part of an imagined community of women, this ode evokes a lyric image to present her as helpless and passive, a calf ready for the yoke.

Yet even if Deianira at the end of this ode is isolated and passive, this marginalization, I have been suggesting, allows for the establishment of a new space at the margins; while she is eliminated from the heroic arena, she develops a new subjective space outside that arena, on the hillside overlooking the contest, or in a walled garden. I would like to propose the garden metaphor as tragedy's imagination of the female subject, a space to which it has no access and which can only be expressed in lyric terms. It is, I admit, only a slight and fragile moment, and we must remember that the garden, no less than the bed, is a fantasy of the text and a product of its ideologies. The imagination of a space beyond or a time before power, as Foucault has argued, is itself a mainstay of power. Moreover, the garden metaphor that protects the woman also confines her and relegates her to insignificance in the root sense of the word. There she is inexpressible, beyond language or meaning; when she leaves that extrasymbolic space, she is immediately subjected to a paternal law that forecloses upon her subjectivity. Nonetheless, the metaphor perhaps offers some hope, a slight indication of the text's awareness of its own hegemonic force and a wish (however impossible to articulate or actualize) to preserve a space beyond that force. Further, the metaphor seems to acknowledge both the possibility of a valid female subject separate from the male and her essential and (if she is to remain truly separate) necessary inaccessibility. The virgin in the garden is thus like Sappho's apple on the highest branches of the tree: it is not that the men don't know she is there, but that they cannot reach her.

The only valid female subject in tragedy, the only female subject uncompromised by male models of self, is thus one who cannot be seen. It is also one who does not watch. Lacan has theorized that the drama of subjectification is a specular event, the child seeing itself in the mirror, seeing itself seeing itself. The specular aspect of subject formation is all the more vital in tragedy, which is, after all, a genre of visibility. But Deianira tries to carve a subjectivity outside of this specular regime. In her opening speech, Deianira describes the *agōn* in which she was won by Heracles, the *agōn*, I argued, that largely defines her as a subjected subject within the play. The precise details of the struggle, she says, she cannot relate, as she could not bear to watch, "but if someone sat there without terror at the spectacle, he could say" (καὶ τρόπον μὲν ἂν πόνων / οὐκ ἂν διείποιμ'· οὐ γὰρ οἶδ'· ἀλλ' ὅστις ἦν / θακῶν ἀταρβὴς τῆς θέας. ὅδ' ἂν λέγοι, 21–23). When the battle is narrated later in the First Stasimon, Deianira is again not in the audience, and again the text calls attention to her nonviewing:

> ἁ δ' εὐῶπις ἁβρὰ
> τηλαυγεῖ παρ' ὄχθῳ
> ἧστο. τὸν ὃν προσμένουσ' ἀκοίταν.
> †ἐγὼ δὲ θατὴρ μὲν οἷα φράζω† [50]
> τὸ δ' ἀμφινείκητον ὄμμα νύμφας
> ἐλεινὸν ἀμμένει ⟨τέλος⟩·
> κἀπὸ ματρὸς ἄφαρ βέβαχ'.
> ὥστε πόρτις ἐρήμα.
>
> (523–30)

> The delicate beauty sat on a distant hill,
> waiting for the man who would be her
> husband. I speak as a spectator. But the
> fair bride who is the prize of the strife
> piteously awaits the outcome. And sud-
> denly she is gone from her mother, like
> a calf abandoned.

The diction—τηλαυγεῖ, ὄμμα, εὐῶπις[51]—draws attention to the specular activity that Deianira seems to refuse. Just as Deianira had removed herself from the tragic *logos*, so, too, she refuses to participate—either as spectacle or as spectator—in tragedy's scopic regime. Again, this is an impossible position for the subject in general, male or female, but even more so for the tragic subject, which is always necessarily constituted by its own visibility. Yet as a fantasy—and here a male fantasy—it is potent, allowing the imagination of an unmediated, undivided, fully self-present subject.

If Deianira does not watch the contest, the chorus does, explicitly positioning itself, in contrast to her, as an audience: "I speak as a spectator" (ἐγὼ δὲ θατὴρ μὲν οἶα φράζω, 526). The same contrast is posed in 21–23: although Deianira herself was too fearful to watch the *agōn*, there is "someone" (ὅστις, 22) who was able to watch, and who watched, moreover, as a spectator watches theater.[52] In each case, the hypothetical spectator is also grammatically male (ὅστις, ὅδε).[53]

This normative male audience, it turns out, includes the chorus: it watches when Deianira cannot. Yet how can it watch with a male gaze? As *parthenoi*, the chorus might be expected to be aligned with Iole; indeed, Deianira introduces the image of the garden to explain the chorus's inability, as *apeiroi* (innocent and inexperienced), to understand her life. But according to the epistemology of the garden, the virgin neither sees nor is seen, and the chorus does both. Is the generalization as audience of the chorus of *parthenoi* another way in which the text tries to appropriate the female space? As *parthenoi* represented—seen and heard—onstage, the chorus offers to expose to view the secrets of woman; closely associated with Deianira, these *parthenoi* are the interlocutors who help bring her motives, desires, and even her actions to light.[54] It is the chorus that fills in the part of Deianira's narrative of her own life that she was unwilling to watch or tell, the *agōn* of Heracles and Achelous, and its version is the androcentric First Stasimon.[55] The chorus is invited to "witness" Deianira's death (896–99), in lines that simultaneously evoke its legitimacy (μαρτυρεῖν) and recall Deianira's denial of its ability, as *parthenoi*, to understand her life (141). Thus the chorus is granted by the text an authority that Deianira explicitly denies it. And with that authority, it does narrate Deianira's death (876–77), filling in the blank left by the Nurse's account. The maidens are made, in the ultimate hegemonic move, to breach the wall themselves.

Yet always coupled with the chorus as audience is Deianira who cannot watch. These *parthenoi* may be coopted, but there is always the shadow of the *gunē* who tries, by not watching, to resist the objectification of the gaze. Deianira refuses to look in the mirror that can show her only as an object or as a failed, subjected, unhappy subject. If she cannot ultimately escape being made into a spectacle, at least she can refuse to watch it. So, too, she refuses to allow the tragic *logos* to speak her life, and in the end is reduced to silence. This protest, this not-speaking and not-watching, is Deianira's last futile attempt to preserve any space for her subjectivity.

This interplay of female visibility and invisibility comes to a head in the last four lines of the play.[56]

> Λείπου μηδὲ σύ, παρθέν᾽, ἐπ᾽ οἴκων,[57]
> μεγάλους μὲν ἰδοῦσα νέους θανάτους,
> πολλὰ δὲ πήματα ⟨καὶ⟩ καινοπαθῆ,
> κοὐδὲν τούτων ὅ τι μὴ Ζεύς.
>
> (1275–78)

And you also, maiden, do not be left behind at the house, you who have seen these terrible recent deaths, many sufferings and new sorrows. None of this is not Zeus.

Who is this *parthenos* who has watched and is invited to watch more? Is it the chorus? If so, even this group of domesticated *parthenoi* is relegated to silence. The chorus has witnessed the scene of Heracles' deterioration and his bequeathal to Hyllus, but in virtual silence (speaking only twice in the last 300 lines). At the very end, then, it would be invited to watch the sacrifice, for it watches with the eyes of men, but it is denied its customary right of closing the play. The other possibility, despite very real practical obstacles, is Iole.[58] As radical other, she promises to speak from the garden, the place beyond ideology, but her words could never be encompassed by tragedy. She has been compared, by structural allusion, to Aeschylus's Cassandra: she might prophesy the truth, but who would heed her?[59]

In the end, perhaps, it makes little difference whether the *parthenos* is the chorus or Iole. Either way, we are left at this final moment with a *parthenos* who neither watches (hence the command) nor speaks. Yet her watching will constitute the sacrifice, and it is her presence, not the awaited apotheosis, that closes the play. The female other is simultaneously shut off from view and put into a place of centrality: she is inscrutable but not marginal. In this silent non-watching, a subjective space is left for the woman, even though it cannot be articulated. *Trachiniae* offers Deianira the options of being either an object or a dangerous and illegitimate subject; it allows her only male models for the definition of her own subjectivity, then shows her inability to use these models and her ultimate entrapment by them. In the scene of her death, it writes man inside of woman. Yet in the silent *parthenos* lies tragedy's preservation of a fantasied space beyond these models, of a female other beyond the control of the male self.

And so we return to the final exchange, in which Hyllus hesitates to accept Iole, the gift who will secure his patrimony, his authority, his masculinity and subjectivity. His hesitation jeopardizes the entire social order that he stands to inherit. Yet we have seen the tremendous psychic investment the text has made in Iole. Inscribed within her are all the lessons of Deianira's tragedy: that although the exchange objectifies her, the woman is never merely an object; that although the male self declares his proprietorship over the female other, there are alternate economies in which self and other are autonomous and equal; that although it cannot be articulated by the tragic *logos*, nonetheless a female subject may exist, maybe even behind the silence of Iole. That Hyllus at least glimpsed these lessons is clear from his recognition of Deianira's innocence and his reiteration, as he carries his father off stage, of the essential mystery to the self of the life of another (1270–74). Accepting Iole as a gift from his father means turning his back on the wisdom gained through suffering, and risking reproducing this suffering in the next generation. How, then, could Hyllus *not* hesitate?

The crisis is brief, and Hyllus does, in the end, yield to the suasion or coercion of the paternal law. But in that momentary hesitation is exposed the cruelty of the law and the price it exacts from its subjects, male and female; the implication of the gods, our divine fathers, and of Zeus himself ("none of this is not Zeus") in this oppressive regime; and the alternatives that are eliminated so that this order might stand unchallenged. In Hyllus's reluctant acceptance of Iole, these foreclosed possibilities— all the possibilities raised by Deianira's life—are buried within the very foundations of the social order, handed down from father to son with the gift of a silent girl.

THE VIOLENCE OF *kharis* IN AESCHYLUS'S *Agamemnon*

✄

FOUR

THE COMMODITY FETISH
AND THE AGALMATIZATION
OF THE VIRGIN DAUGHTER

✄

In Aeschylus's *Agamemnon*, the circulation of women, rather than consolidating male social relations and subjectivities, instead dissolves them. Paris steals Helen; her husband Menelaus and his brother Agamemnon, the Atreidae, wage war against Troy to avenge the theft and take her back. They win the war, but gain neither Helen nor glory, and the Greek soldiers return, not as heroes, but as dust in urns.

The crisis precipitated by this "war fought for a woman" is both economic and emotional: human lives become currency in this play, as men are weighed out on Ares' scales to make up the price of Helen's loss. Iphigeneia is slaughtered like a sheep from a large herd; she is only one of many precious and irreplaceable objects, *agalmata*, that are squandered like cash by aristocrats who seem not to know the difference or not to care. The fatal accountancy surrounding Helen destabilizes an elite economy built upon the distinction between *agalmata* and mere commodities, and calls into question the elite identities grounded upon this economic distinction; it also threatens the fundamental integrity of the male subject, selling men for ashes.

In order to theorize the economic, social, and psychological problems caused by the exchange of women in *Agamemnon*, I adopt as a model Marx's theory of the commodity fetish.[1] The commodity fetish is a description of the dynamics of exchange, and predicts the psychic effects of this economic transaction not only upon the object, but also upon its subjects. Men invest themselves and their social relations in objects; these fetishized objects come to represent, and eventually to replace, their exchangers: subjects are commodified by their commodities. *Agamemnon* dramatizes the violence of this process and the horror of its results. Iphigeneia is fetishized as an object of inestimable worth, but only through her murder, a murder tinged, moreover, with eroticism. Helen, quintessentially fetishized but always liable to disenchantment, reveals the self-deception and misrecognition at the base of the economic process; her seemingly inherent desirability comes to replace not only the relations between Greeks and Trojans that give her her value but also the male exchangers themselves, as the men who fight for her are reduced to corpses. The terror of this objectification, I argue, is the driving force behind the play, and generates defensive fantasies in the characters of Clytemnestra, who punishes the violence of fetishization, and Cassandra, who forgives it and offers sympathy for its fatal effects. But if these defensive figures allow the play to contain the psychological damage, they cannot resolve the problems inherent in the commodity fetish, and, as in *Trachiniae*, male society and subjectivity are rebuilt in the end, but upon a foundation that has been shown to be quicksand.

MARX AND THE FETISHIZED ECONOMY

That women are used as commodities is a basic assumption of much modern feminist theory.[2] But in what sense can a woman be said to be a commodity in the strict definition of the word? The obvious place to start is Marx.[3] Marx defines a commodity on the first page of *Capital* as "an object outside us, a thing that by its properties satisfies human wants of some sort or another" (1906: 41). This definition of a commodity as a use value (an object with inherent utility) gives way later in the text to a definition of commodities based on their exchange value, that is, their value in human labor, as manifested in exchange. A commodity then comes to be defined as an object that, apart from its inherent use value, is produced through human labor and attains its value through exchange.

A table, in Marx's example, is a commodity, produced through labor out of raw material and given value through its relation to other commodities. But the change from raw material to commodity is not a simple one: rather, it is an ontological and somewhat metaphysical change.[4] For the commodity seems to take on a status independent of the labor that produces it, to have an inherent value separate from that of either its labor value or its exchange value, and it comes to seem that the relations of production and exchange are in fact relations among things rather than among people:

A commodity is therefore a mysterious thing, simply because in it the social character of men's labour appears to them as an objective character stamped upon the product of that labour; because the relation of the producers to the sum total of their own labour is presented to them as a social relation, existing not between themselves, but between the products of their labour. This is the reason why the products of labour become commodities, social things whose qualities are at the same time perceptible and imperceptible by the senses. (1906: 83)

This occlusion of the relations of production and exchange in the object is the commodity fetish.[5] The commodity assumes a life of its own: it seems to act autonomously in a free world of commodities, rather than to function as a mere symbol and medium of the relations between its exchangers. Thus the tables are turned, as Marx says, and the commodity takes its owner to market. The human agents are related to one another through their commodities and are defined by them.[6] The final result of the commodity fetish, then, is that the subjects of exchange are commodified by the objects.

Marx's description of the fetishized commodity fits closely a type of commodity specific to Greek economic thought: the *agalma*.[7] An *agalma* is an object the value of which seems to be inherent and eternal.[8] It is unique and irreplaceable, and often is represented as being of divine or miraculous origin.[9] Because *agalmata* have magical, talismanic qualities, to possess them often is to have access to other privileges, such as sovereignty, shamanic power, or immortality.[10] Too valuable to trade lightly, they are kept out of circulation, and are exchanged only on extraordinary occasions. The value of *agalmata* lies not in their price on the market, nor in their use value, nor in the worth of their component materials, but rather in their *kharis*, their charm, grace, and delight. But *kharis* and the related verb *kharizesthai* also bear the economic meaning of a favor or debt: an *agalma*'s *kharis* is thus precisely the fetishization that locates the relations of exchange (*kharis* in the economic sense) within the object itself (*kharis* as grace or charm).[11]

Agalmata, which seem to lead an independent, magical existence, are reintroduced into social relations through gift exchange. In gift exchange, two people, ideally of equal status, generally aristocrats, and generally men, give and receive gifts in order to cement a bond between themselves and their houses.[12] The objects of exchange, usually items of high worth and prestige—*agalmata*—symbolize the relationship and seal it; they gain value from the exchange and in turn confer value upon the relationship. A paradigmatic example is the exchange of armor between Glaukos and Diomedes in *Iliad* 6. The two heroes meet on the battlefield and trade arms to mark their renewed friendship: the movement of the armor symbolizes to the other Greeks the bond between them.[13] The armor is like Marx's fetishized commodity in that it receives value from the exchange (transformed from mere use value into symbolic value), but also by its exchange creates the relationship between the men. It is not until Diomedes has proposed the exchange of armor that the two heroes can trade handshakes and pledges of good faith (6.232–33).

But already here in this paradigmatic instance, we can see some potential problems within the fetishized gift economy. Gift exchange, as we saw in Chapter 2, is part of an elite economy; the symbolic exchange of prestigious gifts is the reserve of the elite, in contrast to the more promiscuous and plebeian buying and selling of commodities in the marketplace.[14] The distinction between the two economies and their two objects—*agalmata* and commodities—is thus the basis for a fundamental social striation. For all its social importance, however, this economic distinction is not ontological but ideological, and is the result of precisely the sort of fetishization Marx describes. There is no inherent difference between the two types of object; the same object can be a commodity at one point in its career and an *agalma* at another, as Herodotus shows in his story of a barbarian king who melts down a golden chamber pot and makes it into a statue for the gods (Hdt. 2.172). In gift exchange, commodities (traded advantageously and subject to reduction to a universal equivalent, money) are misrecognized as *agalmata* (magical things with inherent value), the economic relations obfuscated and enchanted by their investment in the fetishized object.

If there is no inherent difference between these two types of object, and yet this fictional difference is vital to the maintenance of the elite, then there is a potential crisis at each exchange of gifts, a risk of disenchantment, both of the *agalma* and of its noble traders. In the scene between Glaukos and Diomedes in *Iliad* 6, the narrator makes this explicit by disclosing the economics of the deal unrecognized (or misrecognized) by the aristocratic heroes: "But Zeus son of Kronos stole away the wits of Glaukos, who exchanged arms with Diomedes, Tydeus's son, gold arms for bronze, one hundred oxens' worth for nine" (6.233–36). No longer *agalmata,* whose value symbolizes the value of the men and their ancestral bond, the arms become mere commodities, reduced to their market value in a base currency, cattle. The elite exchange becomes a financial transaction, in which one hero profits while the other suffers a loss. The narrator's intrusion acknowledges that the idealized gift exchange—and the elite identities it supports—are built upon a false distinction that is ever in danger of collapsing.[15]

If the fetishized economy always poses for its elite participants the danger of disenchantment, it also offers another, complementary risk: that of objectification. A commodity is fetishized when it comes to symbolize the relationship between its exchangers. But for Marx, the commodity does not merely represent and occlude the relationship between the exchangers; it actually comes to replace its exchangers. So in this Homeric scene, the movement of gifts replaces the friendship between men. The *xenia* relationship between the heroes' fathers is represented by the belt and cup exchanged between them. Diomedes remembers the cup but not its giver; thus the commodity outlives and replaces its exchangers. Supplanted by their commodities, the owners are also defined by them: Glaukos is characterized as a fool because of his role in the exchange. The commodities interpellate their owners, and in the final instance, the fetishism of commodities in turn fetishizes their exchangers.[16]

This dynamic is played out in gruesome clarity in *Agamemnon* as the men who fight for Helen, the quintessential fetishized commodity, are sent back from war as commodities themselves, dust in urns. But before turning to Aeschylus, we must first ask whether Marx's theory of commodities, designed to explain a modern capitalist system, can reasonably be applied to the ancient economy. Vernant, for one, cautions against "overestimat[ing] the spread of exchange value in Greek social life and the hold that the category of commodities had on their minds."[17] Many scholars have argued that the economic sphere as we know it today had little meaning for the Greeks, for whom economic activity was firmly "embedded" within social and political structures.[18] They contend further that the possession of slaves prevented the Greeks from understanding the universal equivalence of human labor, so basic to Marx's theory of exchange value.[19] They would therefore like to maintain a clear separation between the capitalist and precapitalist modes of production and thought, and are wary (as they no doubt should be) of a simple transference of analytical tools.

Though Marx's concern in *Capital* is clearly with postindustrialist economies, he maintains that the commodity as he defines it predates the development of the capitalist mode of production, "though not in the same predominating and characteristic manner as now-a-days."[20] To talk about commodities and their activities, then, does not necessarily imply a free market, the ubiquity of the money form, or other specifics of the capitalist mode of production.[21] In answer to the second point, that the ancient world had no concept of universal human labor, Marx notes that Aristotle (*Pol.* 1.3) recognizes the basic form of equivalence between commodities but can go no further than this because the slave mode of production and the resultant "inequality of men and of their labour powers" allow him no universal basis upon which to equate qualitatively different objects.[22] The extent to which Aristotle did understand exactly the processes Marx describes seems to me to suggest that we are justified in applying the concept of the commodity to ancient economic thought even if we cannot also apply the concept of universal labor. Indeed, the failure to recognize the equivalence between various different sorts of labor merely makes the process of fetishization that much easier for the ancient thinker.[23]

Objection to the application of Marxian principles to a precapitalist society has centered to some extent on the debate over the status of gifts in the ancient world. Following Mauss's famous exposition of the nature of the gift in "primitive" economies, many scholars have been reluctant to see the gift as a commodity.[24] In this view (which stems from a reductive reading of Mauss), the spontaneous, reciprocal exchanges of gifts, intended to create bonds and consolidate social relations, are contrasted to the profit-oriented and essentially selfish motives thought to underlie commodity exchange.[25] But when seen (as Mauss himself suggests they should be) in terms of the exchange of "economic" capital for "symbolic" capital, ancient gift exchanges look less generous and spontaneous.[26] The temporal lag in the exchange of gifts (as opposed to the immediacy of the market) and the invisibility of the "symbolic" rewards purchased in the exchange obscure but do not change the basic economic nature of the transaction.[27] Gift exchange is thus merely an idealized and ideologically invested form of commodity exchange.

For those involved in these prestigious transactions, the imperative to misrecognize commodity exchange as gift exchange was strong, and overt disenchantments like that in the *Iliad* are rare.[28] When they do occur, however (as, for example, in the heroines' critique of the circulation of women in these plays), they strongly suggest that the Athenians did understand, even if they rarely acknowledged, the dynamic of fetishization that Marx describes. In fact, because the ancient aristocrat had more at stake in the misrecognition of commodities for *agalmata* than the modern bourgeois (for whom the free market is an ideological fetish in itself), the Marxian notion of fetishized commodities and the problems that arise from them can be seen as even more urgent for the ancient economic subject than for the modern.

This tension between the aristocratic *agalma* economy and the abjected commercial economy was perhaps particularly marked in Athens in the early fifth century, as the emerging democracy and broadening economic activity put increasing pressure on the old elite.[29] With the shift toward a democratic ideology, aristocrats converted from influence based on direct political power and economic monopoly to a more subtle and symbolic form of power.[30] As we shall see in this chapter and the following two, fifth-century social and economic changes caused a retrenching of ideological positions, both within the aristocracy and in its relations to the *demos*. The *Oresteia* is a central document for the study of this shift: its clear reference to the reforms of Ephialtes, traditionally considered a starting point for Athens's move toward radical democracy, is only the most obvious example of the trilogy's engagement with the "problem" of the aristocracy. This issue is expressed in *Agamemnon* largely through the play's questioning of the aristocratic economy and its relationship to the more democratic commodity economy. The distinction, then, between the enchanted economy of gift exchange and the base economy of the agora is not simply a theoretical or hermeneutic distinction, but a political one: the ways in which the characters relate to these two economies will declare their social status, and the ways in which the text mediates between them will suggest its answers to the question of the role of the aristocrat within a democracy.[31]

Among the items appropriate for gift exchange, women were perhaps the most prestigious, their exchange used to seal the most important connections and surrounded with the most elaborate pomp and circumstance.[32] In Greek literature, women are recognized as *agalmata* from the very first: in Hesiod's account, Pandora, the first woman, is also the first female commodity. Created from raw material through divine labor, she is exchanged as a gift (*dōron*, Hes. *Erga* 85) to mortals and is given her value through that exchange. Created as a punishment for men, Pandora comes to symbolize the mistrustful and postlapsarian relations between mortals and gods, and the relations between her and other commodities (the stolen sacrificial meat, fire, her jar of evils) replace those between their mortal and divine exchangers.[33] Already here, the confusion between *agalma* and commodity is apparent: the phrase that comes to describe her, *kalon kakon ant'agathoio* ("a beautiful evil in exchange for good"), simultaneously fetishizes her (as a thing of inherent evil) and defetishizes her (by hinting at the bad exchange that makes her evil).[34] Finally, the female commodity interpellates the male subject: it is Pandora who defines the conditions of mortality for men.

A woman is the perfect commodity for fetishization.[35] She is easier to invest with inherent value than a table, since she can more easily be seen independently from her producer. Although I have been deemphasizing labor as the basis for the evaluation of commodities, women are also ideal commodities for fetishization because the labor by which they are produced has already undergone a primary mystification.[36] The labor that produces women is no less than the *habitus* of their father, his status, wealth, power, and prestige.[37] Since *habitus* is already mystified (i.e., it presents as inherent or natural a worth that has its foundation in social relations), the commodity it produces is doubly so. Given value through the status of her father and the recognition of that status by her husband, the woman is commodified in the marriage exchange as symbol and seal of the relationship between the two men. The exchange is then romanticized (to varying degrees) and the female commodity fetishized as a bride or wife.

If women are commodities, then the currency of their exchange is desire.[38] It is desire, in the first instance, that mystifies the exchange, transforming use value (reproductive potential) into exchange value, and thereby giving the woman her price on the market. Yet just as for Marx the universal equivalent (the money form) is the ultimate fetishized commodity, so, too, erotic appeal seems to take on more than its own use value. The primary desire for exchange relations (at base, an agonistic desire for social domination) is mistaken for a desire for the object itself; as we saw in *Trachiniae*, the homosocial desire for supremacy is transformed into erotic desire for the woman, agonism fetishized as *erōs*. Finally, this complex desire is projected onto the object, so that the woman herself becomes desirable, just as a table seems "naturally" worth a certain amount of money. A woman's value as an object of exchange, then, is derived from the relations among men—homosocial and agonistic—

that subtend her circulation, and replaces those relations, which are both reified and concealed by her seemingly inherent desirability.

But if the woman is a particularly apt object for fetishization, she is also particularly liable to disenchantment. We saw in Chapter 2 how Deianira critiques the economy that traffics in women by defetishizing the female *agalma*, Iole, calling her a mere commodity and Heracles a trafficker in such base objects. Because they are not actually objects, because their value is impossible to weigh precisely, and yet their evaluation and exchange are so vital to male society, women are precarious *agalmata*; they must be exchanged, but their enchanted status is called into question as soon as they are put on the market, and their disenchantment in turn disenchants their exchangers, exposing the essential falsity of the distinction between *agalmata* and commodities. Given the instability of women as commodities, it is only through extreme manipulations that they are secured as *agalmata*. We shall see when we look at the sacrifice of Iphigeneia the combination of desire and violence by which a female commodity is fetishized, made to bear and conceal the social relations that invest her with value. The violence of fetishization will recoil upon the male exchangers, however, as the war for Helen sends men home as ashes in urns, the commodity commodifying its owners. At the same time, around this incomparable object, the two economies—that of commodities and that of *agalmata*—will converge and collapse, precipitating a crisis of aristocratic identity and opening the way for a new definition of elitism. These two problems of the commodity fetish (the disenchantment of *agalmata* and the commodification of exchangers) will be the focus of the next chapter. First, though, we must look at the sacrifice of Iphigeneia and the process by which a commodity is fetishized and an *agalma* created.

THE OCCLUDED EXCHANGE

Iphigeneia, we are told (*Ag.* 208), is a *domōn agalma*, an invaluable object belonging to the house: the phrase evokes Marx's commodity fetish, for it implies an inherent value and, by locating the commodity within the house, denies its exchange. And yet, what is it that makes this young girl an *agalma*? What is the source of her value? I suggested in the last section that when women are commodities, the source of their value on the market is their sexuality, both reproductive and erotic. With the daughter, this formulation creates certain tensions: a daughter has little use value to her father, as her reproductive potential is unavailable to him directly.[39] Her use value for her father lies in her potential exchange value on the marriage market, and thus she must be traded.[40]

When Agamemnon calls his daughter a *domōn agalma*, he evokes her potential exchange value through marriage, and indeed, as we shall see, there are hints of marriage imagery in the sacrifice scene. The exchange actually transacted, however, is not the anticipated marriage, but rather a different sort of prestation, a sacrifice. Becalmed at Aulis on his way to Troy, Agamemnon must sacrifice his daughter to the goddess Artemis, and it is through this transfer, not through marriage, that Iphigeneia's potential value is actualized and she herself is constituted as an *agalma*. Moreover, in Aeschylus's telling of the scene, the transaction is left extremely obscure: it fails to establish the bonds among exchangers that we might expect; instead, it obscures the relations of exchange—both between mortals and gods and among men—and focuses all attention on the object, Iphigeneia, who emerges from this transaction without transactors as an object of seemingly inherent value, a fetishized commodity, an *agalma*. The result of this occlusion of the relations of exchange and "agalmatization" of the object will be an exchange that is simultaneously a refusal of exchange, a transaction, I argue, that speaks to contemporary concerns about the role of the aristocracy within the Athenian democracy.

But what kind of exchange is the sacrifice? To look at this murder as an economic transaction may seem sheer perversity, and I certainly do not intend to minimize the blasphemy and horror so clearly expressed in the text. Further, the sacrifice may seem to be less an exchange in the normal sense of the word than a unilateral destruction of goods. But as Marcel Mauss has shown, the conspicuous destruction of precious objects, the "potlatch," can be viewed as an extreme form of gift exchange.[41] While such an act appears to be spontaneous and disinterested, it in fact follows a clear economic logic of reciprocity, for this "gift" to the gods demands recompense in the form of divine goodwill and good fortune.[42] The Greeks certainly recognized (with varying degrees of discomfort) that sacrifice was essentially an economic transaction between mortals and gods, a recognition that is exploited to comic effect in Aristophanes' *Birds*.[43]

If the sacrifice of Iphigeneia is an exchange with the gods along the lines of the potlatch, however, Aeschylus leaves the specifics of the deal remarkably vague.[44] First of all, the usual economics of sacrifice, whereby the gods receive honor and respect and mortals in turn receive a certain insurance against disaster and assurance of future prosperity, are perverted here by the abomination of human sacrifice. For this "sacrifice without song or feast" (θυσίαν . . . ἄνομόν τιν' ἄδαιτον, 150[45]) cannot be eaten or shared among the community, and as an offering to the gods, even if demanded by Artemis, it must be a sacrilege.[46] The scene is described in terms that emphasize the blasphemy of the ritual, its details mirroring closely those of a normal sacrifice.[47] The bestialization of Iphigeneia (she is slaughtered "like a she-goat," 232) does nothing to mitigate the aberration, and this "sacrifice," the first of many ritual perversions throughout the trilogy, becomes the most horrific example of the perversity of the whole economy, human and divine.[48]

This transaction between men and gods is flawed not only because the gift itself is blasphemous, but also because it is unclear why or to whom the gift is offered. The text suggests, certainly, but never makes clear that Artemis demanded the sacrifice of Iphigeneia.[49] It is said only that she "demands that the omens be accomplished" (τούτων αἰτεῖ ξύμβολα κρᾶναι, 144).[50] The omen has shown eagles "sacrificing" a pregnant hare (135–36); Artemis "loathes the feast of the eagles" (137), but even if she demands the omen's fulfillment, this is not to say that she commands the sacrifice of Iphigeneia. That the prophet Calchas and the Atreidae blame this awful necessity on Artemis does not help either, for the text leaves their claim unverified.[51] This transaction, so abhorrent to its mortal participants, is not even clearly demanded by the gods.

Not only the economics, but also the sociology of this exchange is obscure. The conspicuous destruction of property, as Mauss shows, is an occasion for social maneuvers. As a public display of wealth, the potlatch is ideally an affirmation of the status of the sacrificer in competition with his elite peers, a performance intended to "put down and to 'flatten' one's rival."[52] Not so much the destruction of property, then, as its exchange for symbolic capital, sacrifices can be seen as a gambit in aristocratic competitive gift exchange, acting both to solidify the group and to establish hierarchy within it.[53] Ian Morris (1986) has identified a similar dynamic in archaic Greek dedications to the gods, which simultaneously demarcated the elite class (since only "top-rank gifts"—*agalmata*[54]— were appropriate for dedication) and created hierarchy within the elite through competitive prestation.[55]

The social dynamic of the potlatch described by Mauss and Morris tallies well with the Homeric world within which Aeschylus's sacrifice scene is located: the sacrifice of Iphigeneia, the conspicuous expenditure of the *domōn agalma*, can be viewed as an attempt on the part of the Atreidae to shore up their prestige in the face of the troops' unrest (188–98), to regain their authority over the army and the control necessary to continue the expedition. The milieu of the sacrifice is a different world from that which we see in Argos; it is one peopled exclusively (if vaguely) by men: the Atreidae, Calchas, the young Greek soldiers (109, 189, 197), and their leaders (200, 230, 240–47); it is "the auspicious command of the expedition by men in authority" (ὅδιον κράτος αἴσιον ἀνδρῶν / ἐκτελέων, 104–5). What is evoked, if only briefly and elliptically, is the male, homosocial world of the *Iliad*. This is one of the very few passages in this play where we are invited to think about Agamemnon's relations to his peers, rather than to the gods, his ancestors, his subjects, or his wife.[56] We have a hint here of the conflict that opens the *Iliad*: there Agamemnon openly upbraids Calchas for what is assumed to be his prophecy at Aulis;[57] here the king is said to agree to the sacrifice, "blaming no prophet" (μάντιν οὔτινα ψέγων, 186).

Agamemnon's conflict is at least in part one between duty to the *oikos* (household) and military duty, a conflict between his two most important roles as an aristocratic male—as head of his *oikos* ("Heavy my fate if I slaughter my child, *agalma* of my house," 207–8) and as king and general ("How am I to become a deserter, failing my alliance?" 212–13).[58] The decision to sacrifice his daughter, then, would seem to be a reaffirmation of Agamemnon's allegiance to his allies (*summakhoi*), a reconfirmation of the homosocial bonds of aristocratic, male society, and the sacrifice itself the enabling factor for the war, that greatest of male-bonding experiences.[59]

The presence of these *summakhoi* is shadowy, however, and their role in the sacrifice is unclear. In a potlatch situation we would expect a manifest and public aristocratic competition; here there is a muted agonism, but its direction and intent are not at all obvious. Whereas in Euripides' version of this scene the power dynamics behind the sacrifice are expressly described, in Aeschylus's version even the players are obscure: the aristocratic community—"first-rank men" (πρόμοισιν, 200), "sacrificers" (θυτήρων, 240), and "war-loving chieftains" (φιλόμαχοι βραβῆς, 230)—is hinted at but never elaborated. Nor are the agonistics inherent in the potlatch explicated. The *brabēs* are not simply chieftains but, more precisely, the umpires or referees of an *agōn*:[60] the *agōn* is evoked, but the details (what is this an *agōn* over? who are the antagonists?) are left vague. As a potlatch, the sacrifice fails to establish hierarchy or even to define the group.

The transaction is thus obscure and the relations subtending it shadowy; all we see clearly is its object, Iphigeneia. This, of course, is precisely the dynamic of the Marxian commodity fetish: relations among people are represented, and eventually replaced, by relations among objects. So the social relations that lie behind the sacrifice (which are explored thoroughly in Euripides' version of the scene) are occluded by the movement of the commodity. The exchange of a woman presupposes a community of men; their social cohesion gives her value and is in turn strengthened by her circulation. Here there is no community. Iphigeneia is given value through the exchange, as we shall see, but it is a value that hides its sources, that pretends to be inherent, and that conceals the relations that produce it. The result of this fetishization is a faulty exchange whereby the owner both sells and keeps his commodity. The fact that she is given but not received allows the pretense that she was never on the market at all: thus, rather than a commodity, she can be a *domōn agalma*, a thing too precious to be traded.

The Agalmatization of the Virgin Daughter

I suggested that when women are commodities, their use value is their reproductive capacity. The father puts his daughter on the market because he cannot himself enjoy her use value, and therefore he exchanges it for something he can use, like advantageous marriage connections. We might read the sacrifice of Iphigeneia as a sort of failed marriage exchange,[61] then, in which the father, rather than giving his daughter away, destroys her, and thus both loses her (gives up his own rights to her use value) and, paradoxically, keeps her for himself.[62] During this exchange that is no exchange, the girl's status as *agalma* is reaffirmed, for she is proven too precious to give away. But what constitutes her value as an *agalma* is quite different from what would constitute her value in exchange: if Iphigeneia's value in marriage exchange would be reproductive potential, her value in this sacrifice is her sexual purity, the purity that makes her a perfect sacrificial victim. This purity is not a given, however, and I argue that we can trace through this scene the transformation of her use value as reproductive potential into use value as virginity, a virginity that itself becomes the desirable alternative to reproductive sexuality.[63]

Iphigeneia in the sacrifice scene is right on the cusp of adult sexuality. She is at the point of perfected virginity, just about to cross over into womanhood, and it is this perfect *hēbē* (youth) in part that makes her such an ideal sacrificial victim.[64] The liminal nature of the moment is marked by the imagery of female initiation.[65] The saffron-colored robes Iphigeneia wears (239) are those worn by brides[66] and also by the girl initiates at the festival of Artemis Brauronia.[67] That the sacrifice in some way marks a transition is further suggested by the repeated and ominous use of the word *proteleia*, a sacrifice specifically associated with initiation, marriage, and war.[68] The word suggests the equation formulated most famously by J.-P. Vernant: marriage is to a girl what war is to a boy, a similar transition, marked often by a similarity of diction and themes.[69] If Iphigeneia's sacrifice is her initiation, though, it is as close to a boy's initiation on the battlefield as to a girl's on the marriage bed.

In the liminality of this moment, there are already hints of adult female sexuality.[70] The "force of the bridle" (βίαι χαλινῶν, 238) that leads Iphigeneia as a sacrificial animal to the slaughter also evokes the trope familiar from lyric poetry of the young girl as a wild animal captured and tamed by her first sexual encounter.[71] This suggests that her sacrifice is also imagined as a defloration.[72] This association is strengthened by the motif of virgin blood, almost an oxymoron in terms of Greek physiology. Unlike the adult woman, who bleeds regularly throughout her life, the virgin was seen as essentially bloodless.[73] Following this logic, the "usual" method of death for virgins in myth, as Helen King has shown, is strangulation, a bloodless death.[74] A bloody death becomes a sort of marriage or defloration in which the girl bleeds for the first time; the piercing of her throat connotes the piercing of her "lower throat," her vagina.[75]

Iphigeneia, then, is at the moment of perfected virginity, just prior to defloration.[76] And yet the sacrifice scene is thoroughly suffused with eroticism: the blood of the virgin is an object of desire (214–16); Iphigeneia herself is beautiful (235–36), and her beauty is specifically erotic. The "piteous shaft of the eye" with which she appeals to her sacrificers (ἀπ' ὄμματος βέλει φιλοίκτωι, 241) is the erotic glance of lyric poetry; in lyric, the eyes are the locus of erotic sensation, and their shaft penetrates the lover.[77] Even at her moment of most perfect virginity,

Iphigeneia is already starting to show signs of sexual maturity and of a dangerous seductiveness.

This hint of eroticism would be even more marked if we were actually meant to imagine Iphigeneia's naked body in this scene. She is said to be "pouring her saffron-dyed robe to the ground" (κρόκου βαφὰς δ' ἐς πέδον χέουσα, 239), but what exactly does this mean?[78] Is it just that her robes are flowing down as she is raised aloft, or is she pushing back her garment, letting it fall? Lloyd-Jones and Denniston and Page reject the latter interpretation more on moral and aesthetic grounds than grammatical; Lloyd-Jones thinks it "an unnecessary piece of exhibitionism," and Denniston and Page claim that neither would it be physically possible (as she is bound), "nor is there the least likelihood that she would do anything so ἀπρεπές [improper] . . . even if she were able."[79] Fraenkel, on the other hand, believes that the text does support this interpretation and, his imagination aroused, he conjures the scene: "With a quick movement of her back and shoulders she lets her robe slip to the ground, and there she kneels, with upturned eyes, naked before the men—she the king's daughter heretofore so modest, so closely guarded."[80] The modern debate does little to resolve the difficulties, and the possibility remains open that we are meant to envision the young maiden naked. This I would see not as a piece of shameless exhibitionism on the part of either Iphigeneia or the text, but rather as a sudden and jolting sexual charge as is always given in tragedy (I believe) by the mention or imagination of the naked female body.[81] I would not want to press this issue too hard given the ambiguity of the text, and there is certainly enough evidence for the erotics of the passage without this. If we do accept this interpretation, however, we are suddenly and shockingly confronted with Iphigeneia's sexuality: she is suddenly exposed to the gaze of the audience (even if only via the imagination of the chorus), just as she is about to be exposed to the sacrificial blade. In the analogy of this scene to a marriage, the derobing parallels the unveiling of the bride, the *anakaluptēria*, where the revelation of the virgin and her penetration by the gaze of the spectators prefigures the "loosening of her girdle" and penetration by her husband.[82]

If the sacrifice is conceived as a perverted marriage, the imagery of defloration makes perfect sense. The deaths of young girls were traditionally represented as a marriage to Hades,[83] and Euripides, in his version of events at Aulis, imagines Iphigeneia as the bride of Hades as well as of Achilles.[84] Here this theme is remarkably absent. Just as Iphigeneia is denied a mortal husband, she is also denied a husband in Hades.[85] But if the sacrifice is a sort of penetration, and this is not the penetration of a husband (Hades or Thanatos), whose is it? We have already seen that the episode is infused with eroticism: whose desire is it?

Agamemnon himself is, of course, the sacrificer (224–25). The introduction of other male participants at the last moment (230, 231, 240–41) does nothing to mitigate Agamemnon's sole responsibility for her death.[86] If the murder is a defloration, then Agamemnon himself penetrates his daughter. The fantasy of incestuous penetration is the erotic counterpart to the failed marriage exchange: the father who fails to give away his daughter must marry her himself. This logic is the driving force behind Marx's notion of exchange: one must exchange what one cannot use oneself.[87] But here Agamemnon does not exchange his daughter, choosing instead to hoard her for himself. I shall suggest at the end of the chapter some potential profits from such a hoarding of resources; for the moment, though, we should recognize the problems inherent in the scenario: the father who refuses to give his daughter in marriage is imagined as penetrating her himself, and the taboo against such incestuous use drives this ambiguous and uncomfortable exchange.

But though the specifically incestuous desire of the scene applies only to Agamemnon, the sadism of this erotic murder is generalized to a larger group of male participants. When Agamemnon makes his decision, he claims that it is "right" (themis) to desire virginal blood:

παυσανέμου γὰρ θυσίας
παρθενίου θ' αἵματος ὀρ-
γᾶι περιόργως ἐπιθυ-
μεῖν θέμις. εὖ γὰρ εἴη.[88]

(214–17)

For to desire maiden's
blood and a sacrifice to
calm the winds with a
passion exceeding passion,
it is right. May it be for
the best.

The text here is tantalizingly uncertain. Who is the subject of ἐπιθυμεῖν ("to desire")? Various attempts have been made to emend the text and, in the process, to supply a clear subject. Agamemnon himself (μ') is one possibility. Triclinius proposes Artemis as the subject. Another alternative is the text Denniston and Page (following Bamberger) print: περιοργῶ σ⟨φ'⟩ ἐπιθυμεῖν ("for them to desire . . ."), understanding the allies as the subject. West's process of elimination is illustrative not only of the confusion caused by the absence of a named subject, but also, I think, of the intended psychological effect: "It can only be the army's craving, arising from their desire for deliverance from the tribulations described in 188–197; Agamemnon himself certainly has no such craving . . . and neither has Calchas. . . . Nor can the goddess herself be got into the sentence. No, the craving is that of the ξυμμαχία [the alliance], understood from 213."[89] For West, the text's obscurity allows Agamemnon to be exonerated: since he is not specifically named, the disturbing hints of incest can be denied.[90]

The lack of clear attribution generalizes the sadism, so that it adheres to all the perpetrators of the act and its witnesses. The sacrifice becomes not only an incestuous penetration, but also a sort of gang rape. This implicates more than the internal audience, the "war-loving chieftains" (philomakhoi brabēs) who urge on the act but do not themselves commit it; we must remember, too, the secondary audience, the chorus, which narrates the event even if, as it claims (248), it did not see the murder itself. The erotics of the sacrifice are as much a part of the chorus's narrative as they are inherent to the act itself; the sadism of the chorus becomes indistinguishable from that of the philomakhoi brabēs. By attributing desire, however vaguely, to the brabēs, the chorus can project and deny its own vicarious interest in the scene, but its vehemence in denying its participation (even as witnesses) in the murder itself merely reinforces the impression that the narrative has something to hide.

Further, there is a third audience implicated, the actual Athenian audience.[91] The Greeks seem to have ascribed to Poe's literary dictum that nothing is so poetic as the death of a beautiful woman.[92] The deaths of women represented in tragedy and in art are often tinged with eroticism: the woman is often figured as naked or nearly so, her body revealed to the viewer's imagination just at the moment that it is penetrated by the weapon.[93] We, too, are implicated in this sadistic voyeurism, asked to imagine the scene and hence to experience the longing for virgin blood. Thus the text's lack of determination as to the subject of the desire allows for concentric rings of denial and deferral. The desire that diffuses outward in concentric circles from the act itself implicates an ever-expanding audience: the brabēs, the chorus, and finally the Athenian spectator. That same inadmissible erotics is then denied by its deflection back toward the center of the circle, as the audience projects its desire onto the chorus, and the chorus onto the *brabēs* and Agamemnon. The final stage in this cycle of disavowal (and this is what makes the scene thinkable) is the projection of the eroticism onto the object of desire itself, Iphigeneia.

The anxiety produced by this fantasy of incestuous, murderous desire is ultimately contained, then, by the deflection of the desire onto its object, so that the dangerous urges inhere within the object rather than within the subject: the object itself seems to create the desire. Iphigeneia is represented as the perfect virgin, but already within her virginity there are, I have argued, hints of the sexual seductiveness of a grown woman, and moreover not just any woman, but specifically Helen, the paradigmatically and dangerously seductive woman.[94] When Iphigeneia, bound and gagged, appeals to her sacrificers with her eyes, striking each one "with the piteous shaft of her eye" (ἀπ' ὄμματος βέλει φιλοίκτωι, 240–41), she anticipates the description of Helen as "a gentle shaft of the eyes, a heart-gnawing bloom of love" (μαλθακὸν ὀμμάτων βέλος, / δηξίθυμον ἔρωτος ἄνθος, 742–43). Helen, at her most desirable, just as she is entering Troy as a bride, recalls Iphigeneia. But Helen goes on, in the next sentence, to Paris's bed (and the beginning of all the trouble), whereas Iphigeneia goes on to her death. It is as if Helen is an Iphigeneia gone bad or, more to the point, as if Iphigeneia must be killed in order to prevent her from becoming another Helen.[95]

This suggestion that Iphigeneia, if allowed to reach maturity, will become another Helen is central to the play's conception of women and of human development in general.[96] The *Oresteia* as a whole has a large stake in genealogical purity, in the notion that like produces like and that children prove, in time, true to their inherited natures. This genealogical understanding of *physis* ("nature," "character," "birth") is central to the aristocratic notion of the self (to which we shall return at the end of this chapter), as well as to the trilogy's concept of transgenerational guilt: men grow up to be like their fathers.[97] For women, on the other hand, genealogical purity seems to mean truth to the *genos gunaikōn*, the race of women, and to its progenitor, Pandora.[98] Like Pandora, who appears beautiful when she first enters the house, but is eventually shown to be a "beautiful evil" (*kalon kakon*), each of her daughters will, in time, reveal her "bitch mind and deceitful ways" (κύνεόν τε νόον καὶ ἐπίκλοπον ἦθος, Hes. *Erga* 67). This developmental model demands and justifies total control over the woman in an attempt to prevent a teleology that seems to be, nonetheless, inevitable. Thus the phylogeny of the *genos gunaikōn*, as represented in the myth of Pandora, is recapitulated in *Agamemnon* in the ontogeny of each individual woman. Each woman will eventually turn out to be bad.[99]

This theme of ontogeny is seen most clearly in the "lion-cub parable" of the Second Stasimon (717–36). A man raises a lion cub in his house. Like Pandora, the lion cub is irresistibly attractive when it first enters the house, and only gradually is revealed to be true to its nature, a *kalon kakon*.[100] This extended metaphor, overtly applicable to Helen (as it is embedded within the story of Helen's arrival at Troy),[101] applies equally well to any woman entering a new house in marriage: would it hold true for Iphigeneia, too, were she to reach maturity?[102] Is Iphigeneia doomed to repeat the story of Pandora, to be true to her *genos*, to become Helen?

The fear that the ontogeny of the individual woman will repeat the phylogeny of the *genos gunaikōn* may lie behind the gagging of Iphigeneia. Iphigeneia's enforced silence is emphasized repeatedly throughout the scene (notably in the pleonasms of 235–38).[103] She is silenced to prevent her curses (237) (not the prayers and cries that she has uttered without effect, 228–29) in an attempt to avoid religious pollution and to maintain the fiction, always necessary in sacrifice, of a willing victim.[104] But we are not told that Iphigeneia wants to utter a curse on the house; rather, she desires to address each man by name (προσεννέπειν θέλουσ', 242–43). This naming of men by a woman perhaps recalls the story told of Helen in *Odyssey* 4: she is said to have walked around the Trojan horse calling by name the Greek leaders concealed inside (4.277–79).[105] Helen knew the men by name because they had all courted her; Iphigeneia could name them, we are told, from serving them at her father's table (243–47). But this, too, is a strange and suspicious image.[106] In Athenian practice, only *hetairae* (call girls) would sing at symposia in the company of strange men. Is Iphigeneia here represented as a virginal *hetaira*? Her presence in this all-male setting, contrary to Athenian custom, simultaneously emphasizes Iphigeneia's anomalous purity and undermines it with hints of sexuality.

If Iphigeneia's virginal status allowed her to speak among men in the past, nevertheless, she is prevented from speech in the sacrifice scene, prevented from articulating her suspicious familiarity with the sacrificers. While the naming of the men would associate her with Helen, Iphigeneia's silence keeps her a virgin. The Greek medical texts discuss the thickening of the throat in a young girl as a sign of defloration; the widening of the upper throat in sympathy with the widened lower passage would deepen the girl's voice and offer proof of her sexual activity.[107] Thus, in these lines, the purity of Iphigeneia's voice when she sings the paean is associated with the fact that she is still a virgin (ἀταύρωτος, 245).[108] If defloration opens the throat and deepens the voice, virginity would mean keeping the throat (upper, as lower) tightly closed; the most extreme and infallible indication of virginity, then, would be total silence.[109] Prevented from speaking her familiarity with other men, Iphigeneia is only allowed to utter one word: "Father."[110]

What is perhaps most extraordinary in this scene is the force necessary to keep Iphigeneia silent.[111] The implication seems to be that Iphigeneia's virginity can only be preserved by dint of violent intervention. It is as if the only way to keep her a virgin is to silence her and, finally, to kill her. Even as it suggests the adult sexuality toward which Iphigeneia is already moving, the text goes to great lengths to preserve her as a virgin. And as a result of this effort, the scene creates an *agalma* of Iphigeneia. It objectifies her, freezes her, just at the point at which she is most valuable: valuable to the narrative (as a focus for purity and pathos), to the *oikos* (as untainted reproductive potential), and to her father (as a loving and loyal daughter). The objectification that this scene performs is underlined by the pictorial image of 242: Iphigeneia is "conspicuous as in a picture" (πρέπουσά θ' ὡς ἐν γραφαῖς).[112] She is captured at this precise moment and fixed, unable to speak, move, or change. It is this *graphē* (picture) that makes Iphigeneia a *domōn agalma*: an invaluable and irreplaceable asset for the house.[113]

Iphigeneia may be agalmatized as a virgin in this scene, but only at the price of extreme violence, both within and to the text. The text spares us no horrific detail of the preliminaries to the sacrifice,[114] and, in contrast to the tradition followed by Euripides, Aeschylus chooses to make Iphigeneia an unwilling victim.[115] The *dussebeia* of sacrificing a manifestly unwilling victim is coupled here with the rarity (in extant sources, at any rate) of a virgin sacrifice represented as involuntary. The association, even before the scene opens, of Iphigeneia's sacrifice with the eagles' slaughter of the pregnant hare, and therefore with all the death of the Trojan War, highlights the violence of the sacrifice. Prominently placed as it is, the sacrifice of Iphigeneia becomes the focal point for all the pathos, violence, and impiety of the war. Moreover, the eroticism surrounding her murder is the first instance of a broader erotics of violence in the play; the collapsing of desire for Iphigeneia with desire for her violent death (the "just" longing for virgin blood) makes it impossible to separate aggression from desire. Iphigeneia is the first victim of the sadism of war, what Clytemnestra will later call a "lust for destruction," ἔρως . . . πορθεῖν (341–42). In this scene, all the horror of war is condensed in the *graphē* of a beautiful, doomed girl.

This image is crystallized by an abrupt break in the narrative: "What happened then I did not see and do not narrate; but the crafts of Calchas were not without fulfillment" (τὰ δ᾽ ἔνθεν οὔτ᾽ εἶδον οὔτ᾽ ἐννέπω· / τέχναι δὲ Κάλχαντος οὐκ ἄκραντοι, 248–49).[116] Presentation of the actual sacrifice would not only violate Greek tragedy's supposed squeamishness on such issues, it would also be unnecessary: Iphigeneia has already been fixed as an *agalma* by a narrative that silences her and preserves her as a *graphē*; the actual murder would be superfluous.[117] Further, it is the break in the narrative itself that closes off the space around her and keeps her a virgin: to describe the sacrifice would be to deflower her. Yet, while the break in the narrative effects the objectification, it also points to the artificiality, the imaginary quality, of the construct. When the chorus claims not to have seen the sacrifice proper, it also raises the question of whether and how it was able to see the events leading up to the sacrifice. Why would the chorus have been at Aulis?[118] Why would it have seen one part but not the other? Did it, in fact, see any of it, or is the chorus's whole narrative simply an imaginative fiction? It is not necessary to resolve this problem, but simply to recognize that it is raised. Attention is drawn to the issues of authority and veracity, and we are reminded that this narrative, whether based on eyewitness or reported accounts, is the chorus's fantasy.

The effect of this narrative manipulation is, as I have suggested, the objectification of the virgin as loyal daughter. In spite of the violence perpetrated against her, Iphigeneia is imagined, much later in the play, as greeting her father with a kiss in the underworld.[119] The loyalty of the virgin Iphigeneia to her father, moreover, is generalized as a loyalty to male society as a whole. Within the sacrifice scene, we get an embedded picture of happier times, when Iphigeneia served at her father's table during symposia:

> πολλάκις
> πατρὸς κατ᾽ ἀνδρῶνας εὐτραπέζους
> ἔμελψεν. ἁγνᾶι δ᾽ ἀταύρωτος αὐδᾶι πατρὸς
> φίλου τριτόσπονδον εὔποτμον παι-
> ῶνα φίλως ἐτίμα.
>
> (243–47)

Often she had sung in her father's hospitable
banquet-halls, and virginal and with pure voice
she honored lovingly the blessed paean at the
libations of her dear father.

The repetition of "dear, loving" (φίλου, φίλως, 246–47) and the emphatic placement of "father" (πατρὸς) at the end of 245 make it clear that Iphigeneia is imagined as absolutely loyal to her father and his company. The *trapeza* (banquet table) in *Agamemnon* is virtually metonymic for male homosocial relations: the guest-host relations broken by the theft of Helen (400–2), or the relations between brothers violated at the feast of Thyestes.[120] Iphigeneia is the only woman allowed to enter into this male world without disastrous results.[121]

All this emphasis on the virgin daughter, typically the least significant and least powerful character in Greek society, may seem odd until we recognize the importance of the father-daughter bond in the trilogy's struggle to establish a secure patriarchal civic and domestic structure.[122] It is a relationship we see repeated over and over: in Cassandra's laments for Priam and Agamemnon, in Electra's reverence for her father in *Choephoroe*, and most importantly, in the figures of the Erinyes/Eumenides and of Athena in the last play.[123] Athena is the ideal daughter, loyal in every way to her father's concerns, actively supportive of the patriarchal structure of *oikos* and *polis*:

μήτηρ γὰρ οὔτις ἐστὶν ἥ μ' ἐγείνατο,
τὸ δ' ἄρσεν αἰνῶ πάντα, πλὴν γάμου τυχεῖν,
ἅπαντι θυμῶι, κάρτα δ' εἰμὶ τοῦ πατρός.

(*Eum.* 736–38)

There is no mother who bore me, and I praise the
male in everything—except for getting married—
with all my heart, and I belong entirely to my
father.

Throughout the *Oresteia*, the positive relationship between father and daughter is contrasted to the dangerous relationship between husband and wife: the virginal Athena replaces Clytemnestra.[124] There is, of course, some gesture made at the end of *Eumenides* toward reestablishing the positive value of the marital bond: the Eumenides are made protectors of marriage and fertility (834–36, 956–67). But this in itself is a problem, that fertility should become the domain of virgins;[125] further, the play, by representing onstage powerful virgin daughters while mentioning only in passing the supposedly recuperated marriage bond, replicates the victory in the *agōn* between Apollo and the Erinyes of paternity over maternity or matrimony. Female sexuality is thus eliminated, and the female, so dangerous throughout the trilogy, is redeemed as a virgin.[126]

Yet if this movement from wife to daughter is presented as a solution of some sort within the terms of the text, it is nevertheless extremely problematic, for in replacing the wife with the daughter, or rather in preventing a daughter from becoming a wife, the trilogy reproduces and codifies the faulty exchange of Iphigeneia's sacrifice.[127] Instead of giving his daughter to another man as a wife, Agamemnon keeps her for himself: the woman is kept pure and loyal, but only at the cost of extreme violence and an incestuous economics whereby the *oikos* is preserved, but is unable to reproduce.

The incestuous relationship between father and daughter enshrined in the *Oresteia* speaks to contemporary anxieties about the reproduction and preservation of the aristocratic *genos* within democratic society and the ways in which the elite could or could not be incorporated into the *polis*. The father-daughter relationship preserves the aristocratic fantasy that "like produces like." This fantasy of endogamy represents a desire to maintain somehow the purity of blood that is one justification of aristocratic hegemony.[128] Yet at the same time, this attempt to preserve genealogical purity is a project manifestly antithetical to democratic concerns, for by discouraging the intermarriage of birth elites and wealth elites, it perpetuates an archaic caste system inimical to the integrative aims of the democracy.[129] Furthermore, endogamy is an ultimately unviable strategy: incest may keep the line pure, but it is unproductive.[130] Thus the imagination of incest is simultaneously an aristocratic fantasy of withdrawal and a democratic imagination of aristocratic corruption. These two viewpoints may be allowed to coexist in the trilogy, but we should remember that the *Oresteia* closes with the unification and harmonization of the *polis* under the rule of Athena, the ideal product of a closed and self-sufficient aristocratic *genos*.[131]

The aristocratic withdrawal imagined in this scene is also economic. By denying the exchange of his daughter, Agamemnon hoards her as his *domōn agalma*, and thus reaffirms the separation between *agalmata* and commodities. We saw in the first section of this chapter that this separation is purely ideological, the product of fetishization and not of inherent differences, but that upon it rest important social distinctions. The preservation of Iphigeneia as an *agalma* likewise preserves Agamemnon's status as the owner of *agalmata*. The narrative manipulation by which this agalmatization of Iphigeneia is effected—the occlusion of the relations of exchange, the projection of desire for the object onto the object itself, the artificial breaking-off of the narrative—serves to conceal the social nature of the distinction, reifying it in the *agalma* Iphigeneia. At the same time, it implicates all the scene's audiences (Agamemnon, the Greek warlords, the chorus, the Athenian spectators) in this obfuscation; we are all made complicit in the social hierarchy this *agalma* inscribes and conceals. The result of this fetishization is an antidemocratic withdrawal of aristocratic wealth from the *polis*. By denying his daughter's commodity status, by hoarding her as his *agalma*, Agamemnon removes her from circulation (and, indeed, denies the possibility of her circulation); thus he transforms his wealth into a type of possession that is inaccessible to the *dēmos*.[132] Economically, as well as genealogically, the sacrifice of Iphigeneia represents an antidemocratic hoarding of aristocratic resources.

This father-daughter relationship, then, encodes a tension between the desire to preserve aristocratic exclusivity, both economic and genealogical, and the need to integrate the aristocracy into the society at large. The sacrifice of Iphigeneia represents a failed exchange at many different levels: as an aristocratic potlatch, it fails either to consolidate the aristocratic group or to define a hierarchy within it; as a marriage, it fails to unite two houses; as an attempt to maintain genealogical purity, it is a strategy ultimately disastrous for both democracy and aristocracy. Rather than creating community, this catastrophic exchange results in an antisocial and incestuous hoarding; Agamemnon keeps Iphigeneia for himself by destroying her, thus realizing the tension inherent in the phrase *domōn agalma* between the need to exchange and the desire to hoard. The violence and sexuality intermingled in this transaction are projected onto the victim, who is fetishized as object of desire and of violence. Finally, she is sacrificed, in a move that at once agalmatizes the object and expunges the dangerous desire of the subject.

꙰

FIVE

Agalma ploutou:
ACCOUNTING FOR HELEN

꙰

THE DISENCHANTMENT OF THE *agalma*

If with Iphigeneia we see the creation of a commodity through exchange and the textual strategies of fetishization, when we turn to Helen, we find the process reversed: already an *agalma*, Helen is defetishized and shown to be a commodity. Helen is said to be priceless, yet *Agamemnon* attempts obsessively to calculate her worth: Was she worth the life of Iphigeneia, who was sacrificed as "an aid in a war to avenge a woman" (γυναικοποίνων πολέμων ἀρωγάν, 225–26)? Was she worth the lives of the Greek soldiers who fell fighting for her (62–67, 445–49, 1456–67)? Was she worth the life of Agamemnon, who died, at least in part, for the price he paid for her? If her worth can be evaluated in terms of some equivalent, then why not take a monetary compensation for her, a solution proffered by the *Iliad*, where a man can pay off the death of another and where Hector is worth his weight in gold?[1] Helen's worth would seem to be beyond calculation, yet the attempt to evaluate her drives the play's economy. Moreover, she is not finally won in the war fought for her, although Troy falls. Much booty is brought home, including a woman, but Helen herself is not: what is gained is not the irreplaceable Helen but, as it were, her weight in gold.

At the heart of the issue of Helen's value is the question of exactly what sort of object she is. Is she an object of innate and incalculable preciousness? Or is she a base commodity, whose value can be calculated in money and expressed in exchange? Is she an *agalma* or a more mundane and material form of wealth, like *ploutos* or *kerdos*? This is a vexed question, not only in this play, but even from the first appearances of Helen in Greek literature. In the *Iliad*, the object of the Trojan War is repeatedly given as "Helen and the goods" (Ἑλένη καὶ κτήματα, *Il.* 3.70, 91, 282, 285, 458; 7.350; 22.114). This linking seems both to differentiate *agalma* from commodity and to conflate them through a hendiadys whereby Helen, the unique and irreplaceable object, becomes inseparable from the more concrete property that moves with her.[2]

In *Agamemnon*, Helen is inherently and quintessentially desirable; we are never invited to ask what makes her so desirable. She is explicitly called an *agalma* (741), and bears many of the features of this enchanted type of object. Like an *agalma*, her origin is divine and, in some versions, magical.[3] In epic depictions, she herself has magical powers: a drug that alleviates pain, the right to confer immortality on her spouse.[4] In *Agamemnon*, she is associated with the terminology of *agalmata*: with the *kharis* of beautiful statues (*eumorphoi kolossoi*), with luxurious materials and beauty.[5] And if *erōs* is the force that fetishizes women in exchange, what woman could be more valuable than Helen, who is the virtual personification of *erōs*?[6] She is infinitely valuable, and all attempts to calculate her exact worth fail: in her unique preciousness, Helen becomes like Zeus in the "Hymn to Zeus" of the Parodos (160–66): she cannot be compared to anything but herself.[7]

Yet at the same time as she is "a very queer thing, abounding in metaphysical subtleties and theological niceties" (as Marx says of the fetishized commodity), Helen is also a regular commodity, given value in exchange. Behind her seemingly inherent worth lie relations among men: the bonds among the Greek princes who wooed her and promised to defend her,[8] the broken *xenia* bond between Paris and Menelaus, the hostility between Greeks and Trojans. Though she seems always to transcend the relations among the men who fight for her, Helen's value lies precisely in these relations. Significantly, almost all the adjectives used to describe her in the play are adjectives of possession rather than description.[9] She is "a woman of many men" (πολυάνορος . . . γυναικός, 62) and "another man's woman" (ἀλλοτρίας . . . γυναικός, 448–49), "wooed in battle, much-contested Helen" (τὰν δορίγαμβρον ἀμφι-νεικῆ θ' Ἑλέναν, 686–87), a woman whose price is measured by men and in terms of men.

Helen becomes a valuable commodity specifically through the *agōn*, the arena par excellence for relations between men.[10] The epic fragments tell of the competition among all the Greek chieftains for the daughter of

Tyndareus: each hero competes with different assets and strengths, but it is Menelaus, who "gives the most," who wins.[11] Thus from the first, Helen is located at the interstices of two different systems of evaluation, the economy of commodities and the economy of *agalmata:* she is simultaneously a prize to be contended for and a commodity to be bought.[12] This peaceable competition is replicated in a more hostile register in the Trojan War. If the Trojan War is "a war fought for a woman," Helen is a woman for whom a war is fought, and whose worth (for all that Aeschylus questions it) is constituted through the war. But whereas in epic accounts, the relations among competitors are obviously what invest Helen with meaning, in *Agamemnon*, the competition among Greeks and Trojans is occluded, and Helen's value seems to exist in a vacuum: her possession or loss bears significance in and of itself, outside of a competitive social framework. Just as Marx describes, the commodity comes to represent and replace the relations that create it.

So, Helen is a commodity in that she is given value through the relations of exchange (the competitive relations among men) and is a fetishized commodity in that this value seems magically to reside within herself. Always embedded within exchange relations and yet always seeming to exceed them, Helen is *Agamemnon*'s universal equivalent. In the final step of Marx's extended form of exchange, a single commodity is taken out of circulation and declared, by social consent, to be the recognized standard of all equivalence.[13] Gold, for instance, is abstracted from the system of commodity equivalence (we don't ask how much a coin is worth in itself) and, by being equivalent to nothing in itself, is made equivalent to everything and allows all other commodities to be compared.[14] The universal equivalent is thus simultaneously a commodity, since it is pure exchange value and the lubricant of the commodity economy, and the supremely fetishized object, in that its value seems self-evident and immanent. So gold acts as a currency, but at the same time, as Pindar says, "like a blazing fire shines out in the night brighter than magnificent wealth" (*Ol.* 1.1–2).

Helen, like gold, is in constant circulation and facilitates the movement of other commodities—Greek soldiers, glory, Iphigeneia, Cassandra—but herself is beyond possession, like "a vision that slips through the arms and is gone" (424–25). Like a universal equivalent, Helen is the standard of all value, but is herself virtually devoid of value. Throughout Greek mythology, she is associated with *mimesis*, representation, imitation.[15] Invested with value by those who fight for her, she becomes a mirror of the desires they project onto her:[16] in the *Odyssey* she can mimic the voices of the wives of all the Greek soldiers; she is no more than their desires.[17] At the same time, there is the tradition that Helen did not go to Troy at all, that she was replaced by an *eidōlon*, an image or copy, while the real woman was in Egypt.[18] These traditions lie behind the elusiveness of the Aeschylean Helen: the locus of all value, she is nothing in herself, a mere image, an *eidōlon*, a copy of an uncertain original.

As universal equivalent, Helen is both commodity and *agalma*, and thus poised between the two economies, she collapses the difference between them. She is an *agalma ploutou* (741), an *agalma* that consists of wealth. This phrase, which is virtually oxymoronic in its conflation of two ideologically distinct registers, locates Helen right at the center of a schism between *agalmata* and *ploutos*, a schism that opens again and again throughout the play as *agalmata* are disenchanted and used as though they were mere *ploutos*. So Iphigeneia is represented as an *agalma* to be treasured at home and circulated only in the most prestigious gift exchange, marriage. But instead of a precious gift, she becomes a monetary recompense, *poinē* (225–26), for Helen. Instead of being preserved as a treasure within the house, she is slaughtered like a sheep from a large flock (1415–17), that is, she is spent like money, not cherished like an *agalma*. She is spent as though she were expendable.

A similar dynamic is at work in the "carpet scene" (905–74). Welcoming home the victorious Agamemnon, Clytemnestra spreads a tapestry for him to enter the palace. The tapestry is described in the diction of *agalmata*: an object laden with symbolic value, its rich purple color (910, 946, 959) represents sovereignty, and its worth stands as a metonymy for the wealth of the entire royal house (948, 958–62). As an *agalma*, it should be treasured within the house or given only as an offering to the gods (922–25, 946); Agamemnon knows the blasphemy of trampling such an irreplaceable object, just as he knew the danger of destroying his child, that other *domōn agalma*,[19] and his hesitation merely heightens the sense that this action, like the sacrifice, will incur the *phthonos* (envy, resentment) of both gods and mortals.

But Clytemnestra forces him to walk the carpet, to act as though it were replaceable rather than unique, utilitarian rather than precious, a "footwiper," as Agamemnon says, rather than an "embroidery" (926). Under Agamemnon's feet, this "purple of the gods" (ἀλουργέσιν θεῶν, 946) becomes mere "wealth and weavings bought with silver" (πλοῦτον

ἀργυρωνήτους θ᾽ ὑφάς, 949). Even as he proclaims the religious pro-
hibitions surrounding this special object, he debases it by reference to its
purchase, its price in silver. But it is Clytemnestra who gives the clearest
expression to this disenchantment:

> ἔστιν θάλασσα—τίς δέ νιν κατασβέσει;
> τρέφουσα πολλῆς πορφύρας ἰσάργυρον
> κηκῖδα παγκαίνιστον, εἱμάτων βαφάς·
> οἶκος δ᾽ ὑπάρχει τῶνδε σὺν θεοῖς, ἄναξ,
> ἔχειν, πένεσθαι δ᾽ οὐκ ἐπίσταται δόμος.
>
> (958–62)
>
> There is a sea—who shall dry it up?—that
> breeds a gush of great purple, equal to silver,
> ever-renewed, a dye for our clothes; and our
> house has a store of this, by the gods' will,
> king, and the palace does not know poverty.

In Clytemnestra's mouth (in a speech designed to maximize the *phthonos*
of such conspicuous consumption) the tapestry is ἰσάργυρον, "equal to
silver," mere currency.[20]

Thus the economy of *Agamemnon*, driven by a war for an *agalma
ploutou*, is trapped between *agalmata* and *ploutos*, slipping constantly
between the two. The war fought for Helen is motivated by profit as well
as by justice: the army, Clytemnestra fears, will be conquered by gain
(κέρδεσιν νικωμένους, 342).[21] Its price is paid in *agalmata*—Iphigeneia, Greek soldiers. Its only visible return, Cassandra, mirrors Helen in
her indeterminacy: she is, on the one hand, a "chosen flower, gift of the
army" (ἐξαίρετον / ἄνθος, στρατοῦ δώρημ᾽, 954–55); but on the
other hand, she is chosen from "many possessions" (πολλῶν χρημά-
των, 954), just one piece of property among others. Like Helen, she is
indistinguishable from the goods. And she, too, will be squandered. By
the end of the play, when every *agalma* will have been spent like cash,
Clytemnestra, in a belated attempt to reverse this disastrous trend, will
bargain with the *daimōn*, the spirit of the house, offering to jettison her
wealth in exchange for something—whatever it may be—that money
cannot buy (1567–76).[22]

At stake in this slippage between *agalmata* and *ploutos* is the play's social hierarchy, and especially the status of those aristocrats who should

trade exclusively in *agalmata*. The carpet scene, like the sacrifice of Iphigeneia, can be read as a potlatch, a conspicuous destruction of precious goods intended to display the power and prestige of the owner who can afford to thus consume them. And like that prior consumption, the trampling of the carpet has an ambiguous effect, for even as Agamemnon and Clytemnestra destroy the *agalma* in an act that should declare their absolute preeminence within the elite world of *agalma* owners, they undermine the very basis of their social distinction by calling the *agalma* a mere commodity, a thing bought with money.[23]

The public display of aristocratic expenditure in the carpet scene takes on an added ambiguity when we recognize its social context, the proto-democratic city of Argos;[24] for its audience is not rival aristocrats (as in Mauss's case study) but the Argive people—the chorus of elders, the slave girls (908), the Herald[25]—and, of course, the Athenian citizens in the theater of Dionysus. On the one hand, aristocratic *megaloprepeia* (magnificence and munificence) was vital to the economic health of the city, financing, among other things, the production of this play.[26] On the other hand, excessive expenditure raised the specter of tyranny, as Leslie Kurke writes: "From the point of view of the city, excessive *megaloprepeia* seems to presage tyranny. The man who spends too much, too ostentatiously is often suspected of aspiring to tyranny and for this reason currying the favor of the populace by his magnificence."[27] Aristocratic largess within the democracy was thus fraught with dangers, and it is precisely these dangers that Clytemnestra seeks to maximize in forcing Agamemnon to walk on the precious carpet. Her hyperbolic praise, easternizing in its excess and inappropriate from a member of Agamemnon's own *oikos*,[28] encourages the *phthonos* of the community, eliminating any potentially positive valences of the act and presenting Agamemnon in the most tyrannical light.[29] And if Agamemnon's walking on the tapestry is potentially tyrannical within a democratic context, within an aristocratic framework, it is déclassé, an act of bad faith, a misunderstanding or misuse of *agalmata* that compromises his status as an owner of such rare possessions. Spending their *agalmata* as *ploutos*, Agamemnon and Clytemnestra are simultaneously excessive aristocrats (conspicuously consuming for their own self-aggrandizement the wealth that might otherwise have enriched the city) and no aristocrats at all, but merely buyers of expensive goods.

Through this blurring of *agalma* and *ploutos*, the play dismantles, interrogates, and reconstructs its social hierarchy. *Agalmata* are defetishized: these unique objects—whether Iphigeneia, Helen, or the tapestry—are traded as though they were mere commodities. This debased use is then moralized by being associated with "bad" (excessive or deficient) aristocrats like Agamemnon and Clytemnestra, and is thus rejected. Meanwhile, the audience (which is made to feel *phthonos* at this misuse of wealth) is identified as true "aristocrats," those who (no matter what their actual socioeconomic status) know the value of an *agalma*. The play acknowledges the socially determined value of objects in order to establish the "right" way to use them, for once value is disinvested from the object in itself, the whole economy of its use and exchange can be brought under moral scrutiny: disenchantment allows for a reenchantment within a newly moralized economy.

This location of value in the use of the object rather than in the object itself has a double advantage: on the one hand, it expresses an ostensibly democratic message, that use of wealth must be subject to moral control (and, by implication, that aristocratic excesses must be curbed); on the other hand, the economy that it reconstructs is still based on the aristocratic ideals of inheritance and excellence.[30] Thus in the Second Stasimon (750–81), *olbos* (prosperity, happiness, wealth) is recognized as a socially determined rather than an inherent value, a commodity rather than an *agalma*. The chorus rejects the ancient saying that *olbos* gives birth to misery, stating its opinion that actions, not wealth in and of itself, determine whether or not the house will prosper. *Olbos* is stripped of its inherent properties (both its desirability and its dangers), and its use is moralized. This would seem to open up the ranks of the elite, allowing both for wealth without disaster and for prosperity based on virtue. This newly moralized economy, however, is a distinctly aristocratic one, in which the just poor know their place ("Justice shines forth in smoky homes and honors the man who knows his place"; Δίκα δὲ λάμπει μὲν ἐν / δυσκάπνοις δώμασιν, / τὸν δ' ἐναίσιμον[31] τίει, 773–75) and unjust wealth is "counterfeit" (justice "does not honor the power of *ploutos* counterfeited with praise"; δύναμιν οὐ σέβουσα πλού- / του παράσημον αἴνωι, 779–80).[32] Furthermore, this "new" economy is expressed in terms of a model of genealogical purity (758–62), which is the traditional concern of the aristocracy: good wealth "breeds" prosperity, and bad wealth, disaster.[33] Thus what looks like a democratic message is articulated within an aristocratic framework: the economy is disenchanted only to be reenchanted again, and still with an elite bias.

The same dynamic governs the use of another type of *olbos*, Helen, in the First Stasimon (355–487). When Paris steals her, it is not just a breach of *xenia*, but also the misuse of an *agalma:* Paris, like Agamemnon, "tramples the grace of holy things" (ἀθίκτων χάρις / πατοῖθ᾽, 371–72), and thus shows himself not only impious (373) but also a counterfeit aristocrat, who turns black like bad copper when rubbed (390–92). Unjust wealth, as in the Second Stasimon, will breed suffering in the bloodline (374–84), and it, too, will prove as valueless as counterfeit metal under the "fortune-reversing rubbing of life" (παλιντυχεῖ τρι‐ βᾶι βίου, 465). Meanwhile, safety is sought in the *sōphrosunē* of the mean (471–74), in the wisdom of knowing one's place.

The proper use of wealth, moreover, is protected by the gods. It is their *phthonos* that Agamemnon risks by trampling the tapestry and their wrath that Paris incurs when he "tramples the grace of holy things." In the latter case, it is not just as protector of *xenia* (362) that Zeus punishes Paris, but as king (355), that is, in his most aristocratic guise, and with him Night, who herself "possesses many ornaments" (356).[34] As aristocrats who appreciate the worth of *agalmata*, the gods punish the misuse of such objects by mortals: they defend the separation of *agalmata* and *ploutos*, and, by implication, the social division based (if only in this newly moralized form) upon it.

Furthermore, in this play's economic confusion, in its disenchantment and reenchantment of *agalmata*, Zeus himself provides the only possible point of stability. I suggested that Helen functions as the play's universal equivalent, the basis of all evaluation and the currency of all exchanges. As such, she exists in both the *agalma* economy (as gold) and the commodity economy (as money), an *agalma ploutou* around which the play's economic tensions crystallize. But in addition to this ambiguous standard, the play suggests another, Zeus himself:

> Ζεὺς ὅστις ποτ᾽ ἐστίν, εἰ τόδ᾽ αὐ‐
> τῶι φίλον κεκλημένωι,
> τοῦτό νιν προσεννέπω·
> οὐκ ἔχω προσεικάσαι
> πάντ᾽ ἐπισταθμώμενος
> πλὴν Διός, εἰ τὸ μάταν ἀπὸ φροντίδος ἄχθος
> χρὴ βαλεῖν ἐτητύμως.[35]
>
> (160–66)

Zeus, whoever he may be, if it is pleasing to him to be called by this name, thus do I address him. I can

compare him, weighing all things in the balance,
to nothing but Zeus, if I may truly cast the vain
burden from my mind.

The issue is both epistemological and economic. If Zeus is accepted as a universal equivalent, then value is inherent and can be known: the play's obsessive calculation of worth, its accounting of the war's profits and losses, its questioning of the value of *olbos* or a tapestry or a life, can yield definite and stable answers. At the same time, a social economy built around this supremely aristocratic fulcrum—for what could be more unique and precious than Zeus?—would itself be aristocratic in the extreme. Whereas Helen, the *agalma ploutou*, structures an uncertain economy and society, Zeus, the ultimate *agalma*, legitimates the *agalma* economy and the aristocratic society built upon it, a society in which everyone knows his place, even if against his will (180–81), and in which the gods' *kharis*—the grace that fetishizes this whole divinely sanctioned economy—is a *kharis biaios* (182), an oppressive grace. "And it comes to them against their will to be wise (*sōphronein*); and there is a violent *kharis* of the gods as they sit at the dread thwart" (καὶ παρ' ἄ-/κοντας ἦλθε σωφρονεῖν· / δαιμόνων δέ που χάρις βίαιος / σέλμα σεμνὸν ἡμένων, 180–83). The alternative to Helen's unstable universe, then, would seem to be the fixed and fetishized aristocratic cosmos ruled by Zeus.

Khrusamoibos sōmatōn:
THE COMMODIFICATION OF THE MALE SUBJECT

Helen, as we have seen, is an ontologically slippery object: perched between two economies, an *agalma ploutou*, she shows up the falsity of the distinction between them, the essential misrecognition inherent in the fetishism of commodities. This misrecognition of *ploutos* as *agalmata*, of exchange relations as inherent value, has as its result the replacement of exchangers by their commodities; the commodities "take their owners to market," as Marx says: they commodify them. In *Agamemnon*, Helen not only contains and conceals the social relations among men that give her value, but in fact destroys them, and in the war fought for her, the violence of fetishization—the *kharis biaios* that agalmatized Iphigeneia by killing her—rebounds upon the men, reducing them to mere commodities, dust in urns.

91

The disastrous results of Helen's exchange in *Agamemnon* are all the more clear in contrast to the *Iliad*'s presentation of the same story, which, despite all its bloodshed and questioning of war, offers a clear illustration of the structuring effects of exchanging women.[36] There the theft of Helen and the war fought over her constitute heroes, social relations, a whole heroic pageant. Paris's theft of Helen establishes a relationship between himself and Menelaus, albeit a hostile one. The war that follows provides the occasion for a larger-scale negotiation of relations between men: not only between Menelaus and Paris themselves, but between the Greeks and the Trojans in general and among the leaders on each side. This exchange of Helen also structures identities, as each side fights for supremacy, and each hero for the title of "best of the Achaeans." And though Helen's worth is questioned in the *Iliad* and the price paid for her is shown to be high,[37] the net results are fairly positive: *kleos aphthiton* (undying fame) is won by all and the will of Zeus accomplished.

Aeschylus's account of this same narrative in the First Stasimon (399–455) opens as if it will be a simple story of *xenia* transgressed and avenged. Paris is introduced as an example of a man who desires too much, like a child chasing a bird, and who, "entering into the house of the Atreidae, shamed the table of his host with the theft of his wife" (ἐλθὼν / ἐς δόμον τὸν Ἀτρειδᾶν / ἤισχυνε ξενίαν τράπε-/ ζαν κλοπαῖσι γυναικός, 399–402). This transgression of *xenia* is punished by the gods, who send the Atreidae against Paris and destroy his city. The narrative of transgression and its punishment is subsumed into the divine scheme of *dikē*, and the values of *xenia* are reconfirmed.[38]

As a structuring of heroic relations and a vindication of heroic values, the Aeschylean account would seem to follow the Iliadic model. As this ode progresses, however, rather than reinforcing the values it transgresses, the theft of Helen destabilizes not only society and its values, but even the male subject. The problems begin with Helen herself, the prize and the object of the war. No sooner is she introduced than she seems to disappear.

> λιποῦσα δ' ἀστοῖσιν ἀσπίστορας
> κλόνους λοχισμούς τε καὶ
> ναυβάτας ὁπλισμούς,
> ἄγουσά τ' ἀντίφερνον Ἰλίωι φθοράν.

βεβάκει ῥίμφα διὰ
πυλᾶν ἄτλητα τλᾶσα.

(403–8)

And leaving for her citizens
the turmoil of shields,
the gathering of forces
and the arming of ships,
and bringing a dowry of
destruction to Ilium, she
had gone lightly through
the gates, daring a deed
beyond daring.

Her first verb of active agency in the play, λιποῦσα ("leaving"), is symptomatic:[39] Helen is always leaving; she is nothing but exchange value, and thus must always be in circulation. Indeed, she is gone before she was ever really possessed: she "had already gone" (note the peculiar pluperfect βεβάκει[40]) and that "easily," "lightly" (ῥίμφα). A subject only of departure, even as an object Helen is defined by absence. She is ὑπερποντίας at 414, "she who is beyond the sea," that which is distant. She is in the empty eyes of a statue (418), an empty pleasure that comes in dreams (422–23), a *phasma*, a vision that slips through the arms of whoever tries to hold her (παραλλάξασα διὰ / χερῶν βέβακεν ὄψις, 424–25); she is always gone.[41]

I suggested in the last section that Helen's instability throughout her mythology and her particular elusiveness here might be related to her role as a fetishized commodity. Because she is given value through social relations that are then denied, her worth seems immanent and self-apparent, but is in fact illusory, as becomes manifest whenever the text tries to put a price on her. Moreover, as a universal equivalent, she is abstracted from the economy that gives her value: in order to become the abstract standard of evaluation, she must herself be evacuated of value. What happens, then, when this supremely fetishized and mysterious object is put back into exchange?

ἰὼ ἰὼ δῶμα δῶμα καὶ πρόμοι.
ἰὼ λέχος καὶ στίβοι φιλάνορες·
πάρεστι †σιγᾶς ἄτιμος ἀλοίδορος

93

άλιστος⁴² ἀφεμένωντ ἰδεῖν·
πόθωι δ' ὑπερποντίας
φάσμα δόξει δόμων ἀνάσσειν·
εὐμόρφων δὲ κολοσσῶν
ἔχθεται χάρις ἀνδρί.
ὀμμάτων δ' ἐν ἀχηνίαις
ἔρρει πᾶσ' Ἀφροδίτα.

(410–19)

Woe, woe for the house, the
house and its princes, woe for
the bed and the man-loving
traces; we can see him there,
sitting apart, in silence, dishonored, not reviling, not beseeching (?); and in longing for her
who is beyond the sea, a ghost
shall seem to rule the house.
And the charm of beautiful statues is hateful to the man; and
in the emptiness of eyes, all love
is gone.

At 410, the elders of the house lament the disastrous marriage of
Helen. These men recall the Trojan elders of *Iliad* 3, bemoaning the grief
brought upon Troy by the marriage of Helen and Paris.⁴³ However, if we
read the whole rest of the strophe (down to line 426, as Page prints) as
the content of their speech, then it becomes clear that these elders must
be Argives, not Trojans, for they can see Menelaus sitting in his empty
house. The "house and its princes," and even more importantly the "bed
and the man-loving traces," seem at first sight to be Trojan, but then
turn out to be Greek. Or rather, it becomes impossible to distinguish
Trojans from Greeks and the bed of Paris from the bed of Menelaus. The
phrase *stiboi philanores* in 411 is similarly opaque. *Stiboi* are imprints or
traces: are they the body traces in the bed, and if so, whose bed, Paris's
or Menelaus's? Or are they Helen's footprints, and if so where is she
going, off to Paris or back to Menelaus? And as for *philanores* (literally
"man-loving"), who is the man? Her husband, Menelaus, or her lover,
Paris? Instead of differentiating the two men who struggle for her, Helen
merges them.

Fully invested in their impossible object, the exchangers themselves disappear. Thus Menelaus is introduced in a series of textually insecure alpha-privatives at 412–13: "Sitting apart, in silence, dishonored, not reviling, not beseeching." His identity is literally obelized. "And in longing for her who is beyond the sea, a ghost shall seem to rule the house. And the charm of beautiful statues is hateful to the man; and in the emptiness of eyes, all love is gone" (414–19). Who is the *phasma*, the ghost who seems to rule the house?[44] Is it Helen, who haunts Menelaus in his dreams? Or is it Menelaus, a mere shadow of his former self? Not only are Menelaus and Paris merged, but also Menelaus and Helen. The subject and object become indistinguishable; they both become *phasmata*. Love then becomes hate: the beauty of statues becomes hateful to Menelaus. But again a precise referent is elusive. The ambiguous phrase *ommatōn d'en akhēniais* in 418 ("in the emptiness of eyes") locates the loss within the eyes, the center and medium of *erōs*, but whose eyes are these? Is it "in Helen's absence from Menelaus's eyes" (as Fraenkel takes it) or "the absence of Helen's eyes" (as Lloyd-Jones prefers), a metonymy for her beauty?[45] Or are we meant to picture the empty eyes of a statue, devoid of life? In this vacant statue, subject and object are merged, lifeless and empty.

The *kharis eumorphōn kolossōn* brings us back to the exchange and the commodity fetish. *Kharis*, I suggested, is the force that fetishizes objects, as exchange relations are transformed into inherent grace or charm.[46] Here this *kharis* reifies Helen as a beautiful statue, an *agalma*, just as Iphigeneia was frozen as a *graphē*, a picture. But rather than giving her the fixity desired in an *agalma* (the fixity of a *domōn agalma*), the image of the statue also recalls the tradition of Helen as an *eidōlon*,[47] an illusory and unpossessible object. At the same time, the *kolossos* also represents Menelaus: its empty eyes are his eyes, longing for the sight of Helen; he, too, has become an object through this exchange. The phrase *kharis eumorphōn kolossōn* thus sums up the dynamic of the commodity fetish: human relations are invested in an object; the fetishized object (an *eidōlon*, always illusory and liable to disenchantment) replaces its human exchangers, reducing them in turn to objects. The exchange itself is then evacuated: its *kharis* becomes an "empty pleasure" (χάριν ματαίαν, 422) and the desire that drives it vanishes: ἔρρει πᾶσ' Ἀφροδίτα ("All Aphrodite is gone," 419).[48]

The merging of object and subject in this ode is part of a larger, more general destabilization of male identity throughout the play and trilogy.

οὓς μὲν γάρ ⟨τις⟩ ἔπεμψεν
οἶδεν, ἀντὶ δὲ φωτῶν
τεύχη καὶ σποδὸς εἰς ἑκά-
στου δόμους ἀφικνεῖται.

ὁ χρυσαμοιβὸς δ' Ἄρης σωμάτων
καὶ ταλαντοῦχος ἐν μάχηι δορὸς
πυρωθὲν ἐξ Ἰλίου
φίλοισι πέμπει βαρὺ
ψῆγμα δυσδάκρυτον ἀντ-
ήνορος σποδοῦ γεμί-
ζων λέβητας εὐθέτους.⁴⁹

(433–44)

For those they sent away they know,
but instead of men urns and ashes
return to each one's house. Ares, the
gold-changer of bodies and holder
of the scales in the battle of the spear,
from the pyres at Ilium sends to their
dear ones heavy dust bitterly wept
for, with ash that was men loading
the easily stowed urns.

Just as Menelaus becomes a ghost through his desire, the men who fight
for this desire become dust, undifferentiated objects. In this play of perverted *nostoi* (homecomings), this is the most dire: rather than returning from war with immortal glory and precious war-booty, these men return as booty themselves. The exchange of women, which should create
bonds between men, destroys them; the objectification of the woman,
which should declare the men subjects, objectifies the men in turn; all
that is left of them is dust.

And even their dust settles in the impossible space between *agalma*
and *ploutos*. The image of "easily stowed urns" at 444 straddles the two
economies, suggesting at once funerary urns and storage vessels:⁵⁰ are
the remains of the men *agalmata* (carefully preserved in a special funerary urn) or commodities (stored in urns along with the other oils and
grains)? If Ares is a gold-changer of bodies, is the men's "heavy dust"
(βαρὺ ψῆγμα) gold dust or just dirt? But even gold dust is not an
agalma, but rather a currency, the quintessential form of *ploutos*. Ares
reduces people to cash, subjecting them to the same process of agalmati-

zation and disenchantment that besets all objects in this play: a daughter becomes an animal for sacrifice, a precious carpet is just the silver it cost to buy, and men are dust. The violence of commodity fetishism—the *kharis biaios* that invests Iphigeneia and Helen with their value—recoils upon the male exchangers, and here on Ares' scales we find the extreme results of these fatal transactions, where men are weighed out to make up the price of a bad deal.

And by the end of the play, it is Agamemnon himself whose body is on the scales. The most deeply implicated in the war's bad exchanges, Agamemnon is turned, literally, into an object; he is displayed on stage as a corpse, Clytemnestra's *ergon*, as she says, her handiwork. He dies in a vessel that recalls the urns bearing the soldiers' ashes (ἐνύδρωι τεύχει. / δολοφόνου λέβητος, "a vessel to hold water, a deceitful murderous urn," 1128–29; ἀργυροτοίχου δροίτας, "a silver-walled tub," 1539–40), and his corpse becomes an *agalma* that testifies to Clytemnestra's supremacy. Agamemnon's murder enacts before our eyes the catastrophe that results from the dynamic of fetishism: the male subject—moreover a king and a hero—is turned into a mere object.

This fantasy of male commodification is the driving force behind the whole play. So terrifying is it that it immediately generates a reparative or compensatory response, an attempt to reclaim the male objects, turning them back into subjects and saving them from the undifferentiation of dust.[51] At the end of the First Stasimon, the dead are given back their identities and subject status through memorialization: "And they grieve, praising them, this man as skilled in battle, that man for falling nobly in the slaughter for the sake of another man's wife" (στένουσι δ' εὖ λέγοντες ἄν-/δρα τὸν μὲν ὡς μάχης ἴδρις, / τὸν δ' ἐν φοναῖς καλῶς πεσόντ', / ἀλλοτρίας διαὶ γυναι-/κός; 445–49). If their bodies can no longer be separated, at least their memories can be; the *ton men* / *ton de* construction—this man skilled in battle, that falling nobly in the slaughter—effects grammatically this memorial differentiation. Through eulogy the dead are made whole again, and in that form can be reincorporated usefully into the *polis*.[52]

οἱ δ' αὐτοῦ περὶ τεῖχος
θήκας Ἰλιάδος γᾶς
εὔμορφοι κατέχουσιν. ἐχ-
θρὰ δ' ἔχοντας ἔκρυψεν.

(452–55)

97

> But there before the wall in
> the land of Troy, the men,
> in all their beauty, have
> their tombs, and the enemy
> land covers its conquerors.

The description of the victorious soldiers' tombs evokes the language of Homeric heroism, in which the hero is immortalized by his glorious death.[53] The passage also suggests the Athenian *epitaphios logos*, the funeral oration spoken over those who have died fighting for their country.[54] The combination of Homeric *kleos* and the Athenian funeral laudation immortalizes the soldiers and reintroduces them as civic heroes into the *polis*.[55] The losses of the play's bad deals are recouped by this good exchange of corpses for heroes.

But the attempt to repair and reincorporate the commodified male soldiers is here at best only partially successful. The very diction that glorifies the dead also recalls their objectification: the *eumorphoi* bodies of the dead Greeks recall the *eumorphoi kolossoi* at 416, in whose empty eyes we saw the drastic results of the commodity fetish.[56] Likewise, the *thēkai*, the "storage places" that are to be their tombs under Troy, recall the dust in the easily stowed urns. The tomb still suggests an amphora, and a corpse, no matter how glorious it becomes in the memory of the living, is still just "ash that was men" (ἀντήνορος σποδοῦ, 442–43). Moreover, instead of being positively reintegrated into society as a point of civic cohesion, these dead soldiers create *phthonos* and revolutionary mutterings (449–51, 457–58).

But if full reparation of the male subject is impossible within *Agamemnon*'s pessimistic vision, nonetheless, this ode hints at the direction eventual reparation will take and at one possible strategy: the deflection of the problem onto the female object. The objectification of exchangers, I have suggested, is the ultimate result of the fetishism of commodities: the problem is structural; it inheres within the economic process. But as a defense against the terror of objectification, this entire complex dynamic is localized within the female object. Thus in the First Stasimon, the reparation of the dead soldiers as civic heroes is accompanied by a recuperation of misogynist discourse: the soldiers die "because of another man's woman."[57] This response is even clearer in the Second Stasimon, which begins where the First left off: Helen is "hell for ships, hell for men, hell for cities" (ἑλένας ἕλανδρος ἑλέπτολις, 689–90[58]). Instead of the detailed process of the First Stasimon, where the objectification of the woman entails the objectification in turn of the men, here the destruction of the men is located directly within the object itself. Her very name shows destruction as immanent within Helen: she *is* the destruction her exchange causes.[59] Thus the violence perpetrated in the name of Helen is projected onto her, just as Iphigeneia's incipient eroticism was made to bear the burden of the men's sadistic longing for virgin blood.

The defensive strategy of projection and disavowal hinted at in these two odes will be traced in more detail in the next chapter, when we look at the roles of Clytemnestra and Cassandra in this process of recuperating the objectified men and redeeming their bodies from the dust. For if recuperation of the male subject is impossible within *Agamemnon*, it is achieved by the end of the trilogy, and the dynamic of the First Stasimon mirrors in microcosm the dynamic of the *Oresteia* overall. The fetishization of women as commodities in *Agamemnon*—the war fought for Helen, the sacrifice of Iphigeneia, the importation of Cassandra—results in the objectification of Agamemnon himself. But *Choephoroe* will mark a movement toward reparation as the dead king is glorified and called upon to aid in familial and civic restitution. Like the dead soldiers in the First Stasimon, Agamemnon will have his identity restored through memorialization and will be saved from the total objectification of death. Finally, *Eumenides* will see a successful reparation of the male subject in the person of Orestes, the legitimate heir of Agamemnon and legitimate ruler of Argos, and the integrity of the male subject will be enshrined in the establishment of the democratic state, a state of male citizens whose autonomy, identity, and individuality are both constitutive of and guaranteed by the *polis*. The movement of the *Oresteia*, then, is the restitution of the male object—the dust in urns—as the Athenian citizen, the transformation of the objectified male body into the glorious democratic body.

SIX

FEAR AND PITY:
CLYTEMNESTRA AND CASSANDRA

Economic processes, as we have seen in the last two chapters, are thoroughly suffused with psychological affect, with desire, aggression, anxiety. The commodity fetish—a dynamic designed to explain an economic phenomenon—is motivated by desires as much erotic as they are economic: the subject invests himself in his objects psychologically as well as financially, defining himself and his relations through them; invested in his objects, the subject becomes inseparable from them, an object himself. The phantasmic terrors generated by this investment give rise in turn to psychic defenses. The dynamic of the commodity fetish, then, occupies a realm where the economic and the psychological, the social and the subjective, intersect and inseparably coexist. In this chapter, I explore *Agamemnon*'s psychological defenses against the commodity fetish. In order to pursue these strategies, it will be useful to shift theoretical vocabulary (although not focus) from the economic to the psychoanalytic, from Marx to Melanie Klein and the psychoanalytic school of object relations.

Object-relations theory, of which Klein is the unofficial matriarch, studies the way in which individuals project their feelings onto external objects (whether inanimate or human), and incorporate these objects as parts of themselves.[1] The world as Klein describes it is alive with objects vivified by the projections of the subject; the subject, in turn, is full of objects it has introjected. The line between the internal self and external reality is fluid and indistinct. The intimate economy of the subject and its objects that we saw in Marx's commodity fetish is theorized in a psychological register by object-relations theory. By shifting register in this way,

I hope to explicate most fully both the economic dimension of the exchange of women and the psychological, and—a project central to this book—to detail their profound and mutual imbrication.[2]

Klein postulates an inherent sadistic instinct in all infants, a desire to attack the mother's breast and empty it of its contents. Thus for her, desire and satisfaction are always enmeshed with violence. But this instinctual sadism creates overwhelming feelings of guilt and anxiety for the child, who imagines that his or her attack has destroyed the loved object. The various strategies adopted to alleviate these feelings structure the child's developing ego. One of the basic defenses Klein identifies against the anxiety of sadism is the splitting of the loved/destroyed object into positive and negative components: a persecutory figure, which bears the projection of all the child's aggression and is imagined to turn that aggression back upon it, and a conciliatory figure, who forgives the child for its attack and offers it comfort.[3]

Without adopting the clinical analogy of child development (which I believe to be more historically determined than most psychoanalytic theorists will admit), I think we can use Klein's theory of sadism and its defenses to understand *Agamemnon*'s responses to the anxiety of the commodity fetish. Indeed, the dynamics of exchange in *Agamemnon*, which in the last two chapters we discussed from a Marxian perspective, could be recast entirely in the terms of Klein's model. The nexus of desire and violence that we saw in the sacrifice scene as the compelling force behind the relations of exchange—the violent grace that creates *agalmata* by destroying them—is Klein's sadism, the desire that destroys its object. The whole play is driven by this urge, a "lust for destruction" (ἔρως . . . πορθεῖν, 341–42), spurred on by a lust for wealth (κέρδεσιν νικωμένους, 342), a passion that links sexuality, acquisition, and aggression under the aegis of a prohibition (ἃ μὴ χρή, 342): sadism. The very act of commodifying a woman, an act at once erotic and violent, can be seen as sadism in Klein's terms: to put a woman on the market is to risk losing or destroying her. Loved objects are murdered, consumed, betrayed. But these lost objects do not disappear; rather, they haunt the subject, evoking the nightmares of male objectification that we saw in the last chapter, fantasies of urns and corpses.

The play's defense against the anxiety of sadism is the splitting of the object that Klein describes, and the imagination of two complementary fantasies of persecution and forgiveness. *Agamemnon* is dominated by a fantasy of persecution, a figure that both embodies and punishes the violence of fetishization, Clytemnestra. Almost completely determined by her transgressive behavior, Clytemnestra literally enacts the objectification of men that Helen (as object of desire and fetishization) threatens: she murders her husband. Though Clytemnestra is usually seen as the root of all the play's problems,[4] I suggest that we see her instead as a defensive gesture: all the traumas of the commodity fetish—the sadism implicit in fetishization, the economic indeterminacy and social instability, the ultimate disintegration of the male subject—are projected onto her; a ubiquitous and systematic crisis is localized within her individual transgressive character, and in that way is acknowledged, contained, expiated, and finally disavowed. This persecutory fantasy is complemented by a fantasy of conciliation, represented by Cassandra. If Clytemnestra embodies and punishes the commodity fetish, Cassandra forgives the violence of exchange and offers sympathy for its disastrous consequences. Associated with both Helen and Iphigeneia, and herself a victim of the play's faulty economics, Cassandra mourns for the male exchangers, and prophesies their eventual reparation.

This reading of these characters may seem too schematic, and admittedly does not account for every aspect of their characterization. I use the theory of the defensive fantasy only to explain in the broadest terms the functions of the two characters within the psychic structure of the play, for it is at the level of the play as a whole and not of the individual character that I believe subjectivity is located in Aeschylus. Though each character in *Agamemnon* has agency and a certain degree of self-reflection, it is in the complex imagery and symbolic intricacy of the play as a whole that I suggest we look for the nexus of material and psychological conditions that constitute subjectivity.[5] Rather than examine the psychic makeup of individual characters (as Klein does in her own reading of the *Oresteia*), I propose to treat the characters as what Klein calls "part objects," those fragmentary fantasies that combine to make up the subject. Clytemnestra and Cassandra are just such fantasies. Between them they allow the play if not to resolve the problems inherent within the fetishization and exchange of commodities, then at least to defend against them, and in this way to move toward the restoration of civic and subjective integrity secured at last in *Eumenides*.

Androboulon kear:
CLYTEMNESTRA'S TRANSGRESSIVE IDENTITY

Our first introduction to Clytemnestra is in the words of the Watchman at 10–11: "Thus commands a woman's man-counseling, hopeful heart" (ὧδε γὰρ κρατεῖ / γυναικὸς ἀνδρόβουλον ἐλπίζον κέαρ). From the beginning, we are prepared for a character who transgresses both gender and political boundaries.[6] She comes to be defined by a phrase she repeats several times in the play: *ouk aiskhunomai*, "I am not ashamed" (614, 856, 1373),[7] a phrase that speaks to both her sexual and her political transgressions. For in *Agamemnon*, as Froma Zeitlin notes, the political and the sexual are inseparable:[8] a wife's murder of her husband is also regicide; so, too, Clytemnestra's sexual perversions overlap with her political tyranny. Furthermore, both transgressions are overdetermined: not only is she sexually active, she is also sexually perverted; not only is she a ruler, she is also a tyrant.[9]

Clytemnestra's regency during her husband's absence is represented as an aberration and an abomination in both sexual and political terms. Following a polar logic that Zeitlin calls the "Amazon Complex," Clytemnestra's transgressive power destroys the play's male rulers, rendering the legitimate (Agamemnon) and the illegitimate (Aegisthus) alike politically ineffectual and sexually abjected.[10] Explicitly referred to as tyrants (1355, 1365, 1633; *Cho.* 973), Clytemnestra and Aegisthus represent the worst possible sorts of aristocrat: autocratic, self-indulgent, ineffectual, yet violent and authoritarian toward the *dēmos.*[11] Not only is she an illegitimate ruler herself (as a woman), but Clytemnestra has also installed on the true king's throne a conspirator and pretender, Aegisthus. An indisputably detestable character in Aeschylus's presentation, Aegisthus is characterized by the same combination of political and sexual perversion that marks Clytemnestra: he is "the fire on Clytemnestra's hearth" (πῦρ ἐφ' ἑστίας ἐμῆς, 1435), a "cowardly lion who stays at home, tumbling in the bed" of Agamemnon (λέοντ' ἄναλκιν ἐν λέχει στρωφώμενον / οἰκουρόν, 1224–25), but also a cruel and violent oppressor of the people (1617–24, 1632–70).[12] As an illegitimate ruler, a stay-at-home associated with deceit and sexuality, Aegisthus is effeminized; with Clytemnestra as ruler, Aegisthus becomes, as the chorus says, "a woman" (1625–27; cf. *Cho.* 302–5).[13]

The effect of Clytemnestra's perverted authority on her husband is no less damaging. In her speech welcoming him home (855–913), while Clytemnestra offers a fiction of herself waiting loyally like a good wife for the return of her city-sacking husband, the similes with which she describes her joy compare her to male figures (father, 898; sailor, 899; traveler, 901), thus assimilating her husband to the infantile (898), bestial (896), and objectified role. This gender inversion is taken further in the carpet scene, where Clytemnestra interpellates Agamemnon as an illegitimate and impossible creature, and he does not have the strength to resist. Her excessive adulation likens him first to an Eastern despot, a most suspicious figure in the Athenian mind.[14] When Agamemnon protests— "Do not gape at me with prostrations and shouts, as at some barbarian man" (μηδὲ βαρβάρου φωτὸς δίκην / χαμαιπετὲς βόαμα προσχάνῃς ἐμοί, 919–20)—Clytemnestra reminds him that Priam would have accepted such honors (935); she urges him to ignore the "talk of the *dēmos*" (938) and to risk their *phthonos* as the price of their envy (939). Against his will—or at least his better judgment—Agamemnon is hailed as barbarian, tyrant, and finally woman, yielding to his wife's "unwomanly desire for battle" (οὔτοι γυναικός ἐστιν ἱμείρειν μάχης, 940). He, like Aegisthus, becomes an erotic object—"the honey of every Chryseis under Troy" (Χρυσηΐδων μείλιγμα τῶν ὑπ' Ἰλίωι, 1439), as Clytemnestra puts it, and "the darling of the city" (ἐράσμιον πόλει, 605), a phrase that, in its insinuation of passivity, speaks to both the sexual and the political abjection of a man under the power of a woman.[15]

But even as she generates illegitimacy, Clytemnestra also becomes its central embodiment in the play. We saw in the last chapter how the carpet scene dramatizes two different modes of unacceptable aristocratic behavior: Agamemnon (at Clytemnestra's urging) exceeds the bounds of aristocratic *megaloprepeia* by squandering his *agalma* (wealth that might otherwise have enriched the city) and, at the same time, falls short by calling that *agalma ploutos*.[16] Both extremes suggested in that confrontation are acted out onstage by Clytemnestra. On the one hand, she is excessive in her autocratic rule of Argos; on the other, she shows herself deficient by her debased economic language. While Agamemnon certainly acts in ways that suggest he does not know the difference between *agalmata* and *ploutos*, it is Clytemnestra who makes this explicit (1415–18) and who forces him to reenact onstage his bad spending— forcing him to sacrifice the carpet as he had Iphigeneia—and to bear the *phthonos* for it. Indeed, she kills him with the very wealth he misuses, wrapping him in "an evil wealth of cloth" (πλοῦτον εἵματος κακόν, 1383). But even while punishing him for his misuse of wealth, Clytemnestra herself speaks the play's most explicit disenchantments: it is she who transforms the tapestry into mere money in her "sea of purple" speech.[17] Hence it is extremely ironic when she advises Cassandra as to the "charms" of old money (ἀρχαιοπλούτων δεσποτῶν πολλὴ χάρις, 1043), for it is precisely that elite *kharis*, the magical investment of objects with value, that Clytemnestra fails (or refuses) to understand.[18]

I argued in the last chapter that the slippage between *agalma* and *ploutos* endemic to *Agamemnon* is rooted within the fetishization of commodities and that the disastrous result of this slippage—the disintegration of the male subject—is inherent in the process. But as part of the psychological defense against this dynamic, both cause and consequences come to be attributed in particular to Clytemnestra: her disenchanted economic language localizes the ubiquitous problem, and her victory over Agamemnon in the carpet scene—forcing him to misuse his *agalma*, and then punishing him for it—pursues its fatal effects, as Agamemnon loses first his status, then his life. Clytemnestra, meanwhile, is defined as a "bad" aristocrat vis-à-vis both democratic ideology and the aristocratic *agalma* economy. She can then be eliminated, in a move that reaffirms both democratic and aristocratic ideals (and shows them to be compatible), and also denies the more systematic and deep-seated economic problems implicit within the fetishism of commodities.

Indeed, the entire dynamic of fetishization that we explored in the last two chapters comes to be located within Clytemnestra herself: not only the slippage between *agalmata* and *ploutos*, but also the sadistic combination of violence and desire that suffused Iphigeneia's sacrifice and the war fought for Helen, and the ultimate objectification of the male subject. The fantasies of virgin blood and soldiers in urns are, after all, the imaginings of the chorus, a group of men disenfranchised by Clytemnestra's tyranny, powerless to oppose her openly, their political action limited to subversive allusions and mutterings (457–60, 548–50).[19] Her presence hangs over the Parodos: the chorus's address to her interrupts its narration of the war, her power (83–103) contrasting to its weakness (72–82); another address to her caps the ode.[20] The sacrifice is thus framed by reminders of her oppressive authority.[21]

If this tyrannical queen generates nightmares of virgin sacrifice and undifferentiated bodies, she also gives these fantasies their clearest expression, translating them from the "imaginary" realm of Aulis and Troy to the "symbolic order" of Argos.[22] In her imagination of the scene at Troy, Clytemnestra would seem to offer a reassuring alternative to the horrors imagined by the chorus. She pictures a clear dichotomy between victorious Greeks and defeated Trojans:

οἶμαι βοὴν ἄμεικτον ἐν πόλει πρέπειν·
ὄξος τ' ἄλειφά τ' ἐγχέας ταὐτῶι κύτει
διχοστατοῦντ' ἂν οὐ φίλω προσεννέποις·
καὶ τῶν ἁλόντων καὶ κρατησάντων δίχα
φθογγὰς ἀκούειν ἔστι, συμφορᾶς διπλῆς.

(321-25)

I believe an unmixed cry is audible in the city. If
you pour oil and water together in the same jar,
you might say they stand apart in no amity. And
so it is possible to hear the voices of the captured
and the conquerors apart from one another,
speaking different fates.

In Clytemnestra's vision of the war, the conflation of the two warring sides, which in the First Stasimon is the initial step toward the dissolving of individual identity and the eventual reduction of men to dust, is denied and refused. For her, there is a real difference between victor and vanquished, precisely the difference that is deconstructed in the logic of the commodity fetish.[23] Clytemnestra's vision of differentiation would thus seem to defend against the merging and disintegration associated with Helen in the First Stasimon.[24]

At the same time as she seems to offer a denial of the fears expressed in the First Stasimon, however, she also speaks those fears expressly:

ἔρως δὲ μή τις πρότερον ἐμπίπτηι στρατῶι
πορθεῖν ἃ μὴ χρή, κέρδεσιν νικωμένους.

(341-42)

But may no lust fall on the army beforehand to
destroy what they should not, conquered by
profit.

Despite the ironic tone of the passage, there is no more express statement of the play's dynamic of fetishism: erotic desire and desire for possession are inextricable, and both are implicated necessarily in violence; the conqueror is conquered by gain, just as the exchanger is taken to market by his fetishized commodity. Clytemnestra expresses openly what the chorus can only whisper.

So, too, it is Clytemnestra who speaks in Argos the sadism of the scene at Aulis. At 1555–59, Clytemnestra imagines Iphigeneia greeting her father joyously in the underworld. The vision recalls the Parodos, where Iphigeneia was remembered singing at her father's banquet tables and where, I argued, she was murdered so as to be preserved as a loyal and virginal daughter. But if Clytemnestra's imagination shows this goal accomplished, it does so with a tone that deconstructs the agalmatization of Iphigeneia, revealing the perversion behind this fantasy of filial loyalty, and the unbearable cost of its maintenance.[25] Clytemnestra's sarcastic vision reanimates Iphigeneia to let her mourn the father who was killed to avenge her; the devotion and forgiveness that the scenario might be hoped to offer Agamemnon are revoked, and the vision stands instead as a taunt (1560) and a justification for his murder.

Clytemnestra speaks baldly the sadism of the scene at Aulis and punishes it with the murder of Agamemnon; what is more, though, she also enacts that sadism herself, taking upon herself its terrible burden of guilt. For Clytemnestra kills not only Agamemnon, but also Cassandra, Agamemnon's young concubine, who (in ways that we shall see below) resembles Iphigeneia. Clytemnestra's murder of this innocent girl reenacts the sacrifice of Iphigeneia and replicates the sadism of her death: if the Greek elders longed for virgin blood, Clytemnestra delights in the slaughter of Agamemnon's lover, she says sarcastically, as "a side-dish to the pleasure of my bed" (εὐνῆς παροψώνημα τῆς ἐμῆς χλιδῆι, 1447).[26]

Thus the play's sadism is not merely expressed by Clytemnestra but enacted by her: she displays on stage the virginal body that the chorus scarcely dares to imagine in the Parodos. The violence and desire implicit in the fetishism of commodities come to be located within Clytemnestra's own sadistic sexuality:[27]

> οὕτω τὸν αὑτοῦ θυμὸν ὁρμαίνει πεσών
> κἀκφυσιῶν ὀξεῖαν αἵματος σφαγὴν
> βάλλει μ' ἐρεμνῆι ψακάδι φοινίας δρόσου,
> χαίρουσαν οὐδὲν ἧσσον ἢ διοσδότωι
> γάνει σπορητὸς κάλυκος ἐν λοχεύμασιν.[28]
>
> (1388–92)

So he falls and gasps away his life; and blowing
out a sharp wounding of blood, he hits me
with a black drizzle of bloody dew, and I
rejoice no less than the crop rejoices in the
god-given rain at the bursting of the bud.

Just as Iphigeneia's sacrifice was a rape, Agamemnon's murder is inter-
course. All the complex psychic forces of violence and desire that we saw
in the sacrifice at Aulis and the First and Second Stasimon come into the
open in this astonishing passage. The sadism of the war, the longing for
virgin blood, which in the odes is so diffuse, so hedged around with denial, is here recognized and claimed by Clytemnestra as her own; she admits openly that violence is a source of sexual arousal. It is as if her
shameless, boastful acknowledgment of her sadistic passion were what
allows the others—Agamemnon, the chorus, the audience—to disown
their own desires, as the eroticized violence that pervades the play is subsumed under her individual, perverse sexuality.

Not only localized, the sadism is also explicitly condemned as blasphemy. Clytemnestra's speech after the murder of Agamemnon (1372–
98) is a virtual litany of ritual perversity: she represents his death as a
sacrifice; the third blow is an offering, as at a sympotic libation, to Zeus
Sōtēr (1384–87); and her curse or vaunt (ἐπεύχομαι, 1394) over her feat
becomes a virtual libation to Agamemnon's corpse (1395–96).[29] The
ejaculatory image of Agamemnon's death, placed between the two perverted libation images and with its own suggestion of natural fertility
perverted, makes Clytemnestra's sexual transgressions a crime against
the gods and nature as well as against her husband and *oikos*. Her sexuality becomes a blasphemy.[30]

And so it is perhaps not surprising that Clytemnestra should be
conflated with that other disastrous woman, Helen. In a choral passage
late in the play, Agamemnon is said to have died "because of a much-
daring woman" (πολλὰ τλάντος γυναικὸς διαί, 1453) and "at the
hand of a woman" (πρὸς γυναικὸς, 1454), but which sister is referred
to? "Mad Helen" (παράνους Ἑλένα, 1455) has destroyed so many
souls, but it is Clytemnestra whom the chorus has repeatedly called mad.
Helen seems to "wreath herself" (1459) with the blood that Clytemnestra has shed, each equally becoming "an unconquerable strife in the
house, a grief for her husband" (Ἔρις ἐρίδματος ἀνδρὸς οἰζύς, 1461).
The two sisters have become indistinguishable, as both are made to bear

the guilt for the perversions and disasters of the play. In a final step, both are associated with the *daimōn* (avenging spirit) of the house of Tantalus, which "works through women" (1469–71). The persecutory fantasy embodied in Clytemnestra is thus taken to its logical extreme: Clytemnestra herself becomes the *daimōn*.[31]

αὐχεῖς εἶναι τόδε τοὖργον ἐμόν.
τῆιδ' ἐπιλεχθείς.
'Αγαμεμνονίαν εἶναί μ' ἄλοχον·
φανταζόμενος δὲ γυναικὶ νεκροῦ
τοῦδ' ὁ παλαιὸς δριμὺς ἀλάστωρ
'Ατρέως χαλεποῦ θοινατῆρος
τόνδ' ἀπέτεισεν
τέλεον νεαροῖς ἐπιθύσας.

(1497–1504)

You claim that this deed is mine,
because you think I am the wife of
Agamemnon. But manifesting itself
in the form of the wife of this corpse,
the ancient, fierce avenger of Atreus,
terrible banqueter, sacrificed him, offering a grown man as payment for
children.

Clytemnestra denies here not her guilt, but her identity, as the wife of Agamemnon, as the queen, as the murderer. She becomes, like Helen and Menelaus in the First Stasimon, a *phasma*, a persecutory *daimōn* "through which there is nourished in the womb a lust to lick blood" (ἐκ τοῦ γὰρ ἔρως αἱματολοιχὸς / νείραι τρέφεται, 1478–79).

And it is as the *daimōn* that she claims to have killed Agamemnon, thus bringing to its inevitable conclusion the dynamic of fetishism she has been made to embody. As a corpse, he becomes her handiwork, her *ergon*:

οὗτός ἐστιν 'Αγαμέμνων. ἐμὸς
πόσις. νεκρὸς δέ. τῆσδε δεξιᾶς χερὸς
ἔργον. δικαίας τέκτονος.

(1404–6)

> This is Agamemnon, my husband and a
> corpse, the work of my right hand, a just
> craftsman.

His body, displayed on stage, literalizes the First Stasimon's terrifying image of men turned to dust in urns.[32]

Clytemnestra is thus implicated in every stage of the commodity fetish: in its sadistic agalmatization, in its disenchantments and economic deceptions, in its final commodification of the male subject. Yet in her overdetermined transgressions, her perversions, blasphemies, and violence, Clytemnestra offers psychic relief. Exacting punishment on Agamemnon, she allows for the expiation of his crimes and of all the crimes of war; as the personification of sadism, she allows the play to deny the sadism inherent within the process of fetishism and exchange. And so, while Agamemnon's corpse embodies this play's nightmare of objectification, it also points the way toward reparation. Whereas the soldiers returning as dust were objectified by the very dynamic of exchange, here the objectification is the act of a specific, perverted woman. Clytemnestra localizes and contains the horror in a form in which, with her death in *Choephoroe* and posthumous defeat in *Eumenides*, it can eventually be eliminated. Agamemnon's body may recall the soldiers' ashes, but his at least is a corpse that can be mourned, and through mourning, in *Choephoroe*, can be reconstituted as the rallying point for the vengeance that moves the trilogy toward its resolution.

A LAMENT FOR THE FATHER

In *Trachiniae*, a silent maiden is introduced into Deianira's house; I argued in Chapter 3 that Iole, the "virgin in the garden," represents a foreclosed space of alterity in that play, a site of absolute difference beyond the play's epistemological and ideological reach. In *Agamemnon*, too, a maiden is brought into the house. Cassandra, like Iole, is a foreign princess, her conqueror's war-booty and concubine; like Iole, she is silent when confronted by the mistress of the house, in a scene so close to *Trachiniae*'s as to suggest a direct influence.[33] At the same time as Cassandra resembles Iole, she also recalls another silent virgin, Iphigeneia, re-presenting the dead girl on stage. Cassandra, like Iphigeneia, is both a bride (1178–79) and a sacrificial victim (1277–78). Iphigeneia died to buy back Helen, but instead bought Cassandra; and if

Iphigeneia is the price paid for Cassandra, Cassandra is killed in part to avenge Iphigeneia.

But whereas Iole was silent and Iphigeneia gagged, Cassandra, after a long and dramatic silence, speaks.[34] Are we to hear, when Cassandra finally speaks, the words that Iphigeneia was prevented from uttering? The words that cannot be forced from Iole? For first in her silence and then in her incomprehensibility, Cassandra would seem to be quintessentially other. Doubly alien as a foreigner and a virgin, Cassandra refuses to answer when hailed by Clytemnestra, refuses to take up her position as a subject within the play's symbolic order. She is also a prophet; she has uniquely privileged insight into the deepest workings of the play, and yet her words are incoherent or disbelieved, taken for lunacy. In her prophetic madness, Cassandra is ecstatic, possessed by the god who gives her her visions. Given her otherness within the world of Argos, will her prophetic ecstasy also be an "ek-stasis," a standing outside and speaking from beyond the symbolic order?[35] Will she be tragedy's "virgin in the garden" given voice?

As the only character from Troy, that fantasied site of psychic wounds, Cassandra would seem able to explicate the play's dynamic of fetishism, and all the more so since she herself has been an object of the play's bad exchanges. Bought with Iphigeneia's death, a prize in the war fought for Helen, Cassandra, too, falls into the gap between *agalma* and *ploutos*: she is Agamemnon's "bride,"[36] his "chosen flower" and gift from the army (954–55), but, as she herself says, her death will be a *misthon* (1261), a wage paid for services rendered,[37] and Agamemnon will pay with his life for bringing her (1263). Her relationship with Apollo is also expressed in economic diction: she is a beggar in his service (ἀγύρτρια, 1273); the symbols of this service enrich her (πλουτίζετε, 1268), and her rejection of them is seen as a repayment (ἀμείψομαι, 1267). Even her death will be nothing more than a financial transaction: "And now the prophet, destroying me his prophetess, has led me to such a deadly fate (καὶ νῦν ὁ μάντις μάντιν ἐκπράξας ἐμὲ / ἀπήγαγ' ἐς τοιάσδε θανασίμους τύχας, 1275–76). Ἐκπράξας ("destroying") can refer to the calling in of a debt: it is as if Apollo had loaned her to herself.[38] She is the play's ultimate female commodity.

And yet, although Cassandra recognizes her objectification, she does not condemn her exchangers; when she finally speaks, it is not her own sufferings she prophesies (as the chorus anticipates, 1083–84), but the sufferings of the male victims of the play's pervasive violence. She sees, in kaleidoscopic visions, the house of Atreus stained with blood (1090–

92), the babies of Thyestes crying for their own slaughter (1095–97), the murder of Agamemnon in the bath (1107–11, 1125–29) and his entrapment in Clytemnestra's net (1114–18), her own impending death (1136–39, 1146–49, 1156–61), and the destruction of Troy (1167–72), the adultery of Thyestes (1186–93), the children of Thyestes again (1217–22), the adultery of Clytemnestra and Aegisthus and their murder of Agamemnon (1223–32), her own murder at Clytemnestra's hands (1258–63, 1277–79), the return of Orestes (1280–84), and the death of Clytemnestra and Aegisthus (1317–19). She does not see Iphigeneia, the very personification of pathos; nor does she see Helen, another victim of the Tantalid *daimōn*; and her comments on Clytemnestra are the most misogynist in the play. Her vision is almost exclusively male-centered.

Moreover, her own suffering is inseparable from that of the men. Her own fate is subsidiary to that of Agamemnon: it is a suffering "poured on in addition" to his (ἐπεγχέασα, 1137³⁹) that she will die with him (ξυνθανουμένην, 1139); her own murder is a "payment" put into the draught of Agamemnon's murder (1260–61), Clytemnestra's revenge upon him, even as she sharpens the blade for his murder (1262–63); she is a preliminary sacrifice for him (1278). "I am going into the house lamenting my and Agamemnon's fate," she says (ἀλλ᾽ εἶμι κἀν δόμοισι κωκύσουσ᾽ ἐμὴν / Ἀγαμέμνονός τε μοῖραν, 1313–14).⁴⁰ Fraenkel commends Cassandra throughout his notes for recognizing her subsidiary role in the saga of the House of Atreus.⁴¹ But her death is not so much secondary to Agamemnon's as inseparable from it: the suffering of men is her own suffering. "Oh father, alas for you and your noble children!" she exclaims as she is about to enter the house (ἰὼ πάτερ σοῦ σῶν τε γενναίων τέκνων, 1305). Who is the father she laments? Her own? Agamemnon as Iphigeneia's father? Thyestes? Atreus? It is all of these; her sympathy is for all the men. And she pities herself as the daughter of her father, her suffering subsumed under his. She becomes the focalizer for all the male suffering in the play; she is indistinguishable from it and can speak of herself only in relation to it.

Cassandra's androcentric vision is generalized as a sympathy for all mankind:

> ἰὼ βρότεια πράγματ᾽· εὐτυχοῦντα μὲν
> σκιᾶι τις ἂν πρέψειεν· εἰ δὲ δυστυχῆι,
> βολαῖς ὑγρώσσων σπόγγος ὤλεσεν γραφήν.
>
> (1327–29)

> Alas for the affairs of mortals; when they are for-
> tunate, one may liken them to a shadow; when
> they are unfortunate, a damp sponge with a
> stroke erases the picture.

Her lament for herself is one for all humanity.[42] The diction evokes the horror of the Parodos and the First Stasimon. To fare well is to be like a shadow, even as Menelaus's desire for Helen turned both him and her into *phasmata* (415). The image of the erased picture recalls the *graphē* of Iphigeneia (242), and the *eumorphoi kolossoi* of Helen and Menelaus (416). In Cassandra's vision, mortals—women and men—are not only objectified, but also obliterated: first made objects, they become destroyed objects. Her final words express all the horror of the commodity fetish and carry that logic to its furthest conclusion, total annihilation. But Cassandra's vision of this objectification, in contrast to Clytemnestra's, is suffused with pity. If Clytemnestra persecutes—embodies and punishes—the play's exchanges of women, Cassandra forgives them and pities their disastrous consequences.

Cassandra, then, may be Iphigeneia given voice, but not to speak the experiences or thoughts of the virgin; rather, she may only bespeak again the male fantasy of the virginal daughter, the fantasy of a woman who forgives her violation and whose only word is "father." Without the violence of gagging, Cassandra says willingly what Iphigeneia said through "the force of the bridle" (238). Further, Cassandra goes to her sacrifice voluntarily, in contrast to the intense struggle put up by Iphigeneia: her resolution at 1290–94 offers the voluntary self-sacrifice that the Iphigeneia scene denied.[43] And not only does Cassandra forgive Agamemnon for her death, she also glorifies him. She represents him, in contrast to Aegisthus and Clytemnestra, as a noble lion (1259), as the leader of the Greek force and conqueror of Troy (1227).[44] Thus Cassandra, Agamemnon's war-booty and concubine, sets in motion his posthumous recuperation, which will culminate in the *kommos* of *Choephoroe*.[45] She is the fantasy of the sacrifice scene come true, a woman loyal to men.

Not only does Cassandra offer forgiveness to Agamemnon, but she also contributes to the vilification of Clytemnestra. Her prophecies are expressed in explicitly gendered terms: it is she who first traces the origin of the curse back to adultery (1192–93) and who explicitly lays out the plot structure in gendered terms: "When a woman dies in compensation for me, a woman, and a man falls in exchange for a man unlucky

in marriage" (ὅταν γυνὴ γυναικὸς ἀντ' ἐμοῦ θάνηι. / ἀνήρ τε δυ-
σδάμαρτος ἀντ' ἀνδρὸς πέσηι, 1318–19). She also expresses the murder of Agamemnon in the starkest gender terms: "A woman is murderer
of a man" (θῆλυς ἄρσενος φονεὺς / ἔστιν, 1231–32). Gender, indeed,
becomes the crux of her enigmatic prophecy: it is this that the chorus is unable to comprehend, the one clue it lacks to solve her riddle (1251–52).

In Cassandra's gendered visions, Clytemnestra is the cow who will attack the bull (ἄπεχε τῆς βοὸς / τὸν ταῦρον, 1125–26). The metaphor
suggests not only the inversion of the natural order (in which the bull
threatens the cow), but also the confusion of sex and violence endemic to
the play but especially attributed to Clytemnestra: the bull must be re-
strained not only to prevent it from damaging the cow but also, more
naturally, to prevent it from mating. Clytemnestra's sexuality is murderous: in Cassandra's elliptical language, Clytemnestra herself becomes the
net in which she kills Agamemnon: "Some net of Hades, but a net that
sleeps with him, accomplice in his murder" (ἦ δίκτυόν τί γ' Ἅιδου· /
ἀλλ' ἄρκυς ἡ ξύνευνος. ἡ ξυναιτία / φόνου, 1115–17).[46] With this
conflation of Clytemnestra and the murder weapon, the dynamic of the
First Stasimon is collapsed even further. Whereas there the commodification of Helen initiated a war that sent men home in urns, here the
woman herself becomes the urn, the engulfing, devouring, suffocating instrument of male objectification.[47]

But even as she reviles Clytemnestra's sexuality, Cassandra's own sexual status is called under suspicion. As the priestess and recipient of
the god, she should be pure of the taint of mortal sexuality.[48] But she
is referred to throughout as *gunē* (a mature woman, not a virgin), and
is presumed by Clytemnestra at least to have had sexual relations
with Agamemnon; however unjust, Clytemnestra's vulgar slur—"This
woman, a captive and a soothsayer, and sharer of his bed, trusted
prophetic bedmate, slut of the sailor's benches" (ἡ τ' αἰχμάλωτος ἥδε
καὶ τερασκόπος / καὶ κοινόλεκτρος τοῦδε. θεσφατηλόγος. / πι-
στὴ ξύνευνος. ναυτίλων δὲ σελμάτων / ἰσοτριβής, 1440–43)—
contrasts sharply with her exclusive devotion to Apollo.[49]

This ambiguous position is complicated by Cassandra's story of her
relationship with the god. At 1178–79, Cassandra promises to unveil the
true meaning of her oracles, analogizing them to a bride pulling back her
veil at the *anakaluptēria* (1178–79). The nuptial image at once points to
Cassandra's sexual liminality and promises to reveal its true nature.[50] In
the image's syncretism, Cassandra herself becomes the unveiled bride,

but what is to be revealed when Cassandra pulls back the veils is that she is not, in fact, a virgin. For the god "was a wrestler, breathing great *kharis* on me" (ἀλλ' ἦν παλαιστὴς κάρτ' ἐμοὶ πνέων χάριν, 1206). At the center of the story is an *agōn*. Though this is a common enough erotic image in itself,[51] here the metaphor is strangely expressed. There is only one antagonist, and the dative ἐμοὶ ("to me") fails to clarify Cassandra's role in the *agōn*: is she an antagonist or the prize? Even here, it seems, Cassandra is Apollo's possession. Moreover, the image places Cassandra at precisely the same intersection of violence and eroticism that we have seen over and over again in this play. The *kharis* Apollo breathes on her in this struggle is both sexual delight and divine grace, the *kharis biaios* of fetishization. If that is the origin of Cassandra's distinctive prophetic ability, then this potential site of otherness and purity is abruptly foreclosed in this line. Far from standing outside the play's sadism, "ek-static," Cassandra emerges from it, another product of its destructive passion.

Finally, this suspicious sexuality—as with Iphigeneia, Helen, and Clytemnestra—is located within the woman herself:

> XO.: ἦ καὶ τέκνων εἰς ἔργον ἠλθέτην ὁμοῦ;
> KA.: ξυναινέσασα Λοξίαν ἐψευσάμην.
> XO.: ἤδη τέχναισιν ἐνθέοις ἡρημένη;
> KA.: ἤδη πολίταις πάντ' ἐθέσπιζον πάθη.
> XO.: πῶς δῆτ' ἄνατος ἦσθα Λοξίου κότωι;
> KA.: ἔπειθον οὐδέν' οὐδέν. ὡς τάδ' ἤμπλακον.
>
> (1207–12)

CHORUS: Did you two come to the work of begetting children together?
CASSANDRA: I promised Loxias, but deceived him.
CHORUS: Were you already seized by your divine craft?
CASSANDRA: I was already prophesizing to my citizens all their sorrows.
CHORUS: How then were you not harmed by Loxias's anger?
CASSANDRA: I have persuaded no one of anything since I committed that transgression.

It is unclear exactly how or why Cassandra deceived the god; all that is clear is that she did.[52] Cassandra's deceit, placed between her visions of the adultery of Thyestes and the adultery of Clytemnestra and Aegisthus, is incorporated into the cycles of sexual betrayal that structure the history of the House of Atreus. Her betrayal of Apollo becomes part of the same narrative as Clytemnestra's betrayal of Agamemnon, her sexuality as suspect and transgressive (ἤμπλακον, 1212) as Clytemnestra's. Thus female purity conceals an essentially criminal sexuality; at the heart of Cassandra lies a potential Clytemnestra, just as there lay within the virgin Iphigeneia an incipient Helen. And like Iphigeneia, Cassandra must be strictly controlled to prevent her from realizing her inherent potential, controlled by the ubiquitous gaze of Apollo (1269–72), by the slavery to Agamemnon, by her ineffectuality in the craft that should give her power, by her inability to control her prophecies, and ultimately by the text itself, which lets her speak only to betray herself. Cassandra may be Iphigeneia given voice, but her words are silenced no less and no less brutally than Iphigeneia's. The play promises an *anakaluptēria*, but in this unveiling of the female other is revealed only a familiar misogynist fantasy. Born of the sadism of exchange—the sexual *agōn* with Apollo, the Trojan War—and ultimately killed by it, Cassandra might uncover the bedrock of cruelty and repression beneath the fantasy of the loyal, virginal, and forgiving daughter. But rather than lamenting the sufferings of Iphigeneia, Cassandra merely replicates them in her own person; rather than exposing the logic of fetishism, Cassandra denies and, with her death, reproduces it.

Yet even as Cassandra replicates the dynamic that resulted in Iphigeneia's sacrifice, she also moves the play toward reparation, forgiving Agamemnon in Iphigeneia's name, and offering willingly the loyalty to the father that was agalmatized in Iphigeneia. Her redemption of Agamemnon and vilification of Clytemnestra will be continued after her death by another loyal daughter, Electra, and ultimately by Athena, who will codify Cassandra's androcentric visions as law. Thus between them Cassandra and Clytemnestra initiate the reparation hinted at in the First Stasimon: the transformation of the male corpse into the civic body. The economic process of fetishization that had sent Greek soldiers home in urns generates the psychic defenses of splitting that Klein elucidates: the economic and the psychological converge in the desire and violence that drive this play's exchanges of women. The terrifying results of these exchanges are contained by projection onto Clytemnestra, who literalizes the nightmare in her murder of Agamemnon. The crimes committed in the "war fought for a woman" become her crimes, and the entire process of the commodity fetish with all its disastrous effects is reified and occluded in her monstrous character. It is the ultimate fetishization. The benefits of this fetishization Cassandra, with her prophetic foresight, predicts: the exchangers of women are exonerated, their crimes forgiven, and their sufferings lamented, and the male subject and social order are finally recuperated and guaranteed for the future under the aegis of a kingly father and his loyal daughter.

MOURNING AND MATRICIDE
IN EURIPIDES' *Alcestis*

⚜

SEVEN

THE SHADOW OF THE OBJECT: LOSS, MOURNING, AND REPARATION

⚜

Euripides' *Alcestis* is a tragedy about mourning. Admetus is allowed to escape death only if he finds someone who will take his place. He asks his father and mother, but they refuse; his wife, Alcestis, however, agrees to replace him and is on the verge of death as the play opens. Admetus bemoans her passing with extravagant and excruciating lamentation, and his grief is a focal point of the play's action. In order to explicate the process of mourning in this play and the ambivalent responses it generates, I shall look to psychoanalytic theories of mourning, in particular those of Melanie Klein on the one hand, and of Freud, Lacan, and Kristeva on the other. These two psychoanalytic camps offer two very different understandings of the process of loss, mourning, and reparation, and their differences on mourning indicate their broader disagreements on the relation between subject and object, between self and other, between child and mother, and between man and woman. By reading *Alcestis* through these two theoretical approaches simultaneously and by playing them off against one another, letting them complicate and critique one another, I hope to lay bare a vacillation within the play between two models of psychic and social well-being, one predicated upon the objectification and exchange of women, the other in which such a commerce is not only unhealthy, but impossible.

For Melanie Klein, the process of mourning encapsulates in miniature the entire process of ego development. In the earliest stages of psychological development, as Klein describes them, the distinctions between subject and object, self and other, the internal and the external, are dynamic and unpredictable. In this state of undifferentiation, the mother is seen not as something fully external to the child, but as a part of itself;[1] nor is she perceived as an autonomous and whole entity, but as a series of split-off "part objects," both good objects that gratify desires and bring pleasure and bad objects that withhold satisfaction and instead persecute the child (it was these part objects that we saw at work in the defensive strategies of *Agamemnon*). The development of the ego is a process simultaneously of separating the external from the internal (the child from the mother) and of integrating the part objects into a "whole object" that combines both good and bad aspects. But this process of synthesis and separation creates ambivalence, as the child comes to realize that the persecutory object it hated is identical to the nourishing object it loved. This ambivalence comes to the fore when the maternal breast, the child's first object relation, is lost in weaning. The loss of the good object, which the child experiences as a loss of part of itself, generates feelings of guilt and anger, guilt that the loss was in some way its own fault, and anger at the thwarting of its desires. If left unresolved, these feelings can lead to psychosis, an inability to form healthy object relations in later life.

This period of ambivalence, which Klein calls the "depressive position,"[2] is a seminal stage in her scheme of infantile development. Ideally, the end result is a reparation of and to the lost object: the child reconciles the loved and hated aspects of the object and is able to see it as something separate and whole in itself, combining both gratification and frustration. It is in this form, as a "whole object," that the lost object—quintessentially the mother—is incorporated into the self, and provides the foundation for the stable organization of the ego. Klein's imagination of psychic health thus entails not only emotional and mental integration at the level of the ego, but also a recognition of the autonomy, integrity, and plenitude of the mother. In her model, a healthy male ego is impossible without an acceptance of the subject status of the female other, and this acceptance is seen as the culmination of his psychic maturation.[3]

The dynamics of the depressive position—loss, ambivalence, reparation—are reiterated, Klein argues, in moments of loss in adult life.[4] Building from Freud's 1917 essay, "Mourning and Melancholia,"[5] Klein develops a theory of mourning that closely parallels her view of the depressive position in normal development: the loss of the object is a loss of part of the self, and gives rise to conflicting feelings of anger (a belief that the object has betrayed the self) and guilt (that the subject has destroyed the object). Mourning is a process of reconciling these conflicting attitudes toward the object and eventually repairing the lost object and recognizing it as a whole object, complete in itself and separate from the subject. Ideally, adult mourning recapitulates the process of loss and reparation of the maternal object that is for Klein so fundamental to the consolidation of the ego.

Again, we need not adopt the clinical schema of child development (rooted as it is in the particularities of the modern bourgeois family) in order to use Klein's basic dynamic of mourning to illuminate *Alcestis*, a play that is structured around the loss of a woman, mourning for her, and her eventual reincorporation into the household. Indeed, the play seems to lend itself quite precisely to the detailed mechanics of Klein's depressive position. The action is initiated by the impending loss of Alcestis. This loss devastates the self and its world: Admetus himself is destroyed by her death (277, 386, 868–69, 897–902, 1083–86), as are his *oikos* and *polis* (414–15, 425–27). The destruction of the ego consequent upon the loss of the object is precisely what Freud describes in "Mourning and Melancholia" as a sign of abnormal mourning (melancholia) and what Klein identifies in the depressive position. The ego remains cathected to the lost object and identifies with it, as Freud explains: "Thus the shadow of the object fell upon the ego, so that the latter could henceforth be criticized by a special mental faculty like an object, like the forsaken object." [6]

In psychoanalytic theory (both Freudian and Kleinian), the object whose shadow falls so heavily upon the ego is, in the first instance, the mother. Though the maternal object is often as much metaphorical as literal,[7] in Euripides' play, Alcestis is represented as a maternal figure, a mother to her children and to the house.[8] Although Alcestis's posthumous glory will be that she died for her husband, she tells us repeatedly that she is dying for her children (164–69, 288, 304–19). And whether Alcestis dies as wife or mother, it is as mother that she is mourned. Her death scene closes with a final farewell to Admetus (390–91), but the lyric lament that follows immediately after her demise is not, as we might have expected, sung by Admetus, but rather by the unnamed child. Why is Admetus's mourning preempted here by that of this ad hoc child?[9] The child speaks for the *oikos* in its relation to Alcestis as mother;[10] through this child, the *oikos* and Admetus mourn the loss of Alcestis as a maternal figure: she is called *matēr* (mother) four times in the space of these twenty-two lines (400, 401, 408, 415). She is also referred to as *maia* (393), a word rare in tragedy, and one that evokes the role of mother as nurse, as nourisher, as the source of goodness.[11] These are precisely the things that Klein feels the child loses at weaning, and it is the loss of these things (symbolized by the maternal breast) that initiates the depressive position.[12] As giver of all goodness, Alcestis is idealized, even deified, after her death:

Αὔτα ποτὲ προύθαν' ἀνδρός.
νῦν δ' ἔστι μάκαιρα δαίμων·
χαῖρ', ὦ πότνι', εὖ δὲ δοίης.[13]

(1002–4)

She died for her husband. Now
she is a blessed spirit. Hail,
revered lady, and may you be
benevolent [literally, "may you
give well"].

Idealization is one of the defensive strategies Klein identifies against the ambivalence of the depressive position: by worshiping the object as wholly good, the child can repress any feelings of hostility or aggression toward it. So Alcestis is imagined as inexhaustibly munificent. Her generosity saves the *oikos* (e.g., 620–22) and gives life to Admetus; thus she becomes his mother, replacing the biological mother who is conspicuously absent in the play.[14] Idealized as beneficent mother, Alcestis is mourned as a good object—perhaps even too good an object, a point to which I return at length in the next chapter.

But the abundance of the maternal body is coupled here with a fantasy of depletion and exhaustion, for Alcestis herself is destroyed by her gift. This sense of having used up the goodness of the object provokes a guilt and anger that works against idealization and reintroduces ambivalence.[15] This ambivalence is reflected in the diction surrounding Alcestis's loss. Why is Alcestis gone? Did she abandon Admetus? Or is it rather that Admetus destroyed her? The text allows both possibilities. When Admetus begs Alcestis repeatedly not to leave him, the diction also accuses her of betrayal (προδοῦναι, 202, 250, 275; προλιποῦσα, 396).[16] At the same time, when Admetus is said to have "lost" Alcestis (ἁμαρτάνεις, 144; ἀπόλλυμαι, 167), the words also imply that Admetus has himself destroyed his object. Alcestis is alternately canonized for saving Admetus and blamed for destroying him, and this ambivalence cripples Admetus and hinders the resolution of his mourning.[17]

If Admetus is unable to reconcile these conflicting feelings toward Alcestis, that is in part because he is unable to distinguish her clearly from himself. Is she a part of him, so that her death is the loss of a part of himself? Or is she something external, which can be lost and mourned? The boundaries between self and object are indistinct; thus the central scenes of the play raise repeatedly the question of whether Alcestis is "inside" or "outside." Although Alcestis is called *othneios* ("foreign," "unrelated," 532–33, 810) and *thuraios* (literally, "outside," 778, 805, 1014), the process of separation is, for most of the play, incomplete and inconclusive. In their first meeting, when Admetus urges Heracles to enter the house, Heracles asks after the identity of the dead woman: "Was it someone foreign (*othneios*) or someone closely related to you by birth?" (ὀθνεῖος ἢ σοὶ συγγενὴς γεγῶσά τις; 532). While Heracles' question assumes a polar relation between internal and external, Admetus's answer shows him incapable of drawing the line so firmly. He replies that she was *othneios*, but nonetheless necessary to the house (*anankaia*: the word also means related or kindred).

To a certain extent, this ambiguity resides in the particular relationship of the woman to the house of her husband.[18] Unrelated by birth to her husband's *oikos*, but connected to it emotionally, economically, and through her children, the woman is in a very basic sense both internal and external to it.[19] Here, however, the confusion runs deeper; it is metaphysical, not just practical, and affects not only Admetus, but even the text itself. At 810, Heracles justifies his revelry on the basis of the dead woman's relation of exteriority to the *domos*. The response of the slave, however, merely serves to blur again the lines between inside and out:

HP.: οὐ χρῆν μ' ὀθνείου γ' οὕνεκ' εὖ πάσχειν νεκροῦ;
ΘΕ.: ἦ κάρτα μέντοι καὶ λίαν ὀθνεῖος ἦν.

(810–11)

HERACLES: Should I not have enjoyed myself because of some stranger's death?
SLAVE: It is too true; she was indeed an outsider [? or "member of the house"].

The codices' readings on line 811 are split between *thuraios* ("an out-sider") and *oikeios* ("belonging to the house"):[20] this textual crux fur-ther obscures Alcestis's relation to Admetus and his *oikos*, and the con-fusion of self and other voiced by Admetus is here reproduced on another level by the play's early transcribers and interpreters.

In this state of undifferentiation, the loss of the object is a death of the self. The confusion of self and other, subject and object, is imagined as a confusion of life and death as well.[21] Thus Alcestis, although dead, lives on as a part of Admetus, as a phantasm that will visit him by night; Admetus, on the other hand, though still alive, loses a part of himself with Alcestis.[22] Throughout much of the play, Alcestis is simultaneously alive and dead.[23] The chorus's first lines call attention to this liminality: no one can say whether Alcestis is alive or dead (80–83); she is a corpse already, it speculates, but not yet buried (93–94), and therefore privately dead but publicly alive, actually dead but officially alive. She is, accord-ing to the slave woman, both alive and dead (141). Her preparations for death (narrated by the nurse) culminate in her appearance alive onstage: there she will die once only to come back to life so that she can die again. Likewise, Admetus escapes death, but lives to envy the dead and to long for death himself (866–69, 895–902). The shadow of his object upon him, Admetus lives or dies with Alcestis: "If you die, I would be no more, for I exist in you, alive or dead" (σοῦ γὰρ φθιμένης οὐκέτ' ἂν εἴην. / ἐν σοὶ δ' ἐσμὲν καὶ ζῆν καὶ μή, 277–78).

Into this world of psychic and existential confusion, difference is in-troduced by Heracles. It is he who demands that Admetus distinguish the external from the internal, and himself from the dead Alcestis: Heracles will not accept hospitality if Admetus is mourning someone intimately related to the house, and thus Admetus is forced to declare Alcestis "out-side" (*thuraios*) before Heracles will come inside. Likewise, it is Heracles who insists upon the separation of life from death:

> ΑΔ.: τέθνηχ' ὁ μέλλων. κοὐκέτ' ἔσθ' ὁ κατθανών.
> ΗΡ.: χωρὶς τό τ' εἶναι καὶ τὸ μὴ νομίζεται.
> ΑΔ.: σὺ τῇδε κρίνεις. Ἡράκλεις. κείνηι δ' ἐγώ.[24]
>
> (527–29)

> ADMETUS: The man on the point of death is dead
> already, and the dead man is no more.

HERACLES: Being and not being are considered
different things.
ADMETUS: You think so, Heracles, but I think
differently.

Although Admetus at first rejects this distinction, unable as yet to separate the two states (even as he is unable at this point to see Alcestis as
fully *thuraios*, 533), he later will attempt to distinguish the two forcibly,
literally locking the door (548–49) between the part of the house that
mourns and the part where Heracles is feasting. Ultimately the distinction is resecured by Heracles' descent into the underworld. This
transgression, the exceptional act of a demigod, reconfirms the rule
that, as Heracles says, "all mortals are bound to die, and there is no living man who knows if he will be alive tomorrow" (βροτοῖς ἅπασι
κατθανεῖν ὀφείλεται. / κοὐκ ἔστι θνητῶν ὅστις ἐξεπίσταται / τὴν
αὔριον μέλλουσαν εἰ βιώσεται, 782–84).

As "the restorer of differences,"[25] Heracles seems to help Admetus
work through the depressive position, to separate himself from his lost
object and to reconcile his ambivalence toward her. In this role, Heracles
functions as what Klein calls a surrogate good object. In Klein's model,
the depressive anxieties over the loss of the mother are worked out partly
within the Oedipal scenario.[26] The child replaces the lost mother with a
substitute good object, the father; with this internal security, the child is
then able to accept the loss of the mother and to repair the mother as a
good internal object.[27] Thus, unlike Freud, who sees the goal of the
Oedipal complex as the abandonment of a cathexis to the mother in exchange for identification with the father, Klein posits an object relation
with the father as a means to the end of reparation to the mother.

If Alcestis is represented as a mother in the play, Heracles is (among
other things) a paternal figure: he, too, gives Admetus life, saving him
from the morbidity of endless lamentation; in this regard he, too, like Alcestis, replaces Admetus's biological parents. As a paternal figure, Heracles not only helps Admetus separate from Alcestis, but, more importantly, effects the final reparation that allows the lost object to be
reincorporated into the ego. To repay his friend's hospitality, Heracles
goes down to the underworld and wrestles Alcestis away from death. In
the final scene, Heracles presents Admetus with Alcestis; husband and
wife are reunited and Alcestis, the lost object, is seemingly repaired and

reincorporated into the household as a whole object, the bearer of restored vitality.[28] Thus, it would seem, with Heracles' help, the depressive position is completed, and we close with the "happy ending" celebrated by so many of the play's readers.[29]

And yet it is difficult to be so sanguine about the end of *Alcestis*, and to read this final scene as a "happy ending" we must close our eyes to the essentially ambiguous tone of the episode and of the play as a whole. For though Alcestis may be returned to life, she is not returned as a subject, but rather as an object, silent, veiled, and half-dead. In the Kleinian model, the mother is transformed from a part object to a whole object, recognized ultimately as a subject in her own right. In this play, however, Alcestis starts out as a strong subject—controlling her house and her own fate—but returns as an object, passively traded between two men. In what sense can this movement really be called a reparation to the maternal object?

The falsity of this reparation is all the more obvious if we contrast the version of the myth told in Plato's *Symposium*,[30] where Alcestis's return is a divine reward for her excellence: "Her deed seemed so noble not only to men but also to the gods, that in admiration for her act, they granted her an honor given to only a few of the many who have performed noble deeds: for her soul to be released again from Hades" (*Symp.* 179c2–d1). Whereas in Plato's Phaedrus's version, the gods restore Alcestis to reward her self-sacrifice and honor her *aretē*, in Euripides' account, Heracles returns Alcestis to reward Admetus's hospitality and to celebrate the *xenia* bond, the bond of guest-friendship, between them. This difference is telling. Throughout the course of the play, the relationship between Admetus and Heracles seems to take priority over that between Admetus and Alcestis, so that rather than Heracles becoming the medium of Admetus's reparation to Alcestis, Alcestis becomes a medium for Admetus's bonding with Heracles. Admetus is forced to choose between Heracles and Alcestis: he cannot both mourn Alcestis and entertain Heracles, for Heracles will not come inside and accept Admetus's hospitality unless the dead woman (Alcestis) is declared "outside" (*thuraios*), unrelated to the house (537–67). Admetus chooses to honor his obligations to his *xenos* at the expense of those to his dead wife, and so Heracles replaces Alcestis in Admetus's house—this quite literally, as the same actor would have played both parts.

In the juxtaposition of Alcestis and Heracles we can see two different models of mourning and two different understandings of the self. Alongside the Kleinian model of loss, mourning, and reparation to the mother lies another model that sees the definitive separation from the mother as a necessary precondition to the socially desirable end of the child's identification with the father. This model is implicit in Freud's understanding of the process of mourning, the end of which is the severance of attachment to the lost object and its transference to a new object.[31] Once the link is made between the lost object and the maternal body,[32] we can see a close parallel in Freudian theory between mourning and the Oedipal complex, for in the latter as in the former, the goal is a libidinal separation from the mother and a transference of the libido to other women. Lacan takes the Oedipal exchange further, making rejection of the mother the essential precondition not only for the bond with the father, but also for the boy's assumption of his rights as a male subject within the paternal symbolic.[33] Thus in the Freudian and Lacanian model, the loss of the mother is not to be lamented and repaired, but actively embraced, a symbolic "matricide," as Kristeva puts it, "our vital necessity, the sine-qua-non condition of our individuation."[34] The final goal in this model of mourning is not reparation of the mother as a subject in her own right, but the cementing, over her dead body, of the bond with the father.

Throughout *Alcestis* these two models of mourning—the Kleinian and the Freudian—are in tension: a pattern of loss, mourning, and reparation is juxtaposed to and in conflict with the Oedipal dynamic of matricide and paternal identification. Is Alcestis's death a loss that will be redeemed with her resurrection in the final episode, or is it a matricide, a murder that grounds the play's social order? The tension between these two models can be seen in the play's mythic paradigms for the return of Alcestis. In its structure, *Alcestis* closely resembles the story of Demeter and Persephone.[35] A women is lost, taken down to Hades; her mourning makes life sterile and deathlike; her return from the underworld restores vitality to the world.[36] But despite the obvious parallels between the two plots, Demeter is never mentioned in the play, and Persephone figures only as queen of the underworld (358, 852). Instead, the mythic model of death and resurrection is Orpheus: at 357–62, Admetus bemoans the fact that he cannot descend to Hades and rescue his wife as Orpheus did (cf. 455–59), and it is Orpheus at 357 who beguiles Persephone into releasing Alcestis.[37] Whereas the myth of Demeter and Persephone celebrates the abundance of the maternal body and the strength, even in the face of death itself, of the maternal bond, the Orpheus myth is associated in *Alcestis* with the male homosocial relations between Admetus and his guest-friends, Apollo and Heracles: like Orpheus, Apollo charmed wild animals and thereby increased Admetus's wealth (579–87); like Orpheus, Heracles undertakes a *katabasis* (a descent to the underworld, 846–54) to restore Admetus's wife. The Orpheus myth eclipses the Demeter myth as the paradigm for Alcestis's death and return. The fact that Orpheus failed in his mission is largely ignored (acknowledged only once in passing, at 963–72),[38] and whereas Plato's linking of Alcestis and Orpheus (*Symp.* 179d2–3) makes it clear that Alcestis succeeded where Orpheus had failed, in *Alcestis* it is Heracles, not Alcestis, who conquers death.

Even as the homosocial bond with Heracles is shown to be life-giving, the maternal cathexis becomes murderous. In his bond with Alcestis, I suggested, Admetus lives in a state of semideath, life and death as indistinguishable as self and other. Heracles, with his miraculous transgression, reestablishes both the separation and the necessary coexistence of life and death: all living things must die, as he says (528, 782–84); life and death are two different things, although for mortals they are mutually defining. Heracles moves the play from an existential confusion of life and death to a philosophical understanding of the mortal condition[39] that is often taken to be the moral of this "fairy tale."[40] But we should note the gendering of this movement. Not only is the confusion of life and death associated with the maternal bond, but death itself is located within the maternal body:

> ἦ βαρυδαίμονα μήτηρ μ' ἔτεκεν.
> ζηλῶ φθιμένους. κείνων ἔραμαι,
> κεῖν' ἐπιθυμῶ δώματα ναίειν.
>
> (865–67)

> To a heavy fate my mother bore me.
> I envy the dead, I long for them,
> desire to dwell in their house.

If the maternal body is imagined as the source of life and all goodness, it is also imagined as the wellspring of death.[41] Alcestis gives Admetus his life, but it is a life that he experiences as a living death (1084–86); indeed, the gift she gives him is not immortality, but the gift every mother gives her child: a brief life that ends in death.[42] Maternity and mortality are linked in an inverted causality that makes the mother the murderer of the child. The only escape from her deadly embrace is matricide.

The movement from mourning to matricide is the focus of the next two chapters. In Chapter 8, I examine Alcestis as a subject and a maternal presence in the beginning of the play, and the crises she generates, crises of gender, genre, status, and economy. The following chapter traces Alcestis's transformation from subject to corpse and the relationships that are negotiated around her; in the relations between Admetus and Pheres and Admetus and Heracles, I shall argue, a new economy and a new aristocratic male identity are forged, literally over Alcestis's dead body. The last section of that chapter returns to the final exchange of the play. *Alcestis*'s final scene, I argue, offers not a reparation to the maternal body but an elimination of the maternal object in favor of a male homosocial bond that is figured as both a mirroring relation between aristocratic male equals and an Oedipal relationship of aristocratic patriliny. The restoration of Alcestis as a silent object is essential to the construction of this bond, and the ostensibly "happy" ending implies that resolution is worth the price of the woman's subjectivity. Yet at the same time, in the sense of uneasiness with which this final scene leaves us, I suggest, we can see hints of resistance: just as the Freudian model makes reparation to the maternal object impossible, the Kleinian model makes an unproblematic homosocial order impossible. In the silent, moribund figure of Alcestis is encrypted the paradox of tragedy's traffic in women, for her presence simultaneously forecloses the possibility of a female subject and incorporates that foreclosed possibility as a point of uncertainty and instability right at the center of the paternal symbolic.

✑

EIGHT

AGONISTIC IDENTITY
AND THE SUPERLATIVE SUBJECT

✑

THE MATRIARCH OF THE *oikos*
AND *Alcestis*'s DOMESTIC POLITICS

If, as I suggested in the last chapter, Alcestis's presence as a maternal figure generates an existential crisis, a confusion of self and other and of life and death, Alcestis herself also causes more concrete problems in the play. Alcestis is not only a biological and nurturing mother to her own children and a maternal object to Admetus, but also the matriarch of the *oikos*, as the servant says, "my mistress who was a mother to me and to all the servants" (ἐμὴν δέσποιναν. ἥ 'μοὶ πᾶσί τ᾽ οἰκέταισιν ἦν μήτηρ, 768–70). Her relation to the household slaves is linked with her relation to her children (189–95), and she is mourned by the slaves as a mistress even as she is mourned by her children as a mother:

> τέκνα δ᾽ ἀμφὶ γούνασιν
> πίπτοντα κλαίηι μητέρ᾽. οἱ δὲ δεσπότιν
> στένωσιν οἵαν ἐκ δόμων ἀπώλεσαν.
>
> (947–49)

And the children fall around my knees and
cry for their mother, and the slaves grieve
for their mistress, such a mistress has the
house lost.

Alcestis's domestic authority is tied to her maternal authority; that is to say, her maternal presence becomes a political issue.

This political aspect to Alcestis's maternal authority is suggested in the maidservant's narrative of her preparation for death (158–95). After bathing and dressing herself, she prays to Hestia and adorns all the altars of the house before proceeding to the bedchamber, where she throws herself upon her marriage bed and says her last farewell both to the bed itself and to the children and servants, who are all in tears. "And she held out her hand to each, and there was no one so lowly that she did not address him and speak with him" (ἡ δὲ δεξιὰν / προύτειν' ἑκάστωι κοὖτις ἦν οὕτω κακὸς / ὃν οὐ προσεῖπε καὶ προσερρήθη πάλιν, 193–95). This episode closely echoes the scene of Deianira's death in *Trachiniae* (900–935), especially Deianira's final apostrophe to the marriage bed at *Trachiniae* 920–22.[1] But whereas Deianira's movement into the interior of the house, as I argued in Chapter 3, is a move toward interiority and privacy, at the center of Alcestis's death preparation we find not, as Burnett puts it, "the purity of Alcestis' private actions,"[2] but a public scene. Alcestis tries to leave the room, but is drawn again and again back to the bed (187), as if she knows that tradition would have her die on it.[3] But rather than culminating in a private death on the bed, a private affirmation of her identity as wife, this scene suddenly becomes peopled with children and servants.[4] In her preparation for death, we see Alcestis not in intimate private reflection, but in semipublic interaction, as a good mother comforting her children, but also as a good mistress, greeting each member of her household in turn, her private bedchamber transformed into the administrative center of the *oikos*.

The designation of domestic master-slave relations as political may seem misplaced unless we recognize the extent to which this play reinscribes the political within the domestic. In a play that opens with the word *domos* ("house") and contains ten references to the *oikos* or *domos* in the first seventy-six lines, and more than eighty references in the text as a whole,[5] there occur only two explicit references to the *polis* (at 156 and 553). Admetus is, we know, king of Pherae: he is referred to as "lord" and "master" (*koiranos*, *despotēs*); we are told of the extent of his domain (588–96) and of his tetrarchy (1154).[6] Yet we see his authority only in relation to his *oikos*. He seems less the king of a city than the master of a house. His only concerns outside the *oikos* are centered on *xenia*, the relation of his household with other aristocratic households abroad. His *xenia* bond with Heracles, for all that it is more than just a personal friendship, is never represented in the play as a specifically political bond; it is not a link between two cities, but between two men and their houses.[7] We might contrast the situation in *Agamemnon*; there, too, the state and the house are conflated, and the political map is crossed with personal connections. Yet in that play, the breach of *xenia* between the house of Atreus and the house of Priam results in a political action, and the murder of the patriarch causes political anarchy: in *Agamemnon*, the domestic is politicized.[8] In *Alcestis*, by contrast, the interstate political relations implied by *xenia* are not made explicit:[9] the relationship is never generalized beyond the two *xenoi* themselves, and there is never any indication that Admetus acts for the city rather than for himself and his *oikos*.

Because the political is domesticated, as it were, in *Alcestis*, the heroine's relationship with the domestic slaves can be seen as a political relationship and her authority within the *domos* as a political authority. Coincident with this female authority is a noticeable weakness in the play's patrilines.[10] The mythic background to the play tells a story of patrilineal disruption: Zeus has killed his grandson Asclepius and enslaved his own son Apollo.[11] The patriarch himself has broken the patriline. The same rupture occurs on the mortal level, where Pheres, by refusing to give his own life for Admetus's, in effect kills his own child and destroys his *oikos*. This disruption is enacted on stage, as Admetus "disowns" his father, thereby making the break official (737–38).

The breach in the patriline is accompanied by a confusion of social order, a leveling of rank that characterizes social relations throughout this play.[12] The opening lines of the text, in which Apollo describes his former servitude to Admetus, reveal a certain confusion in the social and cosmic hierarchy.[13]

Ὦ δώματ' Ἀδμήτει'. ἐν οἷς ἔτλην ἐγὼ
θῆσσαν τράπεζαν αἰνέσαι θεός περ ὤν.

(1–2)

Oh house of Admetus, in which I deigned
to accept a slave's board, god though I am.

The contrast between θῆσσαν ("slave's") and θεός ("god") is remarkable enough, and is underlined by the unique collocation of θῆσσαν with τράπεζαν ("table," "board"), a word that in tragedy most often connotes the equal homosociety of the aristocratic symposium or *xenia*.[14] This conflation of *xenia* relations with the master-slave relation is repeated throughout the passage: Zeus forced Apollo to be a slave (θητεύειν, 6) to a mortal, but as Apollo tells it, Admetus was his *xenos* (8). The relationship between Apollo and Admetus is simultaneously one between slave and master and one between equals.[15]

A similar confusion of status is evident on the mortal level. Admetus, at the critical moment of rupture with his father, not only abjures his genealogical link with Pheres, but even assimilates himself to a slave:

> οὐκ ἦσθ' ἄρ' ὀρθῶς τοῦδε σώματος πατήρ,
> οὐδ' ἡ τεκεῖν φάσκουσα καὶ κεκλημένη
> μήτηρ μ' ἔτικτε, δουλίου δ' ἀφ' αἵματος
> μαστῶι γυναικὸς σῆς ὑπεβλήθην λάθραι.
>
> (636–39)

> You were not truly the father of this body, nor
> did she who claims to have borne me and is
> called my mother really give me life, but born
> from slave blood I was secretly put to your
> wife's breast.

Many critics have been startled by this suggestion (which is extreme whether we print it as a question or a statement).[16] But we should recognize that this assimilation of king to slave replicates precisely Apollo's servitude to Admetus, a servitude again caused by a break with his father. The same paradox is also embodied (although the text does not emphasize this) in the figure of Heracles, the paradigmatic hero-slave.

Thus Alcestis's strong maternal presence and domestic authority coincides with a breach in the patriline and social leveling. Yet, Alcestis herself seems to pose little threat to the patriarchal structures of the play; indeed, it is she who saves the *oikos* and, in theory at least, preserves the bond between father and son (620–22).[17] In her association with Hestia (162), Alcestis embodies the integrity of the *domos*, and while this association means that her death destroys it (415), nonetheless, she dies in order to save it.[18] In her reproach of Pheres, the logic of her priorities is clear. Pheres and his wife should have died honorably and saved Admetus: "For you were their only child and there was no hope that they would have other children once you were dead" (μόνος γὰρ αὐτοῖς ἦσθα, κοὔτις ἐλπὶς ἦν / σοῦ κατθανόντος ἄλλα φιτύσειν τέκνα, 293–94). This is not an argument for parental affection, for she implies that had his parents been able to insure another heir, they would have been justified in letting Admetus die. The argument is clearly for the preservation of the *genos*, and the patriline in particular.[19] And her death saves the link not only between Pheres and Admetus (before they themselves sever it) but also between Admetus and his heirs. Had Admetus died, their children would have been orphaned (288); with her death, they will remain "masters" in Admetus's house (304), and the line of descent will be secure.[20]

Moreover, Alcestis's death preserves not only the link between father and son, the vertical axis of the *oikos*, but also its horizontal axis, matrimony. For Alcestis dies not only to save her children, but also to save her husband (281–84; cf. 154–55).[21] Remarkably absent in this play are any of the common tragic themes of the matron's suicide as a reenactment of marriage or as a marriage in death.[22] Alcestis, unlike Deianira, does not die on the bed, although she does grieve to leave it and tears herself from it reluctantly. Her death—dying for her husband—becomes a public act of self-sacrifice for marriage, rather than, as with Deianira, a private resignation to its fatality.[23] Moreover, Alcestis is not killed by marriage, but rather redeems marriage by her death:

> Ὦ λέκτρον, ἔνθα παρθένει᾽ ἔλυσ᾽ ἐγὼ
> κορεύματ᾽ ἐκ τοῦδ᾽ ἀνδρός, οὗ θνήισκω πέρι,
> χαῖρ᾽· οὐ γὰρ ἐχθαίρω σ᾽· ἀπώλεσας δέ με
> μόνην· προδοῦναι γάρ σ᾽ ὀκνοῦσα καὶ πόσιν
> θνήισκω.[24]
>
> (177–81)

> Oh marriage bed, where I lost my maidenhood to
> this man, for whose sake I am dying, farewell. I
> do not resent you; you have destroyed me alone.
> Because I am loathe to betray you and my
> husband, I die.

These lines have puzzled critics: what does she mean when she says that the marriage bed has killed her alone? Does she mean that it has killed only herself and not Admetus or the *oikos* as well? But Admetus's life was never threatened from this quarter. Dale suggests that this is another claim for Alcestis's unique status among women. But if this is what is meant, it is a strange claim, for one of the central plot-elements of

Greek tragedy is the death of the woman because of, or for the sake of, her marriage.

By claiming that she is the only woman killed by the marriage bed, and by actively embracing that fate, Alcestis redeems tragic marriage. Whereas Deianira sees marriage and trouble as synonymous (*Trach.* 28, 149–50), and dying with her husband as the only possible alternative to living with him, Alcestis rejects this topos. By taking upon herself the sacrifice of her life for her marriage, and by claiming the uniqueness of this action, Alcestis breaks the tragic equation of marriage with disaster and redeems tragic marriage as an institution.[25] Her marriage becomes the ideal, a standard by which all future marriages are to be judged (627–28). Thus this play, unlike *Trachiniae*, can end with a "happy" re-marriage. The very fact that the extremely ambiguous transaction that closes the play can be viewed by so many readers as a happy ending suggests the extent to which Alcestis's unique self-sacrifice accomplishes the end of recuperating tragic marriage, of making her its only victim.[26]

Alcestis, then, preserves the integrity of the *oikos*, insures the patrilineal succession, and redeems marriage. And yet her salvation of the patriarchal order is not a solution to the problem, as it seems,[27] but rather is a problem in itself. For if Alcestis saves the *oikos*, the *oikos* that survives is *hers*, not Admetus's; *her* children will be the masters of *her* house, as she makes Admetus promise (τούτους ἀνάσχου δεσπότας ἐμῶν δόμων, 304). The patriline will be preserved, but only by its transformation into a matriline.

> καὶ σοὶ μέν, πόσι,
> γυναῖκ' ἀρίστην ἔστι κομπάσαι λαβεῖν,
> ὑμῖν δέ, παῖδες, μητρὸς ἐκπεφυκέναι.
>
> (323–25)

And you, husband, will be able to boast
that you wed the noblest woman, and you,
children, that you were born of the noblest
mother.

The phrase μητρὸς ἐκπεφυκέναι ("born of [the noblest] mother") is particularly revealing. The children will be Admetus's heirs, but their *physis* ("nature," "essence," contained in the word ἐκπεφυκέναι) will be hers: she will be their genealogical parent. I discussed in Chapter 4 (in

reference to *Agamemnon*'s lion-cub parable) the importance of genealogical descent in tragedy, the notion that fathers bear sons like unto
themselves, and the particular aristocratic connotations of this definition
of *physis*. In this play, too, *physis* and its verbal derivatives are used elsewhere only of male parentage. Admetus's father is *ho phusas* ("he who
begat," 290, from *phuō*, cognate with *physis*).[28] Admetus's mother, on
the other hand, is always *hē tekousa*, not the one who gives the child its
physis, but the one who physically bears him.[29] Alcestis saves the line of
male succession, but by doing so, she insures that it is her blood, her *physis*, and not Admetus's, that will constitute the *genos*. This suggestion is
realized when Admetus "disinherits" his father—"I no longer consider
myself your child by *physis*" (καί μ' οὐ νομίζω παῖδα σὸν πεφυκέναι,
641)—and takes as his new father Alcestis herself, "a foreign woman,
whom alone I might justly consider both father and mother" (γυναῖκ'
ὀθνείαν, ἣν ἐγὼ καὶ μητέρα / καὶ πατέρ' ἂν ἐνδίκως ἂν ἡγοίμην
μόνην, 646–47). Now she, and not Pheres, will receive the care and respect that are the father's due (666–68). She preserves the *oikos*, but only
to become, after her death, its patriarch.

THE SUPERLATIVE SUBJECT AND HER HUSBAND

This same collocation of feminine strength with masculine weakness re-
curs at the individual level in a contest between Admetus and Alcestis.
The basic premise of *Alcestis* is the exchange of one body for another:
Admetus escapes death by "exchanging another corpse to those below"
(ἄλλον διαλλάξαντα τοῖς κάτω νεκρόν, 14). The original deal assumes the essential equatability of all humans, at least in their most basic
corporeal existence. Yet this economy of equivalence is everywhere belied and contradicted in the play. While Alcestis's body is substituted for
Admetus's, their deaths establish differences between them that obviate the very possibility of equivalence. Admetus, in self-pity for the approaching loss of his wife, equates his suffering with hers (246–47,
257–58). Alcestis, however, rejects this equation: the tragedy is hers
alone (280). Again after Alcestis's death, Admetus imagines the two of
them joined in the grave; he equates his unhappiness, his living death, to
her real death (895–902). But the distinction between the two is always
clear, for Admetus is alive and Alcestis is dead, and life and death, as
Heracles insists, are two different things. Pheres makes this incommen-

surability explicit: Alcestis is dead and glorious; Admetus, alive and shameful (694–96). The play swings between an economy of equivalence (one corpse for another) and an economy of difference, in which equation is impossible.

The basis of this latter economy, and what makes so traumatic the basic exchange the play requires, is the superlative nature of Alcestis.[30] She is, as we are told over and over again, *aristē*, the best and most noble woman (83, 151, 152, 241, 442, 559, 742, 899). As a living subject, she performs an action that shows her superiority to all other women and to her husband; as a corpse, she is canonized by the chorus, praised by Admetus, virtually deified, a "blessed *daimōn*," "honored like the gods" (1003; cf. 996–99). So superlative is Alcestis that equivalencies become impossible. No woman can ever replace her, for "there is no woman so outstanding in noble lineage nor in beauty either" (οὐκ ἔστιν οὕτως οὔτε πατρὸς εὐγενοῦς / οὔτ᾽ εἶδος ἄλλως ἐκπρεπεστάτη γυνή, 332–33). She is not only dear but dearest (230), not only good but best (235). She is unique in her fate and in her fame (179–80, 330, 368, 434, 460, 647).[31]

But if this unique *aristeia* makes her equivalent to no woman other than herself, it also vitiates the exchange of equivalents proposed at the beginning of the play, for the more unique she is, the less can Admetus hope ever to equal her. The initial exchange of body for body sets up an equation whereby both Admetus and Alcestis will be defined in relation to one another. "Oh wretched man, such a husband, you lose such a wife," says the chorus (ὦ τλῆμον. οἵας οἷος ὢν ἁμαρτάνεις, 144): the nature ("such," *hoios*) of Admetus is determined in relation to the nature ("such," *hoias*) of Alcestis.[32] But as it turns out, this relationship will not equate husband and wife as equally good and noble; instead it will define them through contrast and differentiation, and Admetus will suffer in the shadow of his wife's supreme excellence.[33]

Death, then, rather than being a simple exchange that equates them as interchangeable bodies, becomes a competition between them. It is an *elenkhos*, a test (15–18, 640–41, 1058–59),[34] and one that Alcestis clearly wins, her sacrifice making her "the best of women" and "like the gods" (996–1005). Meanwhile, Admetus just as clearly loses: he becomes, in the taunts of his father, the "worst of men, beaten by your wife" (γυναικός. ὦ κάκισθ᾽. ἡσσημένος, 697). To the extent that this contest proves Alcestis *aristē*, best, it proves Admetus *kakistos*, worst.[35]

Beaten by a woman, Admetus is feminized; Alcestis, the victor, is correspondingly masculinized. Alcestis's superlative nature, while marking her specifically as a superlative woman, also assimilates her to masculine figures.[36] She is compared at several points in the play to Homeric heroes,[37] an association reinforced by the repeated epithet *aristē*.[38] Her dying apostrophe to the bed—"Some other woman will possess you, a woman not better, but perhaps luckier"—is reminiscent of Ajax's dying words to his son in Sophocles' play (*Ajax* 550–51), a passage that in turn points back to Hector's farewell to Astyanax at *Iliad* 6.476–78.[39] Like Patroclus, Alcestis will return as a ghost to visit the man for whom she died;[40] like Hector, she will have a "hollow" tomb, a landmark for travelers in the future.[41] So, too, the chorus's farewell to her recalls Achilles' address to the dead Patroclus.[42] Moreover, the emphasis on Alcestis's willing sacrifice, the repetition of *ethelō*, "I am willing," (17, 153–55), likens her to a fifth-century Athenian hero, a hoplite who dies for his *polis*.[43] Alcestis dies gloriously, like a hero, for her husband; she will thus win the *kleos* befitting a hero and will even have something of a hero cult: her tomb will be the object of veneration for passersby (996–1005).

Alcestis's bravery, as Loraux points out, "has the recoil effect of feminizing the well-loved husband."[44] While Alcestis, with her death, has replaced Admetus as hero, Admetus, by living, replaces Alcestis as mother: "You be the mother to these children now in my place," she exhorts him (σύ νυν γενοῦ τοῖσδ᾽ ἀντ᾽ ἐμοῦ μήτηρ τέκνοις, 377). While she is masculinized by death, he will be softened by the passing time.[45] If Alcestis is assimilated to the male heroes of epic, Admetus becomes like their wives: his requests that Alcestis not betray him (250, 275, 280–89) recall Andromache's pleas to Hector (*Il.* 6.407–39)[46] and Tecmessa's to Ajax (Soph. *Ajax* 496–524).[47] If Alcestis's action has heroized her, his has called even his masculinity into question: "And does he seem to be a man at all?" he asks of himself (κᾆτ᾽ ἀνὴρ εἶναι δοκεῖ; 957).

After the death of his wife, Admetus remains in the house, taking the place of the woman.[48] It is he, rather than the woman, who guards the entrances and exits (507–8). He leaves the house only to bury his wife, and only to return to its loneliness. In his spatial displacement—comfortable neither in the outside world nor within the house—Admetus becomes like the bride, who moves from one house to another. When he imagines his marriage in death to Alcestis (a theme usually reserved in tragedy for female virgins' deaths), he imagines going to a house that Alcestis has readied for him in Hades (363–64), joining her there like a bride. At his most desperate, he even wishes to bury himself with her

(897–99) in an inversion of the shared death (*sunthanein*) that represents the morbid extreme of uxorial devotion.[49] Furthermore, the usual gendered division of labor in Greek ritual would have women mourning over the death of a male hero, the situation that would have transpired had Admetus died when he was supposed to. But with the exchange, we end up instead with men—the chorus, but also Admetus—mourning a dead woman.[50] The chorus even goes so far as to recommend suicide (227–29), a traditionally feminine act, and one to which Alcestis's self-determined death is never compared.[51]

Thus the strong maternal presence is manifested as a masculinization of the woman, resulting in a feminization of the man. For it is specifically Alcestis, as mother of the household, who "softens" Admetus. She is mourned by the servant as

> ἐμὴν
> δέσποιναν, ἣ 'μοὶ πᾶσί τ' οἰκέταισιν ἦν
> μήτηρ· κακῶν γὰρ μυρίων ἐρρύετο,
> ὀργὰς μαλάσσουσ' ἀνδρός.
>
> (768–71)
>
> the mistress who was a mother to me and
> to all the slaves; for she saved us from
> countless troubles, softening the tempers
> of her husband.

The maternal presence "softens" Admetus. He will be defined after her death as "her husband," rather than she being defined as "his wife" (323–25; cf. 233).[52] Unable to separate himself from his maternal object, Admetus is destroyed by her loss and by his own idealization of her after her death. She becomes too good an object, an object that can never be repaired, and whose very goodness thus becomes a reproach to the self.

Admetus is incapacitated by his relationship to his wife, alive or dead. Not only is he vilified and feminized in contrast to her heroism, but his basic status as a subject is eclipsed by her brilliance. For while she is alive, Alcestis is insistently a subject. She refuses to be an object of exchange, or rather, if she must be the object, she insists on also being the subject. In the opening scene of the play, Alcestis is the object of a legalistic debate between Thanatos and Apollo: her life is property that they fight over.[53] So, too, in the first formulation of the trade of bodies (14),

Admetus is its subject and Alcestis the "other corpse" that is its object. Yet this is not how the exchange is presented throughout most of the play. Rather, we see Alcestis trading herself to Death in exchange for Admetus's life (282–84, 340–41, 462–63). The continuous emphasis on her willingness to die (as well as the play's refusal to make love for Admetus her sole motive) underscores the fact that her death will be an act of her own determination. Not just an object of exchange (14), Alcestis becomes its subject (17–18), the giver as well as the gift.[54]

And almost inevitably (according to the logic we have seen in *Agamemnon* and *Trachiniae*) when the woman becomes a subject of exchange, the man becomes the object. If in the original terms of the bargain Admetus traded his wife for his soul (δάμαρτ' ἀμείψας, 46), Alcestis reverses this, giving her soul for Admetus (σὺ τὸν αὐτᾶς / ἔτλας ⟨ἔτλας⟩ πόσιν ἀντὶ σᾶς ἀμεῖψαι / ψυχᾶς ἐξ Ἅιδα; "You dared to trade your husband out of Hades in exchange for your own life," 461–62). His life, won a first time in Apollo's *agōn* against the Fates (11–14), now becomes the prize in her contest against Death (259–63): thus she dies not only instead of him, but also "over him" (οὗ θνήισκω πέρι, 178), in a phrase that recalls the fighting over a dead Homeric hero.[55] Admetus himself seems to set his life as the prize in a contest among his loved ones (648–49), a contest and prize that Alcestis wins. Although the trade of Alcestis for Admetus is the central fact of the play, nowhere is Alcestis represented as the pure object of exchange—that is, not until the final scene.

In her death scenes, too, Alcestis refuses objectification. Unlike Deianira, Alcestis dies publicly, onstage; whereas Deianira's death is private and hidden from the audience's gaze, Alcestis's death is a central *praxis* (action) of this play, and one that publicly stages her as a subject.[56] In the ecstatic visions of her approaching demise, we see her last moments through her own eyes, a highly personalized vision of death, in which Charon speaks directly to her (255–57).[57] We see her struggle against death (259–63),[58] her resistance emphasizing the enormity of her decision.[59]

If Alcestis's first, lyric death asserts her position as subject of her own fate, her second death, her rhesis (a speech delivered in a more "prosaic" meter, iambic trimeter), makes this claim even more emphatically.[60] Alcestis pulls herself back from the brink of death to take care of her final business, the "gift" of her children to Admetus and the assurances she expects in return (375–76). Critics have reviled this speech as cold, heartless, and indicative of Alcestis's selfish motives for dying.[61] But what is perhaps most remarkable about this speech, moral evaluations aside, is the degree to which Alcestis separates herself from Admetus. She evokes clearly the alternatives that were available to her:

θνῄσκω, παρόν μοι μὴ θανεῖν, ὑπὲρ σέθεν,
ἀλλ' ἄνδρα τε σχεῖν Θεσσαλῶν ὃν ἤθελον
καὶ δῶμα ναίειν ὄλβιον τυραννίδι.

(284–86)

I die. It was possible for me not to die on your
behalf but to take a husband, whomever I
wished among the Thessalians, and to dwell
in a home blessed with power.

In raising the possibility of remarriage, she suggests that the choice was hers to make freely, whom to marry (with no mention of a *kyrios*, a guardian), whether or not to die for Admetus. Her new house, as she pictures it, would be wealthy (ὄλβιον, "blessed" or "prosperous") and powerful to the point of tyranny (τυραννίδι): her status and power are independent of Admetus in her mind. So is her sexuality: there were other pleasures for her if he had died ("I did not spare my youth, although I have things in which I could delight," οὐδ' ἐφεισάμην / ἥβης, ἔχουσ' ἐν οἷς ἐτερπόμην ἐγώ, 288–89).[62] Imagining an alternative to her self-sacrifice, Alcestis depicts herself as an autonomous, politically potent, and sexual subject, a whole object, in Klein's terms, distinct and independent from Admetus. He echoes these lines in his promise not to remarry (330–31: he will refuse a Thessalian bride, just as she refused a Thessalian husband), but the promise itself denies the possibility of his separation from her and the freeing of his libido from his lost object. Instead of another woman, he will only take her again, as a phantom, a statue, and finally Alcestis herself, returned from the dead.

While Alcestis is alive, then, she insists upon her own subject status, on her separateness from Admetus, and on the self-determination of her action. As a subjective act, Alcestis's death is, of course, ambiguous: it suggests that a woman's only possible choice is the choice of her own death, her only possible action suicide. Though her sacrifice may make her a hero, it is a heroism still strictly circumscribed by oppressive gender roles.[63] Even if Admetus will become "*her* husband" after her death, she dies as "*his* wife": "She is dead, the wife of Admetus is no more" (βέβηκεν, ούκέτ' έστιν 'Αδμήτου γυνή, 392). Her glorious deed still defines her and her *kleos* in relation to her husband and his *oikos*. And it still leaves her dead. Even if we read Alcestis's self-sacrifice as her final claim to subject status, the ultimate effect is objectification: after her death, she becomes a mere body, an object of investigation, conflict, burial, and—finally—exchange.[64]

Compromised though it may be in the final reckoning, Alcestis's subjectivity still presents problems for the play, as I have argued in this section. The strong subjective presence of Alcestis coincides with a confusion of social relations, a disruption of the patriline, and domestic chaos. Alcestis is idealized as the perfect woman and a heroic figure; Admetus in comparison is feminized and abjected. Maternal strength and paternal weakness together create an *aporia* that incapacitates the whole psychic economy of the play, an *aporia* that is not eliminated but rather is crystallized and encrypted with her death, and that will only be resolved by her eventual transformation into a virginal and voiceless object.

FROM TRAGEDY TO THE SYMPOSIUM

I suggested in the last chapter that *Alcestis* is riven by a tension between a strong maternal cathexis and a male homosocial bond. It has often been noticed that this play falls into two halves: the first deals with "the tragedy of Alcestis" and the second with the Heracles plot, although how we should define this latter plot generically—as comedy, satyr play, tragicomedy, romance, or something else entirely—is debated.[65] Indeed, the generic designation of *Alcestis* as a whole is a vexed topic. We know from the hypothesis that this was a fourth play, occupying the time slot in the City Dionysia's schedule normally reserved for a satyr play. Starting from that knowledge, scholars have tried to identify the satyric elements of the play, and have found many: the undignified quarrel between Thanatos and Apollo, and later between Admetus and Pheres; the drunkenness of Heracles; the "happy" ending.[66] There are problems, however, with designating *Alcestis* a satyr play. First of all, it lacks the most definitive feature of satyr plays, a chorus of satyrs. *Alcestis*'s chorus of citizens is fully tragic in its character, diction, tone, and sentiment. Second, for all that *Alcestis* does contain some humorous elements, particularly associated with Heracles, it is far from the slapstick vulgarity of our only satyr play,

Euripides' *Cyclops*.[67] To some extent, then, I think the problem has been blown out of proportion. We can say with confidence that *Alcestis* is closer to tragedy in every way than it is to the satyr plays we know, and therefore the fact that it was performed fourth may simply mean that the "rule" of three tragedies and a satyr play was more flexible than we are accustomed to think.

Or rather, perhaps, the generic definitions of tragedy, comedy, and satyr play are more flexible than we would like. If *Alcestis* does not resemble Euripides' *Cyclops*, it does resemble some of his later tragedies, which Burnett has designated plays of "mixed reversal," plays that were performed, and are recognized, as tragedies.[68] Many of Euripides' tragedies share characteristics with *Alcestis*: like *Alcestis*, many have "happy" endings (*Ion, Iphigeneia among the Taurians, Helen*); like *Alcestis*, many contain scenes that could be called humorous (the miscommunication between Clytemnestra and Achilles in *Iphigeneia in Aulis*, the confusion of seaweed-strewn Menelaus in *Helen*, the parody of *Choephoroe* in the recognition scene of *Iphigeneia among the Taurians*); like *Alcestis*, these other plays use less famous or canonical myths, and thus assume the "fairy-tale" quality that so many critics identify in *Alcestis*. It seems, then, that the generic ambiguity of *Alcestis* may point toward the "new" tragedy of later Euripides;[69] perhaps in 438, this sort of play was felt to be not quite tragic enough (for whatever reasons) to be performed in the time slots normally reserved for tragedies. Within the next decades, however, these tragedies of "mixed reversal" became normalized to such an extent that Aristotle considers *Iphigeneia among the Taurians* a paradigmatic tragedy.[70]

Yet if *Alcestis* seems to be tending toward the generic characteristics of later Euripidean tragedy, still the two different elements—tragic and "satyric" or comic—seem to be less well integrated here than in those later plays. This is not, I think, a function of the play's early date or an immature author (Euripides was in his forties and had been producing plays for over seventeen years by 438), nor to its occupation of the fourth time slot of the festival day. Rather, I believe that the generic issue is intimately related to the psychological tension that structures *Alcestis*, and that the separation of the tragic and the "satyric"—which the play in fact goes out of its way to highlight—is deliberate and significant.

In this division of the tragic and the "satyric," Alcestis, her decision, and her death occupy the tragic position, forming a mini-tragedy within the play.[71] An archetypical tragic decision was posed before the action of the play begins: a choice between life and *kleos*, or between one's own life and the life of a loved one.[72] Faced with this decision, Alcestis makes the tragic choice: death with *kleos*, Admetus's life over her own. Admetus, on the other hand, makes not only an un-tragic choice, but an anti-tragic choice, a choice that seems to be ignorant of the standards and options of tragedy. He seems not to understand (in his decision and throughout much of the play) the guidelines that govern the action of most tragic heroes. Indeed, these tragic norms are the content of his *anagnōrisis:* it is better to die with good repute than to live with bad (939–40). It is as if the action of the play teaches him not only to value his wife but also to understand a certain tragic framework for action.

Admetus, by choosing to live, in effect chooses not to be a tragic hero, and all the tragedy of the play devolves upon Alcestis. Her double death, once in lyric and once in iambic trimeter, allows her to fill the tragic form completely, to occupy both its modes. In contrast, Admetus gets no lyric until late in the play. During Alcestis's lyric vision of death, Admetus answers her in more prosaic trimeter distichs, the contrast in meters underlining the failure of the two to connect on any level.[73] The important lyric lament that should belong to Admetus directly after the death of Alcestis is preempted by the child, and Admetus is denied his moment of mourning. This denial is all the more remarkable for the fact that Admetus begins to mourn in anapests at 273–79 after Alcestis's first, lyric death, but is stopped by her speech. It is as if the doubleness, the formal inclusiveness of her death, silences him. It is only after his negotiations with Heracles and Pheres, nearly 500 lines after her death (861–934), that Admetus can join in the lyric lament, and even there he does not himself sing.[74]

Alcestis's life and death constitute a miniature tragedy: her decision and preparation for death are a *thauma*, a "marvel," narrated by the maidservant to the audience of chorus members: "What she did in the house you will marvel to hear" (ἃ δ' ἐν δόμοις ἔδρασε θαυμάσηι κλύων, 157). This formulation could be taken as a definition of tragedy, as we have seen it in *Trachiniae* and *Agamemnon*; the affairs inside the house, and particularly the deeds of the woman, are externalized in tragedy, so that they become the object not only of narration (*kluōn*, "hearing"), but also of theatrical spectation (*thauma* from *theaomai*, "to be a spectator"). Alcestis's death will be celebrated in music and ritual (445–54), and she will leave behind her a subject of song for poets in "rich and blessed Athens": her story is tragedy.[75]

Moreover, Alcestis herself shows affinities with the most fundamental characteristics of tragedy. Zeitlin (1990) has argued that the basic elements of tragedy—plot, the body, space, and *mimesis*—are associated with the Greek conception of the female, and many of the findings of the past chapters have supported her thesis. Here, Alcestis's sacrifice drives the plot; her occupation of the house and the location of her corpse organize the play's spatial relations; her body, as we shall see, becomes the central signifier in the second half of the drama. She is also associated with *mimesis*, a certain doubleness that is, Zeitlin argues, particularly tragic.[76] One of the fundamental questions of *Alcestis* is whether Alcestis can be replaced after her death. Admetus promises that she will not be, and the chorus's emphasis on her uniqueness suggests that she cannot be; nonetheless, throughout the play she is replaced, first by the statue that Admetus imagines holding in her place,[77] then by the ghost that will visit him in his dreams (354–55), and ultimately in the final episode by Alcestis herself, returned from the dead.[78] Yet if Alcestis at the end recreates Alcestis of the beginning, she also fully becomes the imagined statue, for the new Alcestis is silent.[79] The original and the reproduction never truly merge, and Alcestis remains a copy of herself, the essence of tragic *mimesis*.

Alcestis's life and death, then, are the subject of tragedy, and she is given tragic *megethos* (magnitude) by the chorus's laudation after her death. Admetus, on the other hand, is denied the role of tragic hero.[80] Just as the play does not allow him lyric grief, the chorus does not grant heroic stature to his mourning, but instead trivializes his fate in contrast to his wife's.[81] He is not the first to lose a wife, the chorus tells him (416–19, 892–94); death has taken the wives of many men (930–33). Dale points out that such sentiments are generic,[82] but the effect of this theme, in conjunction with the chorus's ceaseless praise of Alcestis, is, I think, the denial of tragic grandeur to Admetus's suffering. This is especially evident in a peculiar choral exemplum:

> ἐμοί τις ἦν
> ἐν γένει, ὦι κόρος ἀξιόθρη-
> νος ὤλετ' ἐν δόμοισιν
> μονόπαις· ἀλλ' ἔμπας
> ἔφερε κακὸν ἅλις, ἄτεκνος ὤν.[83]
>
> (903–7)

There was a man in my family whose son
died, the only child in his house, worth
lamenting. But still he bore the sorrow well
enough, even though he was left childless.

Whereas Alcestis becomes quasi-divine through her self-sacrifice, Admetus is compared to some unknown relative of the chorus. The play designates her suffering as tragic, and his as ordinary; the *agōn* between Admetus and Alcestis is fought again on the generic level, and again Admetus loses.

If Admetus is denied magnitude as a tragic hero, the solution offered by the play is a retreat from tragedy, and the movement toward a new genre, represented by Heracles. We saw above that Heracles introduces order and structure into the undifferentiated state created by the cathexis to the maternal body: it is he who segregates life and death, which the bond between Alcestis and Admetus had merged and rendered indistinguishable. Likewise, Heracles' arrival initiates a separation of mourning and festivity. Eager to persuade Heracles to stay, Admetus tries to compartmentalize the two genres, as he says, locking the door between them:

ἡγοῦ σὺ τῶιδε δωμάτων ἐξωπίους
ξενῶνας οἴξας τοῖς τ' ἐφεστῶσιν φράσον
σίτων παρεῖναι πλῆθος, εὖ δὲ κλήισατε
θύρας μεταύλους· οὐ πρέπει θοινωμένους
κλύειν στεναγμῶν οὐδὲ λυπεῖσθαι ξένους.

(546–50)

You there, open the guest chamber across
from the house, and tell those inside to provide plenty of food. And make sure you close
the inner doors. For it is not fitting for guests
to be disturbed by groans while they are
feasting.

The artificial separation of life and death, of mourning and festivity, is expressed in generic terms, as the separation of the dirge and the drinking song: Heracles' carousal is characterized by his singing (ἄμουσ᾽ ὑλακτῶν, "unmusical yelping," 760), just as the lamenting for Alcestis is characterized by tears and groans.

The drunken speech (773–802) that results from this enforced separation is generally considered to be the main satyric element of the play.[84] While it is true that the satyrs in *Cyclops* are drunk most of the time and that much of that play is devoted to drunken song, the tone here is quite different. First, this is a rhesis, not lyric; second, the moral and philosophical tenor of this speech associates it less with the satyr play than with the discourse of the symposium, the drinking party that was a central institution of aristocratic male society.[85] The themes of the shortness of life and the uncertainty of the future, with the inevitable corollary, "Cheer yourself: drink!" (εὔφραινε σαυτόν, πῖνε, 788), and the emphasis on camaraderie (ἄνδρ᾿ ἑταῖρον, 776), are all reminiscent of the sympotic tradition of Alcaeus.

If *Alcestis* is medial between two genres, then, those genres are not tragedy and satyr, but rather tragedy and sympotic literature.[86] And if, as Zeitlin has claimed, tragedy had associations in the Greek mind with the female, sympotica was the literature par excellence of aristocratic male homosociality. The former is structured by alterity, a tension between self and other that, as we have seen, is frequently figured as a tension between male and female; the latter is based on similarity and homogeneity within the all-male group. Thus the psychic tension in *Alcestis* between Admetus's relation of alterity with Alcestis and his *xenia* bond with Heracles is replicated on the generic level in the dichotomy between tragedy and sympotica.

Admetus has a firm connection with sympotic wisdom literature outside of this play.[87] The *Admētou logos*, "Admetus's song," a well-attested sympotic song probably originating in the mid-fifth century,[88] celebrates the values of camaraderie and aristocratic reciprocity:

> Ἀδμήτου λόγον ὦ ἑταῖρε μαθὼν τοὺς ἀγαθοὺς φίλει,
> τῶν δειλῶν δ᾿ ἀπέχου γνοὺς ὅτι δειλοῖς ὀλίγη χάρις.[89]

> Comrade, learn the story of Admetus, and take good and
> noble men as your friends, but keep away from cowards,
> recognizing that there is little goodwill with cowards.

If Alcestis is a quintessentially tragic heroine, Admetus is a hero not of tragedy, but of the symposium; she is an exemplary tragic wife, he an exemplary sympotic *hetairos* ("comrade"). This sympotic role is one, moreover, that Admetus explicitly claims for himself in *Alcestis*. Among his renunciations at the time of Alcestis's death are the joys of the symposium: "I will stop the revelry and the sympotic gatherings, the wreaths and the music that used to occupy my house" (παύσω δὲ κώμους συμποτῶν θ᾽ ὁμιλίας / στεφάνους τε μοῦσάν θ᾽ ἣ κατεῖχ᾽ ἐμοὺς δόμους, 343–44). The symposium was part of the *terpsis* that used to characterize his life (345–47),[90] but that has been interrupted with Alcestis's death: it is as if for Admetus tragedy were merely a temporary and unnatural state in his usual life of sympotic entertainment.

For much of the play, Admetus wavers between tragedy and the symposium (as he does between death and life, and between Alcestis and Heracles), trying to admit both, and to "lock the door" between them. But just as the initial confusion of life and death is resolved by a temporary separation of the two, and ultimately their recombination into a more manageable philosophical union, likewise, with the issue of genre, the tragic stranglehold of Alcestis is broken by the introduction of Heracles and his new genre; the two are temporarily separated, but only to be recombined in the end. But rather than providing the "comic resolution" (κωμικωτέραν τὴν καταστροφήν) of the hypothesis and the incorporation of the satyric into the tragic, the final exchange represents a reincorporation of tragedy into the symposium, as Alcestis is reintroduced into Admetus's revitalized household, moribund and silent.[91]

Why is Alcestis silent at the end?[92] If there are only three speaking actors in the play, this means that Alcestis's actor must play Heracles after her death. That is to say, Alcestis must be silent so that Heracles can speak; her tragic lament has been replaced by his sympotic singing. Moreover, we should note that it is wrong not for Alcestis to talk, but rather for Admetus to hear her:

οὔπω θέμις σοι τῆσδε προσφωνημάτων
κλύειν, πρὶν ἂν θεοῖσι τοῖσι νερτέροις
ἀφαγνίσηται καὶ τρίτον μόλῃ φάος.

(1144–46)

It is not right for you to hear her words
yet, before the third morning comes and she
has been purified of her consecration to the
gods below.

In *Trachiniae* and *Agamemnon*, I suggested, the figure of a silent woman is in some sense at the core of the play, her silence emblematic of an otherness tragedy always tries to make speak but can never hear: Iole, the virgin in the garden; Iphigeneia, her cries violently stifled; Cassandra, whose incoherent prophecies placed her beyond the play's symbolic, "ek-static." If Alcestis could speak, it would be with the voice of the other. Her words might reveal the secrets of death, the ultimate alterity, but they cannot be encompassed by the play. It is not her speech that is re-incorporated into the play in the final scene, but her silence, a silence associated here with tragedy itself. The three days of her silence correspond to the three days of tragic performance at the City Dionysia: when she will be able to speak again, the tragic festival will be over.[93] Thus the play moves from the tragedy of a woman, through the homosocial world of the symposium, to a reincorporation of tragedy in the form of a silent woman.

This reincorporation of tragedy into the symposium, of otherness into the homosocial world of sameness, is the formula for Euripides' new tragedy. Alcestis's death was the occasion for tragedy; Heracles' drunken-ness evoked skolion; now new choruses are to be set up to celebrate the recovery of Alcestis (1155–56). These new choruses will combine loss and recovery, tragedy and the symposium, and, at a generic level at least, will represent the achievement of the end of mourning.

NINE

The Mirror of *xenia*
and the Paternal Symbolic

From Impossible *kharis* to the *agalma* Economy

We have seen in the last two chapters how Alcestis's presence—as a maternal figure and a matriarch, as a superlative subject and a too-good object—creates a psychic paralysis that threatens not only the patriline, but also the male subject. This paralysis is also economic: Alcestis's gift—her life for her husband's—operates within and establishes an impossible economy, an economy of excess. Nothing is more valuable than a life, she says, and therefore her gift to Admetus is a *kharis*—a grace, favor, debt—that can never be repaid:

> εἶεν· σύ νύν μοι τῶνδ᾽ ἀπόμνησαι χάριν·
> αἰτήσομαι γάρ σ᾽ἀξίαν μὲν οὔποτε
> (ψυχῆς γὰρ οὐδέν ἐστι τιμιώτερον).
> δίκαια δ᾽. ὡς φήσεις σύ·
>
> (299–302)

> So be it. But now repay your debt of gratitude for these acts; the request I will make is not equal—never, for nothing is more valuable than a life—but just, as yourself will admit.

The demand she makes in return, that Admetus not give her children a stepmother, is *dikaia* but not *axia*, just but not a just return. Even Admetus's hyperbolic promises (to mourn her forever, to worship her statue) cannot match her extraordinary beneficence; moreover, these promises are never fulfilled. Her gift operates according to the logic of the pot-latch, and its result, as Mauss predicts, is to "flatten" Admetus.[1] By giv-ing a gift that Admetus can never return, Alcestis puts him forever in her debt; she wins this economic *agōn*, then dies, leaving no way in which he can ever reciprocate so as to put them back on an equal footing.

The excessive gift generates an economic imbalance in the play that makes equivalence and equation all but impossible.[2] The play is struc-tured by a series of impossible gifts: Apollo's offer to Admetus (1071), Alcestis's gift to Admetus,[3] Admetus's hospitality to Heracles, Heracles' final gift to Admetus. This circulation of excessive gifts works against the equivalence of corpses that the action of the play requires. The chorus tells us over and over again that Alcestis is unique and irreplaceable; be-cause she is unique, Admetus can never give a gift that will equal or repay her gift, nor can he ever replace her (329–33), the object he has lost in this exchange. Her irreplaceability is both theoretical and literal, for the condition of Alcestis's death is that she will not be replaced by another woman (305–16): even if he could replace her, he may not. She imagines that some other woman will occupy her bed (181), but that other woman turns out at the end of the play to be herself.

Alcestis's excessive *kharis* ties back into the problem of her maternal presence: inseparably cathected to his maternal object, Admetus will never be able to accomplish the sublimation that would replace her with another object. The normative substitution of wife for mother in the Freudian model is an act of economic equivalence.[4] It can be expressed precisely in Marx's equivalent form of value: "twenty yards of linen equals one coat" is an expression in commodity form of the Oedipal dic-tum that the mother can (indeed, must) be replaced by another woman. This primary replacement or sublimation, however, opens the way for infinite exchange, for if the mother can be replaced, all women are theo-retically set as equal to the mother, and thus the elementary form of value can be extended into Marx's expanded form: "twenty yards of linen equals one coat equals ten pounds of tea equals forty pounds of coffee, etc." The essential equivalence of all women is the underlying assump-tion and theoretical imperative for the exchange of women. Here, how-ever, Alcestis makes such a string of sublimations impossible. No other woman is ever equivalent or equatable to her.

Perhaps this is why *Alcestis* is so remarkably devoid of eroticism, especially for Euripides, an author notoriously fascinated with female passion.[5] The *philia* ("friendship," "closeness") that inspires Alcestis to die for Admetus, and the *philia* he honors in return, is never represented as *erōs*, erotic love.[6] Unable to replace Alcestis, unable to sublimate, Admetus remains attached to this dead object: Alcestis has taken "the delight (*terpsis*) of life" from him with her death (σὺ γάρ μου τέρψιν ἐξείλου βίου, 347), and other women are for him only a reminder of her (950–53).[7] The first time he speaks of his wife erotically is in describing the statue he will have made of her:

σοφῆι δὲ χειρὶ τεκτόνων δέμας τὸ σὸν
εἰκασθὲν ἐν λέκτροισιν ἐκταθήσεται,
ὧι προσπεσοῦμαι καὶ περιπτύσσων χέρας
ὄνομα καλῶν σὸν τὴν φίλην ἐν ἀγκάλαις
δόξω γυναῖκα καίπερ οὐκ ἔχων ἔχειν·
ψυχρὰν μέν, οἶμαι, τέρψιν, ἀλλ᾽ ὅμως βάρος
ψυχῆς ἀπαντλοίην ἄν.[8]

(348–54)

By the skilled hand of a craftsman your body
will be sculpted and laid out on our bed where
I will embrace it and clasp it to me calling your
name, and I will feel like I am holding my dear
wife in my arms, although I am not. It is a chilly
delight, I know, but still I might be able to drain
the weight from my spirit.

His "chilly delight" is not a sublimation for her,[9] but a libidinal cathexis to his dead object.[10] He fantasizes about lying with her in the coffin, "side by side" (πλευρά τ᾽ ἐκτεῖναι πέλας / πλευροῖσι τοῖς σοῖς, 366–67); he envies the dead, and loves them (ζηλῶ φθιμένους, κείνων ἔραμαι, 866). He knows he should stop grieving, but "some *erōs* leads him" (1080): his only *erōs* is for death itself. It is only with the play's final remarriage, when Heracles has severed Admetus from his lost object, that Admetus is free to "honor Kypris" (790–91) as Heracles recommends.

The impossibility of equivalence or sublimation is also a rejection of signification, for language, too, is a system of equations, the equivalence of signifier and signified.[11] When Admetus states that Alcestis is both

154

alive and dead, Heracles responds, "You speak of something meaning-less" (*asēma*, literally "without signification," 522). Without equivalent, Alcestis bears no value and no meaning; if she is everything, she is also, as she herself says, nothing (381, 390). In the symbolic paralysis that her excessive presence has created, she herself is *asēma*.[12] Thus Alcestis's *kharis* generates a stagnation—libidinal, semiotic, and economic—that stops all sublimation, equation, and signification.

If Alcestis's unanswerable gift occupies one economic pole in this play, the disenchanted monetarism of Pheres represents the other.[13] Both phi-losophies start from the same premise: "Nothing is more valuable than a life" (ψυχῆς γὰρ οὐδέν ἐστι τιμιώτερον, 301; cf. 691–93, 703–4, 712, 722). But starting from this point, Alcestis's economy denies the possibility of an equivalent to life or of equating values at all; Pheres, on the other hand, takes this premise as the foundation for an economy in which everything is equatable. Life may be defined as the most valuable commodity, but it, like everything else, can be measured and given a *timē*, a value.

While Alcestis's economy is one of excessive agalmatization that deals in objects too valuable to part with or pay for, Pheres' disenchantment puts a price on everything. Pheres comes bearing gifts for the corpse (ἀγάλματα, 613); these ornaments (κόσμον) are an attempt to compen-sate Alcestis for her sacrifice and Admetus for his suffering (614–24): the *timē* they represent is honor, but also recompense. Thus they presuppose a very different perspective upon the economics of loss than that de-manded by Alcestis, for whom no repayment will ever be sufficient.[14]

Pheres, for all that he appreciates the material profit her action has brought him, rejects Alcestis's trade of life for *kleos*, calling her choice foolish (728), and subjecting her *kharis* to an accountancy alien to it. Al-though he understands well the material underpinnings of his royal sta-tus, he is completely uncomprehending of the notion and value of sym-bolic profit.[15] He considers the exchange of his reputation for his life a good deal: "A bad reputation is no concern to me when I am dead" (κακῶς ἀκούειν οὐ μέλει θανόντι μοι, 726). He subjects his relation-ships to this same profit-and-loss logic. In his mouth, the *philia* between father and son consists of economic obligations and little more (681–90). The "paternal law" (*patrōios nomos*, 683) to which he subscribes is one of strict economic rules.[16] In this rigid economism, Pheres plays Thanatos to Admetus's Apollo, in a dialogue that clearly echoes the de-bate between the two gods in the opening scene.[17] Between Admetus and

Pheres, as between Apollo and Thanatos, there can be no *kharis* (60–61, 70, 660–61).

So it is little surprise that Pheres is incapable of understanding Alcestis's sacrifice. Although his first words acknowledge Alcestis's unique status (615–16), his later attacks on his son reveal a different conception:

> σοφῶς δ' ἐφηῦρες ὥστε μὴ θανεῖν ποτε,
> εἰ τὴν παροῦσαν κατθανεῖν πείσεις ἀεὶ
> γυναῖχ' ὑπὲρ σοῦ.[18]

(699–701)

> You have cleverly figured out a way to live
> forever, if you will always persuade your
> current wife to die for you.

Pheres imagines Alcestis as part of an economy of easy and unrestricted exchangeability. Whereas Alcestis represents her life as an *agalma* so precious that it can never be exchanged, so precious that it makes exchange impossible, Pheres represents it as a mere commodity, like ten pounds of tea or forty pounds of coffee. This is the crudest expression of the expanded equivalent form implied by the Oedipal exchange of mother for wife, an endless string of sublimations. And if the unique cathexis with the mother is imagined as creating a suffocating confusion of life and death, as I argued above, this string of equivalents defers death endlessly, the sublimation serving a simultaneous end of denial.

Admetus, throughout most of the play, wavers between the excess of Alcestis and the monetarism of Pheres. Like Pheres, he sees filial obedience as a material transaction (660–64) and chooses life over *kleos*. He, too, talks about his relationships (to his father, 660–64; to his wife and children, 334–35) in the disenchanted terms of expenditure and profit and loss. But like Alcestis, he can also be excessive in his *kharis*.[19] His entertainment of Heracles despite his mourning puts Heracles under an onerous debt: letting him leave, Heracles implies, would have been a great, but answerable, *kharis* ("Let me go, and I will give you many thanks," μέθες με καί σοι μυρίαν ἕξω χάριν, 544).[20] But by forcing Heracles to accept his hospitality, Admetus is *agan philoxenos*, an overzealous host (809), and replicates the latent agonism of Alcestis's beneficence.[21]

And yet Heracles is able to answer this gift, to transform excessive *kharis* into reciprocal *kharis*, and thus to forge a new economy between Pheres' crass materialism and Alcestis's excessive prestations.[22] Unlike Alcestis's economy, this is one based on reciprocal *kharis*, gifts that can be and are returned. Unlike Pheres', it is an elite economy, built upon symbolic, not material, profits. This ideal of a reciprocal symbolic economy is enshrined in the relationship between *xenoi*, in the mutually enriching relation between Apollo and Admetus, and in the *xenia* exchange between Heracles and Admetus. This productive bond is consecrated with the return of Alcestis, Heracles' *kharis* in return for Admetus's hospitality:

> δεῖ γάρ με σῶσαι τὴν θανοῦσαν ἀρτίως
> γυναῖκα κάς τόνδ' αὖθις ἱδρῦσαι δόμον
> Ἄλκηστιν Ἀδμήτωι θ' ὑπουργῆσαι χάριν.
>
> (840–42; cf. 1073–74, 1101)

> I must save the woman who has so recently
> died and settle Alcestis once more in this
> house, and do a favor (*kharis*) in return to
> Admetus.

Rather than stopping exchange relations, like Alcestis's gift, or disenchanting them, as Pheres did, Heracles' *kharis* resumes a cycle of reciprocity that insures amicable relations between the two men in the future: Heracles goes off at the end of the play to perform his labor, but with the promise that he will return to Admetus's hearth and hospitality (1151–52).

It is within the context of this economy of reciprocal and profitable *kharis* that we should read Admetus's *anagnōrisis*, his realization too late (ἄρτι μανθάνω, 940) that although he won his life in Apollo's bargain, what he lost was far greater. He recognizes not only the value of Alcestis's sacrifice, but, more importantly, the value of symbolic wealth, the choice of *kleos* over life:

> τί μοι ζῆν δῆτα κύδιον, φίλοι,
> κακῶς κλύοντι καὶ κακῶς πεπραγότι;
>
> (960–61)

> What advantage is there, then, in my living,
> friends, when I live with a shameful name and
> having acted shamefully?

This realization marks Admetus's break from the monetarism of Pheres and the material value he had placed on living,[23] and it embraces Alcestis's choice of *kleos* over life and all the symbolic profits that choice accorded. But this noble choice of material sacrifice for symbolic profit is one Admetus need not make. With the return of Alcestis (which frames Admetus's *anagnōrisis* with Heracles' decision at 837–60 and its execution at 1008) and the exchange with Heracles, Admetus will be allowed to have both the profit and the glory, both to live and to live with *kleos*.

The negotiations through which this new economy is forged take place literally over Alcestis's dead body. While alive, Alcestis's excessive value made all equivalence impossible: nothing could be equal to her except herself, and as a result there could be no value, no exchange, no signification, no *erōs*—in short, no symbolic order. But if her universal value creates symbolic *aporia* while she is alive, once she is dead this same excessive value becomes the standard that enables all other equations. Whereas the living Alcestis was *asēma*, beyond signification, her corpse becomes a *sēmeion* (717), a sign in the conflict between Admetus and Pheres: it is the reproach they hurl at one another (721), a touchstone around which *philia* is renegotiated and new patrilineal relations are formed. As a corpse, she is not only a sign, but *the* sign, the universal signifier of a newly forged symbolic order.

This universal equivalent is reintroduced onto the market in the play's final scene, in a deal that would have been impossible in either her economy or Pheres'. This exchange between aristocratic *xenoi* constitutes an elite economy that displays its unique affinity with the gold standard by trading only in gold. Equivalent to nothing but herself, a *kharis* that can never be equaled, Alcestis is the ultimate *agalma*, and it is as such that she is traded between Admetus and Heracles, a sign of the value of the men and the bond between them. Alcestis then becomes a *kerdos euklees*, a profit that brings with it good repute (1033), the currency in an economy at once prestigious and profitable.

It is in this transformation of Alcestis as impossible subject to Alcestis as universal signifier that we move from the Kleinian model of mourning to the Freudian and post-Freudian. The maternal body is not repaired, but is objectified as a symbol, the universal signifier that grounds the symbolic order. Kristeva marks the necessity of this movement: "What makes such a triumph over sadness [i.e., the end of the depressive position] possible is the ability of the self to identify no longer with the lost object but with a third party—father, form, schema. . . . Such an identification, which may be called phallic or symbolic, insures the subject's entrance into the universe of signs and creation."[24] The dead mother is transformed ("by means of an unbelievable symbolic effort, the advent of which one can only admire") into an eroticized other, and the dead maternal body becomes the repository for the death instinct, an image of "unrepresentable death."[25] Thus Admetus will be able, with the help of Heracles, to buy his own life, his subjectivity, his paternity, his symbolic, but only through the "vital necessity" of matricide.

FROM *physis* TO *praxis*

Alcestis's body functions as a reference point in the forging of new male relations as the play moves from the domination of the maternal presence to the symbolic order under the father. Her superlative corpse provides a gold standard not only for the play's economic transformations, but also for its gradual redefinition of aristocratic identity: it interpellates social as well as economic subjects.

As a subject, Alcestis was the supreme aristocrat.[26] The chorus's almost obsessive references to her *aristeia* praised not only her noble sacrifice, but also her noble status: she was *gennaia* ("of noble birth," 742, 993), *eugenēs* ("wellborn," 332, cf. 920), and *euklees* ("of good repute," 150, 938) as well as *aristē* ("best," "noblest," 83, 151, 152, 241, 442, 742, 899).[27] By contrast, as we have seen, Admetus became *kakistos*— "worst"—with both moral and social connotations (697). So his father accuses him of sophistry (679) and cowardice (694), ending his denunciation with a resounding condemnation in the triple repetition of *kakos:*[28]

κᾆτ᾽ ὀνειδίζεις φίλοις
τοῖς μὴ θέλουσι δρᾶν τάδ᾽, αὐτὸς ὢν κακός·
σίγα· νόμιζε δ᾽, εἰ σὺ τὴν σαυτοῦ φιλεῖς
ψυχήν, φιλεῖν ἅπαντας· εἰ δ᾽ ἡμᾶς κακῶς
ἐρεῖς, ἀκούσῃ πολλὰ κοὐ ψευδῆ κακά.[29]

(701–5)

> Do you reproach your friends for being unwilling
> to do this, when you yourself are a coward (*kakos*)?
> Silence! Consider this: if you love your life, all
> people love theirs too. If you will speak ill (*kakōs*)
> of us, you will hear yourself called many bad names
> (*kaka*), and they are true.

If in contrast to Alcestis's *aristeia* Admetus was branded as *kakos*, af-ter her death he renegotiates the bases of his identity as an aristocrat. The *agōn* with his father calls into question and ultimately rejects the tradi-tional criterion of elitism, birth.[30] Pheres is a king, wealthy and wellborn; he inherited his aristocratic status from his father (675–78), along with his property and political rule. And this is the *patrōios nomos* (paternal law) that guides his actions toward Admetus:[31]

> πολλῶν μὲν ἄρχεις, πολυπλέθρους δέ σοι γύας
> λείψω· πατρὸς γὰρ ταῦτ' ἐδεξάμην πάρα.
> τί δῆτά σ' ἠδίκηκα; τοῦ σ' ἀποστερῶ;
>
> (687–89)

> You rule over many men and I will leave you far-
> reaching lands, for I inherited them from my father.
> What injustice have I done you? What have I stolen
> from you?

This is a traditional definition of aristocracy, yet it is precisely this clean line of descent that is questioned in *Alcestis*. For while Pheres may be an aristocrat by birth, his behavior is distinctly déclassé: he is com-pletely unable to understand the symbolic assets (*kharis, kleos, agalmata*) that we have seen so consistently in these plays as the true measure of the aristocrat. Rejecting *kleos* in favor of his life (726), he in effect relin-quishes his elite status; thus Admetus condemns him as *kakos* ("base," 717, 723), *anaidēs* ("shameless," 727), *apsukhos* ("faint-hearted," 717), and *dusklēes* ("of bad repute," 725). This *agōn*, as Admetus says, is a test of their identity, both Pheres' and Admetus's, as aristocrats: "Entering into the test, you have shown who you are" (ἔδειξας εἰς ἔλεγχον ἐξελθὼν ὃς εἶ, 640). It is a test that both men fail.

Invalidated as the basis for elite status, paternity is rejected: Admetus renounces his filial bond with Pheres. He denies his paternity, since

Pheres by his actions has shown himself to be no father to him. The breach is radical:

οὐκ ἦσθ' ἄρ' ὀρθῶς τοῦδε σώματος πατήρ,
οὐδ' ἡ τεκεῖν φάσκουσα καὶ κεκλημένη
μήτηρ μ' ἔτικτε, δουλίου δ' ἀφ' αἵματος
μαστῶι γυναικὸς σῆς ὑπεβλήθην λάθραι.
ἔδειξας εἰς ἔλεγχον ἐξελθὼν ὅς εἶ,
καί μ' οὐ νομίζω παῖδα σὸν πεφυκέναι.

(636–41)

You were not truly the father of this body, nor
did she who claims to have borne me and is
called my mother really give me life, but born
from slave blood I was secretly put to your
wife's breast. Entering into the test, you have
shown who you are, and I do not consider
myself to be your son.

Admetus hyperbolically declares himself the child of a slave (638–39),[32] fatherless (born from "blood," not a father), a foundling, virtually without *genos*. Finally, he "disowns" his father:[33]

εἰ δ' ἀπειπεῖν χρῆν με κηρύκων ὕπο
τὴν σὴν πατρῶιαν ἑστίαν, ἀπεῖπον ἄν.

(737–38)

If it were possible for me to disown your
paternal hearth by proclamation, I would
disown it.

This is more than just a denial of his aristocratic identity as Pheres' son; it is a rejection of patriliny as the basis of aristocratic status and, ultimately, a rejection of *physis*, the genealogical definition of the self.

But how does Admetus redefine himself as an aristocrat, having rejected *physis*? Pheres had accepted his elite status as an asset, inherited just like property: for him, Admetus is an aristocrat because his father was. But the breach in the patriline opens the way for a new definition of aristocratic identity. The chorus sings in the Third Stasimon (just before the *agōn* with Pheres) of Admetus's kingdom and the extent of his property. It is because this "always liberal and extremely hospitable house of Admetus" (569) once welcomed Apollo that it is now so rich in flocks and lands (569–96). Admetus's wealth and aristocratic status, in this ode, are derived not from his inheritance, not from his patriline, but from his *xenia* relations. It is his hospitality to Apollo that defines him as an aristocrat, and his hospitality to Heracles reconfirms this identity, so that it becomes innate:

τὸ γὰρ εὐγενὲς
ἐκφέρεται πρὸς αἰδῶ.
ἐν τοῖς ἀγαθοῖσι δὲ πάντ᾽ ἔνε-
στιν· σοφίας ἄγαμαι.
πρὸς δ᾽ ἐμᾶι ψυχᾶι θράσος ἧσται
θεοσεβῆ φῶτα κεδνὰ πράξειν.

(600–5)

The noble birth comes out in his
respect for others. Everything is
possible for the good and noble.
I admire their wisdom, and there
sits in my heart confidence that this
god-fearing man will fare well.

This ode proposes an alternate model of aristocracy, one based not on birth but on lifestyle and actions, not on patrilineal relations but on *xenia* relations, not on *physis* but on *praxis*. Because he has behaved like an aristocrat (*philoxenos*), Admetus has shown himself *sophos* ("wise"), *eugenēs* ("wellborn"), *agathos* ("noble") and *theosebēs* ("god-fearing").

Yet this distinction between aristocracy by birth and aristocracy by action is a false one. Admetus may redefine his aristocratic identity as originating in his behavior toward his *xenoi*, but the very fact that he was in a position to enter into *xenia* relations with gods and heroes is due to his royal paternity. This redefinition of inherited prerogative as a matter of *praxis* is an attempt to mask the inherent inequality of a birth elite, to give the impression that aristocracy is simply a matter of choosing from options that are available to anyone. That is to say, it naturalizes social inequality (including inequality of birth) by misrecognizing it as a matter of ethics.

Nonetheless, the *philoxenia* ode seems to be a turning point in the chorus's relation to Admetus. Always unambiguous in its praise for Alcestis, the chorus is more wary in its appraisal of Admetus. Although joined to him by a bond of sympathy (109–11, 138–39) and *philia* (212, 369–70), the chorus reinforces the comparison that is so detrimental to Admetus's characterization, implying that he won't keep his promise to Alcestis (326–27), that his people are alienated (210–12), that he is wrong to entertain Heracles while the house is in mourning (551–52) and to conceal his suffering from his friend (561–62). Indeed, the chorus's implicit criticism is clear enough to provoke a vehement defense from Dale and from Admetus's other supporters.[34] But in this ode, the chorus seems to offer Admetus its full support, a move that coincides with its explicit recognition of his wealth, status, and power. Not only is the ode a recantation of the chorus's earlier criticism of Admetus's *xenia*, but it is also an expression of faith in his behavior in general as an aristocrat. In the final strophe, the exact actions that were condemned as folly earlier (551–52) are ascribed to respect, *aidōs*, and in particular an *aidōs* that is inherently, innately (in the root sense of the words) aristocratic: "The noble birth comes out in his respect for others" (τὸ γὰρ εὐγενὲς / ἐκφέρεται πρὸς αἰδῶ, 600–1).[35]

Thus, in this ode, aristocracy is stripped from *physis* and predicated upon action, but that action—at least in the eyes of the nonaristocratic chorus[36]—is then reattributed to *physis*, an aristocratic *physis* that behaves correctly because it is inherently *sophos* ("wise"). Here, as in *Agamemnon*, elitism is disenchanted only to be reenchanted on newly moralized terms, terms on which—ostensibly—anyone might compete. In *Agamemnon*, *agalmata* were stripped of their inherent properties, and their value (whether positive or negative) was shown to reside rather in the way they were used. The moralization of their use, though, was articulated within an elitist framework: a true aristocrat was no longer simply a possessor of fine things, but someone who knew how to manage them. Likewise in *Alcestis*, elitism is separated from noble birth and reestablished on a seemingly more democratic basis, proper behavior. But then the behavior that is to define the elite is derived from an innate elitism, an inborn sense of *aidōs* or *sōphrosunē*. In both cases, traditional criteria of excellence are reinscribed in new form. And, as in *Agamemnon*, it is around a female object that this "new" elitism is negotiated, and through her exchange, as we shall see, that it is secured.

HERACLES AND THE MIRROR OF *xenia*

The movement from *physis* to *praxis* is also a movement from the maternal cathexis (with all the problems it is imagined as creating) to a new homosocial bond. When Admetus breaks from his father and denies his *physis*, that is also a break from the maternal. By separating his birth from his nurture, Admetus denies his link to the maternal body and all the anxieties that accompany that cathexis. He breaks free of the matrix within which birth entails death, for he is no longer the son of a mother who bore him to grief and mortality (865). Thus he denies his biological mother (who is disowned along with Pheres, 637–38), but also Alcestis, who gave him life a second time.

This broken bond with Alcestis will be replaced by the bond with Heracles, at the most literal level, if the same actor played both parts. He is "the best guest-friend" (*aristos xenos*, 559) just as Alcestis was the "best wife" (*aristē gunē*, 83, 151, 241–42, 442). She saved Admetus's life by giving herself; Heracles saves Admetus's life again by giving her back. When Admetus refers to his savior at 666–68, the language leaves it unclear whether he refers to Alcestis or to Heracles:

> τέθνηκα γὰρ δὴ τοὐπὶ σ'. εἰ δ' ἄλλου τυχὼν
> σωτῆρος αὐγὰς εἰσορῶ, κείνου λέγω
> καὶ παῖδά μ' εἶναι καὶ φίλον γηροτρόφον.[37]
>
> (666–68)

> I am dead as far as you are concerned. But if
> I still see the light because I happened upon
> another savior, I consider myself *his* child and
> the dear nourisher of his old age.

If Alcestis replaces Pheres as nurturing parent, Heracles will replace them both, allowing Admetus to escape the suffocation of the maternal bond and to discover a new mode of self-definition based not on alterity but on similarity, not on *physis* but on *xenia*.

I suggested in the last chapter that Admetus's relationship with Alcestis was one of mutual definition based on difference and competition, so that her superlative *aretē* necessarily compromised his own. With Heracles, on the other hand, the relationship is based on similarity: the ratio between them is direct, rather than inverse, the *aretē* of the one reflecting, not diminishing, the *aretē* of the other. This mirroring relationship is apparent from their first mutual hailing:

ΑΔ.: χαῖρ', ὦ Διὸς παῖ Περσέως τ' ἀφ' αἵματος.
ΗΡ.: Ἄδμητε, καὶ σὺ χαῖρε, Θεσσαλῶν ἄναξ.[38]

(509–10)

ADMETUS: Greetings (*khaire*), son of Zeus and offspring of Perseus.
HERACLES: Admetus, greetings (*khaire*) to you as
well, king of Thessaly.

This mutual *kharis*, prefiguring the concrete *kharis* that will be exchanged at the end, hails Admetus as king and Heracles as a son of Zeus. The reciprocity of the *xenia* relationship declares them equals and equally aristocratic.

Likewise, the *xenia* exchange that closes the play will define the two heroes in direct proportion. If his offer of hospitality proved Admetus *gennaios*, his return of the favor will prove Heracles the same:

καὶ πέποιθ' ἄξειν ἄνω
Ἄλκηστιν, ὥστε χερσὶν ἐνθεῖναι ξένου,
ὅς μ' ἐς δόμους ἐδέξατ' οὐδ' ἀπήλασεν,
καίπερ βαρείαι συμφορᾶι πεπληγμένος,
ἔκρυπτε δ' ὢν γενναῖος, αἰδεσθεὶς ἐμέ.
τίς τοῦδε μᾶλλον Θεσσαλῶν φιλόξενος,
τίς Ἑλλάδ' οἰκῶν: τοιγὰρ οὐκ ἐρεῖ κακὸν
εὐεργετῆσαι φῶτα γενναῖος γεγώς.

(853–60)

I trust that I will be able to lead Alcestis back
up and place her in the hands of my *xenos*,
who welcomed me into his house and did not
drive me away; although he was struck by a
heavy misfortune, he hid it, like the nobleman that he is, out of respect for me. Who
in Thessaly is a better *xenos* than this man,
who in all of Greece? Therefore he will not
say that he, being born noble, did a base man
a good turn.

With the gift of Alcestis, Heracles proves himself a "noble *xenos*" (γεν-
ναῖον ξένον, 1120), wellborn and semidivine (1136); Admetus, similarly, shows himself to be master of a "noble house" (γενναίων δόμων,
1097), just and pious (δίκαιος, εὐσέβει, 1147–48),[39] and worthy of future exchanges with Heracles (1152). The final exchange is a second
test of Admetus's character (1058); this time, both he and Heracles
win, and each comes out a winner in proportion and in relation to the
other.[40]

This new relationship with Heracles will define Admetus as a subject
through a homosocial mirroring. In the Freudian developmental scheme,
the male subject moves from a cathexis with the mother to identification
with the father, from a relationship based on alterity to one based on
similarity. Lacan localizes this transition in the "mirror stage," the moment when the child first sees himself in the mirror and recognizes himself as a discrete subject, unified in himself and separate from his mother.
The primary relationship with the maternal object gives way to a relationship with himself, and difference is replaced by sameness, as the mirror reflects what appears to be him.[41] For Lacan, it is only through this
identification, and not through the chaotic alterity of the maternal bond,
that the child gains subject status within the symbolic order. The relationship between Heracles and Admetus, I am claiming, is precisely such
a mirroring; it is through this relationship that Admetus emerges from
the shadow of his lost object, breaks free of the maternal cathexis, and
lays claim to his prerogatives as a subject, a man, and a king. *Xenia* is the
mirror in which Admetus sees himself as Heracles, and the mutual recognition is a reciprocal *kharis*.

Lacan's mirror stage represents not only the birth of the subject
through his identification with the mirroring other, but also the subject's
entry into the world of language and law. In this sense, the mirror stage is
a direct precursor to the Oedipal crisis.[42] Again, identification is the basis
of identity, as the boy takes up his place within the symbolic order by
identifying with an idealized reflection of himself, the father. Renouncing
his bond with his mother, he submits to the authority of the father and
gains in return the promise that he, too, will one day wield paternal
authority. The relationship between Admetus and Heracles is Oedipal
as well as mirroring, restoring in new form the patrilineal bond that is
broken in the *agōn* between Admetus and Pheres. The conflict that destroys the latter relation (a conflict that centers on the maternal body) is

resolved in the former, as Oedipal antagonism is transformed into a shared authority (and a sharing of the maternal body) under the banner of *xenia*.

The dynamic of the *agōn* between Pheres and Admetus is purely Oedipal.[43] Pheres, by refusing to give up his life and power to his son, deprives him of Alcestis (both wife and mother, as in the Oedipal scenario); Admetus, meanwhile, would kill his father in order to take his place (alive and as king of Pherae) and the woman.[44] This antagonism—over their own lives, but also over the life of Alcestis—precludes the son's identification with the father or his submission to paternal authority, and the law of the father (*patrōios nomos*) is not merely broken, as we have seen, but rejected altogether. Throughout this failed Oedipal transition, the maternal body, which should ideally be the means of identification between father and son, the gift that seals the Oedipal pact, instead divides them: Alcestis's corpse, occupying center stage throughout this scene, physically separates the two men, reinforcing visually the breach caused by the conflict over her.

The Oedipal identification that fails between Admetus and Pheres succeeds between Heracles and Admetus. While Pheres' selfishness would deprive Admetus of his own life and of Alcestis, Heracles vouchsafes both, saving Admetus's life with the restoration of Alcestis. Heracles becomes the "savior" whom Admetus will take as his father (666–68), and to him Admetus transfers the respect and *philia* withdrawn from Pheres. Alcestis, rather than a symbol of paternal weakness and the failure of the patrilineal bond, becomes now the conduit of identification, as "father" passes her to "son" in the play's final episode.

But even here there is a latent antagonism. When Heracles asks Admetus to take Alcestis, he offers her not as a gift, but rather as a loan (1020–24). He presents her as his prize from the *agōn*, an embodiment of his own prowess. Admetus is to hold her while Heracles is off performing another labor, but he will only get to keep her if Heracles fails to return (and we have already been alerted to the danger of this mission, 479–506). The "son" would seem to get the woman only if the "father" dies. Admetus sees this transfer as an *agōn* between them and his capitulation as a victory for Heracles ("Take your victory now," νίκα νυν, 1108; cf. 1065), suggesting a repetition of the hostile Oedipal dynamic with Pheres; but Heracles assures him that they will share this victory ("But when I win you win along with me," νικῶντι μέντοι καὶ σὺ συννικᾶις ἐμοί, 1103). The antagonism implicit in the Oedipal exchange is here transformed through *xenia* into a reciprocity in which both men emerge equally victorious; the paternal bond and the homosocial *xenia* bond are conflated, and the latent antagonism of the exchange is thereby denied. The transfer then becomes a marriage—the most formal, prestigious, and positive exchange—as Heracles hands over Alcestis, veiled like a bride,[45] in a gesture reminiscent of the marriage ritual.[46]

In this Oedipal bargain, Admetus gives up the maternal object but gains adult sexuality. Within the maternal cathexis, as we saw, there could be no *erōs*. Aphrodite is introduced into the play by Heracles, who praises her in his drunken speech:

τίμα δὲ καὶ τὴν πλεῖστον ἡδίστην θεῶν
Κύπριν βροτοῖσιν· εὐμενὴς γὰρ ἡ θεός.

(790–91)

And honor Kypris, the sweetest of divinities
for mortals, for she is a kindly goddess.

The goddess, in her only mention in the play, is described as *eumenēs*, "kindly." This word, which is very rare in reference to Aphrodite,[47] appears only once before in the text, in Alcestis's apostrophe to her orphaned daughter: "nothing is kindlier than a mother" (οὐδὲν μητρὸς εὐμενέστερον, 319). Aphrodite thus replaces the mother, just as Heracles predicts that "a wife and a new marriage" will stop Admetus from longing for death (1087).[48]

Heracles reintroduces *erōs* into the house along with the mysterious woman. Although he gives the woman to Admetus as a servant (προσπολεῖν, 1024), Admetus immediately sees her in a sexual role, as he ponders where she could stay. If she is put in the men's quarters, her virginity will be in danger, for "it is not easy to rein in a man in the vigor of youth" (1053–54): the house is suddenly bursting with male sexuality. But how can he put her in Alcestis's chamber, "let her into her bed?" (1055–56). If he should, he would fear the blame of both his dead wife and his people that he had betrayed Alcestis by "falling into the sheets of another young woman" (1059). And if Admetus rejects the possibility here, this is precisely what he accepts at the end of the play. The final exchange transforms love for the dead, which is a love for the maternal, into love between husband and wife. No longer a maternal figure,

Alcestis is restored to youth (1049–50, 1059) and virginity (ἀκραιφνής, 1052); and Admetus, having eliminated (with the help of Heracles) the maternal presence and finally eradicated the overpowering ghost of Alcestis, can take to bed his virginal new bride.

With this remarriage, the patriline is restored. Throughout the play, while the line of descent between Pheres and Admetus had been broken, and that between Zeus, Apollo, and Asclepius troubled, the lineage of Heracles and Zeus was secure. Indeed, Heracles sets the return of Alcestis as a test of his legitimacy (837–39), a test that he passes. Admetus's expression of thanks to Heracles is an expression of hope for the reestablishment of positive relations between father and son: "Oh, nobly born son of mightiest Zeus, may you be blessed, and may the father who begat you protect you" (ὦ τοῦ μεγίστου Ζηνὸς εὐγενὲς τέκνον, / εὐ-δαιμονοίης, καί σ' ὁ φιτύσας πατὴρ / σώιζοι, 1136–38). The confusion in the patriline that accompanied the maternal presence on both the divine and human level is thus resolved, and the authority of Zeus, who, as Heracles' father, enables this fortuitous miracle, is reaffirmed.[49]

Along with this restoration of the patriline comes a restoration of positive relations between mortals and gods. *Alcestis* can be read as a reworking of Hesiod's myths of Prometheus and Pandora, but here the exchange of the woman becomes the occasion for reconciliation between mortal and divine, rather than a breach.[50] The play begins with a rift between mortals and gods in the death of Asclepius.[51] Before this, men and gods were less absolutely polarized, for death, the defining factor of human existence, was not final or irreversible. But with the death of Asclepius, men and gods are separated, as is represented by the condition of Admetus's mortality, which is the condition for the action of the play. In Hesiod, the deceit of Prometheus to help mortals results in a rupture between men and gods symbolized by woman, the necessity of reproduction and death. Here Alcestis, like Pandora, is a gift from god to man (1071), but one that creates positive bonds of exchange and even bridges the ontological gap between them, for she is living proof that mortality is not an inevitable barrier. Asclepius is restored in the form of Heracles, another semidivine figure who can move between earth and the underworld. Alcestis's exchange thus reverses the separation between the immortals and mortals initiated by the death of Asclepius. And once more, this restored relation is represented as a relationship of *xenia* between aristocrats, whether mortal (Admetus), semidivine (Heracles), or divine (Apollo).

Thus the homosocial bond between Admetus and Heracles resolves the problems that seem to accompany a strong maternal cathexis in this play. The patriline, shaken by the death of Asclepius, the enslavement of Apollo, and the fight between Admetus and Pheres, is restored on the divine level and reformulated on the human level as *xenia*, the potential antagonism of the Oedipal relationship transformed into the reciprocity of a bond between equals. Around this reciprocity a new economy is formed, an elite and productive economy based on the exchange of gifts and *kharis*. The elite subjects who engage in this exchange declare, in mirroring interpellation, each other's aristocracy, masculinity, and subject status.

Moreover, the benefits for Admetus and his house extend also to his people. Having bid farewell to his *xenos* and expressed hope that he will visit again (1153), Admetus issues an order to all the townsfolk and his entire tetrarchy to offer sacrifices in celebration of his good fortune (1154–56). The whole kingdom, formerly in mourning, is revitalized by the private good fortune of its king. The chorus's final lines about the unexpected ways of the gods (words vague enough to close four other Euripidean tragedies[52]) generalize Admetus's good luck further still, so that the "resolution into joy and pleasure" (εἰς χαρὰν καὶ ἡδονὴν καταστροφή) mentioned in the hypothesis is extended to the audience as well: we, too, reap the rewards of this happy association.[53]

This new bond and renewed social order are founded, of course, upon the dead body of the mother. When Heracles first appears on the scene, Admetus greets him by the rare patronymic "blood of Perseus" (509). This connection to the mythic gorgon-slayer is reiterated later in the play: when Admetus reluctantly agrees to take the woman, and to touch her with his hand as Heracles insists, he does so, as he says, "as if he were cutting off the head of the gorgon" (1118).[54] The work of Loraux and Vernant on the symbolism of the gorgon suggests that she was a daimonic figure associated with the maternal body, and specifically with her genitals.[55] Cutting off the gorgon's head, then, is both a desexing and a decapitation of the mother. As Kristeva predicted,[56] the mother is demonized as gorgon, the bearer of paralysis and death, and is slain. So with the help of Heracles, the grandson of Perseus (who has a troubled maternal bond of his own[57]), Admetus is saved from petrifaction, and the male subject, his patriline and kingdom, and the entire symbolic order are resecured, rescued at last from the mother's stony grip.

THE FINAL EXCHANGE

The end of mourning would seem to be matricide. And so we have moved from the Kleinian model of loss, ambivalence, and reparation to the Freudian model of separation from the mother and identification with the father. Like *Trachiniae* and *Agamemnon*, *Alcestis* rejects the maternal bond in favor of the paternal, as Admetus chooses Heracles over Alcestis. The maternal cathexis is imagined as deadly: Admetus is suffocated and crippled—deprived of authority, social status, masculinity, even tragic magnitude—by his superlative wife, and is destroyed by her gift of life. The solution to the problems of the maternal bond is found in a new paternal and homosocial relationship, and the seemingly ineluctable and essential geometry of the exchange of a woman is rediscovered once again as the foundation for the symbolic order and its elite male subjects.

Admetus heralds this exchange as a new beginning, and orders choruses to celebrate the inaugural moment. Many modern readers have heeded his call and joined in the celebration.[58] To be sure, we are made to hope for Alcestis's return: who would be so churlish as to take the part of Thanatos against Apollo, or to wish Alcestis dead? And yet, can we blithely accept this transfer—with its prior matricide—as a "happy" ending and leave the theater cheerful at the thought of the "better life" (1157) it inaugurates?

Judging the tone and intent of the final scene is one of the most notorious problems in scholarship on *Alcestis*. Nielson speaks for many scholars in tracing the problem back to the question of Admetus's character: "Euripides' *Alcestis* presents its audience with a curious problem. Why is a blatant coward rewarded?"[59] Those who find this ending happy must claim either that Admetus was worthy throughout (as a good *xenos*, as a decent fellow) or that he grows throughout the play and his true repentance makes him worthy of forgiveness and the return of his wife.[60] Those who find Admetus undeserving of this reward find the ending unsatisfying and ironic.[61] Admetus lets Alcestis die for him, yet is given her back; he betrays her again, yet is reunited with her; he lies to Heracles, and is forgiven and rewarded. Euripides does nothing to mitigate the gravity of each mistake: to let Alcestis die was murder (694–96); Admetus's own reluctance to accept the silent woman emphasizes the seriousness of the betrayal; Heracles criticizes Admetus openly for having deceived him (1008–17). And still Admetus is rewarded at the end with the return of Alcestis.

But the problems are broader than this. The return of Alcestis from the dead makes nonsense of the play's final ode, the hymn to Necessity (*Ananke*):[62]

τόλμα δ'· οὐ γὰρ ἀνάξεις ποτ' ἔνερθεν
κλαίων τοὺς φθιμένους ἄνω.
καὶ θεῶν σκότιοι φθίνου-
σι παῖδες ἐν θανάτωι.

(986–90)

Bear up, for you will never raise the dead
up from below with crying. Even the sons
of the gods fade, obscured in death.

So much seems to be the clear and valid moral of this play, a reaffirmation of human mortality and the necessity of death. But this moral is contradicted and Necessity gainsaid when Alcestis returns from Hades in the final episode. Heracles' *katabasis* not only transgresses the limits of the human condition but also defies the will of Zeus, completing an act that Zeus explicitly forbade with the punishment of Asclepius. Is Zeus so completely attenuated by the notoriously "atheistic" Euripides that his displeasure does not trouble this happy moment? Does the end of resolution justify the means of transgression?

These transgressions, moreover, are specifically aristocratic. The moral ultimately seems to be not that there is an impassable barrier between life and death (as the initial punishment of Asclepius might have led us to expect), but rather that for supreme aristocrats, no rules are unbreakable. In the prologue, as Apollo and Thanatos debate the economics of death, Apollo suggests that a wealthy burial makes a corpse more valuable (and therefore Thanatos should defer taking Alcestis until she is older). Thanatos replies that this law would favor the wealthy, who would be able to purchase longer lives (56–59). Apollo's plutocratic logic runs counter to the basic equivalence of bodies that the play's action depends on, and yet if there is any conclusion to be drawn in the end, it would seem to be that the wealthy can, in fact, buy longer lives.[63] Admetus does cheat death, buying back his wife not with money, but rather with *kharis*, the hidden currency of aristocratic commerce. The moral posed by the chorus in the last ode (no one can cheat death, 985–90) is supplanted by another: "Be just and honor your *xenoi*" (1147–48). Admetus admits he has been lucky (1158), but this is not the random luck that the chorus ponders in its final lines, but rather the *eutukhia* (good luck) that follows upon *eugeneia* (good birth).

The final episode is thus built upon transgression, illegality. It is also suffused with violence. This exchange, like so many we have seen throughout these three plays, is shadowed by the *agōn*.[64] The gift in this *xenia* exchange is the prize of prior *agōnes*, the struggle between Heracles and Thanatos (1140–42) and the athletic competition in which Heracles claims to have won Alcestis (1025–36). The agonism behind this transaction is repeated, although in muted mode, within it. While Heracles' gift is a return for Admetus's hospitality, it is also a gift that Admetus does not want; thus it replicates the dangerous generosity of Apollo's gift or Alcestis's. Heracles deceives Admetus, concealing the woman's identity just as Admetus had concealed the identity of the dead woman so that he could entertain Heracles.[65] Admetus is obviously reluctant to take Heracles' gift, and makes it clear that accepting her means betraying his vows to Alcestis. But Heracles forces him: "Obey," he says, "for perhaps this *kharis* might fall where you need it" (πιθοῦ· τάχ᾽ ἂν γὰρ ἐς δέον πέσοι χάρις, 1101; cf. 1109, 1115). The exchange that grounds the symbolic order here is founded on deceit, coercion, and betrayal. Like Hyllus in *Trachiniae*, Admetus must accept a woman against his will and accede blindly to a paternal authority that seems cruel and tyrannical. The *kharis* Heracles offers him is the *kharis biaios* of Agamemnon, the grace of gifts bought at too high a price.

At the center of this transgressive and violent exchange is the woman. The prize of the *agōn* and the gift of *xenia*, Alcestis unites the two, for she is a gift that Admetus is forced to accept against his will, and is won only through betrayal.[66] The agonism latent between the two men can remain latent because it is projected against her; if, as Heracles claims, both men are winners in this transaction, she is their prize, but also the loser, allowed to die and then betrayed so that Admetus might seal his bond with Heracles.

At the same time, she becomes the other to the new male self that emerges from this relationship. If the relation between Heracles and Admetus is mirroring, it is also necessarily divisive and alienating. The recognition by which Lacan's child becomes a subject is a misrecognition of the mirror image for the actual self; it is part of the labor of the symbolic to conceal this ontological and irreparable difference. But in this final scene, alienation is denied by its projection onto Alcestis, the token of the similarity of Heracles and Admetus and the guarantee of their mirroring subjectivization. The final exchange replaces Alcestis with herself, but the fit is never quite perfect. The new woman is similar in stature and appearance to Alcestis (1062–63); looking at her, Admetus seems to see his wife (1066–67), just as (at 352) he imagined he would hold her when he held her statue. The new Alcestis seems to Admetus to be a *phasma* (1127), like the dream-vision he predicted she would be (354–55). This silent woman seems like the woman he buried (1129), like the corpse of Alcestis. Finally, Admetus likens her to his living wife (1131). Yet, in this final equation, Alcestis both is and isn't restored to her original self. Although the silent woman is equated with the original Alcestis, the medium of identification, speech (1132), is also the marker of disparity, for while Alcestis is returned in bodily form, she cannot speak: she is returned just as a body.

> ΗΡ.: πρόσειπ'· ἔχεις γὰρ πᾶν ὅσονπερ ἤθελες.
> ΑΔ.: ὦ φιλτάτης γυναικὸς ὄμμα καὶ δέμας,
> ἔχω σ' ἀέλπτως, οὔποτ' ὄψεσθαι δοκῶν.
>
> (1132–34)
>
> HERACLES: Address her, for you hold all that you
> wanted.
> ADMETUS: Oh, eyes and body of my dearest wife, I
> hold you now, beyond all hope, since I thought I
> would never see you again.

Thus, the identification of Alcestis combines in this new woman all the other Alcestises of the play—living, dead, real, and fantasied—but fails to reconcile them; the original subject Alcestis is never truly recaptured, and this new Alcestis is a silent body housing an essential schism,[67] a schism that for Lacan is the tragic truth of subjectivity. This existential alienation is denied, and the male self authenticated as whole and self-present by the projection of division, alienation, lack onto Alcestis, who (by her silence, her objectification, her gender, her liminal ontological status) is set as truly other to both Heracles and Admetus. Each of them can be undivided within himself and in his relationship to the other because Alcestis is divided both within herself and from them.[68]

With Admetus's betrayal, Alcestis is replaced; she is subjected to the metonymic substitution that her own self-determined sacrifice forbade. No longer unique and heroic, Alcestis is reduced to a supplementary prize in an unknown competition: she is an added prize thrown in with the cattle (1032). So, too, in her return to the *oikos:* she died as the matriarch, but returns as a concubine.[69] More importantly, she died as a subject, but returns as a silent object. With this exchange, Alcestis is not repaired but reduced. Critics have lauded Alcestis's silence as an indication of Euripides' delicacy (what could she say?);[70] but when we contrast this woman to the woman at the opening of the play, we must recognize the violence done to Alcestis. It is not enough for her to have been killed; her corpse must be exhumed and resurrected to bear witness to the power of her murderers.

If *Alcestis* moves from tragic loss to a "happy" resolution, alongside this trajectory is another, the reduction of the woman from subject to object, from self to other, from plenitude to utter lack. We see the maternal cathexis represented as a deathlike embrace, trapping and paralyzing the male subject. We see the maternal body rejected for an Oedipal bargain sealed over her headless corpse; we see this body resurrected but not repaired, imperfectly reconstituted to stand as lacking other to the male self, traded passively as a gift in an exchange that grounds the paternal symbolic. This trajectory is all the more clear for the alternatives evoked—the possibility of reparation, of the woman as a whole object, of the maternal cathexis as a source of security and stability—and rejected.

But if these alternatives are eliminated in favor of an Oedipal homosociality all too familiar to readers of tragedy, nonetheless, these abandoned options persist, I think, and cast a pall—the shadow of the lost, now murdered, object?—over what should be an auspicious moment. Both alternatives, the failed reparation and the successful matricide, are encrypted in the mute body of Alcestis. And so Alcestis, dead, joins Iole and Iphigeneia, the tragedies' silent virgins, as a figure of radical unknowability, foreclosed subjectivity, and potential, if voiceless, resistance. Tragedy kills the woman off, only to revive her and reincorporate her, silenced and veiled, right at the heart of the new order it celebrates, the order to which she was sacrificed. She stands as a silent reproach, a reminder of the price and precariousness of the paternal symbolic, and of the alternatives that had to be eliminated that this symbolic and its subjects could stand, a reminder of the mother not mourned but murdered.

CONCLUSION
Too Intimate Commerce

*Men are affected as much as, and more than, women by a commerce
that is too intimate; they lose only their moeurs, but we
lose our moeurs and our constitution.*

—JEAN-JACQUES ROUSSEAU,
LETTER TO M. D'ALEMBERT ON THE THEATRE

In his *Letter to M. D'Alembert*, Jean-Jacques Rousseau decries the depravity of the theater. Rousseau dreams of a homogeneous, homosocial Geneva, a polity founded upon classical models and maintained through the rigorous segregation of the sexes. He sees in the theater a deadly peril to that community: not only would it introduce immorality, sloth, and higher taxes, but it would also—and this seems to be its most pernicious effect and provokes the most vitriolic rhetoric—encourage the intermingling of the sexes. This "too intimate" commerce, Rousseau imagines, would destroy social mores for both sexes, and for men, their very constitutions. Theater poses a threat of difference, particularly gender difference, that is figured as inimical and ultimately devastating to this virtuous and virile republic.

While Rousseau's Geneva is patterned explicitly after Sparta and Rome, it is in many ways similar to classical Athens. Athens, too, was a society built upon sameness: not only the democratic ideology of equality but also the very practice of radical democracy was made possible by the homogeneity of the citizen body, a homogeneity attained through the

177

rigorous marginalization and disenfranchisement of various others, such as slaves, barbarians, and women. If the Athenian democracy, like Geneva, was a homosocial polity, tragedy was (as Rousseau, with panic, intuited) a genre of difference. Structured at the most basic level by the alterity between the individual protagonist and the corporate chorus, tragedy explores otherness, be it the otherness of barbarians (for example, in Aeschylus's *Persians*), of the social underclasses (most notoriously in Euripides' dramas), or, as in the plays we have examined, of women. In its constant focus on and display of the other—in particular the female other—tragedy staged a drama of difference for its civic audience. And although that audience was constituted as a cohesive citizen body precisely through such shared rituals, at the same time, as Zeitlin has argued, tragedy allowed Athenian men to experience otherness, "playing" the other or watching it played. In the theater of Dionysus, Athenian men were invited to enter into sustained empathy with fictional women—women constructed and performed by men—in a way that must have been difficult, given the gender arrangements of Athenian daily life, with real women. The stage's commerce between the sexes—if only in this fictionalized form—was indeed intimate, but was it "too intimate"? Did it pose the threat to the *polis* that Rousseau predicted? In tragedy's representation of the female other and of the traffic between male and female, were Athenian men's *moeurs* and constitutions somehow at risk?

At first glance, tragedy would seem to prove Rousseau's fears unfounded, for although they may explore alterity, the tragedies we have seen do in the end reinscribe sameness, whether by eliminating the other entirely or by colonizing it, turning it into a fantasied reflection of the self. The tragic Zeus governs a symbolic order that, conflating Sedgwick with Irigaray, we might call "hom(m)osocial," a unified, uniform, and masculine universe. His "most noble law" (*kallistos nomos*) legislates endless prerogatives for its law-abiding citizens, but only by declaring others disenfranchised or illegitimate. This is the law of the Oedipal bond, an identification based on identity between father and son, and guaranteeing the identity of the next generation with the last. It is the law of *xenia* and of the symposium, institutions that do not merely reinforce homosocial relations in practice, but raise them to an art and a cultural and moral imperative. Zeus's law and the society of male subjects it governs are challenged—often from the direction of the woman—but ultimately resecured and reconsecrated at the end of each play: in the paternal pact between Hyllus and Heracles in *Trachiniae*, in the acquittal of Orestes at the end of the *Oresteia*, in the *xenia* bond between Heracles and Admetus that closes *Alcestis*. In each case, homosocial relations, whether between father and son, guest and host, or citizens and ruler, are shown to be productive solutions to the problems that had beset the plays, and foundations for a secure social and subjective order for the future.

This reinauguration of a kingdom of equal male subjects is possible, of course, only through the elimination of the female other. Female subjectivity is introduced, as we have seen, only to be foreclosed, a foreclosure that reaffirms the exclusionary logic that predicates the male subject upon a female object. The heroines in these plays reject that position of object, but their actions show them as weak, dangerous, or illegitimate subjects. The female other, then, becomes a site of articulation for the law of sameness, the *kallistos nomos*. Owned completely and known entirely, she is a fantasy of absolute proprietorship, of male self-presence and epistemological certainty, like the female house that in *Trachiniae* conceals a male bed, the heroine's deathbed. The divisive female subject is rejected and reduced; her murdered body becomes the token in the Oedipal identification between father and son, a fetishized gift that binds men one to another.

There are, without doubt, lessons to be learned from tragedy's elimination of difference and imposition of sameness; there is a certain value to merely identifying modes of domination, to uncovering the secret and local intricacies of power, and documenting oppression that we may better resist it. Tragedy affords (and the preceding chapters have catalogued) a depressing wealth of examples for this sort of education: critiques are raised only to be silenced; problems that are in fact structural are deflected onto the woman and thus are denied rather than addressed; female virtue is figured as dangerous, female vice is greeted as expected and oddly reassuring; any resistance is ultimately subsumed within the system it seeks to withstand. The structures of oppression are seemingly without bound, as economic, social, and subjective forces combine to form an inescapable and unassailable matrix. The subject itself (male or female) is a testament to the limitless power of the dominant ideology; hailed by it, the subject must accede to it as a condition of its birth; the subject, if it is to be a subject, is implicated in and reproduces its hegemony.

But if tragedy is a case study in domination, it also reveals the artificiality and violence of the systems it eventually reaffirms. The exchange of women, as we have seen, does reconsecrate tragedy's social world and male subjects, but only after a struggle, an exposure, a rupture. Father and son are joined, but first paternity is called into question and the cruelty of the paternal law laid bare; male subjects are guaranteed, but only after their ashes have been weighed out on the scales. The homosocial world is reinaugurated, but in the process attention is drawn to its constitutive exclusions, its brutal, often murderous denial of difference.

At the same time as it reveals the founding violence behind tragedy's (and by extension, Athens's) social order, this drama of exclusion also gives lie to its ostensibly tranquil homogeneity. The equality of the exchange—the equality conferred upon the two male givers by their opposition to the female gift—is shadowed always by the inequality and aggression of the *agōn*. The desire for the female object conceals a desire for domination, a sadism that threatens always to transform a reciprocal trade of gifts into a contest to the death. The woman, as object of both desire and violence, becomes a symbol of this inadmissible nexus. If the exchange is built upon a repressed agonism, it also participates in a larger structure of inequality, as the woman's value as a precious object naturalizes a social and economic elitism largely denied in Athenian democratic ideology. These relations of exchange—agonistic, homoerotic, elitist—are both disowned and commemorated in the fetishized commodity, woman.

The tragic exchange institutionalizes these violent exclusions and hidden aggressions even as it reveals them to critique, establishing them as the necessary, if suspect, groundwork of the social order. But if the exchange produces and reproduces an oppressive sociality, from this brutal transaction there also emerge alternatives—alongside the *kallistos nomos*, glimpses of another law and another world: when Deianira imagines herself as an exchange partner with her husband, or Iole as an active, desiring subject; when we see through Clytemnestra's eyes her "much-lamented" daughter, Iphigeneia, or await in Cassandra's revelations the secrets of the other; in Alcestis's life-giving bond with Admetus, or the possibility—left open until the very end of the play—that his grief will recall her from death; finally, in the hesitation of Hyllus to take Iole, the hesitation of Admetus to betray Alcestis, the hesitation even of Orestes when faced with his mother's breast in *Choephoroe*. These moments are fragile and fleeting, almost imperceptible. And they are always repressed, prevented from having lasting effects or from derailing the anticipated resolution. But if they cannot forestall the gentlemen's agreements that close these plays, they do subvert the closure these transactions should bring. For the alternatives eliminated do not evanesce, but rather persist in a sense of unease, a sense of misgiving, a particularly tragic suspicion that full and certain truth has eluded us at the end.

These ambiguous endings reveal the frailty of the familiar tragic world. The exchange of women creates that world and gives birth to its citizens, but in the very course of dramatizing this genealogy, tragedy disrupts its seemingly inevitable ontology. When the heroines resist their roles as gifts, they may not be able to occupy the position of valid subjects, but they do make impossible the facile and unquestioning assumption of a female object. When a woman refuses to be exchanged and exchanges men instead, she may be branded a monster, and may ultimately (by the horror she inspires) reaffirm the system she resists, but still her actions challenge the ineluctable asymmetry of the exchange. The female other is not born lacking in tragedy, but has lack imposed upon her, and in the process of that imposition is challenged the necessity or universality of female lack and therefore of male self-presence and plenitude, the obviousness with which the male is interpellated as dominant and legitimate subject. Genealogy becomes a form of critical resistance, as not just the subject but the interpellating law itself is opened to scrutiny, its cruelty revealed and its contingency, ideological investments, and temporality exposed. The result of this exposure is not an overturning of the Law or an escape from the Symbolic—it would be naive to expect that. Rather, it is the realization that *this* law, *this* symbolic, is not the only possible one, and its seeming permanence and inevitability is not a question of nature, but of politics; it is the result of hegemonic struggles and subject therefore to revision. Their necessity and normativity thus contested, perhaps men's *moeurs* and constitutions are, as Rousseau feared, "lost" in tragedy's exchanges of women.

At the same time, of course, Rousseau's dire predictions of social breakdown were not realized in Athens: watching drama did not make Athenian men effete and eviscerated, nor was the *polis* taken over by its women, newly emboldened by the example of the tragic heroines. We should not forget—as feminist activists accuse feminist scholars of doing—that real lives are at stake in ideological debates, nor fancy that these frail moments of resistance within tragedy made for practical improvements in the lives of Athenian women. And yet, perhaps there is still room for the faintest hope, because Athens did not, like Geneva, ban the theater, but rather incorporated tragedy and its various possibilities—hegemonic and subversive—right at the center of its polity. And in this admittedly circumscribed, limited, and carefully controlled space, it reintroduced difference into the midst of sameness.

For tragedy, despite its undeniable oppressions, does not banish the female other completely. Instead, it reinstalls her within its new world precisely as its other, as the subaltern that legitimates the dominant order and justifies its cruelties, but also as a site of foreclosed possibilities, excluded alternatives, and repressed subversions. This otherness is encrypted at the very heart of these plays in the person of the silent virgin, whom I have proposed as a figure for tragedy itself. The silent woman is a testament to the symbolic order grounded upon her exchange; she is a guarantor of the male subjects who exchange her, a precious object that declares their sovereign masculinity. But if she is a precious object, it is a pearl, whose lustrous beauty congeals around a prior wound. The woman's fetishization both reveals and conceals the painful process of her own production as an object and the man's as a subject. This subaltern cannot speak, as Gayatri Spivak says, but her silence is eloquent, for in it tragedy acknowledges, after its various strategies of domination, interpellation, and colonization have either failed or succeeded, an irreducible otherness, a limit to and space beyond its own symbolic, and it installs this recognition as its very condition of possibility.

In the silent woman is crystallized not only the history of her oppression, but also the words she might have spoken, words potentially other, potentially subversive. These radical potentials are handed down from father to son with the woman as tragedy reinaugurates its social world, transferring from one generation to the next not only modes of repressing alternatives, but those repressed alternatives themselves. Perhaps we should read tragedy, then, for precisely those reasons that Rousseau rejects it, for the challenges and subversions it contains, for the other it preserves rather than for the other it exiles, for its temporary disruption rather than for its ultimate reinscription of sameness, and for the opportunity it affords to think both antiquity and ourselves differently. For if Athens, fearing the effects of so intimate a commerce, was unable to realize these potentials or embrace these alternatives, perhaps we, tragedy's modern audience, can.

Notes

Introduction

1. I return to this passage in greater depth in Chapter 2.

2. E.g., Harrison 1968; Richter 1971; Pomeroy 1975, 1991; Just 1975, 1989; Schaps 1979; Gould 1980; Foley 1981a; Keuls 1985; Sealey 1990; Rabinowitz 1993: 3–9; Fantham et al. 1994.

3. Gomme (1925: 25) takes the most extreme position in denying the seclusion and oppressed status of Athenian women altogether; contra see Gould 1980; Patterson 1986; Cohen 1989. On the debate on women's status more generally, see Foley 1981a; Blok 1987; Rabinowitz 1993: 3–9; Seidensticker 1995: 151–67.

4. A full archeology of the practice of exchanging women in ancient Athens has yet to be written; it is a fascinating project and would no doubt provide valuable insights on the tragic exchanges of women. For some investigations of the topic, see Harrison 1968: ch. 1; Benveniste 1969: 239–44; MacDowell 1978: 84–98; Schaps 1979: 25–60, 74–88; Vernant 1980: 55–77; Gould 1980; Foley 1981b: 129–32; Gernet 1981c; Just 1989: 40–75; Sealey 1990: 25–36; Rabinowitz 1993: 3–9; Seaford 1994: 206–20.

5. Lévi-Strauss 1963: 59–60; 1969. Of course, exogamy and the incest taboo had been concerns of anthropology long before Lévi-Strauss, but he was the first to formulate the corollary social law of exchanging women. Strictly speaking, marriage is a "complex" structure of kinship for Lévi-Strauss; by "elementary structures" he means preferential marriage (i.e., marriages in which the choice of spouse is closely circumscribed). See 1969: xxii–xxiv. Although ancient Greek marriage systems were by and large complex, nonetheless Lévi-Strauss's observations seem relevant, and he himself allows for a large degree of overlap between the two systems (ibid.: xxiv).

6. Rubin 1975: 174. She sees three results from a social system that functions through exchange of women: "Gender [that is, the division of biological sex into

social masculinity or femininity], obligatory heterosexuality, and the constraint of female sexuality" (ibid.: 179).

7. Ibid.: 177; cf. 179, 182, 196–97. For other feminist work on exchange, see Weiner 1976; Irigaray 1977; Leacock 1981: 214–42; Hirschon 1984; Hartsock 1985: 267–301; Sedgwick 1985; Strathern 1988; Cowie 1990.

8. Rabinowitz 1993. Despite the differences indicated here, there are many similarities between Rabinowitz's study and mine, besides the basic structure of the exchange of women: an explicitly feminist slant, an interest in literary and psychoanalytic theory, a conviction of the ideological function of tragedy, and a recognition of the subordination of women to the relations between men, both in exchange and in literature. The more specific disagreements on readings of texts (in particular *Alcestis*, the only play we treat in common) will be noted as they become pertinent. I highlight our general theoretical differences here in order to position the present study within the dialogue between feminism and classics (to which Rabinowitz has made such a valuable contribution) and in the hope that it will provoke as much productive discussion and disagreement as her book has.

9. Ibid.: 12–14, 26–27, 220–22. "Women in the ancient audience may have, like many later readers, resisted this structure [i.e., gender hierarchy] proposed to them, by focusing on the power and the women's community behind the text" (14). A similar supposition informs Rabinowitz 1986.

10. Rabinowitz does acknowledge that "while . . . all of tragedy shared this desired ideological function for the dominant order, it was not monolithic, it did not equally and at all times foreclose the possibilities of resistance; tragedy may even inscribe resistance" (1993: 12). This resistance, however, is attributed to Euripides *qua* iconoclast, and not to tragedy as a genre.

11. Similar objections are raised in the review articles Zeitlin 1994; Dellner 1994; Foley 1995.

12. Podlecki 1990 gathers all the relevant citations; cf. Gould 1980: 38 n. 2; Henderson 1991; Rabinowitz 1993: 2; Goldhill 1994. Since I assume the general complicity of women in male culture, the presence of women would make little difference to my argument.

13. Elsewhere, however, Rabinowitz allows for women in the audience taking on a masculine subject position (1993: 24; cf. 1986: 178–83 and 1992: 38: "The ideal spectator identifies as if 'it' were male, regardless of whether there were women in the actual audience"). On cross-gender identification, see, e.g., Silverman 1988; Clover 1992. Equally problematic, to my mind, is Rabinowitz's predication of the domination of women upon a presumed gynephobia. This is an unfalsifiable claim (repressed fears can be found everywhere and are difficult to disprove, as readers of Freud well know) and is not always justified: there are other motives for domination than fear. Again, this assumption locates resistance as external to tragedy, in its unconscious, as it were, as a subtext that it does not recognize, cannot control, and would vehemently disown.

14. In this way, I follow more closely the position advanced by Rose (1992). Looking for a way to reconcile art as "a mere vehicle for class ideology" and art as a utopian dream (25), he adopts Fredric Jameson's model of double hermeneutic, a dialectic inherent within every work of art between a negative hermeneutic ("a rigorous, even ruthless elucidation of all the aspects of the work of art which reveal its active ideological support for the status quo," 35) and a positive hermeneutic (which "aims at restoring to consciousness those dimensions of the artwork which call into question or negate the ruling-class version of reality," 36). Rose's methodology is sophisticated and yields extremely interesting readings of the ancient texts; where I differ from him is in the extent to which he privileges great art as a site of such dialectic (I would rather see it in all ideological activity); in his focus on class (my focus being more on gender); and in his emphasis (implicit in the term "hermeneutic") on the critic as the site of articulation for the text's tensions.

15. It is for this reason that I prefer the term "hegemony" to "domination" or "oppression" in discussing tragedy's ideological operations. Whereas the latter terms imply an organized and repressive application of power, "hegemony" in the sense I use it refers to a temporary, contingent, and historically specific articulation of power relations based on the attraction or subsumption of a majority of ideological elements to the discourse of a single group. Hegemonic power is thus creative and contested ("persuasive," as Rose [1992: 30] puts it), not unitary and repressive. On hegemony, see Gramsci 1971: 12, 57–59, 180–83; Mouffe 1979; Laclau and Mouffe 1985: 134–45, 65–71; cf. Foucault 1978. For similar readings of tragedy as hegemonic, see Rose 1992; M. Griffith 1995.

16. Foucault 1978: 95: "Where there is power, there is resistance, and yet, or rather consequently, this resistance is never in a position of exteriority in relation to power. . . . Their [power relations'] existence depends on a multiplicity of points of resistance: these play the role of adversary, target, support, or handle in power relations. These points of resistance are present everywhere in the power network."

17. Laclau and Mouffe 1985; see especially 176–93. Strictly speaking, they would not allow for the hegemonic nature of power in tragedy, since they see hegemony as a political form evolving only in the industrial period; in this periodization I believe they underestimate the ambiguous and fluid nature of Athenian social relations, which, after all, had no clearly defined parties or classes.

18. Ibid.: 152–53: "Although we can affirm, with Foucault, that wherever there is power there is resistance, it must also be recognized that the forms of resistance may be extremely varied. Only in certain cases do these forms of resistance take on a political character and become struggles directed towards putting an end to relations of subordination as such."

19. It is here that I part paths with Vernant, whose important studies of tragic ambiguity have been so influential; I concur with him (and, e.g., Segal, Zeitlin,

Loraux) in seeing "tensions and ambiguity" as the generic core of tragedy, but I believe, to a greater extent I think than he, that tragedy ultimately limits the openness of the questions it asks. Gellrich 1995 offers a penetrating critique of the Paris School and its influence on the study of tragedy.

20. Althusser 1971. I argue below that this is a reductive reading of Althusser. If we take seriously his definition of ideology as "the imaginary relationship of individuals to their real conditions of existence" (1971: 32–44), then ideology should be as variegated and variable as human fantasy. For a thoughtful adaptation of this definition, see Ober 1989: 38–42. Rabinowitz (1993: 11–12) cites Althusser and Foucault to argue that tragedy generated gendered subjects, but instead of developing the deconstructive tenets inherent in their work (as I do below), she focuses on the more repressive aspects of their theories of power (in this she is not alone: see below). That she conceives of tragedy as an instrument of repression is clear from her statement that "texts can misfire" (12). Tragedy becomes an ideological gun trained at the head of its captive audience, and resistance to this ideology can be seen only as accidental, attributable either to the text's error or to Euripides' supposed radicalism.

21. See Pickard-Cambridge 1946; Goldhill 1990a.

22. Seaford 1981; Segal 1982: 158–214; Vernant and Vidal-Naquet 1988: 161–79; Winkler 1990a and 1990b: 39–40; Goldhill 1990a; Zeitlin 1990: 66; Heiden 1993; M. Griffith 1995.

23. When I speak of tragedy's material conditions, what I am speaking of is tragedy's representation of Athenian social relations; thus there is already an ideological filter, and to seek the material conditions external to tragedy is to be caught in an infinite regression that prevents our ever reaching a non- or pre-ideological stratum.

24. Thus while some chapters focus more explicitly on economic issues (especially the *Agamemnon* chapters) and others on psychoanalytic issues (the *Alcestis* chapters), in no section will one approach be exclusive. Foley (1981b: 139–40) calls for such an approach toward the role of women in tragedy. DuBois's (1988) study of the ancient representation of the female body combines materialism and psychoanalysis to excellent effect (see especially 1988: 7–36).

25. These are not, of course, the only two possible roads to travel; another profitable route would be semiotics, as Lévi-Strauss suggests when he calls the woman in exchange a sign to be communicated (1969: 492–96). For this approach to the exchange of women, see Cowie 1990; Goux 1990; Rabinowitz 1993: 16–17.

26. On the debate between materialism and psychoanalysis, see P. Smith 1988: ch. 1; for various attempts to synthesize the two, see, e.g., Deleuze and Guattari 1983; Žižek 1989; Goux 1990; Silverman 1992: 15–51.

27. This is not to deny that there are feminist theorists whose work falls substantially outside of other formal theoretical models; although writers like Julia

Kristeva or Luce Irigaray are influenced both by psychoanalysis and by semiotics or materialism (respectively), their work falls strictly into neither category. I acknowledge such explicitly feminist models as I use them.

28. On the problems of a feminist Marxism, see Rubin 1975: 160–64; Kuhn and Wolpe 1978; J. West 1978; Sedgwick 1985: 11–15; M. Barrett 1988; Strathern 1988: 23; C. A. MacKinnon 1989: 3–12; Rose 1992: 14 n. 26. On the position of women in a Marxist schema of the ancient Greek class structure, see de Ste. Croix 1981: 98–111.

29. See, for example, Mitchell 1975; Rubin 1975: 184–204; Chodorow 1978 and 1989; and the helpful introductory essays by Mitchell and Rose to Lacan 1982.

30. Cf. Cowie 1990; she offers a similar constructivist corrective to Lévi-Strauss, whose theory of exchange, she notes, assumes the gender inequality it claims to explain (121). Thus I situate myself firmly in the "constructivist" camp of feminism: see Butler 1990: 1–6; 1993: 4–12; Cowie 1990: 113–33; Mouffe 1993: 74–88.

31. On the tension between hierarchy and equality in Athens, see, e.g., Connor 1971; Donlan 1980: ch. 4; Vernant 1980: 11–27; de Ste. Croix 1981: 31–80; Finley 1973: 35–61, 1981: 62–94; J. K. Davies 1981; Ober 1989. On the mediation of this tension in tragedy, see Vernant and Vidal-Naquet 1988: 22–28, 33–34; Ober and Strauss 1990; M. Griffith 1995.

32. By a member of the "elite" ("aristocrat," "noble") I mean a person distinguished, whether by lineage, wealth, political power, or prestige, from the average Athenian citizen. Though to a large extent these different advantages overlapped still in the fifth century (see Connor 1971: 3–34; Finley 1973: 45–61; Donlan 1980: ch. 4; J. K. Davies 1981; de Ste. Croix 1981: 81–98; Gernet 1981b; Ober 1989: 11–17), it is not desirable to be more specific, because it is precisely the composition of the elite as a class that is under negotiation in tragedy's exchanges. When I refer to the elite as a "class," I mean this in a generic sense (as an identifiable but flexible group), not in the strictly Marxian usage.

33. This elitism was mediated (and is obscured) in part by the "democratization" of traditionally aristocratic values such as *eugeneia* ("nobility of birth") and *kalokagathia* ("nobility and goodness") throughout the fifth century (Ober 1989: 259–70; cf. Donlan 1980; Gernet 1981b). This diffusion, however, should not blind us to the fact that although Pericles might imply that the whole *dēmos* is "noble" (*gennaios*, Thuc. 2.40–41), all Athenians knew that in the strictest sense of the word, some were more noble than others. As Bourdieu has argued (1984), this downward diffusion of aristocratic values serves to support rather than to undermine elitism.

34. Ober 1989: 35–52; Ober and Strauss 1990; M. Griffith 1995, esp. 107–24. Of course, such mediation was not always successful, and these tensions

erupted in violence several times over the course of the fifth century; see de Ste. Croix 1981: ch. 5.

35. Vernant and Vidal-Naquet 1988: 33–34. Vernant sees this structural tension between the corporate *dēmos* and the individual aristocratic hero as an essentially diachronic problem (that is, a tension within tragedy between a civic present and a heroic past), rather than as a negotiation of a synchronic conflict between mass and elite (as, e.g., Ober and Strauss [1990] do). Thomson (1966: 165–72) and Rose (1992: 190) propose a similar dialectic between mass (chorus) and elite (protagonist) in their Marxian-oriented discussions of the evolution of tragedy.

36. Bourdieu 1977: 10–15; Kurke 1991: 94.

37. Bourdieu 1977: 14; Herman 1987: 39; Mauss [1950] 1990: 35–42.

38. On conflict and consensus as two organizing poles of Athenian society and politics, see Gouldner 1965: 13–15, 44–55; Ober and Strauss 1990: 241; Seaford 1994: 7.

39. Sedgwick 1985; cf. Irigaray 1977: 192.

40. E.g., Finley 1973; Gernet 1981a; Morris 1986; Gabrielsen 1986; Herman 1987; Kurke 1991.

41. Mauss [1950] 1990; Gernet 1981a; Kurke 1991: 96–97.

42. It should be noted that the distinction I am drawing between gifts and commodities is a synchronic and ideological split between two coexisting systems, and not the diachronic, historical development from an exchange to a market economy. I return to this issue in Chapter 4.

43. I concentrate on the first part of Volume 1 of *Capital*, where the commodity is defined and its behavior examined. For a fuller discussion of the theory and its application to the ancient economy, see Chapter 4.

44. Bourdieu 1977: 171–97; 1984; 1990a: 112–34.

45. Lévi-Strauss 1969: 63–65; cf. Finley 1955; Vernant 1980: 60; Redfield 1982; Kurke 1991: 116–18.

46. M. Griffith 1995: esp. 75, 107–24; cf. Bassi forthcoming. For a similar dynamic in Xenophon, see Johnstone 1994.

47. On "bad faith" and the aristocratic economy, see Bourdieu 1977: 173; 1990a: 114–15.

48. As Laclau and Mouffe (1985) argue, such articulations of one set of relations to another are not necessary and permanent, for all that they may be remarkably persistent. Rather, they are the temporary and contingent effects of ongoing hegemonic struggle. On modern scholarship's nostalgia for the elite male subject of Greek tragedy and its complicity in his production, see Bassi forthcoming.

49. Indeed, in formulating his exchange theory of value, Marx posits a "mirror stage" for commodities that eerily anticipates Lacan. In a footnote, Marx (1906: 61 and note) points out the psychology implied by the fact that the value

of commodity A is reflected in the body of commodity B: "In a sort of way, it is with man as with commodities. Since he comes into the world neither with a looking glass in his hand, nor as a Fichtian philosopher, to whom 'I am I' is sufficient, man first sees and recognises himself in other men. Peter only establishes his own identity as a man by first comparing himself with Paul as being of like kind. And thereby Paul, just as he stands in his Pauline personality, becomes to Peter the type of the genus homo." On the parallelism between Marx's basic equivalent form of value and Lacan's mirror stage, see Goux 1990: 13–14.

50. That is not to say that men are never exchanged in tragedy (Heracles himself is sold into slavery, as we shall see in Chapter 1) or in real life. The point is rather that men are exchanged only exceptionally and under very extreme circumstances, whereas women are exchanged as a rule. Cf. Rubin 1975: 175–76.

51. Lévi-Strauss 1969: 496 (the penultimate page of *The Elementary Structures of Kinship*). He goes on to speculate that the role of woman as both "sign" and "value" explains "why the relations between the sexes have preserved that affective richness, ardour and mystery which doubtless originally permeated the entire universe of human communications." Rubin's critique is by now as famous as the original claim: "This is an extraordinary statement. Why is he not, at this point, denouncing what kinship systems do to women, instead of presenting one of the greatest rip-offs of all time as the root of romance?" (1975: 201; quoted in Sedgwick 1985: 50 and n. 3).

52. Vernant 1988; the essay appeared in an earlier form in *Belfagor* 6 (1979): 636–42.

53. Vernant 1988: 240. Cf. Zeitlin 1990. In taking up Vernant's suggestion that tragedy generated a tragic subject, I am not arguing that tragedy "invented" the subject. For various attempts to find the origins of the modern subject, see Barker 1984; Fineman 1986.

54. J. Jones [1962] 1980. Starting from a radical re-reading of Aristotle's *Poetics*, Jones argues that "we have imported the tragic hero into the *Poetics*, where the concept has no place" (13). Jones's caveats are important ones, as we would not want simply to assume a unitary, transhistorical notion of or fascination with the subject—and much less, an actual transhistorical, unitary subject. Nevertheless, I believe it is possible to talk about the subject in tragedy without reverting immediately to the Romantic notion of the tragic hero. Even if character is, as Aristotle claims, merely "moral coloring" for action, the colors chosen are still an important part of the play (as Jones admits, [1962] 1980: 31). On the debate over character in tragedy, see further Wilamowitz-Moellendorf 1917; Snell 1953: 90–112 (with the critique by Halliwell [1990: 37–42]); Lloyd-Jones 1972; Easterling 1973, 1977; Gould 1978; Vernant and Vidal-Naquet 1988: 29–38; Vernant 1988; Pelling 1990.

55. Althusser 1971: 48–49. Althusser explains that the self that answers the interpellation is already a subject-in-ideology: because children are born into

ideology (so that, for example, their gender, male or female, is already expected before their birth), "individuals are always-already subjects." Thus he allows us to answer those modern theories that draw a distinction between the dramatic mask or type and the "genuine self." See, e.g., Vickers 1973; Gill 1990: 2–8, where "character" (by which Gill means moral agency) is distinguished from "personality" (which is associated with the "real" or "authentic" self); Halliwell 1990: 33: "There remains . . . an irreducibly personal element of responsibility." This appeal to a "commonsense" self also informs the earlier works of Easterling on tragic character (1973, 1977; but see her more current thoughts on the issue, 1990: 89).

56. Deleuze and Guattari take the logic furthest: they dissolve all boundaries between the internal and the material in their concept of "desiring-machines," which simultaneously produce material reality and psychic fantasy (1983: 22–35).

57. When translated from the real world to the world inside the play, this continuum between the material and the psychological allows us to see the total implication of the character within the symbolic structures of the play. Thus to say, as for example J. Jones does ([1962] 1980: 72–137), that a tragic character is constituted wholly within the *oikos* and the *polis*, circumscribed by fate and the gods, and inseparable from the language, imagery, and conventions of the play is not to deny that there is a subject, but rather is to locate the subject in the relationship of the individual to these defining forces. Cf. Gould 1978; Goldhill 1990b: 105–11.

58. The Althusserian subject answers point for point Jones's objections. The continuum between society and the individual deprives the post-Romantic subject of his majestic individuality and freedom, thus automatically undermining the primacy of the "hero" to which Jones objects. Further, Althusser's subject is manifested in practice, so for him, as for Jones and Aristotle, *praxis* is the only valid category through which subjectivity can be examined. Finally, though Jones may be right that the psychological individual was not in itself interesting to tragedy, there can be no doubt that the individual in society was, and this latter is what Althusser's subject is.

59. P. Smith (1988: 17–21) rejects Althusser's theory of the subject largely on these grounds. Rose (1992: 30–33) seconds Smith's criticism, arguing that Althusser offers "too pessimistic a picture of the process of ideological reproduction. . . . The status quo seems to have all the advantages in its ceaseless and relentless brainwashing of passive subjects, whom Althusser presents precisely as 'subjected' to reigning hegemonic ideas" (ibid.: 33).

60. On the other hand, Althusser's essay could also be read as constructing a more heterogeneous subject; note, for example, the very different interpellations imagined at 1971: 46 (a friend at the door), 46–47 (Althusser as author hailing the reader), 48 (a policeman), 50 (parents hailing a newborn infant), and 51ff.

(God hailing Peter). Althusser does not make it clear whether these different hailings could conceivably all call the same individual or whether they must call different individuals. On the theoretical advantages of a heterogeneous subject, see Mouffe 1993: 77.

61. A heterogeneous subject also means that we need not (indeed, should not) require absolute psychological coherence from tragic characters. Thus we avoid one of the worst traps facing scholarship on the tragic subject, the logic that cannot accept psychological complexity without also having psychological consistency.

62. Butler 1993: 120–24; cf. Laclau and Mouffe 1985: 178–81; Silverman 1992: 15–51.

63. Althusser's essay "Freud and Lacan" (1971: 147–71) discusses psychoanalysis (primarily Lacan's) specifically as a scientific and theoretical methodology, but does not clarify the debt he owes to Lacan in his theories of the subject. On the relationship between Althusser and Lacan, see P. Smith 1988: 18–23; Žižek 1989; Silverman 1992: 29–34.

64. Lacan 1977: 1–7. Strictly speaking, the mirror stage is assigned to the presymbolic realm of the "imaginary"; Lacan maintains that the mirror is not ideological, but, as Silverman (1983: 160) shows, cultural determinants can be seen at work in the scene and, furthermore, the mirror stage takes on significance only in retrospect, from the standpoint of the symbolic and in the light of the Oedipal complex.

65. Lacan 1988: 261–62; 1977: 67. Although Lacan is at pains to distinguish this abstract paternal authority from the biological father, this distinction seems somewhat disingenuous given his emphasis on the power and determination of language. A similar blurring of the symbolic and the literal confuses the phallus (the universal signifier) and the penis (the anatomical organ). In both cases, the Lacanian term denotes not only the authority of the male subject within the symbolic, but also his alienation from absolute power in the register of the "real." See Lacan 1977: 281–91; Rose in Lacan 1982: 39–41; Silverman 1983: 182–87; 1992: 42–48.

66. Rubin 1975: 193.

67. Lacan distinguishes between "other" (an object or person not fully separate from the subject, the "objet petit autre") and "Other" (a fantasied site of certainty and meaning, associated with God, language, and the phallus). The woman can occupy either of these two positions. See 1977: 139–40, 304–5; 1988: 235–47. I here use the lowercase form and employ it in a generic, non-Lacanian sense, meaning that which is not the self.

68. The exchange of women is also analogous for Lacan to the exchange of signs, language, which is virtually synonymous with the symbolic: 1977: 66; 1988: 259–64.

69. "The fact that the woman is thus bound up in an order of exchange in

which she is object is really what accounts for the fundamentally conflictual character, I wouldn't say without remedy, of her position—the symbolic order literally subdues her, transcends her" (Lacan 1988: 262).

70. Silverman 1992: 46; cf. 1988: 13–22; Rose in Lacan 1982: 48–53.

71. By "lacking" and "castrated" I do not mean lacking only the penis, but the phallus as well. As Zeitlin points out (1994: 547; cf. duBois 1988; Winkler 1990b: 35), female sexuality was not figured as lack in antiquity so much as difference (the uterus, not the vagina, contrasted to the penis). The significant lack in Lacan's model is not anatomical but symbolic; this is an important difference because symbolic characteristics, as we shall see, are constructed and can be resisted and reconfigured, while anatomy generally cannot.

72. Keuls 1985 offers an exhaustive survey.

73. Strauss 1993: esp. 61–99.

74. See Gould 1980: 46; Patterson 1986; Loraux 1993.

75. Hall 1989; Halperin 1990a; Cartledge 1993.

76. Zeitlin 1990 first appeared (in slightly different form) in *Representations* 11 (1985): 63–94, and has now been reprinted in Zeitlin 1996: 341–74. Heiden (1993) imagines the humbling experience of "playing the other" (and acting in general) in Athens and suggests that it helped foster a flexible, self-critical, and empathetic civic body.

77. Zeitlin formulates it somewhat differently, emphasizing more than I the ultimate inclusion of the female within the male, but I believe that we agree in our conclusions: "In the end, tragedy arrives at closures that generally reassert the male, often paternal, structures of authority, but before that the work of the drama is to open up the masculine view of the universe. It typically does so . . . through energizing the theatrical resources of the female" (1990: 86–87). Loraux (1987: 60) comes to similar conclusions in her discussion of tragic women's deaths.

78. For Lacan, the primary alienation of the subject is a function of his situation within signification—language, but also such structures as kinship. The exchange of women, then, even as it secures the male subject within the symbolic, also represents his alienation from his real drives, which are circumscribed by the incest taboo (1977: 65–67; 1988: 262). Ironically, a genuine and undivided male self would only be possible in a world in which women were not circulated.

79. See Rose in Lacan 1982: 48–52.

80. Halperin 1990a: 11.

81. Of course, Lacan himself would be the first to emphasize the artificial nature of gender, which is merely the symbolic representation of the "real" of sex. The phallus that distinguishes and hierarchizes men and women is a signifier with no fixed or stable referent. See Lacan 1977: 151; Rose in Lacan 1982: 41–42.

82. Kristeva 1980: 237–70; Silverman (1988: 101–26) psychoanalyzes Kristeva's fantasy. The idea of woman's "ecstasy," her existence outside of the sym-

bolic, is implicit in Lacan's association of women not only with the fact of loss but also with what has been lost, *jouissance*, a primary relationship to the self and the body, the "real."

CHAPTER I

1. DuBois (1982: 95–106; cf. 1979) emphasizes the importance of the exchange of women in establishing civilization in *Trachiniae*. See, too, Rabinowitz 1992: 46.

2. The text of *Trachiniae* adopted throughout is Lloyd-Jones and Wilson's (1990b). The translations throughout are my own.

3. There is much debate on the issue of whether or not Iole is present during this transaction, and the answer has a bearing upon the much-disputed question of the speaker and addressee of the last lines of the play, to which I shall return at the end of Chapter 3. See Webster 1936b: 175; Easterling 1982 ad 1275; 1981: 70–71. M. Davies (1991), Jebb (1892), and Kamerbeek (1959) agree that Iole is not present at the end of the play.

4. Cf. Foley 1982b: 2: "It is hard to read the conclusion of the play as anything but an insensitive assertion of patriarchal authority by Heracles." For more optimistic readings of the ending, see, e.g., Segal 1975: 50; 1977: 135, 152; 1981: 103; Rehm 1994: 80–83 and n. 31. Reactions to this scene and to Heracles' behavior toward Iole and Hyllus have polarized critics; cf. note 30 below. My intention is neither to vindicate Heracles nor to condemn him, but rather to analyze how (and why) the text allows for both impulses.

5. Loraux 1990: 23–24; cf. Hoey 1972: 143; Nagy 1979: 318; contra, Fuqua 1980: 15–16.

6. Heracles is not the king of Trachis, but this fact is largely elided in the play. Although Deianira points out their position as strangers and guests in the land (39), Cyex, the king of Trachis, is mentioned only obliquely as their host (ξένῳ παρ' ἀνδρὶ ναίομεν, 40). The chorus of Trachinian women accords to Deianira and Heracles all the respect usual from a chorus of natives toward the royal protagonists, referring to Heracles as king at his entrance (1045).

7. Musurillo (1967: 68) sees Heracles in this *agōn* as "a symbol of all men's fantasy of wish-fulfillment"; likewise Bowra 1944: 132; Gardiner 1987: 130.

8. For a detailed and subtle reading of the two narratives, see Heiden 1989: 53–64, 67–71. Ormand (in a work in progress) examines the interplay of the homosocial and heterosexual in *Trachiniae*'s two versions of the sack of Oechalia.

9. Unfortunately, the text is corrupt at 267–68 and does not allow certain reading. It does seem clear, however, that Eurytus is taunting Heracles with his servitude to Eurystheus (so Jebb [1892], Kamerbeek [1959], and schol. ad loc.), and thus insulting him personally, as well as transgressing the rules of *xenia*.

10. Plut. *Thes.* 6.6; cf. Loraux 1990: 36. Sophocles does not include these details, but does emphasize Heracles' ignominious sale with an abundance of economic terms (ἐμποληθείς, 250; πραθείς, 252; πρατόν, 276; cf. πράκτωρ, 251, which beyond its more usual meaning ["accomplisher"] can also refer to a bailiff who executes a judgment for debt [LSJ II.1]).

11. Note the personal involvement of Zeus in Heracles' affairs. With him as the "executor" (πράκτωρ, 251) of Heracles' punishment, the whole incident can be seen as a stage in Zeus's grooming of his son for apotheosis.

12. Loraux 1990: 39. Diodorus puts an even more positive spin on Heracles' stay with Omphale. Not only did Heracles willingly submit to being sold (4.31.5)—and for more than a fair purchase price—but he also cleared Lydia of criminals and bandits while he was there, earning his freedom and an offer of marriage from Omphale (4.31.8).

13. Heiden (1989: 60–61) also notes that Lichas mitigates Heracles' condemnation by delaying the word δόλῳ ("deceit," 277), by specifying that Iphitus was distracted (272–73, and thus his failure to see Heracles does not necessarily imply treachery), and "by making the description itself so elliptical and confusing that no clear picture of the event can be drawn from it" (ibid.: 60).

14. Ἔρως δέ νιν / μόνος θεῶν θέλξειεν αἰχμάσαι τάδε ("Eros alone of the gods seduced him into this attack," 354–55). This seems to be the version told in the (now lost) epic *Capture of Oechalia*; see especially Eust. 330.41, which speaks of Iole, "for whose sake Heracles sacked Oechalia" (Ἰόλης δι' ἣν ἐπόρθησεν Ἡρακλῆς τὴν Οἰχαλίαν).

15. On Lichas's lies, see Heiden 1981 and 1989: 53–77; Halleran 1986. Although Lichas defends his master and denies his complicity in these lies, Heracles' own deceit is virtually inseparable from Lichas's in this narrative. Thus the secrecy with which Heracles introduces Iole into his house (360) will repeat the original stealth against Iphitus for which Heracles was sold to Omphale.

16. Cf. note above. In the light of this indenture, Heracles' whole heroic career becomes a series of servitudes (34–35, 70, 267–68, 829–30), a point to which I return in Chapter 2. Note, however, that Sophocles draws a rigorous distinction between *latris* ("lackey," "servant," the word used throughout for Heracles) and *doulos* ("slave," used of characters like the Nurse and the captive girls). The former refers to debt slavery, which was circumstantial and temporary; the latter is more usually chattel slavery, a state into which one was born and from which it was difficult to escape, a condition inherent to one's nature, according to Aristotle (*Pol.* 1.2.7; cf. Finley 1981: 150–51; Garlan 1988: 19–22). The distinction is important, because it differentiates the exchange of Heracles, which is marked as highly anomalous, from the exchanges of women, who are defined as exchangeable by nature. On this difference, see Rubin 1975: 175–76.

17. For the parallels, see Musurillo 1967: 71ff.; Ryzman 1993: 76.

18. So Plutarch (*Per.* 24.9) links Deianira with Omphale and Hera (as paral-

lels to Aspasia), presumably as women who controlled their men (and Heracles in particular). See Faraone 1994: 126.

19. For the parallels and discussion, see below, Chapter 3.

20. Loraux 1990: 33–40. Although Heracles is often shown in a *peplos*, the robe in which he is killed is generally given as a *khitōn*, a man's garment (D.S. 4.38.1–2; Apollod. 2.7.7). In *Trachiniae*, the poisoned robe is repeatedly referred to as a *peplos* (602, 613, 674, 758, 774), and the feminine associations of the gown are emphasized, for example, at 602 (ταναυφῆ πέπλον, "a floor-length gown") and at 764 (by Heracles' delight in the "ornament and gown," κόσμῳ . . . καὶ στολῇ). The gown is also at times referred to as a *khitōn* (580, 612, 769). A scholiast's disapproval underlines the oddity: οὐκ εὖ δὲ τὸν ἀν-δρεῖον χιτῶνα πέπλον φησί ("Sophocles sloppily calls a man's *khitōn* a *peplos*," ad 602).

21. The "feminine" nature of death by the robe is even more pointed in contrast to Deianira's masculine death by the "double-edged sword" (ἀμφιπλῆγι φασγάνῳ, 930). Whereas the sword is the death instrument of the hero in battle, women in tragedy most commonly die by hanging (Loraux 1987). Faraone (1994: 123) adduces further the emasculating effects associated with love potions both in Greek tradition in general and in this scene in particular.

22. Halperin 1990a: 11–12.

23. Reading μηδέν pronominally rather than adverbially. Heracles plans to redeem this nothingness by punishing Deianira (1107–11), reclaiming his status through a display of physical prowess (χειρώσομαι, 1109, picks up the apostrophe to his formerly heroic χέρες at 1089). In this way he hopes to determine the significance of Deianira's death, making it bespeak his strength (1110–11).

24. Zeitlin 1990: 72, 74; she takes *Trachiniae* as her test case for this argument. Loraux (1990: 29) discusses agony as a man's "means of experiencing femininity in his body." Cf. Loraux 1981: 41–66 (now translated in Loraux 1995: 23–42), and on Sophocles' Heracles, particularly 60–64: "Héraklès est travaillé par une souffrance qui n'a d'égale que celle des femmes en couches" (62).

25. The juxtaposition of παρθένος ("maiden," 1071) and βέβρυχα ("bellowed," 1072) is striking: βέβρυχα is the epic vocalization of heroes in pain (e.g., *Il.* 13.393, 16.486). In this play the word is used of the death cries of both Heracles and Deianira (at 805 and 904); cf. Loraux 1981: 61 n. 135.

26. Heiden (1989: 140) tentatively suggests that Heracles' genitals have been mutilated by the disease and thus his self-exposure offers proof of his feminization. We do not have to take Heracles' self-proclaimed ruination so literally in order to see its effect on Heracles' masculine identity: it is the phallus he has lost, not necessarily the penis (as Heiden acknowledges, ibid.).

27. Seaford 1986: 57; Rehm 1994: 79. For the metaphor, see Aes. *Ag.* 1178–79, 690–91; Eur. *IT* 372. See Carson 1990: 160–64 and Rehm 1994: 141–42 on the *anakaluptēria* in the marriage ceremony: for the bride, the unveiling is an

extremely perilous moment, exposing her for the first time to the penetrative public gaze; cf. Redfield 1982: 192. Ormand (1993) also notes the nuptial imagery in lines 1053–55, where the robe is said to "live with the passages of his lungs"; cf. Pozzi 1994.

28. The connection between weakness, femininity, and servility is not accidental. Women and slaves were considered analogous in their permeability: women could be penetrated; slaves could be beaten. So here, Heracles becomes like a woman and a slave when he is permeated by the disease (605, 767; see Pozzi 1994: 583–84). On the homology between women and slaves, see Arist. *Pol.* 1.1–7; Vidal-Naquet 1981.

29. Notice that the command (προσθοῦ δάμαρτα, "make her your wife," 1224) is immediately surrounded by the paternal oath (πατρῴων ὁρκίων, 1223) and an injunction against disobedience to the father (μηδ᾽ ἀπιστήσῃς πατρί, 1224). Ryzman (1993) explores the tension between Heracles' traditional representation as champion of *nomos* and his transgressions of *nomos* in *Trachiniae*. Her debate over whether Heracles acts within *nomos* or beyond it becomes moot when we realize that the *nomos* itself can be cruel and self-interested.

30. Some critics believe that this final exchange also redeems Heracles as a character, showing his concern for Hyllus or even for Iole. Bowra (1944: 192–93), for example, sees in this act "an unsuspected trait of tenderness and justice." Norwood (1920: 156–57) sees the exchange as Heracles' belated recognition of his true attachment to Deianira. Cf. Sorum 1978: 70–71; Easterling 1981: 68–69. Others take an opposite view: Kirkwood (1941: 203), for example, writes of Heracles' "callous and selfish spirit"; cf. Webster 1936b: 179 ("cruelty . . . coupled with true heroism"); Musurillo 1967: 64 ("brutal"); Wender 1974: 14 ("utterly self-absorbed, violent and vengeful"); Winnington-Ingram 1980: 85 ("outrageous and offensive"). J. K. MacKinnon (1971: 41) sensibly discards both interpretations, showing that if this scene characterizes Heracles at all, it is as a Homeric hero concerned primarily with maintaining his status and property; cf. Rehm 1994: 80–81. On the critical urge to justify Heracles, see Kirkwood 1941: 204–5.

31. Winkler 1990a. One need not accept Winkler's entire theory of the City Dionysia as an initiatory ritual in order to see that many tragedies do stage, among other things, the (successful or unsuccessful) social education of a young man.

32. In Hyllus's first scene, the root *klu-* occurs three times in five lines (68, 71, 72). The model for the young hero's reclamation of his father's *kleos* is Telemachus's quest in the *Odyssey*; see Kurke 1991: 18 and 15–61.

33. There is a clustering of aristocratic diction in Hyllus's first scene: Deianira's injunctions to Hyllus are expressed as part of an aristocratic ethics of shame (τὸ μὴ πυθέσθαι ποῦ 'στιν αἰσχύνην φέρειν. "to not know where he is brings shame," 66) which is especially marked, coming as it does just after the discourse about slavery and freedom between Deianira and the Nurse. This sug-

gests that social prerogative will be an essential component of Hyllus's character, as it is of Heracles'.

34. The separation from and rejection of the mother is a fixed element in ephebic mythology: see P. R. Slater 1968: esp. 63–70, 161–92. Heracles himself, with his ambivalent relation to his stepmother Hera, is a prime example (ibid.: 337–88), but one may also think of Orestes, Perseus, Pentheus, Achilles, and Telemachus.

35. She greets him at 61, "Oh child, oh son" (ὦ τέκνον, ὦ παῖ; cf. 68, 76, 82, 92); he addresses her as *mēter* ("mother") three times in their first dialogue (64, 78, 86). Easterling (1982) at 67 identifies "a warm relationship between mother and son."

36. "Give into my hands your mother, taking her from the house yourself with your own hands, so that I may know truly which you grieve more to see: my outraged form or hers, abused justly" (1066–69). The impossibility for Hyllus of this choice between pity for his father and for his mother is implied even within Heracles' command: line 1069 does not make it clear whether the pitiful form (*eidos*) is Heracles' or Deianira's.

37. Hyllus uses every discursive attack he can muster against her. His speech deploys the aristocratic discourse of praise and blame, honor and shame (773, 811), the juridical discourse of guilt and innocence (808, cf. 814), the religious discourse of right and wrong (the triple repetition of *themis*, 809–10), and the misogynist discourse of female deceit (773–74). I have argued elsewhere in reference to Telemachus and Penelope that a contest over words with his mother is one of the first tests of the ephebe's emerging autonomy and authority (Wohl 1993: 38–39). Here, Hyllus's victory is definitive, as Deianira leaves the stage in silence without answering his charges.

38. Adkins 1960: 156–68; Donlan 1980: 4; Ober 1989: 259–61.

39. I return to the parallels between Deianira and Iole in the next chapter. Whether Iole is intended as Hyllus's wife or his mistress is not particularly important for my argument. J. K. MacKinnon (1971) has noted that tragedy in general blurs the distinction between legal marriage and concubinage, and in this scene, as he shows, all the language referring to Iole could be taken either way (he nonetheless argues that Heracles meant Iole to be Hyllus's concubine). This ambiguity, I think, serves to legitimize a violent and lawless exchange of a woman: Heracles was explicitly denied Iole as a legitimate wife and for that reason stole her as his "secret bedmate" (359–60). This final exchange, though less violent, is also illegitimate by reason of its incestuous, or at the very least endogamous, nature; by confusing wife with concubine, the text can, on the one hand, neutralize the incestuous overtones (as there seems to have been no stigma against father and son sharing a concubine: see J. K. MacKinnon 1971: 39; contra Heiden 1989: 154), and, on the other hand, position Iole as a potential wife and worthy mother of the Heracleidae.

40. Pherecydes (*FGrH* 3.82a, and quoted by schol. ad *Trach.* 354) makes

Heracles take Iole for Hyllus, thus resolving the problem of competition between father and son. A similar dynamic can be seen in the myth of Heracles' first marriage: after slaying his children, Heracles gives his wife Megara to his nephew and charioteer Iolaus (Apollod. 2.6.1; D.S. 4.31.1). P. R. Slater (1968: 376) notes the Oedipal overtones in these myths and points in addition to the myth of Heracles' gift of Hesione to Telamon, another mistress to another favorite young assistant (Apollod. 2.5.9, 2.6.4; D.S. 4.32, 4.42).

41. Note that Heracles, too, complies unwillingly (ἀεκούσιον, 1263) with the enigmatic will of *his* father, Zeus; cf. Sorum 1978.

42. In this scene, all relations other than the patrilineal are occluded. For example, at 1010–14, the Greek men whom Heracles had saved he now reproaches for not helping him; only Hyllus will be able to do that. Likewise at 1155–56, Hyllus offers the help of those who are present (masculine plural), but Heracles responds (1157) to Hyllus alone in the singular. The absence of Heracles' other children (1147–54) again distills all familial relations to a single element: the relationship between father and son.

43. Hence the functionalist explanations of the ending, which argue that since the audience would know that Hyllus and Iole were the forebears of the Heracleidae, the play must somehow effect the transition of Iole from Heracles' bed to Hyllus's. For this line of argument, see Jebb (1892) on 1224; Segal 1977: 151–52; Easterling 1982: 10–11. For a summary and rejection of the functionalist argument, see Kitto 1966b: 170–71; J. K. MacKinnon 1971: 33.

44. There is a sinister slippage between compulsion and volition in this scene: the formulation of the *kallistos nomos* (1177–78) urges Hyllus to discover for himself the compulsion of the law; likewise, at 1217 and 1229, Heracles represents Hyllus's obedience as a *kharis*, a favor freely given, masking external constraint behind a pretense of spontaneity.

45. Heiden 1989: 155.

46. J. K. MacKinnon 1971: 34–41.

47. Webster 1936b: 179; Kirkwood 1941: 203; Musurillo 1967: 64; Wender 1974: 14; Winnington-Ingram 1980: 85.

48. Lines 1245–46 suggest that what he has learned from his father is *dussebeia* in the name of obedience, or how to subordinate all other considerations to the pleasure of his father.

CHAPTER 2

1. Lévi-Strauss signals this when he notes that women can be the producers of signs as well as signs themselves (1969: 496); cf. Cowie 1990.

2. Heiden 1989: 65–66 and n. 58; Kraus 1991: 87.

3. Deianira says of herself: "For I sat struck with fear lest my beauty someday

win me sorrow" (ἐγὼ γὰρ ἤμην ἐκπεπληγμένη φόβῳ / μή μοι τὸ κάλλος
ἄλγος ἐξεύροι ποτέ, 24–25); and of Iole: "I pitied her most when I saw her,
since her beauty destroyed her life" (ᾤκτιρα δὴ μάλιστα προσβλέψασ᾽, ὅτι /
τὸ κάλλος αὐτῆς τὸν βίον διώλεσεν, 464–65).

4. On male homosociality, see Sedgwick 1985. Ormand (in a work in progress) is analyzing *Trachiniae* (and in particular the marriage of Deianira and
Heracles) in the light of Sedgwick's theory of homosocial desire.

5. Easterling 1982: 133; Heiden 1989: 77.

6. On *klimakes* in ancient wrestling, see Poliakoff 1987: 51 and illustration 47; cf. Burton 1980: 57. ῥαβδονόμει is a *hapax*, but the official umpires
at the festival games were called ῥαβδοῦχοι. Hesych. s.v. ῥάβδοι· καὶ ὁ βρα-
βευτὴς ῥαβδονόμος. Cf. Thuc. 5.50.4; Ar. *Pax* 734; Plat. *Prot.* 338a8; and
M. Davies 1991 ad 516.

7. Burton (1980: 55) suggests further that the "two clauses describing the
wrestlers in answer to the question at the end of the strophe sound like the official
announcement by the herald of the competitors' names and home towns."

8. *Suneimi* often means to live with in marriage or sleep with; see, e.g., Hdt.
4.9.3; Soph. *El.* 276; Ar. *Ec.* 619; Arist. *Pol.* 1262a33.

9. On the erotic triangle, see Girard 1972: 1–52; Sedgwick 1985: 21–27.

10. E.g., *Il.* 23.704; cf. Theogn. 994; see Detienne 1967: 84.

11. Thus the ode replicates grammatically the union it depicts, progress-
ing from the differentiation of the ὁ μὲν . . . ὁ δέ construction at 508–10 ("the
one . . . the other") to the dual (ἀμφοῖν) at 522.

12. Hoey 1977: 285–86. For the erotic connotations of *terpsis*, see *Il.* 9.337;
Od. 5.227, 23.301; *h. Aphr.* 72, 226; Hes. *Theog.* 206; Sappho 78.7 (P); Mimn.
1.1, 2.4, 5.3; Sem. 7.52 (W); Theogn. 256, 1019, 1345; Eur. *Andr.* 208, 290;
Suppl. 453; *Herc.* 1376–77; *Bacch.* 774; Eur. fr. 26.2; Ar. *Lys.* 553.

13. When Deianira herself spreads a bed at 915–16 in preparation for her suicide, Easterling comments that "in Homer, when a woman 'makes a bed' for a
man she goes to bed with him." Easterling does not, however, notice the similarity between the passage at 915–16 where Deianira prepares the bed and that at
901–2 where Hyllus does, despite a marked overlap of diction.

14. When Hyllus first greets Heracles in Malis, he is "pleased with longing"
(ἄσμενος πόθῳ, 755), a phrase that, apart from the usual sexual overtones of
the word *pothos*, also recalls Deianira's first reaction to Heracles (ἀσμένη δέ
μοι, "to my pleasure," 18: the adjective occupies the same position in each line).
We might also notice, in arguing for an eroticism of the patrilineal bond here, the
peculiar similarity between Hyllus's name and that of Hylas, Heracles' heroic
helper and, in later tradition, his *erōmenos* (Theocr. 13; A.R. *Arg.* 1.1187–
1357); a similar convergence of names links Iole to Iolaus, another one of Heracles' mythic sidekicks.

15. At 938, Hyllus lies "side to side" with his dead mother (πλευρόθεν /

πλευρὰν παρεὶς ἔκειτο, 938–39) in a passage that Easterling remarks "pathetically and ironically suggest[s] a lover embracing his beloved" (1982 ad 932–42); at 1225–26, Hyllus will lie by the woman who has lain at Heracles' side (τοῖς ἐμοῖς πλευροῖς ὁμοῦ / κλιθεῖσαν), thus moving from an eroticized connection with his mother to one with his father mediated by Iole. Hoey (1970: 15) notes the Oedipal overtones in Hyllus's grief for Deianira.

16. Cf. Halperin 1990b for the same dynamic in Plato's *Symposium*.

17. Dover 1978: 100–9; Halperin 1990a: 10; cf. Richlin 1983.

18. This last phrase is Jebb's (1892). I return to the problems of line 526 and to a closer reading of this passage in Chapter 3.

19. I return to the epistemological issues raised by this passage below, Chapter 3.

20. On this narrative, see Kirkwood 1941: 204; Kitto 1966b: 150; Reinhardt [1947] 1979: 27. This is the only narrative prologue in Sophocles' extant plays, and some critics have seen in both its form and its content a Euripidean influence: see Norwood 1920: 159; contra Kamerbeek 1959: 10; Kitto 1966b: 161.

21. Both are agonistic words: ὑπερβάλλω: *Il.* 23.637, 847; ἐξαίρομαι: *Od.* 5.39, 10.84; Pi. *Ol.* 9.10; Theocr. 24.122.

22. Perhaps we might connect to this nexus of agonism and eroticism the bizarre image of 539–40: καὶ νῦν δύ' οὖσαι μίμνομεν μιᾶς ὑπὸ / χλαίνης ὑπ-αγκάλισμα ("And now we await his embrace, two women under one cloak"). Two people under one cloak is probably an erotic image (Easterling 1982 ad 539; cf. M. Davies 1991 and Jebb 1892 ad loc.; Long 1968: 118–20; Dover 1978: 98–99; Heiden 1989: 85 n. 10); the combination of homoerotics (the women, like lovers, under one cloak) and heteroerotics (the women wait for Heracles' embrace) suggests the dynamic of the *agōn* in the First Stasimon. Moreover, the attribution of active and passive roles here is extremely obscure: Heracles seems to be objectified, both grammatically and logically, while Iole and Deianira act as subjects of this lying-together; the noun can alternately be construed passively, making the women the object of Heracles' embrace (so Long 1968: 118–20). The two women are competing, in this interpretation, not to be subjects, winning the prize of Heracles, but rather to be his objects. So, too, when, Deianira imagines her fading beauty in contrast to Iole's youth, she suggests a competition, the prize of which is to be plucked by Heracles (547–49).

23. McCall 1972: 150.

24. Jebb 1892 ad 494.

25. This play shows a profound ambivalence toward *tekhnē* in general (Segal 1981: 85–86): Deianira's death, too, is a *tekhnē* (928). The products of this *oikos*'s *tekhnai* are fatal: its one literal product is the poisoned robe. The poison is preserved carefully in the home (556, 578–79, 685–86, 692), guarded as if it were a household treasure; the wool it is rubbed on is home-produced (689–90). Both the disintegration of the wool and the melting of the robe are described with

craft metaphors: the wool disintegrates like the sawdust of cut wood (699–700); the robe sticks close to Heracles' limbs ὥστε τέκτονος (768), an obscure phrase (see Easterling 1982 ad loc.), but one that clearly connects the disease to artisanship. This fatal *tekhnē* is part of a larger economic instability; this *oikos* not only produces fatal objects, but also consumes everything that enters. This is expressed most vividly by the imagery of consumption associated with Heracles' disease, which is repeatedly described as devouring him (1054–56; cf. 676, 700, 771, 987, 1084, 1088).

26. Bergren 1983: 71–75. Cf. Redfield 1982: 194–95.

27. On the robe's associations with magic, see Bowra 1944: 127–28; Segal 1977: 111–12 and 1981: 92; Faraone 1994.

28. The meaning and reading of this phrase are disputed: for the full repertoire of conjectures, see M. Davies 1991 ad 554. The manuscripts' λυτήριον λύπημα is plausibly explained by Lloyd-Jones and Wilson as an idiom analogous to ἄκος τομαῖον, a cure that requires painful and serious measures; the pain, according to them (1990a ad 554) would refer to Deianira's reluctance to resort to magic. Binding is a common theme in magic; see Detienne and Vernant 1978: 279–318; Faraone and Obbink 1991: 3–10.

29. Easterling finds this line so close to the *Agamemnon* lines that "it should be read as an actual reference to that famous episode" (1982: 21–22). She lists as other parallels ἀφράστῳ τῇδε χειρωθεὶς πέδῃ (*Trach.* 1057) with πέδαις γ'ἀχαλκεύτοισι θηρευθείς (*Cho.* 493) and πέδας τε χειροῖν καὶ ποδοῖν ξυνωρίδος (*Cho.* 982). Cf. Garner 1990: 108–9. These clear references to the *Oresteia* provide the only secure *terminus post quem* for *Trachiniae*, the date of which is otherwise unknown, though most generally is presumed to have been in the (early?) 440s. See Earp 1944: 77–79; Schwinge 1962; Reinhardt [1947] 1979: 239–40; Winnington-Ingram 1980: 341; Easterling 1982: 19–23. On the hazards of dating plays based on literary allusions, see Earp 1939: 113–14.

30. Webster 1936b: 164–80 draws out the comparison most fully; cf. Garner 1990: 102–4.

31. The potential danger of a woman's gift is here compounded by the associations between Deianira's robe and Nessus's poison. Deianira's gift is an enactment and a reactivation of Nessus's gift, and her role as gift-giver is doomed in advance because of this association. Segal (1977: 106–27) has argued that the movement of this play is from barbarity to civilization; if we accept his structuralist progression, then Deianira must be seen as an impediment to this teleology, a recursion of the monstrous past into the present. Cf. duBois (1979 and 1982: 95–106), who identifies an impingement of the bestial upon civilization in Achelous's and Nessus's attempts to enter into the circuit of Deianira's exchange.

32. On gift exchange in ancient Greece, see, e.g., Finley [1954] 1988: 64–68; Morris 1986; Kurke 1991: 92–97.

33. I discuss and deconstruct this distinction between gift exchange and com-

modity exchange in Chapter 4. As will become clear there, the distinction, though not ontological, is socially useful, and it is that socially ordained difference (and its transgression) that I am focusing on here.

34. On *agalmata*, see Gernet 1981a; Morris 1986. Kurke (1991: 94–95) identifies Gernet's *agalmata* with the top-rank goods discussed by anthropologists.

35. Heracles' robe also has religious associations (it is a robe to sacrifice in), it is always concealed (556, 622, 692), and it has a magical lineage and otherworldly origin (given its real, though unrecognized, link with Nessus). Heracles receives it κόσμῳ τε χαίρων ("rejoicing in the ornament," 764).

36. φόρτος in Herodotus, for example, always implies merchandise traded by a traveling merchant, one of the more marginal figures in the Greek economic and social world. On the ancient Greek attitude toward merchants, see Finley [1954] 1988: 68–70; Kurke 1989: 538 and n. 6.

37. Explicit economic language is otherwise reserved for lower-class characters like the heralds: see, e.g., 230–31 and note 48 below.

38. On Heracles' *latreia*, cf. line 830, and above, Chapter 1, notes 10 and 16.

39. Jebb (1892 ad loc.) remarks upon the oddness of the line: it would more logically be the ascertaining that brings gain, not the thing ascertained.

40. Kurke 1991: 228–32.

41. *Pace* Finley 1955; see Vernant 1980: 49–52; Kurke 1991: 118 and n. 26.

42. A ναύτιλος is usually a sailor, not a ship's captain (as all the translations and commentaries have it: "master of a shipping vessel" [Jebb 1892], "ship's owner" [M. Davies 1991], "ship's master" [Easterling 1982]).

43. Note, too, Deianira's prior economic dealings with Nessus, who ferries people for a fee (560), and promises her a profit (570) from the transaction.

44. Fuqua (1980: 40–41 n. 108) notes "her respect for ξενία, . . . her sense of αἰδώς, the very Homeric conviction that words must be the same as deeds, and her belief that birth and status are important determinants of her behavior."

45. Deianira's opening dialogue with the Nurse, with its language of slavery and freedom (52–53, 61–63), establishes a clear hierarchy between them.

46. As captives from an enslaved city (πόλις . . . δούλη, 283), these women would become slaves to their captor, regardless of their former social position. Deianira feels pity for their fallen state (298–302), but her recognition of the arbitrary nature of slavery and freedom for the women, "who were once perhaps born of free men, but now hold a slave's lot" (αἳ πρὶν μὲν ἦσαν ἐξ ἐλευθέρων ἴσως / ἀνδρῶν. τανῦν δὲ δοῦλον ἴσχουσιν βίον, 301–2), does nothing to alter the fact that she is mistress and they are slaves.

47. "But then to live with her, sharing the same marriage, what woman could bear it?" (τὸ δ' αὖ ξυνοικεῖν τῆδ' ὁμοῦ τίς ἂν γυνὴ / δύναιτο. κοινωνοῦσα τῶν αὐτῶν γάμων; 545–46). See Faraone 1994.

48. Lichas is called by Hyllus "the herald from the house . . . Lichas who belongs to the house" (κῆρυξ ἀπ' οἴκων . . . οἰκεῖος Λίχας, 757), the repetition

of domestic diction suggesting not only that Lichas is more closely part of the female, domestic world of the *oikos* than a man should be (thus implying sexual abjection), but also that Lichas belongs to the household, that he is Heracles' possession. Even the ease with which Heracles (and the text) tosses him aside when he has fulfilled his purpose (777–82) argues for his marginality. Note, too, Lichas's use of economic imagery. Like most tragic heralds, Lichas is not coy about his expectation to profit from his services, and this is expressed in monetary terms (230–31: ἄνδρα γὰρ καλῶς / πράσσοντ' ἀνάγκη χρηστὰ κερδαίνειν ἔπη, "The man who fares well should reap the profit of a good report"; the Messenger expresses similar sentiments at 189–91). The form of this statement shows the complex social barriers set around upper-class values: though Lichas recognizes the aristocratic distinctions of *kalos/kakos*, and tries to employ them, he can do so only imperfectly, and it is precisely in this misuse of aristocratic discourse that Lichas shows himself to be a nonaristocrat.

49. Though this form of address seems not to be particularly rude (in *OT*, Jocasta is called γυνή both by the messenger, 934, and by her husband, 642, 700, 726, 755, 767, 964, 1054), it acknowledges the queen as a married woman, and not specifically as a monarch.

50. Mastronarde 1979: 95: "Sophokles appears to have tolerated what seems (on extant evidence) to be a break of the etiquette of social hierarchy in order to carry out the entrapment of Lichas in the most lively fashion (Deianira, after all, is too much of a 'lady' to treat Lichas with the roughness required)." McCall (1972: 149) smooths over this irregularity by assuming that the Messenger answers after a moment of silence.

51. McCall (1972) sees this scene as evidence of Deianira's lack of resolve and independence. Fuqua (1980: 80–81) and Jebb (1892 ad 401–4) counter that Deianira deliberately avoids a confrontation that would demean her royal dignity. Thus for them Deianira is here proving, by her silence, her queenly stature.

52. Note, too, 423–24: ἐν μέσῃ . . . ἀγορᾷ, "in the middle of the public square."

53. The emphasis in this passage on education (μαθών, 449; μάθησιν, ἐκμανθάνεις, 450; παιδεύεις, 451) also ties into the dichotomy between "natural" aristocracy (inherent nobility) and the learned traits that signify the diffusion of aristocratic values downward through society.

54. For the antiaristocratic connotations of ἀγνώμων, see, for example, Theognis 895, 1260.

55. Yet, though θνητὰ φρονεῖν ("to think as mortals should") is gender-neutral, the form in which it is stated (with the participle φρονοῦσαν in the feminine form) reminds us grammatically of Deianira's femininity; gender is inescapable.

56. Foley 1982b: 4: "Once [women] have crossed the boundary into the political sphere they adopt the male heroic code, or a distorted image of it."

57. This question is further suggested by the heroic themes that surround Deianira in her mythology; her name probably means "destroyer of men" (Jebb

1892: xxxi: "It denoted an Amazonian character"); according to Apollodorus (1.8.1), she drove a chariot and practiced war before marrying Heracles. Webster (1936b: 164) suggests that audience expectations would have been prejudiced by the associations of her name; cf. Errandonea 1927: 146–50; Bowra 1944: 117. Against this, Deianira's perceived passivity has come in for harsh criticism from some scholars. McCall (1972: 155) remarks: "Deianira is no Sophoclean hero at all . . . those qualities which mark Sophoclean heroes—raw force, authority, obduracy—are absent from the passive Deianira." Cf. Wiersma 1984: 49–52. Whitman, on the other hand, argues that Deianira's gentleness and intelligence comprise a sort of heroic *aretē* (1951: 113).

58. Loraux 1981; cf. Huston 1986.

59. The scholiast develops this theme by referring repeatedly (26, 27, 28) to her mental anguish in Heracles' absence as an ἀγώνισμα, a struggle.

60. κἀφύσαμεν δὴ παῖδας, οὓς κεῖνός ποτε, / γῄτης ὅπως ἄρουραν ἔκτοπον λαβών, / σπείρων μόνον προσεῖδε κἀξαμῶν ἅπαξ, "We had children, but Heracles sees them as often as a farmer visits his outlying field, only when he sows and reaps," 31–33.

61. Heiden 1989: 29–30; duBois 1988: 39–85 and esp. 73 on this passage. Segal (1981: 75) notes that in locating the field on the margins, Sophocles confuses cultivation and wilderness, a symptom of the play's ambivalence toward birth and nurture.

62. Lloyd-Jones and Wilson (1990a and 1990b ad loc.), M. Davies (1991 ad loc.). Easterling (1982) prefers the emendation στρέφει (defended by Hooker [1977: 71–72]), as does Jebb (1892). Another destructive maternal image occurs at 833–35, where the poison that kills Heracles is born of death but raised by the snake (αἰόλος δράκων). There is also perhaps a pun there on the roots ΤΑΚ- ("to wither") and ΤΕΚ- ("to give birth").

63. Note the use of the word παῖς ("child") in Heracles' official appellation at 98 (if the text is secure; Lloyd-Jones and Wilson [1990b] reject the word). Dover (1976) argues that the image of Sun as messenger (ἅλιος κῆρυξ) at the beginning of the Parodos comes from the practice of sending out a proclamation for a lost child.

64. Wender 1974; Parry 1986.

65. Halperin 1990b.

66. The word εὐνάζειν ("to put to sleep") in itself carries these multiple connotations: maternal, sexual, and destructive. These associations are even stronger if (as M. Davies [1991] and Jebb [1892] ad loc. suggest) the "wretched bird" (ἄθλιον ὄρνιν) of 105 is properly read as a reference to the story of Tereus and Procne, another myth about the destructive effects on children of the parents' sexuality.

67. King 1983; Loraux 1987: 15.

68. Loraux 1981: 66.

69. The term *parthenos* is ambiguous: it can imply sexual inexperience (vir-

ginity in the modern sense) or social status (an unmarried woman). See Sissa 1990a: 339–43 and 1990b: 76–78.

70. King 1983: 112.

71. γυνή (400, 447, 486); δάμαρ (428, 1224); ὠδίνουσα (325); παρθένος (1219; 1275?); κόρη (352, 536); νεᾶνις (307); παῖς (585).

72. See J. K. MacKinnon 1971; Wet 1983: 221–22; for the conflation of concubine and wife: 428, 460, 486, 841–44, 857–58, 1139, 1224. Sophocles further emphasizes the problem by placing Heracles' marriage to Deianira early in the hero's career (so that it becomes a long-standing marriage, as opposed to Heracles' numerous other short-term "marriages") and by rejecting the tradition that makes Heracles win Iole for Hyllus (schol. ad *Trach.* 354). On the multiple "wives" of heroes and tyrants, see Gernet 1981c.

73. It is unclear where the corruption lies. If we are to salvage the line, I would prefer to preserve the sense of "household"; this could be done either by reading οὐσίας in its technical sense of "property" (admittedly a tragic *hapax* in this meaning) or by adopting Reiske's ἑστίας or Pearson's οἰκίας. See Easterling (1982) on 910–11 for a summary of other possible emendations.

74. Musurillo 1967: 75.

75. See Harrison 1968: 13–15 on "less formal unions" in classical Athens, relations that were more than just casual, but unsanctioned by the formal elements of the *enguē* and *ekdosis*. Wet (1983) examines *Trachiniae* in the context of Athenian marriage practice; she sees the play as an argument in favor of love and monogamy in marriage.

76. Mikalson 1986 discusses the representation of Zeus as a father in *Trachiniae*.

77. Heracles' apotheosis is suggested but not represented; see Bowra 1944: 159; Musurillo 1967: 79; Hoey 1977: 270; Segal 1977: 132–33, 138–39; 1981: 99–100; Easterling 1981: 67; Friis Johansen 1986: 55–61; Kane 1988: 209; Holt 1989.

78. Especially if Hyllus, rather than the chorus, speaks these last lines. Hoey (1977: 286) remarks that no other extant Sophoclean work "is so bitter so close to the end. . . . It comes so near to being the last word of the play that the proverbial serenity of Sophoclean final impressions seems endangered." Cf. Mikalson 1986: 91–92. Norwood (1920: 159) finds in the cynicism of these lines a Euripidean influence; contra, see Bowra 1944: 158. Page (1960: 317) and Musurillo (1967: 79) read it optimistically; McCall (1972: 162), pessimistically.

79. See the Hellenistic epigram (*AP* 11.381, quoted in Carson 1990: 148): πᾶσα γυνὴ χόλος ἐστιν· ἔχει δ᾽ ἀγαθὰς δύω ὥρας· / τὴν μίαν ἐν θαλάμῳ, τὴν μίαν ἐν θανάτῳ, "All of woman is bile. She has two good seasons: one in the marriage chamber, the other in death."

80. Loraux 1987. Faber (1970) takes a different tack, psychoanalyzing the "case histories" of tragedy's "suicidal individuals." (See his ch. 4 on *Trachiniae*.)

81. Loraux 1987: 7–30.

82. Bergren 1983; King 1983: 118, 121, 125 n. 4; Cantarella 1985; Loraux 1987: 10. Diodorus Siculus (4.38.3) and Apollodorus (2.7.7) make Deianira hang herself.

83. For the diction, cf. *Il.* 10.256; Pindar *Nem.* 8.23.

84. Knox (1964: 44 n. 48) points out that Deianira uses "heroic formulas" only before her death. Loraux (1981: 64 n. 151) remarks that the reference to the Nurse as *parastatis* represents Deianira's death as that of a hoplite.

85. Loraux 1981: 46. Devereux's (1975: 136) suggestion that Deianira's manly death reveals Sophocles' latent homosexuality is rightly rejected by Winnington-Ingram (1980: 81 n. 28).

86. Loraux 1987: 3–4; she later rejects this original supposition, 62–63. Cf. Heiden 1989: 129–30.

87. Loraux reaches similar conclusions (1987: 30, 62–64).

CHAPTER 3

1. See, e.g., Reinhardt [1947] 1979; Gardiner 1987: 124 n. 10.

2. The temptation to "fill in" the blank Iole has also affected modern critics: Jebb, addressing the issue of how Iole is physically distinguished from the other captives, interpolates a psychology alien to the inscrutable character in the text: "Iole . . . is feeling not only bitter grief (326), but the new shame and embarrassment caused by the presence in which she stands" (1892 ad 313). Likewise, Webster (1936b: 168) comments upon her "silent disdain," whereas Bowra (1944: 123) attributes her silence to the fact that she is "broken with misfortune and misery."

3. Lloyd-Jones and Wilson 1990a ad 463; the scholiast also takes Heracles as subject. Easterling (1982 ad 462–63), though equivocal, takes a line closer to my own; cf. Winnington-Ingram 1980: 81 n. 27.

4. Heiden 1989: 74. Rabinowitz (1992: 44) discusses the ways in which the play constructs Deianira's sexuality as murderous.

5. Easterling (1982) ad 313. Waldock (1966: 87) imagines that the other captive women are cheerful, while Iole is the only one "who really looks like a captive." Seale (1982: 188–89) suggests that her "special look" may have been represented by "a stance of proud composure, which would contrast very effectively with the dejection of the group as a whole." Easterling (1982 ad 313) summarizes some of the other attempts to imagine how this difference was staged. On *physis* in line 308, see Hajistephanou 1975: 51–52; cf. *Phil.* 874; *OT* 740–41.

6. I do not seriously entertain the attribution of 379 to the Messenger (by the close group of manuscripts, AUY, followed by Jebb [1892]); see M. Davies (1991) on 379 for a summary of the scholarship.

7. In thinking about the spatialization of gender, I am indebted to the work of

Padel (1990 and 1992), who has most fully articulated the tragic connection between the feminine and the interior, and the ramifications of that connection for the experience of tragedy. I differ from her in my formulation of the gender-specific relation between internal and external in the individual and also in my focus on the ideological underpinning and consequences of these models.

8. On the external definition of the Homeric hero, see Donlan 1980: 5–8. He identifies "external appearance as an index of human worth" as a "constant theme in the developing aristocratic self-conception" (6) and argues that *kalokagathia* did not lose its aristocratic connotations until the fourth century (129 and n. 25).

9. The one major exception is, of course, Odysseus, but he is marked precisely as an exception. Attention is continually drawn to the incongruence between his inner wisdom and strength and his external appearance. However, it is the Achilles type of hero that is generalized and idealized in tragedy, not the Odysseus type. In fact, when Odysseus appears in tragedy, it is to raise these very issues.

10. Thus, an evil king can be represented as something of a paradox, a "cowardly lion," as Aegisthus is called in *Agamemnon*. This ideal is also reaffirmed by the outrage expressed (by Aristophanes at any rate) toward Euripides' protagonists, noblemen inside, but externally beggars, farmers, or castaways. So, too, tragedy's aversion to male *dolos* (on which see Zeitlin 1990: 81–83) could be seen as stemming from the ideal of internal and external congruity.

11. Winkler 1990b: 36–37. Note the difficulty Lichas has in living up to this ideal. Feminized by his deceit, he is charged (by a woman, no less) with being one thing while seeming to be another (451–54).

12. Loraux 1978 (translated in Loraux 1993: 72–110); Zeitlin 1981: 207–8 and 1996: 53–86; Vernant 1981: 51–52.

13. Bergren 1983; Zeitlin 1990: 85. In Xen. *Oec.* 10.2, even the "perfect wife" of the economic philosopher Ischomachus paints her face, and this adornment is represented as a deceit (ἐξαπατᾶν, κίβδηλον, 10.3); after she has been chastised, the wife asks how she can *be*, not *seem*, beautiful (ὡς ἂν τῷ ὄντι καλὴ φαίνοιτο. ἀλλὰ μὴ μόνον δοκοίη, 10.9), a neat reference to the male philosophical ideal. On gender in *Oeconomicus*, see Murnaghan 1988.

14. So Heracles dies outside in public, consumed from the skin inward by an external disease; Deianira dies inside the house, destroyed "by nothing external" (οὐδενὸς πρὸς ἐκτόπου, 1132). Whereas Deianira externalizes her physical beauty (she separates it from herself and personifies it, 25), Heracles internalizes his physical strength, so that *biē Hērakleeiē* becomes his identity.

15. MacDowell (1978: 113–16) discusses the distinction between intentional and unintentional homicide in Attic law, citing a passage from Aristotle that is particularly appropriate to *Trachiniae*'s situation: οἷόν φασί ποτέ τινα γυναῖκα φίλτρον τινὶ δοῦναι πιεῖν. εἶτα τὸν ἄνθρωπον ἀποθανεῖν ὑπὸ τοῦ φίλ-

τρου, τὴν δ' ἄνθρωπον ἐν 'Αρείῳ πάγῳ ἀποφυγεῖν· οὗ παροῦσαν δι' οὐθὲν ἄλλο ἀπέλυσαν ἢ διότι οὐκ ἐκ προνοίας ("They say that a woman once gave a man a potion to drink, and when the man died from the potion, the woman was acquitted in the court of the Areopagus for no other reason than lack of preconceived malice," Arist. *Eth. Meg.* 1188b29–38). On the question of Deianira's guilt or innocence, see Webster 1936b: 164–80; Bowra 1944: 122, 127–29; P. R. Slater 1968: 361–62; Gellie 1972: 67; McCall 1972: 144; Gardiner 1987: 120–30; Winnington-Ingram 1980: 78 and n. 21; Ryzman 1991, 1993; Gasti 1993; Faraone 1994. The most extreme position is taken by Errandonea (1927: 156–60), who argues that Deianira knows the true nature of the supposed love charm all along.

16. Note the recurrence of forms of *kalos* and *kakos* in these passages: κακὰς δὲ τόλμας μήτ' ἐπισταίμην ἐγώ (582); δοκεῖς παρ' ἡμῖν οὐ βεβουλεῦσθαι κακῶς (589); ἀθυμῶ δ' εἰ φανήσομαι τάχα / κακὸν μέγ' ἐκπράξασ' ἀπ' ἐλπίδος καλῆς (666–67); ζῆν γὰρ κακῶς κλύουσαν οὐκ ἀνασχέτον, / ἥτις προτιμᾷ μὴ κακὴ πεφυκέναι (721–22); ἐν τοῖς μὴ καλοῖς βουλεύμασιν (725).

17. Cf. 596, where the chorus is to "cover" her deeds with silence. Heracles and (initially) Hyllus show no interest one way or the other in Deianira's intent, but concentrate solely on her deed. Thus for Hyllus, her deed and plan are identical, and both are blameworthy: τοιαῦτα, μῆτερ, πατρὶ βουλεύσασ' ἐμῷ / καὶ δρῶσ' ἐλήφθης ("You have been caught plotting and doing such things against my father, mother," 807–8). It is not until after she is dead that Hyllu learns that Deianira killed Heracles unwillingly (ἄκουσα, 935), and deems the murder unintentional manslaughter rather than malice aforethought (ἥμαρτεν οὐχ ἑκουσία, 1123, cf. 1136).

18. Padel 1990: 344; cf. Vernant 1983b. On the house as "the principal locus for the objectification of the generative schemes" of a society, see Bourdieu 1977: 89–91; 1990a: 271–83.

19. J. H. Finley 1966: 1–2; Segal 1975: 34–35; Foley 1982b: 2.

20. Segal 1977: 125, 1981: 64; Zeitlin 1990: 76–77.

21. Bourdieu 1977: 91–92; cf. Vernant 1983b.

22. In fact, the only house he enters in the narrative is Eurytus's and this, as part of the masculine system of *xenia*, is a domestication that poses no threat. Movement into the house is governed by the metaphor of the wedding, which i applied repeatedly to both Heracles (185–86, cf. the hymenaion at 205ff.) and Iole (428, 857, 894), though paradoxically not to Deianira. On Heracles represented as a bridegroom, see Loraux 1990: 26 and n. 22.

23. Hyllus, on the other hand, can approach Heracles and stand near him (797, 1076, 1155), and Deianira's final line, in emphasizing Hyllus's proximity to Heracles, emphasizes her own distance from her husband: ποῦ δ' ἐμπελάζεις τἀνδρὶ καὶ παρίστασαι; ("Where did you approach the man and stand next to him?" 748).

24. This is how I interpret the strange idiom ἐξ ἀκινήτου ποδός ("from motionless foot") of 875; for an interesting alternate explanation, see Loraux (1987: 20), who takes this as a reference to Deianira's death on the ground, as opposed to the aerial death of hanging. See Kraus 1991: 93 on Deianira's "final journey" (τὴν πανυστάτην ὁδῶν, 874–75).

25. Compare the chorus's longing for flight (953); whereas Deianira is drawn irresistibly inward in death, the chorus longs to escape outward, beyond the bounds of the play.

26. Zeitlin 1990: 77.

27. For a trenchant critique of this mode of alterity, which prioritizes and inscribes sameness under the guise of difference, see Irigaray 1977. Her identification of this mode as specifically male is belied by the situation in *Trachiniae*, where Deianira creates in Iole an other that reflects herself; as we shall see, this role may be phallic, but it is not necessarily male. (At the same time, though, we must of course remember the male playwright; it is under his auspices that Deianira takes up the masculine position vis-à-vis the female other, the position of the poet himself.)

28. Dawe (1978: 80–81) rejects the passage, pointing to the peculiarity of αὐτοῦ in 145, as well as the content: "The chorus may be young and lovely, but why on earth should we imagine that they, alone of mortals, are untouched by heat, rain, or wind?" The authenticity of the passage is defended by Easterling (1982 ad loc.) and West (1981: 324). Seaford (1986: 51) notes that "the point of αὐτοῦ is that the unmarried girl has not yet made the transition to an alien household."

29. There may have been a practical basis to this metaphor. One of the ways of ascertaining that a bride was a virgin was to deflower her: the breaking of the hymen, with all the blood and pain involved, was a cognitive experiment; see Hanson 1990: 324–30; Sissa 1990b: 83–86.

30. Loraux 1987: 21–22.

31. Winnington-Ingram 1980: 81 n. 28; Parry 1986: 109; Heiden 1989: 129–30; Rehm 1994: 77. Her breast, the symbol of female eroticism, is evoked as she pulls the brooch from it (925), but not shown, even narratively (only her side and arm are bared at 926); again we hear of but do not see the site of her wound (ὑφ' ἧπαρ καὶ φρένας, 931).

32. Kraus 1991: 93: "Sophocles could have chosen to end the play by displaying Deianeira's dead body; instead, the body actually exposed is that of Heracles who is, of course, played by the same actor who took Deianeira's part. We expect a body and we get one, but not the one we expect."

33. Rabinowitz (1992: 45) calls the Nurse's narrative pornographic for its intrusion upon Deianira's privacy and its linking of death to *erōs*.

34. A scholiast condemns Sophocles for being anachronistic (since Deianira must predate Solon) and paraphrases Herodotus on Solon. Easterling (1982 ad loc.) attributes the sentiment to Solon, but also comments that it is "one of

the great Greek commonplaces." Cf. Easterling 1968: 58–59 and Kraus 1991: 79, 81.

35. *Ajax* and *OT* end with similar sentiments. The opening is all the more remarkable here for the fact that this play closes without such a *logos*. See Winnington-Ingram 1980: 75; Kraus 1991: 78.

36. Zeitlin 1990: 84: "The problem of accurately reading the other is a continuing, obsessive concern in Greek tragedy which increases in urgency as the genre displays a greater self-consciousness with regard to its own theatrical resources." Cf. Whitman 1951: 110–11; Lawrence 1978; Easterling 1981: 58 and nn. 8–10; Hall 1989; Kraus 1991. Thus Deianira feels it is a misfortune not to know (εἰδέναι, 321) Iole's identity, and the Messenger gives her his information so that she will learn (μάθῃς, 336) what she should know (ἐκμάθῃς, 337).

37. See Segal 1977: 101 for critical condemnation of *Trachiniae* as a play with "no universal apprehension about life." Segal himself believes that Heracles does gain true insight at the end of the play. So, too, Hoey 1977: 284; Sorum 1978: 67; Friis Johansen 1986: 53–61; Holt 1987: 215–16; contra, Heiden 1989: 12–15.

38. Kraus (1991: 78) notes the ring composition but believes that it "suggests that a final interpretation is possible now that she is dead."

39. Whitman 1951: 107; Seale 1982: 182. Segal (1981: 105) sees in Deianira's death "the circularity and interiority of feminine experience."

40. Sappho 2, 81b, 94, 96 (P); Ibycus 286 (*PMG*); Winkler 1990c: 180–87. Easterling (1982 ad 144–47) cites Homeric parallels to this image (*Il.* 18.56–57; *Od.* 4.566, 5.478ff., 6.43–44, 6.162–63).

41. Winkler 1990c: 184.

42. This fantasy of a female community (that is, a community of female subjects) contrasts sharply to the reality of the female community established by the introduction of Iole into Deianira's *oikos*. The flower that was a young girl in Deianira's nostalgic vision becomes Iole's beauty, which is plucked while Deianira's own wastes away (547–49). The homoerotics of the Sapphic garden are ironically twisted in the erotic image of two women awaiting one embrace under a single cloak (539–40), and in Deianira's refusal to live with Iole in marriage (545–46).

43. E.g., Anacreon 396.2 (*PMG*); cf. Meleager (*A.P.* 12.48.1–2); Soph. fr. 856.13N.

44. Carson 1986: 12–17, 26–33.

45. Ποθουμένα γὰρ φρενὶ πυνθάνομαι / τὰν ἀμφινεικῆ Δηϊάνειραν ἀεί, / οἷά τιν' ἄθλιον ὄρνιν, / οὔποτ' εὐνάζειν ἀδάκρυ- / τον βλεφάρων πόθον.

46. Jebb (1892) on 103: "A midd. found only here, yet not suspicious, since the context excludes the passive sense." M. Davies (1991) and Easterling (1982) ad loc. closely echo this decision. Compare a similar distrust of the grammar at 444 and 463, discussed above.

47. Carson 1986: 30–45. Here subject and object are further entangled by Deianira's own *pothos* (107), her desire for tearless eyes, but also the desire that her eyes inspire, in a traditional association of love with the eyes. We should retain, then, the reflexivity and reciprocity implied by the middle voice.

48. Contrast to this sympathetic, feminine viewing a scene of male viewing, Lichas's performance of the "Sack of Oechalia" to an audience of Malian men (194–99). The passage shows an unexpected erotic emphasis. Line 196 presents, as Easterling (1982) notes, "a notorious difficulty," but clearly juxtaposes words of cognition (ἐκμαθεῖν) and erotics (ποθοῦν, ξύνεστιν). Yet, unlike the empathetic, reciprocal *pothos* that characterizes the women's watching, the homoerotics of this scene seem to be nonconsensual, as the construction οὐχ ἑκών ἑκουσίοις in 198 suggests.

49. Anacreon 408 and 417 (*PMG*); for other references, see below, Chapter 4, note 71. Seaford (1986: 53) notes that the metaphor of woman as abandoned animal is common in wedding songs for describing the reluctance of the virginal bride.

50. Lloyd-Jones and Wilson print ἐγὼ δὲ μάτηρ μὲν οἷα φράζω in their text but obelize the passage and consider its difficulties unresolved (cf. Lloyd-Jones and Wilson 1990a ad loc.). I am reading θατήρ, Zielinski's emendation for the codd. reading of μάτηρ. Zielinski 1896: 529; cf. Hesych. θατήρας· θεατάς. Easterling defends this emendation (1982 ad 526–28), as does M. Davies (1991) and (with minor alterations) Campbell (1958); Kamerbeek (1959 ad 526) supports the transmitted reading μάτηρ, hesitantly translating "I tell the story as my mother told it me"(against which see Page 1960: 318); cf. Musurillo 1967: 76 n. 1: "I tell the story as a mother might."

51. τηλαυγεῖ can have an active meaning ("far-seeing"), although it is less common than the passive sense ("far-seen" or simply "distant"): Kamerbeek 1959 ad 534. The metonymic description of Deianira as ἀμφινείκητον ὄμμα at 527 also draws attention to the problem of specularity, but again it is unclear whether this is an eye that watches or, by a common synecdoche for "face" or "beauty," an eye that is watched and fought over.

52. *Thakoi* are the seats in a theater, hence the verbal form should rightly mean to sit as in a theater; cf. Hesych. a 949.1: ἁ γώνιοι θᾶκοι; *thea* properly describes a spectacle such as a drama.

53. The generic masculine (like *anthrōpos* or *tis* in its o-declension forms) often does refer to women, but this is always a generalization. *Anthrōpos* is both "man" and "mankind": in Greek as in English, the masculine form is unmarked, effecting grammatically a conflation of the masculine with the human; see Bourdieu 1990b: 7 n. 10; Beauvoir [1952] 1974: xv–xxxiv and passim. So, too, the indefinite pronoun τις (ὅστις) is masculine in form (that is, it can decline like the largely masculine o-stem nouns as well as like the third-declension nouns) but serves for both male and female referents, generalizing the masculine subject as the normative subject. See Moorhouse 1982: 12–13; Renehan 1985: 168;

Easterling (1982) on 151–52; Barrett (1964) on Eur. *Hipp.* 1102–5: "The 'generalizing' masculine plural of a woman or women . . . is not masculine used as feminine, but masculine used *as masculine* with reference to a woman."

54. On the close relationship between Deianira and the chorus, see Kirkwood 1954: 4; Musurillo 1967: 76; Burton 1980: 41; Gardiner 1987: 122–29.

55. Kraus 1991: 87. If we apply strict logic, however, the chorus cannot be both young girls in the present and witnesses of an event so far in the past (Burton 1980: 57–58). The chronological incongruity marks the slipperiness of the attempt to represent the chorus as simultaneously hegemonic and other.

56. Both the speaker and the addressee of these lines are uncertain. See Easterling 1982 ad 1275 and 1981: 70–72 for a summary of the problems and possibilities. If the lines are addressed by Hyllus to the chorus, they violate the Sophoclean pattern of a final choral gnome, and the singular would be peculiar. Likewise if the chorus is addressing itself, the singular is anomalous. The only other possibility is Iole, addressed either by the chorus or by Hyllus. She is a singular and silent woman; however, she has not been onstage since 330, and a silent entrance would be quite extraordinary and awkward. Easterling favors the chorus as the addressee, despite the oddity of the singular (so, too, M. Davies 1991 ad loc.); contra, see Hoey 1977: 288–89.

57. The manuscripts are divided between ἐπ' and ἀπ', but most editors defend the former: Jebb (1892), Easterling (1982), Lloyd-Jones and Wilson (1990a and 1990b), M. Davies (1991).

58. Burton (1980: 81–82) argues for this possibility, suggesting that her silent presence would offer a vivid reminder of Κύπρις ἄναυδος (silent Aphrodite), who guides the action of the play. I agree with him that the logistical problems of bringing the woman back onstage unannounced would not have been insurmountable, and one can imagine a number of ways in which this could have been effected less obtrusively than in K. F. Slater's (1976: 65) elaborate production, with Iole appearing with Deianira's dead body on an *ekkyklēma* at the end.

59. I return to the similarities between Iole and Cassandra in Chapter 6.

CHAPTER 4

1. The *Oresteia* has been a popular object of attention from Marxian classicists. George Thomson's doctrinaire reading (1966) is notorious and, as Rose says, "weighs painfully on anyone who would attempt today to convince readers of the classics that Marxism has a valuable contribution to make to the understanding of the literature of ancient Greece" (1992: 191 n. 10; cf. de Ste. Croix 1981: 41). Rose's own reading of the *Oresteia* (1992: ch. 4), though it differs in many ways from my own, is an invaluable corrective to Thomson's excesses. The reading offered here makes no claims to Marxian orthodoxy, nor to engaging

with Marx on issues beyond exchange; the adjective "Marxian" is intended to signal my use of Marx as a theorist without the overwrought political connotations of the term "Marxist."

2. Irigaray 1977: chs. 8–9; Rubin (1975) implies but never specifies women's commodification in exchange (e.g., 174, 177, 182).

3. Materialist feminists have been at something of a loss as to how to fit women into the rigid structures of Marxism. Although women are obviously both part of the relations of production in society (to the extent that they are part of the workforce) and part of the means of reproducing the means of production (in that they care for and propagate the working classes), their exact class status and role remain difficult to reconcile with Marxian taxonomies. For various discussions of the problems, see Rubin 1975: 160–64; J. West 1978; de Ste. Croix 1981: 98–111; Hirschon 1984; Moi 1991.

4. Marx 1906: 81–82. Marx's tone throughout his discussion of the "metaphysics" of the commodity form is heavily ironic; however, for all that he will try to strip away the mystification that surrounds commodities, he does not take lightly its real effects for the exchangers. The commodity fetish may be a form of false consciousness, but it has real, material ramifications.

5. Ibid.: 83. The process of fetishization is begun the moment that the value of one commodity is expressed in terms of another: in saying that twenty yards of linen are worth one coat (to use Marx's example), we objectify the labor required to produce the coat and embody it within the coat. Therefore the commodity fetish (despite subsequent misuses of the term; see Baudrillard 1981: 88–101) follows logically from Marx's analysis of exchange at its most basic level. In Marx's study, the relations of production (including class relations and the relation of the worker to his own labor) take precedence over the relations of exchange. In my own use of his theory, however, I focus on the latter to the exclusion of the former, first, because very little can be said about production in antiquity (perhaps as a result of a primary fetishization on the part of our elite-oriented texts), and second, because it is exchange, not production, that is at issue in the transfer of women.

6. Marx 1906: 82–83; see 96–97: "In order that these objects may enter into relation with each other as commodities, their guardians must place themselves in relation to one another, as persons whose will resides in those objects. . . . The persons exist for one another merely as representatives of, and, therefore, as owners of, commodities." Bourdieu 1984 is largely an investigation of this phenomenon. Cf. Baudrillard 1981: chs. 1–2.

7. Gernet 1981a is the classic study of *agalmata*. Cf. Morris 1986; Kurke 1991: 94–97. The root meaning of *agalma* is "a delight, a glory, a thing that causes delight, an ornament" (from the verb *agallein*, "to glorify, exult"). In Homer, it generally refers to a pleasing gift: see, e.g., *Od.* 3.274 (where it is glossed by ὑφάσματά τε χρυσόν τε, "weavings and gold"), 4.602, 18.300.

From a general gift, it comes to refer more specifically to gifts for the gods, a process traced by Morris (1986). By the fifth century, it most often means "a statue of or offering to the gods"; but it is clear from Pindar (Kurke 1991) and the usages in *Agamemnon* that the earlier meanings had not been lost, and that a fifth-century audience could still be expected to understand an *agalma* as a precious object or delightful gift.

8. Marx 1906: 81: "A commodity appears, at first sight, a very trivial thing, and easily understood. Its analysis shows that it is, in reality, a very queer thing, abounding in metaphysical subtleties and theological niceties." Gernet 1981a: 115, 119, 120–21; Mauss [1950] 1990: 10–13, 24, 43–44; Kurke 1991: 96–97.

9. Gernet 1981a: 118; Mauss [1950] 1990: 10–13.

10. Gernet 1981a: 125; cf. Mauss [1950] 1990: 44.

11. On *kharis*, see Kurke 1991: 67, 103–6. For the semantics of this word, see Benveniste 1969: 159–61; Kurke 1991: 67 n. 20; MacLaughlan 1993: 3–11 (and 124–46 on *kharis* in the *Oresteia*).

12. Finley 1955; [1954] 1988: 63–66; Herman 1987: 73–82; Mauss [1950] 1990; Kurke 1991: 85–107.

13. "Let's exchange arms with one another, so that the rest may know that we are guest-friends from our fathers' time" (τεύχεα δ' ἀλλήλοις ἐπαμείψομεν, ὄφρα καὶ οἵδε / γνῶσιν ὅτι ξεῖνοι πατρώϊοι εὐχόμεθ' εἶναι, 6.230–31). *Xenia*, the institutionalized relationship of guest-friendship, is a privileged site of gift exchange, as we shall see when we look at *Alcestis*.

14. Needless to say, significant economic changes occurred between the Homeric period and the classical, but the distinction I am discussing is synchronic—an ideological distinction within fifth-century Athens—not diachronic, and is present in some degree in the most "primitive" economies and the most "advanced" (see, e.g., Bohannan 1959; Appadurai 1986; Mauss [1950] 1990). It seems reasonably clear that commodity exchange existed even in Homeric Greece, and that there was considerable overlap between it and gift exchange, despite epic's ideological foregrounding of the latter and almost total occlusion of the former: see Finley 1955; [1954] 1988: 51–73; Humphreys 1978: ch. 7; Donlan 1981; Seaford 1994: 13–25 (esp. 18–20) and 194–204.

15. For a different interpretation of the economic problems with this scene, see Donlan 1989; he argues that this exchange sets up a relation of dominance and submission between the two *xenoi*, and that "the point of lines 234–236 is not that Glaukos outgave, for that was conventionally expected, but that he was so bewildered he gave at the humiliating ratio of 11 to 1" (13).

16. See Baudrillard 1981: chs. 1–2; Bourdieu 1984: 6: "Taste classifies, and it classifies the classifier." In the exchanges studied by Mauss, the object itself is considered to be alive and active; the resultant intermingling of the spirit of the gift with the spirit of the exchanger means that in exchange the partners give and receive not merely objects, but parts of themselves ([1950] 1990: 20, 46).

17. Vernant 1980: 16 n. 9; cf. 26–27. He himself, however, uses Marxian principles to great effect. The strictest Marxian interpretation of the ancient economy, G. E. M. de Ste. Croix's *The Class Struggle in the Ancient Greek World* (1981), shows both the strengths and the limitations of such an approach. Though de Ste. Croix's class paradigm allows him to assimilate huge amounts of economic information and to focus on the lives of average Athenians, his emphasis on the purely economic (rather than the ideological, etc.) aspects of the means of production leads him to underestimate (in my view) the importance of symbolic capital in ancient Athens. What is needed is a synthesis of the hard economism of de Ste. Croix's Marxian approach and the more flexible Weberianism of someone like Finley. See Austin and Vidal-Naquet 1977: 21–26; Garlan 1988: 1–14; Ober 1989: 11–13.

18. Polanyi 1968: 7: "Man's economy, as a rule, is submerged in his social relationships." See also Finley 1973: 17–34; Austin and Vidal-Naquet 1977: 3–11; Mauss [1950] 1990: 29. Arguing against the concept of the embedded economy is de Ste. Croix (1981). Bourdieu's theory of the interconvertibility of economic and symbolic capital (e.g., 1977: 171–83, 185–86) by and large obviates this debate, allowing us to see that the "social" and the "economic" are merely different modalities of the same forces and behaviors, and therefore economic theories (like Marx's) and social theories (like Weber's) need not be incompatible.

19. Vernant 1980: 20 n. 18; cf. Finley 1973: 62–94 (esp. 65–66, 81). Contra, see de Ste. Croix 1981: 49–69.

20. Marx 1906: 94. That he also understood the notion of an embedded economy is apparent from the note to this same page: there he admits the total interdependence of economic, social, and political structures, but argues that "the mode of production determines the character of the social, political, and intellectual life generally."

21. Appadurai 1986: 7–9.

22. Marx 1906: 68–69. On Aristotle as an economic theorist, see Polanyi 1968: 17 and ch. 5; de Ste. Croix 1981: 69–80.

23. Erik Gunderson (in an unpublished paper) has analyzed in this light Aristotle's aristocratic bias against trade and his limitation of exchange to use value (*Pol.* 1256b40–1258b8).

24. Finley 1955; [1954] 1988: 51–73; Polanyi 1968: 8; Morris 1986. See Mauss's distinction between "objects of consumption" and "the precious things belonging to the family" ([1950] 1990: 43). Appadurai (1986: 11–16) has an excellent discussion of this debate. He attributes the "exaggeration and reification of the contrast between gift and commodity in anthropological writing" to an oversimplification of the thoughts of both Marx and Mauss, to a misrecognition of the "embeddedness" of modern economies, and to a romanticization of preindustrial societies. In part, too, the problem goes back to Marx himself, whose

fanciful account of the ancient economy must be largely abandoned. On Marx's use of classical material, see de Ste. Croix 1981: 23–28.

25. Appadurai 1986: 11. Morris (1986: 4–7) extends gift exchange into class and early state economies, but resists collapsing it with commodity exchange.

26. Mauss [1950] 1990: 3: gifts are "apparently free and disinterested but nevertheless constrained and self-interested." Cf. Bourdieu 1977: 171–83; Appadurai 1986: 11–12; Kurke 1991: 93.

27. Bourdieu 1977: 171–72; Mauss [1950] 1990: 33–46.

28. Bourdieu 1977: 172. For ancient warnings against participation in the abjected commodity economy, see, e.g., *Od.* 8.159–64; Plato *Rep.* 371c5–d3; Arist. *Pol.* 1256b28–1258b8; Theognis's warnings against money (e.g., 119–24, 149–50, 183–202, 699–718, and 53–60, on which see Kurke 1989); and Aristophanes' lampoons of the nouveau-riche Kleon (e.g., at *Knights* 128–43).

29. On the opening-up of economic opportunity in the fifth century, see J. K. Davies 1981: ch. 4.

30. The degree to which this reformulation of aristocratic power was voluntary is debated. Ober (1989: e.g., 332–39) argues for a "discursive hegemony" of the masses, and sees the changes in aristocratic self-presentation as a defensive gesture. See also Donlan 1980: xiii for the aristocratic ideal as a "defensive standard." I believe that this shift of strategy was pragmatic, but not defensive, and that elite hegemony persisted, albeit in changed and no doubt restricted forms, under the democracy (see Wohl 1996). On the possibility of the cultural domination of an elite within an ostensibly egalitarian society, see Bourdieu 1984: 11–97.

31. On the political aspects of Aeschylean tragedy, see, for example, Dodds 1960; Thomson 1966; Podlecki 1986 and 1993; Maitland 1992; Rose 1992; Crane 1993; M. Griffith 1995.

32. Lévi-Strauss 1969; cf. Finley 1955; Vernant 1980: 55–77 and 1983b: 139–41; Redfield 1982; Kurke 1991: 116–18. Rabinowitz (1993) also uses the concept of fetishization to discuss the tragic exchange of women, but means it mostly in the Freudian sense.

33. On the structural logic of exchange in Hesiod's myths of Prometheus and Pandora, see Vernant 1981: 43–79. Although the relations of Pandora's production and exchange are not occluded by her fetishization in Hesiod's account, with the race of women descended from her, the relation between man and woman (owner and bad commodity) replaces that between men and gods.

34. Hesiod seems to organize this confusion chronologically: when she is among the gods, Pandora is an *agalma* (note the abundance of gold and the role of *kharis* and the personified Kharites in her creation; *Erga* 65, 72–75; *Theog.* 573–84, 587), but once she is traded to men, she becomes a commodity, a *dōron*, whose negative exchange value (as *kakon*, *dolon*) is a reification of the bad relations of her exchange.

35. Vernant (1980: 60) compares women in exchange to *agalmata*; cf. Gernet 1981a, 1981c. (But see Finley's hesitation as to whether or not the bride is part of the dowry, 1955: 186.) Marx himself suggests this application of the commodity logic to women in a footnote (1906: 96 n. 1) where he mentions a medieval French market in which were sold, among the other commodities, "femmes folles de leur corps." I am focusing here exclusively on female literary figures, not on real women and their conditions of exchange, although a similar analysis could no doubt be done for them.

36. Irigaray 1977: 175.

37. On *habitus*, see Bourdieu 1977: 72–95; 1990a: 52–65. Note the abundance of terms of investment derived from the metaphor of child rearing in Greek: a child is an investment (*tokos*) that will pay back the cost of its upbringing (*Ag.* 728–29); similarly, a parent "labors" over a child in order to get some return (Eur. *IA* 690: Agamemnon will lose the child over whom he has labored; cf. *Ag.* 53–54: δεμνιοτήρη πόνον . . . ὀλέσαντες, "losing their labor of guarding the nest").

38. Irigaray 1977: 177; cf. Goux 1990: 34–38.

39. Redfield 1982: 187. For her father, the daughter's use value consists in household production such as weaving, washing clothes, and so forth, tasks that, though valuable to the household economy, could be equally well performed by slaves.

40. Irigaray 1977: 186: "The virginal woman . . . is pure exchange value. She is nothing but the possibility, the place, the sign, of relations among men. In and of herself, she does not exist." Compare Marx 1906: 96–98 on commodities: for its owner, a commodity's only use value is in its exchange value: "All commodities are non-use-values for their owners, and use-values for their non-owners. Consequently, they must all change hands" (97).

41. Mauss [1950] 1990: 6–7. "Potlatch" properly refers to the "total system" of exchange among the Pacific Northwestern Indians Mauss studies, but it has come to refer specifically to its extreme case, the destruction of property. Mauss cites sacrifices to the gods as one form of potlatch (ibid.: 16–17, 37–38). Crane (1993) also applies the potlatch model to *Agamemnon*, but focuses primarily on the carpet scene.

42. Mauss [1950] 1990: 16: "The purpose of destruction by sacrifice is precisely that it is an act of giving that is necessarily reciprocated." See the discussion of the false dichotomy between commodity and gift above.

43. On sacrifice as exchange, see Vernant 1981: 44–61, and esp. 49–50. That the gods received the bad end of the deal was a problem for Greek religious thought, and can be seen as the motivation for the Prometheus story. The plowing under of the economics of sacrifice shows the effects of the same fetishization characteristic of ancient aristocratic gift exchange, to which exchanges with deities were assimilated. For a deliberately tendentious disenchantment, see Plato

Euthyphro 14E–15A (ἐμπορικὴ ἄρα τις ἂν εἴη . . . τέχνη ἡ ὁσιότης θεοῖς καὶ ἀνθρώποις παρ' ἀλλήλων, "Then piety, it would seem, is some sort of art by which men and gods do business with each other").

44. This in contrast to other versions of the sacrifice, where Iphigeneia is Agamemnon's payment either for the killing of Artemis's stag (Proc. *Chres.* 104.12–14 [Allen]; Soph. *El.* 566–73) or for his failure to carry out a promised sacrifice of a golden ram (Apollod. *Epit.* 3.21, 2.10). Brulé (1987: 180–82) and Dowden (1989: 9–19) discuss these various myths.

45. The text throughout is Page's unless otherwise stated.

46. Cf. μιαίνων ("polluting," 209); δυσσεβῆ τροπαίαν / ἄναγνον, ἀνίερον ("an impious change of direction, impure, unholy," 219–20). Burkert (1985: 59–60) points out that uneaten sacrifices were common only before battles and at the burial of the dead, and that, because of their already anomalous nature, such sacrifices were not infrequently represented in myth as human sacrifices. On the question of human sacrifice in ancient Greece, see Henrichs 1980; Dowden 1989: 35–37.

47. The raising of the animal above the altar (232, 234–35), the purity of the victim (245), even the prohibition of *dusphēmia* (235–36), are all elements of the normal Greek sacrifice, on which see Burkert 1985: 56. On the conflation of terms taken from the realm of sacrifice (δαΐζω, 208; παρθενοσφάγοισιν, 209; etc.) and terms for murder, see Loraux 1987: 32. Zeitlin 1965 and Lebeck 1971: 60–63 treat more generally the theme of corrupted sacrifice in the *Oresteia*.

48. Zeitlin 1965; Seaford 1994: 368–78. The sacrifice is described by the chorus in the Parodos; the scene takes place far from the world of Argos where the play is set, and occupies a different register from the dramatic action, although the two do interpenetrate.

49. Lawrence 1976: 109. The ambiguity is heightened by the paradoxical antithesis between Artemis as the protectress of young animals and as the one who demands the murder of this young girl. On the effect of Aeschylus's occlusion of Artemis in this scene on the question of human responsibility in the trilogy, see Lloyd-Jones 1962; Hammond 1965: 46–48; Lesky 1966: 80–85; Peradotto 1969: 249–61; Dover 1973; J. Jones [1962] 1980: 76–82.

50. See Denniston and Page (1957) on 140–45. The causal relations within this passage are virtually impossible to untangle. For various attempts, see Kitto [1939] 1966a: 68–69; Peradotto 1969: 237–48; Dover 1973: 61–62; Lawrence 1976; Sommerstein 1980; Nussbaum 1986: 32–38.

51. "The prophet shrieked out, putting forward Artemis" (μάντις ἔκλαγξεν προφέρων / Ἄρτεμιν, 201–2). Cf. 206, where the object of πιθέσθαι is not stated, and 248, where the chorus's summation of the event refers to Calchas's prophecy, not to the demand of the god.

52. Mauss [1950] 1990: 37, cf. 39–42. This aristocratic, agonistic prestation is a central means of social organization in the strictly hierarchized Indian clans

Mauss studied. I examine in Chapter 5 some of the problems that result when the potlatch is performed—in Agamemnon's trampling of the carpet—in a democratic context.

53. C. A. Gregory (1982: 60–61) notes that the destruction of wealth is the simplest strategy for an individual to gain preeminence in a gift society. However, his notion of "conspicuous destruction" is economically simplistic: first of all, as this scene illustrates, the circumstances under which such a destruction could occur and the status of the participant individuals were carefully regulated, so that the event was prevented from becoming a venue for parvenus; second, the term "destruction" fails to recognize the extent to which the wealth destroyed is not lost but rather is transformed into its symbolic equivalent. The fact that such a transaction is represented as though it were a pure and unilateral destruction is part of the obfuscation that makes it such a perfect vehicle for aristocratic manipulations.

54. The primary meaning of *agalma* in the fifth century is "an offering to the gods" (Morris 1986: 12); thus aristocratic exchange is fetishized and mysticized, as Gernet (1981a: 117) remarks, by a trajectory that ultimately ends in the temple.

55. Morris argues that the shift in the eighth century from gifts-to-men to gifts-to-gods "was linked to a need to represent aristocratic competition as having a wider communal value at a time of great social stress, when aristocrats were facing serious problems in legitimising their privileged positions" (1986: 13). Even in democratic Athens, the sacrifice—with all its concomitant processions, feasts, and competitions—was an arena for aristocratic display, and many of Athens's most important priesthoods remained gentile throughout the fifth century; see Wade-Gery 1931; Hammond 1961: 76–79; J. K. Davies 1971: 369, 10–11; 1981: 105–14; Roussel 1976: 65–78; Wohl 1996.

56. Others are during his discussion of his true and false friends among the Greek leaders (838–44) and in the Messenger's speech about the fate of Menelaus (638ff.). M. Griffith (1995) argues for the importance of the homosocial *xenia* bond in effecting the trilogy's resolution; in *Agamemnon*, of course, such a positive bond is not yet possible.

57. See especially *Il.* 1.106–8, generally taken to be a reference to the prophecy at Aulis.

58. Adkins 1960: 31–36; Podlecki 1986: 78, 90–91; R. D. Griffith 1991. Rosenbloom (1995) analyzes this conflict against the historical background of Athenian imperialism, suggesting that the "figure of Aeschylus' Agamemnon condenses and presents in analogical form the character of Athenian naval hegemony" (106). He sees in the conflict between father and commander a critique of Athenian naval power as "a source of violence outside the community that activates hatred and violence within it" (107).

59. Gagarin 1976: 91: "Although Agamemnon's decision to kill his daughter

is a difficult one . . . it is the only course of action consistent with his role as representative of a strongly male point of view."

60. Fraenkel (1950 ad 230) follows Blomfield in assuming a primary meaning of "arbiter in a prize-fight." Both he and Denniston and Page, however, wish to see a more generalized meaning in this passage (Denniston and Page 1957 ad 230: "Normally 'judge' or the like; here and *Pers.* 302 the context requires 'chieftains,' an idea easily derived . . ."). LSJ suggests "chief, leader" for this passage and *Pers.* 302 only, and provides more numerous contemporary tragic occurrences of the word in its technical sense (Soph. *El.* 690, 709; Eur. *Or.* 1650; *Med.* 274), so I see no lexicographic compulsion to rule out the more precise meaning in this passage.

61. This is the slant that Euripides (following Stesichorus) gives this scene. In his *Iphigeneia in Aulis*, Agamemnon lures Iphigeneia to Aulis on the pretext that she is to be married to Achilles. Although not a seal between Agamemnon and Achilles, the exchange of Iphigeneia does become the point of mediation in the various relations among men in the play, and eventually a point of reconciliation. The marriage to Achilles is also a pretext for the sacrifice in the *Cypria* (Proc. *Chres.* 104.15–20 [Allen]) and Stesichorus 217 (*PMG*), and thus was a tradition well known to both Aeschylus and his audience. See Dowden 1989: 13 on the antiquity of this theme, and Rehm 1994 for its prevalence in tragedy. The same dynamic is at work in Aeschylus's *Suppliants*, where Danaos simultaneously trades on his daughters' value and tries to preserve it for himself.

62. See Vernant 1983b: 139–42 on the tension in marriage between the woman's fixity and her mobility (between endogamy and exogamy, hoarding and commerce).

63. That reproductive potential is here conflated with female sexuality, and is thus circumscribed by all the negative discourse that surrounds female sexuality, speaks to the trilogy's mistrust of female reproductive capabilities and its ultimate devaluation of maternity in favor of an androgynous virginity, represented ultimately by Athena. On this process, see Zeitlin 1984 (now reprinted in Zeitlin 1996: 87–119).

64. Loraux 1987: 33 and n. 7; on *hēbē* and the death of male heroes in battle, see Vernant 1991: 59–61; Loraux 1995: 63–74. This notion of completion or perfection lies also behind the word *telos*, which unites the themes of marriage and sacrifice throughout the play: see Lebeck 1971: 70–73.

65. See Brulé 1987: 179–261; Dowden 1989: ch. 2, on the link between the Iphigeneia myth and female initiation rites.

66. On the virgin sacrifice as a marriage, see Loraux 1987: 37–42; Rehm 1994. Cunningham 1984 and Armstrong and Ratchford 1985 provide artistic parallels.

67. On the cult of Artemis Brauronia, see Ar. *Lys.* 645 and schol.; Sourvinou 1971; Stinton 1976; Brulé 1987: 179–261; Dowden 1989: 20–34; Perlman 1989. For the connection between this cult and the myth of Iphigeneia, see

Henrichs 1980: 198–208; Lloyd-Jones 1983; Brulé 1987: 203–17; Dowden 1989: ch. 2; Bowie 1993: 19–22.

68. *Ag.* 65, 227. Denniston and Page (1957) routinely rule out the nuptial associations of the word, but see Fraenkel 1950 ad 65: "By the word προτέλεια an Athenian understands in the first instance not a preliminary sacrifice in general but, in accordance with what is by far the most frequent use of the word, a sacrifice offered before marriage." See Zeitlin 1965: 465; Lebeck 1971: 70; Goldhill 1984: 14–15; Seaford 1987: 108–9; Brulé 1987: 317–18. Note the frequent ironic use of the term in Eur. *IA* (e.g., 433–39, 718).

69. Vernant 1980: 34–35; cf. Loraux 1981; Foley 1982a.

70. Carson (1990: 145–48) argues that in Greek thought, as soon as a woman is ripe, she is already overripe; as soon as the virgin can be looked at sexually, she can already be assimilated to the cultural model of female sexual wantonness. The dividing line between a woman's "unripe virginity" and "overripe maturity" need not be anything so definite as defloration or first sexual experience, however, but can come with the mere identification of the girl as a sexual object, as this passage suggests. This notion of a more flexible boundary between virginity and womanhood is consistent with Sissa's (1990a and 1990b) claim that the Greeks had no awareness of the hymen and that the whole conception of virginity was therefore vague and in need of constant surveillance, regulation, and intervention (1990a: 357–59). In her reading of the medical texts, the vagina is analogized to a mouth that opens and closes (ibid.: 360), rather than, as for Hanson (1990: 324–28), to a jar that once unsealed cannot be restoppered. The liminal nature of this scene suggests both a penetration (by both gaze and sword) that fails to make Iphigeneia a *gunē* and, paradoxically, an active sexuality that precedes defloration. On this same paradoxical combination of chastity and sexual excess in the rites of Artemis, see Vernant 1991: 201 n. 14.

71. At 245, Iphigeneia is "unbulled" (ἀταύρωτος). On the virgin as an untamed animal, see, e.g., Anacreon 408 and 417 (*PMG*); Ar. *Lys.* 217; Eur. *Hec.* 142, *Andr.* 621, *Hipp.* 546; Aristophanes fr. 582 (Kock); Epikrates fr. 9 (Kock); *AP* 5.292; Hsch. s.v. πῶλος. On the metaphor of taming in lyric, see Carson 1990: 144 n. 22; in tragedy, Loraux 1987: 36 and n. 14; and in ritual, Calame 1977: 411–20.

72. This theme is elaborated in Eur. *IA*, esp. 460–61: τὴν δ' αὖ τάλαιναν παρθένον—τί παρθένον; / Ἅιδης νιν ὡς ἔοικε νυμφεύσει τάχα ("The wretched maiden—but why 'maiden'? For it seems that Hades will wed her soon"); see Loraux 1987: 38–39.

73. King 1983: 119–20. This notion is aided by the temporal contiguity of menarche and defloration for most Greek girls (Paus. 2.33.2; *AP* 7.600, 9.245; Soranus *Gyn.* 1.33.4, 33.6; King 1983: 112).

74. King 1983. In tragedy, however, because it is a genre of transgression, the usual is by and large rarer than the unusual.

75. Loraux 1987: 61; Hanson 1990: 326, 328–29; on the upper and lower

throat, see the Hippocratic *Diseases of Women* 3.230, 2.169, 2.127, 2.151; Soranus 1.9 and passim.

76. The ambiguity of her status is reflected in the vague relationship between Iphigeneia and the pregnant hare (119) that somehow prefigures her death. Is Iphigeneia to be associated with the young inside the hare or with the hare itself? Both are under the protection of Artemis, a figure who in herself reiterates this paradoxical connection between the virgin and the woman in childbirth (on which see Vernant 1991: 200–1). Cf. Sissa 1990a: 339–43 and 1990b: 76–78 on the ambiguity of the term *parthenos* as physical virgin or as unmarried woman.

77. Alcman 3.61–62 (*PMG*); Anacreon 417 (*PMG*); Ibycus 287 (*PMG*); Carson 1986: 20. καλλιπρώιρου ("beautiful faced," 235) also seems to have erotic connotations: at *Septem* 533, Parthenopaeus, in the bloom of manhood, is described as βλάστημα καλλίπρωιρον. Thalmann (1993: 143–46) contrasts the diffuse eroticism of Aeschylus's sacrifice of Iphigeneia to the overtly pornographic nature of the sacrifice of Polyxena in Euripides' *Hecuba*. He argues that Euripides "emphasized the erotic overtones he found [in Aeschylus's scene]. . . . And by doing so he constructed a scene that was frankly pornographic" (146). As shall become clear, I believe that this scene, too, is pornographic.

78. Triclinius ad 238b: ῥίψασα εἰς τὴν γῆν τὰς τοῦ κρόκου βαφάς. χέουσα· ῥίψασα. Cf. the dispute over the meaning of the ambiguous phrase πέπλοισι περιπετῆ at 233: is Iphigeneia wrapped round in her robes (Fraenkel 1950; Headlam and Thomson 1938); falling around Agamemnon's robes (Lloyd-Jones 1952: 132–35); or with her robes falling to the ground around her (Lebeck 1971: 83)? On this debate and a possible solution, see Cunningham 1984. Edgeworth (1988) suggests that the κρόκου βαφάς are her tears.

79. Lloyd-Jones 1952: 132–35; Denniston and Page 1957 ad loc.

80. Fraenkel 1950 ad 239. Lebeck remarks (1971: 81 n. 8) that whereas Fraenkel imagined Iphigeneia stripping voluntarily, Wilamowitz had pictured her clothes being torn off in her struggle: "An interesting difference in Zeitgeist."

81. This is not to say that the only meaning of the female body is sexual (in tragedy or elsewhere), but rather to suggest that in tragedy the female body is always highly charged and its revelation (more often heard about than seen, of course, given the sex of the actors) always shocking to an ancient audience (as it seems to shock some modern readers).

82. See Redfield 1982: 187–90; Carson 1990: 160–64; Oakley and Sinos 1993: 25–26; Rehm 1994: 141–42. Cunningham (1984) and Armstrong and Ratchford (1985) make this allusion to the *anakaluptēria* explicit in their claim that κρόκου βαφάς refers to a veil rather than a robe. Both articles bring artistic evidence to bear and build a convincing case for their interpretation. The dropping of the veil, though a less dramatic image than that of disrobing, also connotes a woman's shedding of her modesty: see, e.g., *Il.* 22.460–72;

Od. 1.331–34, 207–10; 21.63–65; and the discussion of the motif in Nagler 1974: 44–60, 64–67.

83. Seaford 1987: 106–9; Loraux 1987: 37–47; Rehm 1994 in general, and on this scene in particular, 50–51. The theme receives its most complete treatment, of course, in the myth of Persephone (e.g., *h. Dem.*). On Thanatos as a lover, see Vermeule 1979; Vernant 1991: ch. 5.

84. *IA* 460–61, 687–90; see Loraux 1987: 38 and nn. 24–25 for other references and discussion. Cf. Foley 1982a and Redfield 1982.

85. Loraux 1987: 40: "After a close reading of these texts one comes to the strange conclusion that a sacrificed virgin loses her *partheneia* (virginity) without winning a spouse. . . . Neither woman nor virgin, but something between the two, like a *nymphē*. A *nymphē anymphos*, however, a bride without a husband." Cf. Vernant 1991: 201 n. 14. I agree that Iphigeneia in Aeschylus's version of the story is stuck in this liminal position between *gunē* and *parthenos*; as shall become clear, though, I think the text goes to great lengths to maintain this precarious balance.

86. Loraux 1987: 37 n. 18. There are hints of incest in Euripides' *IA*, too (e.g., at 635ff.), but these are diffused by the theme of marriage (to Achilles or Hades) and by the fact that Agamemnon does not himself slit his daughter's throat (1578).

87. The same logic also underlies the incest taboo in Lévi-Strauss's analysis: "The prohibition of incest is less a rule prohibiting marriage with the mother, sister, or daughter, than a rule obliging the mother, sister, or daughter to be given to others. It is the supreme rule of the gift" (1969: 481; cf. Rubin 1975: 171–77).

88. I print the reading offered by the codices and supported by Fraenkel (1950) and West (1990: 178–81) (cf. Headlam and Thomson 1938 ad 225–27).

89. West 1990: 178. Cf. Headlam and Thomson's translation (1938) of their reading (ὀργᾷ περιόργως): "And the host eager for war crieth for that virginal blood righteously."

90. Likewise, it is difficult to assign to any single agent the intense emotion indicated by παντὶ θυμῶι ("with whole heart") at 233: is this eagerness and intensity Iphigeneia's as she supplicates her father, Agamemnon's as he gives the order, or the attendants' as they lift the girl for slaughter? See Lebeck 1971: 83 for a discussion.

91. Triclinius suggests this connection by glossing εἶδον ("I saw") with ἐθεασάμην ("I was a spectator").

92. "The Philosophy of Composition," Poe 1967: 486.

93. Loraux 1987: 33. On the erotics of the maiden's death in art, see Vermeule 1979: 150 and n. 9; and on death and *erōs* more generally, Vernant 1991: ch. 5.

94. See Carson's contention (1990: 145–48; referred to above in note 70) that the Greeks could imagine no middle ground between total virginity and total wantonness.

95. There are numerous parallels between Helen and Iphigeneia, both structural and verbal. Iphigeneia is sacrificed to win back Helen (her death is "an aid in a war to avenge a woman," γυναικοποίνων πολέμων ἀρωγὰν, 225–26), and to that extent the one is exchanged for the other. Both are further referred to as *agalmata* (208, 741). The lion-cub parable, as Knox (1952) argues, applies equally to both. In Eur. *IA*, Iphigeneia sacrifices herself so as not to become, like Helen, the cause of war (1392–94, 1417–20).

96. Surprisingly perhaps, it is never suggested that Iphigeneia might grow up to be like her mother. This possibility is, however, allowed for Electra in *Cho.*: αὐτῇ τέ μοι δὸς σωφρονεστέραν πολὺ / μητρὸς γενέσθαι χεῖρά τ᾽ εὐσε-βεστέραν ("Grant it to me to be more wise and modest by far than my mother, and purer of hand," 140–41).

97. This genealogical determinism does, however, leave room for some improvement: Orestes is noble like his father, but distinctly more civic-minded. On the aristocratic appeal to *physis* in the fifth century, see Donlan 1980: 131–39. Donlan suggests that although *eugeneia* did not automatically imply political prerogative in the fifth century, it was deployed by aristocrats as "the wellspring of those qualities of mind and spirit that made a nobleman a superior person" (139). Cf. Hajistephanou (1975: 1–8) and Halliwell (1990: 49), who argues that nature (*physis, eugeneia*) in Isocrates "functions as an ultimate sanction and justification for the (hierarchal) structuring of human relations."

98. On Pandora and the "race of women," see Loraux 1978.

99. The exception that proves this rule is, of course, Athena in *Eumenides*, a female figure purged of all negative female characteristics. Winnington-Ingram (1983: 125–31) analyzes her as the positive inversion of Clytemnestra; cf. Zeitlin 1984: 182. A goddess is, of course, radically distinct from a mortal woman; thus it is only in the most schematic sense that Athena represents a "solution" to the gender problems that plague the mortal characters of the first two plays. On this sort of resolution of human problems through their displacement to the divine level, see Zeitlin 1984: 172–73, 183–84; Arthur 1982.

100. The lion cub is also like Pandora in its associations with the stomach (γαστρός, 726); see Vernant 1981: 51–52.

101. Knox 1952: 17; cf. Nappa 1994.

102. Note echoes of the Iphigeneia scene in the lion parable: φιλόμαστον (719) recalls δρόσοις ἀέπτοις μαλερῶν λεόντων . . . φιλομάστοις of 141–42; the προτελείοις of 720 echo 227, where the sacrifice of Iphigeneia is a προτέλεια ναῶν. See Knox 1952: 20–21. Knox has argued persuasively that the lion-cub simile can be applied to the male characters of the play as well as to the female. Undoubtedly the men of the play, like the women, prove themselves true to their genealogy: this is the point of Orestes' actions in *Choephoroe*. I have suggested above one way in which we may divide the notion of "truth to type" implied by the parable along gender lines: for the male characters of the trilogy,

truth to *genos* refers primarily to the relationship of the individual to his ancestors, whereas for the women it carries the additional sense of truth to their generic category, that is, their gender.

103. στόματός τε καλλιπρώι/ρου φυλακᾶι κατασχεῖν / φθόγγον ἀραῖον οἴκοις. / βίαι χαλινῶν τ᾽ ἀναύδωι μένει, "And by the guarding of her beautiful mouth to prevent the cry that would curse the house; by the force of the bridle and the might that prevents speech" (235–38).

104. Burkert 1985: 56.

105. Cf. the Teichoscopia of *Iliad* 3, where Helen points out and names each of the Greek warriors from the walls of Troy.

106. Fraenkel 1950 ad 245ff.: "The part played by the daughter in the sacrificial ritual of a company of men consisting by no means solely of her near relations . . . would hardly be conceivable within the limits of Athenian custom"; he attributes the use of the image here to deliberate Homericizing on Aeschylus's part. Cf. O. Murray 1990: 6, 80 and n. 44.

107. Armstrong and Hanson 1986: 99. See Hanson 1990: 328–29 for other examples and medical sources.

108. Armstrong and Hanson 1986: 97–100.

109. Sissa 1990a: 360. Thus strangulation is the virginal death par excellence, as it closes the throat completely and forever (see King 1983: 117–20). Perhaps connected with this association between silence and virginity is the prolixity of Clytemnestra, to which attention is drawn repeatedly throughout the play (916, 1229; cf. Thalmann 1985: 225–28); see Parker 1987: ch. 1 on the association of dilation (and narrative dilatoriness) with women.

110. "Her prayers and cries of 'father'" (228: λιτὰς δὲ καὶ κληδόνας πα-τρώιους). Goldhill (1984: 30) comments on the repetition of forms of *patēr* in this passage (at 231, 244, 245). Contrast Soph. *El.* 548, where Clytemnestra assumes that Iphigeneia, if she could speak, would condemn Agamemnon.

111. Note at 238 the "force of the bridle and the might that prevents speech" (βίαι χαλινῶν τ᾽ ἀναύδωι μένει).

112. Much debate has surrounded the question of whether Aeschylus had a particular piece of art in mind: see Fraenkel (1950) and Denniston and Page (1957) ad loc.; Holoka 1985. Prag 1985: 61–67 and Armstrong and Ratchford 1985 offer artistic representations of the Iphigeneia scene.

113. By the end of the fifth century, *agalma* was commonly used in the general sense of an image: see, e.g., Eur. *Hel.* 705; *Trag. Adesp.* 126; Plato *Tim.* 37c7; *Symp.* 216e5; *Rep.* 517d9.

114. Loraux 1987: 43: "Aeschylus is careful to emphasize the scandal of it all."

115. Ibid.: 42–43.

116. For a different reading of this narrative rupture, see Goldhill 1984: 31–33.

117. It would also spoil the revised version of Iphigeneia's sacrifice in *Proteus*, if Mark Griffith's (unpublished) reconstruction of the play is correct. He suggests that the satyr play developed a plot twist similar to that in Euripides' Iphigeneia plays, where Artemis rescues the girl at the last minute, and spirits her off to be her priestess. Such a happy ending in *Proteus* would be strained if the chorus had already claimed to have witnessed Iphigeneia's death in *Agamemnon*.

118. Fraenkel's injunction (1950 ad 247) against such a question is marked with all the naturalizing and justificatory terminology of a subjective claim: "Naturally the spectator has no right—and if he is the kind of spectator for whom Aeschylus wrote, no reason—to inquire why the old men followed the expedition from Argos as far as Aulis."

119. "But his daughter, Iphigeneia, meeting him gladly, as a daughter should, by the swift ferry of sorrows, will throw her arms around him and kiss him" (ἀλλ' Ἰφιγένειά νιν ἀσπασίως / θυγάτηρ. ὡς χρή. / πατέρ' ἀντιάσασα πρὸς ὠκύπορον / πόρθμευμ' ἀχέων / περὶ χεῖρα βαλοῦσα φιλήσει, 1555–59). I return to the problems of tone in these lines in Chapter 6.

120. For association of the *trapeza* with *xenia*, see *Od.* 14.158, 17.155, 21.27–28, 35; Pind. *Ol.* 1.16–17, 3.40; *Nem.* 11.8–9; *Isth.* 2.39–40; Eur. *Hec.* 789–94; *Ion* 651–55; *IT* 949; *Rhes.* 337. The word ἀνδρῶνας here ("men's quarters") emphasizes the all-male nature of the scene.

121. The only other time in the play female figures are found in a sympotic setting is in the image of the perverted *kōmos* of the Erinyes, sitting within the house drinking blood and singing dirges (1189–93). Clytemnestra, too, uses sympotic imagery only to pervert it (1384–87).

122. Arthur (1982 and 1983) and Zeitlin (1996: 53–86) make a similar argument for the *Theogony*; cf. Vernant 1983b on the importance of the virginal Hestia in the Greek pantheon. Here, the forging of a bond between father and daughter is also a preemptive strike against the possibility of an uncompromised mother-daughter bond. Not only is this bond represented as dangerous throughout the trilogy (the Erinyes, for example, are daughters of their mother, Night), but it is also Clytemnestra's only claim to sympathy and justice, and a force that motivates her murder of her husband. The issue of Iphigeneia's loyalty is thus a serious one; the sacrifice scene's preservation of Iphigeneia as a virgin and as a daughter loyal to her father undercuts preemptively Clytemnestra's use of her as self-justification later in the play.

123. Zeitlin explicates the similarities between Athena and the virginal Erinyes/Eumenides as solutions to the trilogy's gender conflicts: "Both agree that female will be subordinate to male within the family in patriarchal marriage and that the family itself will be subordinate to the city. Each is content with daughter status, for the father-daughter relationship is the purest paradigm of female dependence, while the oxymoron of virginal maternity promises fertility without its dangerous corollary of sexuality" (1984: 182); cf. Redfield 1982: 187.

124. Winnington-Ingram 1983: 125–26; Zeitlin 1984: 182.

125. This is only a problem in practical terms; the mythic imagination encompasses the paradox of the virginal goddess of fertility and birth (Artemis, Hestia, Eileithuia).

126. Cf. the etymologization of *Dikē* as *Dios korē* (*Cho.* 949), on which see Goldhill 1984: 61–62, 196, 209. Rose (1992) takes a more positive view than I do toward the resolution offered in *Eumenides*. He emphasizes the extent to which Aeschylus "maximizes the enduring positive contribution of females to the new order and specifically rejects a version that represented them as the threat to be beaten and obliterated" (258). In my view (which follows more closely Zeitlin 1984), the very form in which the female is incorporated into the city—virginal, desexualized, submissive to paternal authority—represents obliteration of the female "threat" posed by Clytemnestra. I find it difficult to see how *Eumenides'* "utopian" solution to the trilogy's gender problems is anything other than the preemptory cutting of that knot.

127. A prime example of this is Electra in *Cho.*; literally *alektra* ("without a marriage bed"), she is ready for marriage but is forcibly kept a maiden. It is part of Orestes' restoration of normalcy that Electra will be free to marry.

128. J. K. Davies (1981: 76) cites a number of cases of aristocratic endogamy within bilateral kinship, with the result of retaining or reuniting the family's property holdings and status. On the tendency toward endogamy in classical Athens, see Just 1989: 79–82. Seaford (1994: 217) also associates endogamy and the accumulation of wealth.

129. Rose (1992) argues for the essentially aristocratic bias of the concern with genealogy, and offers an interesting reading of the lion-cub parable along class lines, interpreting the lion cub as the aristocracy itself (199–202). I agree that the lion-cub parable and the Second Stasimon as a whole imply a critique of certain modes of aristocratic behavior (i.e., that displayed by Agamemnon and Clytemnestra), but I do not see that the notion of inherited *hybris* constitutes a "fundamental ideological attack on the aristocracy" (Rose 1992: 193) as a whole class; I argue in the next chapter that the inheritance of *hybris*, like the inheritance of *aretē*, merely reinscribes within a democratic context the aristocratic preoccupation with genealogical descent.

130. Endogamy and incest are a recurring problem throughout the saga of the House of Atreus, in the adultery of Atreus's wife with his brother, in the incestuous union of Thyestes with his own daughter (from which Aegisthus was born), in Aegisthus's relationship with Clytemnestra. Though such illegitimate unions are part of the House's curse, note that exogamous marriages are no less problematic, be it Pelops's wooing of Hippodameia, the double union of the Tyndaridae with the Atreidae, or the theft that joins the House of Priam with the royal lines of Argos (see M. Griffith 1995: esp. 68–72). Such interstate aristocratic marriages, which created a network of connections between individual aristo-

cratic *genē* independent of the interests of the *polis*, seem to have been a matter of some concern in mid-fifth-century Athens, and may have been the intended target of Pericles' citizenship law of 451 (Humphreys 1974: 93–94; Walters 1983: 329–30; Maitland 1992: 37–40). The fantasy of aristocratic endogamy imagined in the *Oresteia* in general, and the Iphigeneia scene in particular, is an extreme solution to the same problem.

131. Of course, divine society is endogamous by nature, and in this respect sharply differentiated from human society. Nonetheless if, as I have argued, the virgin daughter is enshrined as the ideal female on the human level (as she is on the divine level), then the line between divine endogamy and human exogamy becomes more confused (and confused, moreover, precisely among that class of humans within the social hierarchy—the aristocrats—who claim to most closely approximate the divine).

132. Aristocratic wealth could also be hoarded in commodity form, as "invisible property" (ἀφανὴς οὐσία, on which see Hasebroek 1933: 88; Finley 1952: 54–55; J. K. Davies 1981: 39, 91–105; Gabrielsen 1986; Kurke 1991: 225–28; Aesch. 1.101; Dem. 14.25, 29.49; Isaeus 11.4.3; Din. 1.70). The antisocial nature of hoarding was a common motif in fourth-century oratory (e.g., Dem. 28.24; 42.21–23; 21.154–55; 38.25–27; Din. 1.70; [Lysias] 6.48; Isaeus 5.36–38, 43; 7.40; 11.43–46; cf. Ober 1989: 215–17) and also perhaps in comedy, if we may judge from the seven attested uses of the title *Thesauros*. Gabrielsen (1986: 104–5, citing Ar. *Ran.* 1065ff. and *Eccl.* 601ff.) argues that such hoarding was already a problem in the mid-fifth century, a conclusion possibly favored by the discovery of fifth-century coin-hoards in Attica: see Kraay 1964: 76–79; Starr 1970: 77–78; Kraay, Thompson, and Mørkholm 1973: no. 47; Gabrielsen 1986: 109.

CHAPTER 5

1. It would be interesting to know whether or how Aeschylus treated these same themes in his lost play, "The Ransom of Hector."

2. The money problems surrounding Helen throughout her appearances in Greek literature, and especially the issue of *agalmata* and *ploutos* in *Agamemnon*, were suggested to me by Leslie Kurke. I am indebted to her for the idea of Helen as an *agalma* and a site for economic tensions in *Agamemnon*, as well as for inspiring readings of individual passages (in particular those of the First Stasimon). She takes up these issues in Kurke (forthcoming), where she examines the political ramifications of *Agamemnon*'s tension between a costly economy of gift exchange and the disembedding of excessive commodification.

3. In Homer, she is the daughter of Zeus, a tradition that is suppressed in *Agamemnon*. The *Cypria* (fr. 7 Allen) makes her the daughter of Nemesis by Zeus.

4. *Od.* 4.561–69. Menelaus's eventual retirement to the Elysian fields may also have featured in Aeschylus's *Proteus*. On Helen's *pharmakon*, see *Od.* 4.220–32; Dupont-Roc and le Boulluec 1976: 32, 10–12; Suzuki 1989: 66–67.

5. 690–92, 738–43. On the *kharis* of *kolossoi*, see Vernant 1983a: 305–20. This phrase is virtually a gloss on *agalma*, combining the word's two primary evocations, beauty/value/desirability, and a statue to the gods; I return to the phrase later in this chapter. Helen is also associated with *habrosunē*, a luxuriousness that characterizes the aristocratic lifestyle (Kurke 1992 and 1996).

6. Loraux 1984: 12 (= Loraux 1995: 194–210): "'Hélène' peut servir de nom grec à la chose sexuelle."

7. Her uniqueness is expressed in the repeated juxtaposition of her singularity to the plurality of the men who die to win her back: "One woman destroyed the souls of many Greek men" (ὡς μία πολλῶν / ἀνδρῶν ψυχὰς Δαναῶν ὀλέσασ', 1465–66; cf. 1456–57). I return to the parallel with Zeus at the end of this section.

8. *Suitors of Helen* (in the fragmentary epic *Catalogue of Women* [*Ehoiai*]) links her to most of the major heroes of the Trojan War, as they all vie for her hand (*Ehoiai* fr. 196–204M). There is also a tradition, which Aeschylus does not use, that she was abducted as a child by Theseus (*Cypria* fr. 10 Allen; Plut. *Thes.* 29, 31). Thus her desired possession (as reified in the oath of the suitors) defines the membership of the heroic group. Cf. Gernet 1981a: 117.

9. Contrast the *Iliad*, where most of the adjectives describing her refer to her nationality ('Αργείης: 2.161, 2.177, 3.458, 4.19, 4.174, 6.323, 7.350, 9.140, 9.282), her beauty (λευκωλένῳ: 3.121; ἠϋκόμοιο: 3.329, 7.355, 8.82, 9.339, 11.369, 11.505, 13.766), or her divine origin (Διὸς ἐκγεγαυῖα: 3.199, 3.418, cf. 3.426; δῖα γυναικῶν: 3.171, 3.228).

10. Appadurai (1986: 21) calls such high-stake exchanges "tournaments of value": "What is at issue in such tournaments is not just status, rank, fame, or reputation of actors, but the disposition of the central tokens of value in the society in question."

11. ἀλλ' ἄ[ρα πάντας / Ἀτρε[ίδ]ης ν[ίκησε]ν ἀρηίφιλος Μενέλαος / πλεῖ[στ]α πορών (*Ehoiai* fr. 204.85–87M; cf. 200M).

12. Another *agōn* invests her with a divine value: she is the prize in a beauty contest among the goddesses. They, like the Greek princes, compete for the prize of superiority, though Helen here is bestowed rather than received by the winner. See *Il.* 24.28–30; *Cypria* 102.14–20 (Allen); Eur. *Tro.* 924–34.

13. Marx 1906: 106–62; cf. Goux 1990: 10–12, 16–34.

14. It seems likely that money was in fairly common use by the fifth century: see Kraay 1964 and 1976: 55–74; Finley 1973: 166–69; Austin and Vidal-Naquet 1977: 56–58; Morris 1986: 5–6; Seaford 1994: 202–4. For my purposes, however, it is not essential that money be widespread as a currency, but

only that there be the concept of a universal equivalent, which there clearly was as early as Homer's evaluation of arms in terms of cattle in *Iliad* 6. Again, the distinction I am exploring between *agalmata* and *ploutos* is synchronic and ideological, not diachronic and historical; see above, Chapter 4, note 14.

15. On Helen and *mimesis*, see Zeitlin 1981: 200–11; 1990: 84–88; Bergren 1983: 79–86.

16. For the commodity as mirror, see Irigaray 1977: 176–77; Marx 1906: 61.

17. *Od.* 4.227–29.

18. Hdt. 2.112–20; Eur. *Hel.* A story told about Stesichorus reveals the same doubleness: struck blind for having slandered Helen, Stesichorus recants: the story is not true, she never sailed to Troy (Stes. 192 [*PMG*]; cf. Pl. *Phdr.* 243a–b; *Rep.* 9.586c). On *eidōla*, see Vernant 1983a: 308–9.

19. On the connection (symbolic and moral) between this scene and the sacrifice at Aulis, see Conacher 1987: 38 and n. 71; Lebeck 1971: 74–79; Dover 1987: 154; Crane 1993: 121.

20. It is no accident that a woman speaks most clearly the play's disenchantment; as we shall see in the next chapter, her blatant economism becomes another example of Clytemnestra's transgressive and tyrannical character, and helps justify her eventual elimination, as a "bad aristocrat," from the social world of Argos.

21. Although in Clytemnestra's mouth, this charge is largely wishful thinking, it is reiterated by the Herald at 527–28, and by Agamemnon at 819–20. The profit motive behind the war is suggested at 126–30, in the reference to "all the public herds placed before the walls" (πάντα δὲ πύργων / κτήνη πρόσθετα δημιοπληθῆ, 128–29). Rosenbloom (1995: 109–11) sees *Agamemnon*'s exchange of life for profit as exemplary of the sort of thinking behind Athenian naval hegemony in the fifth century.

22. The theme of jettison runs through the play (e.g., 1005–17), as the burden of excessive wealth threatens to sink the house; see Crane 1993: 126–27 on the topos.

23. Crane's interpretation of the scene proposes the potlatch as a potentially positive model for Agamemnon's action, and suggests that Agamemnon's real fault is the pusillanimous way in which he performs this act (ibid.: 128–29). In his adoption of Mauss's model, I believe that Crane underestimates the differences between the position of a chief in the explicitly hierarchical society of the Kwakiutl (see Mauss [1950] 1990: 6) and that of the aristocrat in democratic Athens.

24. Although strictly speaking Argos is, of course, a monarchy, there are places in the text where the *polis* seems distinctly democratic: see, e.g., 456–57, 816, 845–46, 855, 883, 938, 1210, 1346–71, 1409–13, 1615–16, 1639. For the development of democratic sentiment throughout the trilogy, see Dodds 1960; M. Griffith 1995: 76–78; cf. Pope 1986; Podlecki 1986: 93 and 1993:

76–79. A similar retrojection is at work even more obviously in *Suppliants*, where Pelasgos, king of Argos, speaks like a good democrat (for example at 365–75).

25. Griffith 1995: 72–81.

26. Xen. *Oik.* 2.5–7; Arist. *Nic. Eth.* 1122b19–23a5; Thuc. 6.16.1–3. Kurke (forthcoming) notes that if the aristocratic *chorēgos* was responsible for providing all props for the plays, then his "expenditure" of the carpet for the benefit of the *polis* can be seen as the positive inverse of Agamemnon's self-interested expenditure.

27. Kurke 1991: 176. Crane 1993: 123: "Athenians were long used to watching their victors for new and unacceptable ambitions."

28. Kurke 1991: 26–28; Crane 1993: 120.

29. It is indicative of her total domination over Agamemnon that he is unable to counter her negative representation of his act (as excessive and potentially tyrannical) with a more positive interpretation of his own (for example, as the display of grandeur appropriate to a victorious general). I return to this issue in Chapter 6. On the question of why Agamemnon yields, see, e.g., Fraenkel 1950: 441–42; Lloyd-Jones 1962; Simpson 1971; Easterling 1973; J. Jones [1962] 1980: 86–87; Meridor 1987; Konishi 1989.

30. On the theme of inherited excellence in the *Oresteia*, see Rose 1992: 185–265.

31. ἐναίσιμον, "righteous," "in accordance with one's lot," is related to *sōphrosunē*, the virtue of moderation and knowing one's place in the world. Both virtues, I believe, are implicitly elitist, reinforcing social stratification and discouraging upward mobility. Compare, e.g., 1425: "You will know, having learned too late, how to be wise" (τὸ σωφρονεῖν; cf. 1620); 180–81: "It comes to men against their will to be wise (σωφρονεῖν)." Cf. Headlam and Thomson 1938 ad *Eum.* 520. On the aristocratic connotations of *sōphrosunē* even in the fifth century, see North 1966: 33; Vernant 1982: 89–91.

32. On the metaphor of the counterfeit coin for a bad aristocrat, see, e.g., Theogn. 117, 119, 417, 450, 965.

33. In Hesiod (*Erga* 182–84) children who resemble their parents are the tokens of moral, if not social, superiority. Rose (1992: 208–10) analyzes this same passage, but concludes that "wealth is reaffirmed as the most relevant contributory factor [in crime]" (209). Rather than seeing, as I do, a reformulation (and reaffirmation in new form) of aristocratic ideology in the idealized vision of the reproductive prosperity of the just, he argues that the metaphor "subverts aristocratic ideology where it was most confident . . . that is, the natural processes of sexual reproduction, of birth and inheritance, by giving them the most sinister connotations" (220; but see a somewhat less optimistic view at 225).

34. On Zeus as supreme aristocrat in the *Oresteia*, see M. Griffith 1995: 104–7.

35. The most complete discussion of the "Hymn to Zeus" is P. M. Smith

1980. Smith starts from the question of why the chorus so emphasizes the uniqueness of Zeus at this juncture in the play: "For why on earth should anyone have thought that there *might* be someone to compare to Zeus?" (5). He attempts to solve this problem by taking the sacrifice of Iphigeneia as the direct object of προσεικάσαι, translating "I cannot find an identity [for it] / [although] putting everything into the scales / save Zeus . . ." (17). While I feel that this reading diminishes the strength and focus of the strophe, his interpretation highlights the double status of the universal equivalent as both within and beyond the equivalencies it measures. His reading is not necessarily incompatible with mine: Zeus is still the signifier for every signified, be it the sacrifice or Zeus himself. See the discussion in Weglage 1991. To say this is not, I hope, to fall back into the implicit Christianizing that Smith rightly condemns (1980: vii). Goldhill (1984: 25–27) offers an interpretation similar to mine, although he works from a Derridean (semiotic) rather than a Marxian (economic) notion of value. He equates Zeus with Derrida's "transcendental signified" (ibid.: 26), and he, too, draws the comparison between Helen and Zeus.

36. This according to the "classical" (anthropological and psychoanalytic) model of the traffic in women, on which see Introduction.

37. In *Iliad* 3 the Trojan elders, gazing at Helen, remark: "There is no blame on the Trojans and well-greaved Achaeans that for such a woman they have suffered sorrows for so long, for she is terribly like a goddess in her face. But even though she is such a one, let her go away in the ships and not be left behind as a pain for us and our children" (3.156–60). Suzuki (1989: 29–43) sees the *Iliad*'s ambivalence toward Helen as an expression of its ambivalence toward the war and the heroic code in general.

38. The social importance of the transgression and its punishment is underlined by legal and aristocratic diction: *klopē* is the technical term for the theft of property; *aiskhunē* implies the aristocratic values transgressed and reaffirmed; the *xenia trapeza* is a virtual synonym for aristocratic homosocial relations.

39. Helen's movement is again referred to at 690–98, again with nuptial imagery. Helen is never allowed any interiority in this play, which in this respect, too, moves away from the tradition of the *Iliad*, where she has an extraordinary degree of subjectivity and insight. In *Agamemnon*, in the only passage where we might hear her thoughts, where she may be the subject of an emotive verb, the text is troubled: †παμπρόσθη πολύθρηνον / αἰῶν' ἀμφὶ πολιτᾶν† / μέλεον αἷμ' ἀνατλᾶσα ("She has endured a lamentable life of destruction through the piteous bloodshed of her citizens," 714–16). She is denied, by the vagaries of textual transmission if not by Aeschylus himself, even this moment of subjectivity.

40. Both Fraenkel (1950) and Denniston and Page (1957) follow Keck's emendation of βεβάκει for the manuscripts' perfect βέβακεν. Such a "Homeric" perfect is still extremely rare in Aeschylus; see Fraenkel ad 653. The collocation

of λιπεῖν and βαίνω seems to be something of a fixed element in the story of the daughters of Tyndareus: in Sappho (16.9P) Helen καλλίποισ' ἔβα 'ς Τροίαν; in Hesiod's account, Timandra is subject of the same actions: προλιποῦσ' ἐβε- βήκει (Ehoiai 176.3M). Cf. Stesichorus 223 (PMG), where Helen and her sisters are διγάμους τε καὶ τριγάμους . . . καὶ λιπεσάνορας.

41. Loraux 1984: 25–31. The play of presence and absence is also contained in the image of the kolossos in line 416: see Vernant 1983a: 307.

42. Page prints ἄδιστος; ἄλιστος is Tafel's suggestion. ἄπιστος (Schwerdt; see Fraenkel 1950 ad loc.) is another possibility, but so far the text has resisted certain emendation. See Fraenkel (1950) and Denniston and Page (1957) ad loc.; M. L. West 1990: 186.

43. Denniston and Page (1957 ad loc.) see these men as elders of the House of Atreus, whereas Fraenkel (1950) retains the meaning "seer," but does not specify the household. Knox (1952: 17) makes the analogy to Il. 3 (cf. Headlam and Thomson 1938: 52).

44. Fraenkel (1950 ad 415) takes this apparition to be Helen (justifying his choice by an appeal to "personal experience or the power of imagination"); Denniston and Page (1957) leave the question open, with dissatisfaction at the grammatical irregularities of either interpretation. See Loraux 1984: 28.

45. Fraenkel 1950 ad 418; Lloyd-Jones 1979 ad 418: "And in the absence of her eyes, gone is all the power of love."

46. See the discussion in Chapter 4.

47. Fraenkel 1950 ad 415: "The question so often raised . . . , whether Aeschylus had Stesichorus' εἴδωλον of Helen in his mind here, can hardly be an- swered. In any case, the thought of such a 'reference' must not be allowed to blind us to the complete dissimilarity: in Stesichorus we have a peculiar and mythical miracle, here a piece of general and purely human experience." Fraenkel's need to naturalize this scene speaks to its air of unreality, fantasy. On kolossoi and eidōla, see Vernant 1983a: 305–20, and on this passage, 309–10. Vernant argues that the kolossos, which was originally a substitute or double for someone lost or dead, signifies absence even as it tries to evoke presence.

48. Cf. 728–30, where kharis becomes atē, disaster, when Helen is trans- formed into an Erinys; MacLaughlan 1993: 128: "She is a charis that is not in fact a charis."

49. This is Aratus's reading for the codices' εὐθέτου.

50. As funerary urn: Aes. Cho. 686; Soph. El. 1401; as a container for liquids: Soph. Trach. 556; Od. 19.386. εὐθέτους further suggests the storage of urns in a storeroom or thēsauros and the laying out of the corpse for burial (Supp. Epigr. 1.449; Dio. Chrys. 40.49).

51. See Vernant 1991: 50–74 and especially 67–72 on the terror of an un- identified death for Homeric heroes: "The reduction of the body [of a Homeric

hero] to a formless mass, indistinguishable now from the ground on which it lies, not only eradicates the dead man's unique appearance; such treatment also eliminates the difference between lifeless matter and a living creature" (70).

52. Redfield 1975: 179–82; Loraux 1986b: 47. On lamentation as a political act, see Foley 1993: 101–8.

53. Compare to *Ag.* 446, μάχης εἰδότε, *Il.* 2.823, 5.11, 5.549, 12.100; Vernant 1991: 50–74.

54. On the *epitaphios logos*, see Loraux 1986b.

55. On the issue of hero cult in the *Oresteia*, see Garvie 1986: 137–38, 177–78; Loraux explores the cult associations of the *epitaphios logos* (1986b: 38–42).

56. Lebeck (1971: 44) notes the connection, arguing that the contrast implies criticism of Menelaus and Agamemnon.

57. Fraenkel 1950 ad 448 remarks on the strength of διαì as a causal-instrumental preposition; he quotes Plüss: "Helen is not merely the guilty cause, but also medium and instrument."

58. My translation is adapted from Fagles 1966: "Hell at the prows, hell at the gates, hell to the men-of-war."

59. Goldhill 1984: 59–60. Compare, too, the tradition that makes her the daughter of Nemesis (Apollod. 3.10.7; Paus. 1.33.7; Loraux 1984: 20–25): the genealogical fallacy is parallel to the onomastic.

CHAPTER 6

1. Klein has not given rise to the kind of orthodoxy that surrounds Freud or even Lacan; however, the British and American object-relations theorists— Winnicott, Loewald, Josephs, etc.—even if they do not identify themselves as Kleinians, were all heavily influenced by her work on the relationship between the child and the mother.

2. Marx himself suggests the psychological dimension of his theory by pointing constantly to the irrational and mysterious nature of the relationship between exchanger and commodity, a relationship that he repeatedly (and mostly ironically) describes by analogy to religion. I referred in the Introduction to his almost Lacanian imagination of the mirroring relation between subject and object. The relations between exchangers and between owner and object are always invested for him with desire, and the exchange itself becomes a locus of self-formation for the exchanger vis-à-vis both his partner and his objects. The theoretical parallels between Marx and Freud and Lacan have been fully studied (see, e.g., Rubin 1975; Goux 1990), but those between Marx and Klein have not yet, to my knowledge, been explored.

3. See "A Contribution to the Psychogenesis of Manic-Depressive States" (1984, 1: ch. 17) and "Notes on Some Schizoid Mechanisms" (1984, 3: ch. 1). Klein herself wrote an essay on the *Oresteia*, psychoanalyzing the main characters: "Some Reflections on the *Oresteia*," in Klein 1963.

4. An extreme example is Vickers 1973: 347–437.

5. This stance is anticipated by Gould 1978: 62: "The play as a whole [*Agamemnon*] . . . is the 'meaning' that is to be humanly intelligible, the play as a whole being an image, a metaphor of the way things are, within human experience—not a literal enactment of 'the way people behave.'" A similar point is made by John Jones ([1962] 1980: 63–137), who argues that we should not inquire into the motivations and thoughts of individual agents in tragedy nor attempt to extricate individuals from the structures in which they are embedded—the *oikos*, the *polis*, the divine cosmos, the poetry. On character in Aeschylus, see further Dawe 1963; Vickers 1973: 347; Gagarin 1976: 58; Gould 1978; Winnington-Ingram 1983: 101–2; Goldhill 1990b.

6. Clytemnestra's various transgressions are already well studied; see, e.g., Zeitlin 1965: 472–80 (religious transgression); Vickers 1973: 348–88 (natural); Taplin 1977: 299–300 (spatial); Winnington-Ingram 1983: 101–14 (political and sexual); Goldhill 1984: 33–42, 89–95 (verbal and sexual). Winnington-Ingram (1983) takes this interpretation of Clytemnestra's character furthest and psychologizes it with his thesis that Clytemnestra killed Agamemnon out of jealousy for his status as a man.

7. Goldhill 1984: 89.

8. Zeitlin 1984: 163; cf. Winnington-Ingram 1983: 114.

9. Perhaps such overdetermination is, in part, unavoidable, the anomaly of a politically active woman immediately suggesting this extreme. But Aeschylus elsewhere presents strong and politically dominant female characters in less extreme terms: the Queen in *Persae*, for example, or (more to the point) Athena in *Eumenides*. On Athena as the positive inverse of Clytemnestra, see Winnington-Ingram 1983: 125–31; Zeitlin 1984: 182.

10. This logic "envisions that woman's refusal of her required subordinate role must, by an inevitable sequence, lead to its opposite: total domination, gynecocracy, whose extreme form projects the enslavement or murder of men. That same polarizing imagination can only conceive of two hierarchic alternatives: Rule by Men or Rule by Women" (Zeitlin 1984: 163; cf. Pembroke 1967; Bamberger 1974; Vidal-Naquet 1981; Rabinowitz 1992: 41–43). Thus although the chorus declares that it is "just" for Clytemnestra to rule while her husband is gone and that it honors her power (258–60), that power is always anomalous and threatens a dangerous excess. For a similar linking of gynecocracy and tyranny, see Ar. *Lys.* 616–35 and Henderson 1987 ad loc.

11. M. Griffith 1995: 84. Rose (1992: 203) points out the slippage in the *Oresteia* between legitimate aristocracy and monarchy on the one hand and

tyranny on the other. He argues from this that Aeschylus's explicit condemnation of the latter entails an implicit critique of the former. While I agree with him that this whole aristocratic *oikos* is discredited, I disagree with Rose's central thesis that this constitutes an attack on the aristocracy as a class (204–21); whereas Rose sees Clytemnestra, Aegisthus, and Agamemnon as exemplary aristocrats and thus views the whole trilogy as essentially antiaristocratic (e.g., 205–6, 214), I take these characters as exceptional, exemplary only of the worst excesses of the aristocracy, and thus see in the text's rejection of these "bad" aristocrats an implicit acceptance of a "good" (i.e., less extreme, more democratized) aristocracy. sFor a similar viewpoint, see Podlecki 1986; M. Griffith 1995; Kurke forthcoming.

12. Zeitlin (1984: 163) points out the similarities between Aegisthus and Paris. Although he does have his own role in the story of the house of Atreus, in Aeschylus's version (as opposed to that told at *Od.* 1.32–43 and in artistic representations, most famously the calyx of the Dokimasia Painter), his role as avenger of Thyestes is secondary to that as Clytemnestra's lover. He is only the coconspirator in Clytemnestra's plot, a fact that the chorus holds against him (1633–37, 1643–46), suggesting that he is not man enough to avenge his father himself.

13. M. Griffith (1995: 84 n. 80) sees in the characterization of Aegisthus as both tyrannical and effete "two overlapping models of 'undesirable aristocrat' in democratic ideology." He further notes that it seems to have been a charge leveled against certain elite men that they were ruled by their women. Thus Pericles was said to be "another Heracles," ruled by Aspasia (Plut. *Per.* 24; cf. Semonides 7.57–70; Ar. *Nub.* 1ff.; Plato *Rep.* 549d).

14. On the Eastern parallels to the carpet scene, see Wilamowitz 1927; Flintoff 1987: 123–24; Hall 1989; Crane 1993: 122–25.

15. Halperin (1990a) discusses the link between sexual passivity and political disenfranchisement.

16. I discussed this above, in Chapter 5. These two extremes are complementary and by no means mutually exclusive. Kurke (forthcoming) sees disembedding as associated with tyrannical tendencies.

17. Rose 1992: 206–7; M. Griffith 1995: 88 n. 92. Aegisthus's language is even more explicit: at 1638–42 he states baldly that he will use Agamemnon's wealth to gain control of the city.

18. Compare Clytemnestra's treatment of Cassandra. The girl is introduced by Agamemnon as a *xenē* (950), and her relationship with the chorus is amicable and equal, assimilated to a relation of *xenia* (1062, 1093, 1315, 1320). Clytemnestra, however, will not recognize a relationship of *xenia* with Cassandra. She will admit her into the house only as a *doulos*, a slave (1045) and an addition to the household wealth (1036–39). Clytemnestra thus mistakes this *xenē* for a *doulē*, just as she had *agalmata* for *ploutos*, and Cassandra's death becomes yet another violation of *xenia* in the saga of the House of Atreus. On this theme in the *Oresteia*, see Roth 1993.

19. It is only with Agamemnon's return that they can voice a political opinion,

if only in retrospect (799–806); they must still be oblique in referring to the present political situation (807–9). On the social character of this chorus, see Gantz 1983; Griffith 1995: 76–77 and n. 55; on Aeschylean choruses more generally, Podlecki 1972; Rosenmeyer 1982: 145–87.

20. She may even be present onstage during this ode. Taplin 1977: 280: "Whether Clytemnestra was present throughout the first song (Parodos) of *Agamemnon* or whether she only entered at the end of it must be one of the most disputed stage directions in Greek tragedy." He argues, though, for a late entrance (1977: 280–85; cf. 1972: 89–94).

21. The First Stasimon is likewise framed by the chorus's address to her (351–54) and her speech (489–500).

22. Clytemnestra reaches this site of fantasy through her deployment of the beacons (281–316). This geographical catalogue describes not mythical places but real, practical geography; this is not a literary trope, but the strategic plan of a naval commander familiar with the topography: Clytemnestra's power is always on male terms. Further, although geographical catalogues are common in Aeschylus, there are no others in which the narrator himself has not traversed the terrain he describes. Thus Clytemnestra controls imaginatively even the space she cannot occupy physically. Goldhill (1984: 39) sees in Clytemnestra's imaginative control of space a recognition of the "arbitrary connection between signifier and signified in Clytemnestra's manipulation of signs (language and beacons)."

23. Mingling causes disaster in this play: cf. 650–52, where the oath between fire and water destroys the Greek fleet. So at 321, unambiguous good fortune is the distinction between the Greek victors and the Trojan losers. Rabinowitz (1981) explains this theme by drawing a parallel to cosmogonic myths, with their movement from chaos to order.

24. See Clytemnestra's charge against Helen (1467) of killing many men and causing ἀξύστατον ἄλγος, "a sorrow that won't congeal," again a terrifying image of lack of differentiation.

25. The tone of this passage is open to question. Denniston and Page (1957 at 1551–59) read it as cynical, partly in response to Fraenkel's theory that Clytemnestra has a change of heart after the murder and weakens at the end of the play. I believe that it is possible to read this passage sympathetically (as a genuine expression of maternal grief), especially in light of Clytemnestra's previous lament (1525–29). Potential sympathy is undercut, however, by Clytemnestra's tyrannical diction (e.g., at 1421–25), and her references to Aegisthus (1434–37) and the murder of Agamemnon (1528–29, 1551–54). Any maternal associations Clytemnestra may have in relation to Iphigeneia, moreover, are denied in her relationship to Orestes (e.g., at *Ag.* 877–85 and throughout *Cho.*). I suggested above (Chapter 5, note 122) that one reason for the sacrifice was to strip Clytemnestra preemptively of any claim to Iphigeneia's loyalty by preserving her as her father's daughter.

26. Denniston and Page (1957) ad 1446–47: "The text and the detail of the

meaning remain uncertain." The sexual connotations of χλιδή, however, are clear: see, e.g., Aes. *Supp.* 1003; Aes. *Pers.* 544; Eur. *Cycl.* 500; Xen. *Symp.* 8.8.2; Plato *Symp.* 197d7. Lloyd-Jones's comment is apropos: "Some scholars find it unthinkable that Clytemnestra should say that the pleasure of having killed her husband's concubine should heighten her own sexual satisfaction. This seems to be an insufficient reason for refusing to accept the meaning that the words appear to bear" (1979 ad loc.).

27. Rose (1992: 230–31) also calls Clytemnestra's transgressive sexuality sadism; he argues that this excessive, perverse *erōs* is specifically aristocratic in *Agamemnon.* Cf. Rabinowitz 1992: 43.

28. On this passage, see Peradotto 1964: 380; Zeitlin 1965: 473–74; duBois 1988: 70–71; Goldhill 1991: 24. Vickers (1973: 381) calls the metaphor "brilliant, if sickening."

29. Zeitlin 1965: 473–74; Burian 1986: 335.

30. Perhaps related to this intersection of sexual and religious perversion is Clytemnestra's role, hinted throughout the play, as sorceress or *pharmakeus* (φαρμασσομένη χρίματος ἁγνοῦ / μαλακαῖς ἀδόλοισι παρηγορίαις, / πελάνωι μυχόθεν βασιλείωι, "Charmed by the guileless soft seducings of the pure ointment, a royal offering from deep within," 94–96; cf. 1407–10; see, too, her frequent allusion to apotropaic devices: 341–50, 933–34, 1567–76). In this role Clytemnestra resembles her sister, who in the *Odyssey* is also a *pharmakeus*, her drug allowing the audience to hear tales of sorrow without suffering (*Od.* 4.219–33). Like Helen's drug, Clytemnestra's is associated with her sexuality: her sacrifices are feminine persuasions; the "offerings from the inner recesses" (πελάνωι μυχόθεν, 96, both words charged with sexual connotations for tragedy) suggest the dangerous secrets of the female body. On Clytemnestra's *pharmaka*, see Goldhill 1984: 18.

31. Later she will become inseparable from the very murder weapon: I return to this in the next section of this chapter.

32. For parallels, see above, Chapter 5.

33. Easterling cites this scene among the numerous parallels between the two plays (1982: 21–22 and ad 293–313 and 536–38). But whereas *Trachiniae*'s scene provided an opportunity for intersubjectivity and self-definition, *Agamemnon*'s emphasizes the impossibility of communication between the two women. Cassandra will not speak, and Clytemnestra (in contrast to the chorus, which believes the problem to be merely linguistic and calls for an interpreter) takes the silence as an affront, evidence of Cassandra's pride, madness, or malice (1064–68). Rather than opening up the issue of subjective interiority (as the scene in *Trachiniae* does), this interview closes off individual subjectivity, instead reaffirming the overdetermined roles of these characters as defensive fantasies within the larger psychic structure of the play.

34. Cassandra's prolonged silence is quite extraordinary, compounded by the

fact that the first thirty of her 250 lines of silence focus explicitly on the fact of her silence. Moreover, as Taplin (1977: 316) notes, after Clytemnestra's exit, we expect to hear Agamemnon's death cries, but instead "hear" Cassandra's silence. See further ibid.: 318–22; Taplin 1972: 77; Knox 1979: 42–47; Thalmann 1985 on its dramatic effect (and cf. the charge against Aeschylus in Aristophanes' *Frogs* 833–34, 919–27, on which see Taplin 1972: 52–76).

35. On "ek-stasis," see Cixous 1976; Irigaray 1977: 28–29. Cassandra has been a popular character in modern feminism. For example, Christa Wolf's *Cassandra*, a narrative told from the point of view of the prophetess herself, imagines in Cassandra's struggle against objectification the forging of a specifically female consciousness. Madness is often taken in feminist theory as a privileged site of female subjectivity: see Cixous 1976; Cixous and Clément 1986: 22–26; this view is also implicit in Kristeva's notion of "the abject," which she associates with the female and sees as a space of potential resistance to the phallic symbolic (see, e.g., 1982: 32–55). American feminists have by and large rejected the French romanticization of madness; see, for example, Chesler 1973; Marcus 1989; and the excellent discussion in Felman 1975. On madness and women in Greek thought, see Padel 1992: ch. 8.

36. Note the nuptial diction at 1138–39: ἤγαγες, ξυνθανουμένην.

37. The exact nature of the transaction imagined here is vague: is the payment to Agamemnon for bringing her (which makes her a commodity), or to her for coming (which makes her a wage-laborer)? Either way, the term associates her with the debased commodity economy.

38. See Fraenkel (1950): "Cassandra herself is the debt owed to the god: he has now called in (*exegit*) her person and her life. . . . By bestowing on the maiden his own gift of prophecy, in order to seal the bond of love for which he was striving, Apollo made her his own; now he has reclaimed his property: the consequence is that she must die." Denniston and Page (1957) reject this interpretation of the verb as obscure and translate: "The seer, having finished the business of the seeress."

39. This is the codices' reading, but it is hypermetric. Denniston and Page (1957) want to retain the meaning of the verb, if not its form (they suggest ἐπεγχέαι, an epexegetic infinitive). All that my reading really requires is the sense inherent in the prefix.

40. Cf. 1324, where Agamemnon is inserted next to her in Denniston and Page's reconstruction of the text (δεσπότου τιμαόροις).

41. For example, on 1263: "Here, as in 1137 and 1325f., Cassandra holds fast to the idea that hers is only a secondary part in the whole fearful story." It is true that in the broadest narrative structure of the trilogy, Cassandra's death is less important than Agamemnon's; however, in the poetics of this play, her death is given more space and more emotional elaboration. In fact, her anticipation and lamentation of her own death replace his death in the linear development of the

play: he goes in to his death, but what we see next is her visions; then when she goes in to her death we hear his death cry. Thus, while his death may be more significant to the narrative, in terms of dramatic effect, hers replaces his.

42. Liviabella Furiani (1990) suggests that women in Aeschylus function as men's consciences, showing up the horrors of war.

43. She prays to die ἀσφάδαιστος (1293), without struggle or convulsion. For her courage, Cassandra is praised in the terms of male *aretē* (she is called *sophē*, 1295). Her desire (doomed, of course) to persuade the chorus is a desire to prove her *kleos* as a prophet (κλέος μαντικὸν, 1098), and to maintain her status even in these reduced circumstances. In the end, she will die to prove her prophecies true, and the *kleos* she wins will be for her death, not for her prophetic ability. For Cassandra, alone among the characters of this play, is allowed to die a noble death: ἀλλ᾿ εὐκλεῶς τοι κατθανεῖν χάρις βροτῶι ("But it is a *kharis* for a mortal to die with good *kleos*," 1304). This expression of Cassandra's noble death is especially remarkable considering how sparingly *kleos* is allowed in this tragedy. (Denniston and Page 1957 ad 1304 mark the peculiarity: "The fact must be faced that εὐκλεῶς κατθανεῖν is quite out of place here, a cliché used without sufficient regard for the context; we need 'bravely,' not 'gloriously.'") She dies nobly, receiving the *kharis* that is denied to Agamemnon and to the Greek soldiers at Troy. Schein (1982: 13) contrasts her noble death to Agamemnon's ignominious defeat.

44. Although he had been praised in such terms previously in the play, she is the first to repeat this characterization since his defeat in the *agōn* against Clytemnestra.

45. See Alexiou 1974: 10–14 on the tradition of foreign women lamenting the death of a noble man; cf. Briseis and the other captive women lamenting Patroclus at *Il*. 19.24, 18.339.

46. Again at 1129, she herself becomes the "deceitful murderous urn" (δολο-φόνου λέβητος) in which he is killed. She is also "an amphisbaina, a Scylla, . . . a raging mother of Hades" (1233–36), in a list that prefigures the intensely misogynist First Stasimon of *Choephoroe*.

47. Fraenkel (1950 ad loc.) seems to intuit this in his attempt to understand the exact meaning of ξύνευνος: "Though it is far from certain, it should perhaps be considered as a possibility whether the idea of 'the embracing one' could not be found in σύνευνος, which normally means 'wife.'"

48. The Pythia, to whom Cassandra is explicitly compared at 1255, could be a married woman, but was required to be chaste while she was in service to the god (Lucan 5.141, 161; schol. Eur. *Orestes* 165; Diod. Sic. 16.21.6; Sissa 1990b: ch. 4). This requirement presumably stems from some sense of a union with the god; in later sources, she is imagined as being penetrated by his *pneuma*, which was said to emanate from the Delphic rock (Plut. *de Pyth. Orac.* 405c; Sissa 1990b: 51–52). But on the vested interests behind this representation of the Pythia, see Maurizio 1995: 69–71.

49. On ἰσοτριβής as an obscenity, see Koniaris 1980 and Tyrrell 1980.

50. Rehm 1994: 44–52. Lebeck (1971: 54–55) suggests further that in the swift succession of images in this passage—bride, brightness, waves—Cassandra evokes the sudden transformation of Helen from bride into Fury in the Second Stasimon. On this passage, see also Goldhill 1984: 85.

51. See, e.g., Ar. *Ach.* 271ff.; *A.P.* 12.206; Kovacs 1987; Fraenkel 1950 ad loc. Poliakoff 1980 examines wrestling as a central metaphor in the *Oresteia*.

52. Did she promise to bear Apollo a child, then not bear one? Or did she bear it, then secretly murder it? Was she perhaps unfaithful to the god? Or did she promise to sleep with him and then cheat him of this (as in Apollodorus's account, 3.12.5)? Such literal-minded questions are not intended to be answered, of course, but only to highlight the obscurity of the crime (but see Kovacs 1987 for some proposed answers). The ambiguity rests in the two possible meanings of ἐψευσάμην (to cheat or to deceive) and in the interpretation of 1207: τέκνων εἰς ἔργον could mean sex rather than actual childbearing (the two might be synonymous in conjugal relations). Denniston and Page (1957) hedge the question with their translation: "Were you really *lovers*?" Fraenkel (1950) adduces parallels that could support either interpretation: Semon. 7.48–49 (W) (πρὸς ἔργον ἀφροδίσιον) would suggest that the phrase here means sex, but the parallel with the marriage formula (γνησίων παίδων ἐπ᾽ ἀρότῳ) makes the referent more naturally childbirth. The choice of the final word of the line (Butler's ὁμοῦ versus the codices' νόμῳ) seems to me to make little difference to this issue.

CHAPTER 7

1. The normative psychoanalytic child, for Klein no less than for Freud, is male. At the risk of inelegance, I refer to the child throughout in the neuter in order to avoid prejudging the gender of the subject.

2. Klein defines and elaborates her theory of the depressive position most fully in "A Contribution to the Psychogenesis of Manic-Depressive States"(1935) and "Mourning and Its Relation to Manic-Depressive States" (1940). A convenient summary of her developmental model can be found in "Some Theoretical Conclusions regarding the Emotional Life of the Infant"(1952). All of these essays are collected in Klein 1984.

3. Klein 1984, 1: 269, 285–89, 353–54.

4. Ibid.: 344: "My contention is that the child goes through states of mind comparable to the mourning of the adult, or rather, that this early mourning is revived whenever grief is experienced in later life."

5. Freud 1963: 164–79. In this paper more than anywhere else, Freud lays the groundwork for the theories of object relations associated with Klein. The "shadow of the object upon the ego" (170) is the realm and focus of object-relations psychoanalysis.

6. Ibid.: 170. Segal (1992) also invokes Freud's "Mourning and Melancholia" to explain Admetus's mourning process; he focuses on mourning as a period of transformation for the mourner, culminating in an acceptance of his loss. Cf. Segal 1993: 52–72.

7. The metaphorical nature of the maternal body becomes even more apparent in later object-relations theory; for Winnicott (1971), for example, the mother is reduced to an "environment," which can be hostile or nurturing. Separating the structural function of the mother (as environment, as other, or as object) from the physical, biological mother helps psychoanalytic theory's claims to transhistorical relevance, for it allows for a variety of child-rearing practices (such as wet-nursing, communal parenting, etc.). By arguing that Alcestis bears maternal aspects in the play, I do not mean to literalize the developmental model; rather, I wish to show how the problems generated by Alcestis as a too-good object are expressed in the imagination of the play through (among other means) the fantasy of an overpowering mother. For a similar approach to Shakespearean tragedy, see Adelman 1992.

8. Dyson 1988: 13–16.

9. It is not insignificant that the child is a boy, singing on behalf of himself and his sister; thus here, as in psychoanalysis, the archetypal object relation is imagined as that between a mother and her male child.

10. We might think of him as the juvenile hypostasis of Admetus and the *oikos*; see Dale 1954 ad 393–415: "The child sings the sentiments its elders feel for it" (cf. Dyson 1988: 17). If, as Dale has suggested (xx), the part of the child is sung by the dead Alcestis, this would create a sense that child and mother are not fully distinct; I return to this point later in this chapter.

11. Dale (1954 ad loc.) suggests that it "belongs to nursery language."

12. Klein 1984, 1: 345: "The object which is being mourned [in the depressive position] is the mother's breast and all that the breast and the milk have come to stand for in the infant's mind: namely, love, goodness and security. All these are felt by the baby to be lost."

13. The text is Diggle's (1987) unless otherwise specified.

14. Admetus's real mother is totally occluded; she is linked with Pheres as a bad parent (16, 290, 338–39, 516–17), but in Pheres' defense of his selfishness, he seems to speak for himself alone. The only time she is mentioned in her own right (637–39), it is to be explicitly rejected. Idealization is often accompanied by splitting, which allows the good object to be unambiguously good by projecting all hostility onto a "bad" object. So here, Alcestis is idealized as munificent mother, while Pheres and his wife are villainized as bad parents.

15. Depressive anxieties are closely bound up for Klein with greed and envy: the loss of the object is felt to be the result (either through direct destruction or through retaliatory withholding) of the child's greedy attacks on the breast and its contents. See "Envy and Gratitude," Klein 1984, 3: ch. 10.

16. "Leave," but also "forsake, abandon," LSJ s.v. προλείπω I.1; s.v. προ-

δίδωμι II.2, 3. Pheres literalizes Admetus's ambivalence, charging him with having murdered Alcestis (696, 730). W. D. Smith (1960: 30) rightly links this theme to the question of betrayal in the final exchange. Rosenmeyer (1963: 222) also has a psychological reading of this diction, but sees it as indicative of Admetus's selfishness and resentment (likewise Scully 1986: 140).

17. The causal confusion surrounding the loss of Alcestis, which I am regarding as inherent within the necessarily ambivalent object relation, may explain why so much of the scholarship on *Alcestis* focuses on the question of guilt. Is Admetus guilty of destroying his wife, and then indulging in egotistical self-pity at the effects of his selfishness? (See Grube 1941; Beye 1959; Hartigan 1991.) Or is he, rather, innocent and pious, and deserving of our pity? (See Dale 1954; Burnett 1971 and 1983; Lloyd 1985.) Does Alcestis offer herself precisely because she knows of the rewards that await her, her death a self-interested and aggressive act rather than a selfless sacrifice? (See Beye 1959; Von Fritz 1962: 256–321; Rosenmeyer 1963: 227; G. Smith 1982. Kott [1973: 91] calls Alcestis's self-sacrifice "revolting.") Or is her sacrifice wholly generous? See the discussion in Lloyd 1985. As J. Gregory (1979: 259 and n. 4) points out, both sides adduce the same passages in support of their views.

18. See Buxton 1985: 75–78; Thury 1988: 203–5; Seaford 1990; Rabinowitz 1993: 73–74. For Rabinowitz this liminality makes the woman threatening to male social categories, and she sees this threat and its containment as the basic dynamic of the play. Starting from the Freudian concepts of the "uncanny" and the "fetish," she builds a sophisticated and detailed analysis of Alcestis's movement from the former to the latter. The dynamic of loss and mourning developed here is not so different from the cycle of threat and containment that she identifies, although I locate the primary "threat" in a different place (not in female sexuality but in the loss and subsequent demonization of the maternal object) and identify different defensive strategies (in particular, the Oedipal relationship with Heracles). We agree on the homosocial emphasis of *Alcestis*, but where Rabinowitz sees this play as reaffirming the status quo (98–99), and seeks resistance in the possibility that a feminist reader might focus on Alcestis's strength rather than on the reduction of that strength (the threat, that is, rather than the containment of the threat), I argue that in juxtaposing two different modes of mourning (and two corollary understandings of the structure of the ego and the relation between male self and female other), the play stages both the hegemonic and the counterhegemonic, and allows the two to coexist even until the final scene. My broader theoretical differences from Rabinowitz's provocative book are discussed in the Introduction.

19. She is, as Heracles says, a θυραῖον κῆδος (828), a marriage connection from outside, a grief from outside (cf. 778, θυραίου πήματος, "an outside pain").

20. The scholia and the stronger manuscript tradition (according to Dale [1954]) read *oikeios*, as do most editors (Hayley [1898]; see discussions in Thury

1988: 203; Riemer 1989: 182–83). Dale proposes *othneios* (which, she comments, we might have expected echoing 810) and argues against *oikeios* as "giving the show away prematurely." Diggle (1987) also prints *othneios*.

21. J. Gregory's (1979) conclusions are similar, although she starts from different premises. She argues that if death becomes differentiated, life (and ideas, judgments, and categories) becomes undifferentiated. Cf. J. Gregory 1991: 26–46.

22. Burnett (1971: 37) puts this nicely: "*Philia* means living with two souls instead of one . . . and the full experience of what this can mean, when one of those is dead, reaches Admetus on his return from the tomb."

23. J. Gregory 1979: 263. From the time of her agreement to die for Admetus, though living, she has really been dead, for her imminent death is certain (520–21, 524–27). Verrall (1913: 79–82) takes the most extreme steps to explain away these ambiguities, maintaining that Alcestis was never really dead at all.

24. This is the reading of the majority of the manuscripts; Diggle (1987) prints for 527 Jackson's emendation κἀνθάδ' ὢν οὐκ ἔστ' ἔτι.

25. J. Gregory 1979: 267. Segal (1992: 154) notes that Heracles introduces "a degree of self-consciousness about the outside, male, political world." For an alternate view, see Luschnig 1992: 32: "As long as Alcestis was alive, . . . the house had structure, now [with the entry of Heracles] it has become chaotic."

26. On the connection between the depressive position and the Oedipal complex, see Klein 1984, 1: ch. 9 ("Early Stages of the Oedipus Conflict") and ch. 21 ("The Oedipus Complex in the Light of Early Anxieties"), and the summary at 3: 76–83.

27. Ibid., 3: 79–80.

28. Reparation is by no means the same thing as resurrection; thus I reject the (all-too-common) reading of *Alcestis* as a proto-Christian tale of piety and miracles (an egregious example is Verrall 1913: 79).

29. On the "happy ending," see Wilson 1968: 1–13; Burnett 1971; Halleran 1982; G. Smith 1982; Lloyd 1985; Garner 1988; Hartigan 1991; Luschnig 1992: 33–34; Rehm 1994: 95–96. The view of Rosenmeyer (1963: 215) is representative: the ending is "for the most part a genial fairy tale rather than a bitter drama of conflict and betrayal." For dissenting opinions, see Drew 1913: 319; Von Fritz 1962: 256–321; Nielson 1976; Goldfarb 1992: 122–26. Kott (1973: 79) remarks that for those who do not consider the ending happy, there are only two options: "Either to regard *Alcestis* as a failure, or to consider it as a shocking drama, with an unusual degree of venom and perfidy." It will become apparent that I think there are other possible positions.

30. Plato's may be the older version: see Dale 1954: xi–xii; contra, Conacher 1967: 329–30. Apollodorus (1.9.15) knows both versions. The definitive study of the mythic and "folktale" background to *Alcestis* is Lesky 1925.

31. Freud 1963: 170.

32. This is a connection that Freud himself does not make, despite his famili-

arity with Karl Abraham's work on mourning (ibid.: 164 n. 2), which Klein acknowledges as her strongest influence.

33. This same necessary correlation of separation from the mother and identification with the father is developed further in Lacan's association of the symbolic (language, law, society) with the Father and the Phallus. Cf. Introduction above.

34. Kristeva 1989: 27–28. Kristeva in many regards combines aspects of post-Freudian psychoanalysis and object-relations theory, but in her approach to mourning is generally closer to the former. Silverman (1988: 101–26) offers an excellent analysis of Kristeva's views on the maternal body.

35. Zeitlin (1982 and 1981: 194–200) discusses the Demeter story as a paradigm in ritual and theater.

36. Alcestis's struggle with Hades as she is about to die suggests a rape, like Persephone's rape by Hades, and the negotiations between Apollo and Thanatos in *Alcestis* parallel those between Zeus and Hades in the *Homeric Hymn to Demeter*.

37. In the version of the Alcestis myth used by Apollodorus, it is Persephone herself who sends Alcestis back to Admetus (1.9.15). The alternatives presented at 846–53 between Heracles' fight with death and his persuasion of Persephone suggest that Euripides was familiar with this version. See Dale 1954 ad 837.

38. Rabinowitz (1993: 83) goes further: "Do Euripides and Admetos forget that Orpheus's gaze kills Eurydice?"

39. See, by way of comparison, *Il.* 9.487ff.; Callinus 1.12–13; Simonides 520, 521 (*PMG*). A particularly close parallel is Apollo's advice to Admetus at Bacch. 3.76–84 (to which I return below). For a general discussion of life and death in *Alcestis*, see Buxton 1985: 78–83; Bradley 1980.

40. Lesky 1925; D. M. Jones 1948; Conacher 1967: 327–33; G. Smith 1982; Burnett 1983: 254–55, 270–71; J. Gregory 1991: 43–44. Segal 1992: 157: "When Admetus regains his wife from death, it is after he has come to recognize, experientially, these conditions of mortality."

41. Rabinowitz (1993: 70) also sees death as linked to the female in this play, but connects this to castration anxiety rather than to the maternal body.

42. This way of thinking about maternity was common in Greek literature: we may think of Thetis's lament that she bore Achilles to die young (e.g., *Il.* 1.416–18) or the myth of Althaea (Apollod. 1.8.1–4; Phrynicus fr. 6N; Bacch. 5.93ff.), with a firebrand to mark the span of her son's short life (and the similar story of Demeter and Demophöon at *h. Dem.* 235–91).

CHAPTER 8

1. Or perhaps foreshadows it. Since the dating of *Trachiniae* is insecure, it is impossible to tell which way the lines of influence run. Arguments on stylistic

grounds are inconclusive as borrowings are documented for each poet from the other. See Easterling 1982: 19–23. Riemer 1989: 84–85 n. 211 has complete bibliography for the supporters on each side. On the parallels and difference between the two scenes, see Earle 1902: 5–13; Lesky 1976; Lloyd-Jones's note in Reinhardt [1947] 1979: 245–46; Riemer 1989: 84–90.

2. Burnett 1983: 258; Segal 1993: 39–41.

3. Loraux 1987: 23–24.

4. Dyson (1988: 15) believes she leaves the bedroom before greeting the slaves and children; the text is ambiguous on this point.

5. Burnett 1983: 257; cf. W. D. Smith 1960: 138–39. Note, too, that the only two "messenger" speeches (by the male and female servants) report events from within the house, not, as is more common in this type of speech, from the world beyond the *oikos*.

6. This word may have technical political connotations. In Euripides' day, as Dale points out (1954 ad 1154), it referred to the administrative organization of Thessaly, which Euripides projects onto the mythic past. The other uses of the word occur in more technical contexts (e.g., Dem. *Phil.* 3.26.8; Jacoby 1a.4F. fr. 52). Perhaps it is significant to note here that Admetus's domain is not a *polis* but an *ethnos*; the city of Pherae, unlike that of Argos, Thebes, or Athens, is not a political unit in itself. This fact would add to the diffusion of the political, and facilitate its conflation with the domestic.

7. Admetus justifies his acceptance of Heracles into the mourning *domos* on the grounds not of political expedience, but of the useful *xenia* bond this hospitality will create for him: αὐτὸς δ' ἀρίστου τοῦδε τυγχάνω ξένου / ὅταν ποτ' Ἄργους διψίαν ἔλθω χθόνα ("I have this man as the best host whenever I go to the dusty land of Argos," 559–60): note the first-person-singular verbs.

8. Zeitlin 1984: 163.

9. On the relation between the personal and the political in *xenia*, see Herman 1987. On *xenia* and *philia* in *Alcestis*, Schein 1988; Stanton 1990; Goldfarb 1992.

10. The causal connection between maternal strength and paternal weakness is unclear. While within the dramatic action of the play, it seems that Alcestis's strength gives rise to Admetus's weakness, if we look at the mythic background, the reverse seems to be true. It is only through textual manipulation, as we shall see, that the maternal object comes to seem debilitating to the male subject and to the patriline, the cause of all their problems.

11. Thury (1988) analyzes this same problem in her article on intergenerational strife in *Alcestis* and Athens. Rabinowitz (1993: 69) takes the opposite view from mine, seeing in the mythic background "material that indicates the father's power."

12. This theme may link *Alcestis* with *Telephus*, which was part of the same tetralogy, and also seems to have dealt with status confusion in its depiction of

the king in rags. The social leveling may also be connected to the play's satyric or prosatyric character.

13. Elferink (1982: 47) imagines that Apollo enters the stage at a run and dressed in rags like a slave, not assuming his divine garb until line 9. He also argues that there is no friendship between Admetus and Apollo, and sees Apollo in the prologue as "choking with anger because of the humiliation he has suffered" (48); the rest of the action can then be read as Apollo's vengeance. This over-reading draws out to the fullest the status inversion implied in the prologue.

14. See Chapter 5, note 120 on *trapeza*. Θῆσσαν τράπεζαν is a *hapax legomenon*.

15. "Holy myself, I found a holy man," says Apollo (ὁσίου γὰρ ἀνδρὸς ὅσιος ὢν ἐτύγχανον, 10). The unusual use of *hosios* to describe a god emphasizes the tension between the relationship of inequality (between man and god) and that of reciprocity and likeness (as Scodel [1979: 59] notes).

16. G. Murray (1963) prints 636–39 as questions; Dale (1954 ad 636ff.) follows him, arguing that reading these lines as questions "gives an entirely different tone to the whole passage, which becomes a highly effective *reductio ad absurdum*." For a discussion of the passage, see M. Griffith 1978: 83–86. Griffith rejects Murray's punctuation, identifying in 636 a rhetorical formula used here to express not a literal disavowal of paternity but rather "the paradox, that Pheres, Admetos' natural father, is no *true* father" (86).

17. ἥτις γε τῆς σῆς προύθανε ψυχῆς, τέκνον. / καί μ' οὐκ ἄπαιδ' ἔθηκεν οὐδ' εἴασε σοῦ / στερέντα γήραι πενθίμωι καταφθίνειν ("She died for your life, son, and did not render me childless or allow me to wither in sorrowful old age deprived of you"). See Scully 1986: 138; Thury 1988: 204–5.

18. W. D. Smith 1960: 136; Burnett 1971: 34–35; 1983: 260; Vellacott 1975: 101; Dyson 1988: 15; Rabinowitz 1993: 76. On the woman's association with the preservation of the *oikos* in Greek myth, see Vernant 1983b.

19. Compare Alcestis's support of her own *genos* and patriline: in the myth of Medea's plot against Pelias, Alcestis is the only one of Pelias's daughters who refuses to join in his murder: Diod. Sic. 4.52.2. This myth may be evoked elliptically at 535, as well as in Alcestis's common appellation, daughter of Pelias.

20. Her emphasis specifically on the patriline is clear from the way Alcestis imagines her children's future in her absence: it is her daughter who will suffer most under the sway of a hostile stepmother, while her son will have the protection of his father (311–12). Note, too, the occlusion of the daughter in the lamentation of Alcestis onstage. The boy appears and sings (indeed, his is the largest child's role in extant Euripides), but the girl is not seen. Dyson (1988: 16) points out, however, that Alcestis's daughter is the only female child even mentioned in Euripides.

21. *Pace* Beye (1959: 122–24), who sees Alcestis as "strikingly devoid of any feeling for Admetus" (123) and laments "the sterility of their relationship" (124).

Likewise Rosenmeyer 1963: 224: "Alcestis has naturally come to despise the man who caused her to commit herself." To say, as I do, that Alcestis dies for her marriage is not to speculate either way upon her feelings for Admetus.

22. Loraux 1987: 23–26.

23. Thus Alcestis falls between Loraux's two main categories for the tragic deaths of women: she dies like a matron for her husband but also sacrifices herself like one of Euripides' patriotic virgins.

24. Diggle (1987) prints μόνον ("you alone") for μόνην ("me alone"), following Markland's emendation of the codices' reading, and πάρος for πέρι (a textual problem to which I return below, note 55). See Dale (1954), Hayley (1898) ad 178–80 for the scholarship.

25. When the chorus generalizes at 238–43 that marriage is misery, it refers not to the death of Alcestis, but to the grief of Admetus.

26. Vellacott (1975: 102), however, believes that "the tragedy lies in the assumptions of marriage itself, which imposes an obligation without postulating its necessary motive of love." O'Higgins (1993) argues similarly that the play shows marriage itself to be a system that devitalizes women; cf. Rabinowitz 1993: 93–94.

27. It is taken as such by, e.g., Rabinowitz (1993: 75), who sees it as "allay[ing] male anxiety about the outsider woman": "The sacrifice itself and the motivation for it define Alcestis as no longer a suspect outsider but rather a woman totally committed to the house of Admetos. Thus the problem of the outsider woman is eliminated by bringing her more securely within" (76). Cf. Vernant 1983b.

28. 290; 515, 641, 662, 686. If Winkler (1990c: 217–20) is right in seeing *physis* as a euphemism for the male genitals, we might say that Alcestis, by prioritizing her own *physis* over Admetus's, figuratively takes the phallus; but we needn't go that far to see the control she claims over the patriline in these lines.

29. According to the distinction drawn in *Eumenides* and supported by Aristotle *De gen. an.* 729a, 738b.

30. On the "scholarly adoration" of Alcestis, see Rabinowitz 1993: 77. I see Alcestis's superlative status as deriving from Admetus's (and the play's) idealization of her as a lost object, an idealization that causes more problems than it solves. Rabinowitz (ibid.: 72) takes an interesting approach to this question, arguing that Alcestis's canonization constitutes a form of fetishism that helps contain the threat of female sexuality and liminality.

31. Thus I cannot agree with the opinion of Vellacott (1975: 101) that the audience would have accepted the sacrifice of Alcestis's life for Admetus's as normal; though he may be right that "in every society known to Hellenes or barbarians it is unquestioningly accepted that, in the broadest terms and in the last resort, woman's life is at the service and disposal of man's" (101), nonetheless, Euripides goes to great lengths to emphasize how extreme and extraordinary is Alcestis's sacrifice. For a critique of Euripides' supposed misogyny, see March 1990.

32. This mutual definition is even more noticeable if we read the line as a question (Dale 1954 ad 144).

33. Freud identifies this denigration of the ego and idealization of the lost object in mourning as a form of splitting, with the introjection of the bad object as a part of the self, culminating often in suicide (1963: 167; cf. Klein 1984, 1: 268–69). The only time Admetus and Alcestis are equated (915–25) is in Admetus's memory of their marriage, long before this test differentiated them. Amost all critical literature on *Alcestis* sides with either one or the other of the protagonists. By saying that Alcestis wins and Admetus loses, I do not wish to indicate my own personal preference (which seems to be the sole basis for any such adjudication) for one character over the other, but rather to identify a relationship of inverse proportion between them and to show why the canonization of Alcestis in the play is necessarily problematic for Admetus's characterization.

34. The diction suggests a trial (12–15). The primary effect of Euripides' telescopic chronology (that is, the eclipse of time between the decision and its execution) is that the death itself and not the decision becomes the occasion of the trial. On death as a test in *Alcestis*, see Bradley 1980.

35. If Admetus loses this test, so do Pheres and his wife: see 648–49. I return to Pheres in the next chapter.

36. Alcestis is repeatedly referred to in relative clauses by the masculine generalizing pronoun (49, 76, 381, 527, 530). While female characters can be referred to with masculine pronouns in Greek tragic diction when their situations are being generalized to all "mankind," nonetheless, the grammatical transgendering can be more or less jarring. In *Alcestis*, where the central debate of the play focuses on the gender (and therefore identity) of the corpse, such variation between the feminine and the masculine is quite marked. Consider, for example, the movement between genders in this passage in which Admetus conceals the identity of the dead body:

> HP.: ἆ, μὴ πρόκλαι᾿ ἄκοιτιν. ἐς τότ᾿ ἀμβαλοῦ.
> ΑΔ.: τέθνηχ᾿ ὁ μέλλων. κοὐκέτ᾿ ἔσθ᾿ ὁ κατθανών.
>
> . . . .
>
> HP.: τί δῆτα κλαίεις; τίς φίλων ὁ κατθανών;
> ΑΔ.: γυνή· γυναικὸς ἀρτίως μεμνήμεθα.
>
> (526–27, 530–31)

> HERACLES: Do not mourn your wife now, but put it off
> until the time comes.
> ADMETUS: The man about to die is dead already, and the
> dying man is no more.
> HERACLES: Why do you cry then? Which of your friends is
> the dying man?
> ADMETUS: A woman; we mentioned a woman just now.

37. Garner 1988: 58: "Euripides shaped his portrait of Alcestis with Patroclus in mind." See, too, O'Higgins 1993: 77–82.

38. On the heroic associations of the word in this play, see Garner 1988: 61; Bassi 1989: 25–26; and in general, Nagy 1979: 26–41.

39. σὲ δ' ἄλλη τις γυνὴ κεκτήσεται, / σώφρων μὲν οὐκ ἂν μᾶλλον, εὐ-τυχὴς δ' ἴσως (Alc. 181–82). Cf. Soph. Ajax 550–51: ὦ παῖ, γένοιο πατρὸς εὐτυχέστερος, / τὰ δ' ἄλλ' ὁμοῖος ("Child, be luckier than your father, but like him in all else").

40. Alc. 354–56; Il. 23.65–107.

41. Alc. 898, 996–99; Il. 24.797–98, 7.84–91. These examples and others are discussed in Garner 1988. Luschnig (1992: 24) also notes parallels with the Odyssey, with Alcestis playing the part of Odysseus and Admetus that of Penelope.

42. ὦ Πελίου θύγατερ, / χαίρουσά μοι εἰν Ἅιδα δόμοισιν / τὸν ἀνάλιον οἶκον οἰκετεύοις ("Oh daughter of Pelias, may you dwell happily in the house of Hades, a sunless abode," 435–37). Cf. Il. 23.179: χαῖρέ μοι, ὦ Πάτροκλε, καὶ εἰν Ἀΐδαο δόμοισι ("Farewell, oh Patroclus, even in the house of Hades"). Mark Griffith alerted me to the Homeric sound of the "epic" correption in this dactylic line of Alcestis. See, too, the linking of Alcestis and Achilles as self-sacrificing lovers in Pl. Symp. 208d2–4 and 179b4–180a4.

43. Loraux 1987: 26–29 and n. 57; 1986b: 98–118. Wilkins (1990) discusses the parallels between a hoplite's self-sacrifice and the self-sacrifices of virgins in Euripides, although he does not include Alcestis in his discussion. Rabinowitz (1993: 68) ties this theme to the historical context of encroaching war: "The Alcestis played its role in supporting Athenian social goals by defining female excellence as dying on behalf of men and the family: that is, as a corollary to men's dying for the city."

44. Loraux 1987: 29; cf. Rabinowitz 1993: 80.

45. χρόνος μαλάξει σ'· οὐδέν ἐσθ' ὁ κατθανών ("Time will soften you; the dead man is nothing," 381); note the masculine article (ὁ κατθανών): in the same line he is softened and she masculinized.

46. Garner 1988: 63–64. Wilson's (1968: 3–8) argument that Admetus's "heroic" act of hospitality is equal to Alcestis's heroic self-sacrifice generalizes the sense of "heroic" (and equality, for that matter) beyond all recognition.

47. J. Gregory 1979: 265.

48. Loraux 1987: 29. See also Segal 1992: 148 n. 21; 1993: 60 and 63 n. 34.

49. Loraux 1987: 25; Segal 1992: 145.

50. Alexiou 1974: 10–14. Cf. Foley 1993; Rosenmeyer 1963: 229: "Admetus, the passive, contemplative man, plays the traditional role of women or choruses." On fifth-century attitudes toward male tears (and their bearing on interpretation of Alcestis), see Segal 1992: 148–57. Segal points out that the feminization of male mourning is compounded here by the fact that it is himself

whom Admetus laments. He attributes the gender reversals in *Alcestis* to the extremity of death, one of "the places where the rigid dichotomies of male and female behavior in this society collapse and where there is even an overlapping of male and female roles" (152).

51. Loraux 1987: 7–21.

52. The agonistic nature of the mutual definition of Admetus and Alcestis perhaps explains the difficulty critics have had in coming to grips with Admetus's character. Reactions to Admetus have varied wildly: Myers (1917), Dale (1954), W. D. Smith (1960), Wilson (1968: 1–13), Burnett (1971, 1983), Lloyd (1985), and Dyson (1988) find him heroic and of equal stature to Alcestis, whereas Verrall (1913), Drew (1913), Beye (1959), and Hartigan (1991) dismiss him as weak, foolish, or a cad.

53. Note the legal diction (νοσφιεῖς, 43; ἀφοριζόμενος, 31). Her life is the focus of a dispute over jurisdiction, just as her corpse will be the focus of Admetus's and Pheres' *agōn*, which in many ways replays this divine conflict.

54. Moreover, this exchange never elicits glimpses of other, prior exchanges in which Alcestis did not dispose of herself; unlike in *Trachiniae*, where Iole's objectification recalls for Deianira memories of her own marriage exchange, here Alcestis's marriage is never mentioned. We know from Apollodorus (1.9.15) a version of the myth that made Alcestis the prize of a wedding contest; here there is no hint of this objectifying tradition. Nor is Alcestis's death explicitly represented as a marriage to Hades. Though Alcestis's preparations for death do have nuptial overtones (158–62), these preparations culminate not in marriage to Hades, but in her remarriage to Admetus at the end.

55. Dale (1954 ad loc.) points out that the use of πέρι for ὕπερ is unparalleled in tragedy; she rejects this reading of the preposition and considers the Homeric parallels "irrelevant, since they all contain expressions of fighting or competing, with the idea of a prize set in the midst." She tentatively supports Wilamowitz's emendation of πέρι to πάρος; Diggle (1987) also prints πάρος.

56. *Pace* Burnett (1971: 28), who sees her death as "a private affair." It is private compared to the virgin sacrifices in Euripides (for a comparison, see ibid.: 23–27 and Lloyd 1985: 121–23), but not compared to the deaths of tragic wives (see Loraux 1987: 21–24). O'Higgins (1993: 80–81) and Segal (1993: 73–86) discuss the interplay of public and private in this scene.

57. This speech is unique in Greek tragic literature in that it presents a natural death onstage and a vision of death through the eyes of one on the verge of dying. On the visual imagery of the passage, see Barlow 1971: 56–57. On the naturalism of death in *Alcestis*, see Segal 1993: 51–72.

58. Rosenmeyer (1963: 226) imagines that Charon actually appears onstage.

59. In this death lyric, Alcestis perhaps recalls Cassandra. Through her ecstatic visions (Dale 1954 ad 238–43), she speaks as someone already dead; in effect, she speaks from beyond the grave. If Alcestis, like Cassandra, speaks with

the voice of the other, she is an other separated not only by gender difference, but by the most basic ontological divide. I return to this possibility at the end of the chapter.

60. Luschnig (1992: 30) remarks that Alcestis's demand of Admetus "keeps the plot going and leaves her (though dead) in control of it." Rabinowitz (1993: 79) likewise views this speech as reflecting Alcestis's self-sufficiency, but also sees in it Alcestis's recognition of "her powerlessness as a woman surviving her husband" (76–77).

61. Drew 1913: 318–19; Beye 1959; Rosenmeyer 1963: 226: "It is a most unpleasant speech." The interpretations of Alcestis's act as selfish rely on a Christian notion of self-sacrifice that is alien to this culture and text. To die for one's own *kleos* is heroic, not selfish; the valorization of the hoplite's self-sacrifice for his country is the result of intense rhetorical and ideological manipulation (Loraux 1986b: 98–118).

62. For the erotic connotations of *terpsis*, see above, Chapter 2, note 12.

63. Rabinowitz (1993: 77) emphasizes the domination inherent in Alcestis's "free choice": "She is made less threatening not only because she appears to choose to die but also because she chooses to die having identified totally with the family she has married into." Thus, while I take the sacrifice as one of the main problems in the play (as an act of heroism that Admetus can never match), Rabinowitz reads it as a defense against anxiety: "Sacrifice is used to help satisfy a male need for control, specifically by allaying male fears of both death and female sexuality" (67). On the ambiguous gender associations of Alcestis's death, see Segal 1993: 77.

64. If I seem to go back and forth on the interpretation of Alcestis's death, it is because I agree with Loraux that there is a fundamental ambivalence in tragedy's representations of women: "It is not necessary to choose one view [that is, death as defeat or as self-affirmation] over the other: each has its truth, and in fact it is impossible not to accept, in each case, both at once. This is what is meant by ambiguity, and there must have been an ambiguous thrill to the *katharsis* when, during a tragic performance, male citizens watched with emotion the suffering of these heroic women, represented onstage by other male citizens dressed in women's clothes. Women's glory in tragedy was an ambiguous glory" (1987: 28).

65. W. D. Smith 1960; Rosenmeyer 1963: 212–13; Conacher 1967: 333–39; Wilson 1968: 3; Burnett 1971: 29; Kott 1973: 83; Buxton 1985: 88–89; Segal 1993: 37–50. Castellani (1979) goes so far as to posit a formal division of the play into two mini-dramas, positing a "first exodos" before the break (606–746) and a second prologue following it (747–860).

66. Aristophanes the Grammarian, in his hypothesis of the play, explains the satyric position by pointing to the happy ending: τὸ δὲ δρᾶμά ἐστι σατυ-ρικώτερον. ὅτι εἰς χαρὰν καὶ ἡδονὴν καταστρέφει παρὰ τὸ τραγικόν ("The drama is rather like a satyr play in that it changes toward happiness and

pleasure, in contrast to tragedy"). Other arguments include the length of the work (Dale 1954: xix; although at nearly 1,200 lines, it is barely shorter than many other tragedies and significantly longer than *Cyclops*), the emphasis on hospitality (Burnett 1971: 31; although this is a theme in many tragedies as well), and the prominence of wine, including Apollo's intoxication of the Fates (Rosenmeyer 1963: 213; Burnett 1971: 32).

67. The fragments of other satyr plays (Aeschylus's *Diktuoulkoi* and *Theōroi*, and Sophocles' *Ikhneutai*, for example) suggest that such humor was a generic characteristic. However, the scene of Heracles' drunkenness here is little more humorous than the guard's rhesis in *Antigone*, a play that no one would dream of associating with satyrs.

68. For this generic designation, see Burnett 1971. Barnes (1968: 26–28) calls *Alcestis* a tragicomedy, a term that would have been more useful had she not defined it specifically to explain this play and the Euripidean tragedies (*Ion, Helen, Orestes*) that resemble it.

69. Burnett (1971: 22) also sees *Alcestis* as Euripides' first experiment with "compound plots."

70. Arist. *Pol.* 1452b2–8, 1454b31–36, 1455a16–21, 1455b2–15.

71. Wilson 1968: 3; Burnett 1971: 44; Kott 1973: 83: "Alcestis is a heroine of tragedy, but has a husband taken from comedy."

72. See Lloyd 1985: 120–21 on similar occlusions of the tragic decision in other Euripidean plays and the effect of this strategy here.

73. Dale 1954 ad 238–43, 246–47; Barlow 1971: 57; Mastronarde 1979: 75; Scully 1986: 140.

74. Dale 1954 ad 861–934.

75. These lines (and especially 452: λιπαραῖσί τ'ἐν ὀλβίαις 'Αθάναις) are generally taken as self-referential; see Dale 1954 ad loc.; O'Higgins 1993: 82; Segal 1993: 46–47.

76. Zeitlin 1990: 84–88.

77. Sophocles' satyr play *Pandora* may have concluded with the breathing of life into a statue, a scene perhaps alluded to in the passage on Alcestis's statue (Burnett 1983: 261 n. 10). Euripides may also have drawn upon his own *Protesilaus* (fr. 647–57 Nauck), in which Laodameia creates a statue of her dead husband. For a comparison of the statue theme in *Alcestis* and the fragments of *Protesilaus*, see O'Higgins 1993: 85–88. Segal (1993: 38) suggests the statue as a self-conscious metaphor for Euripides' artistry. On statues as a means of communication with the dead, see Vernant 1983a (and on this statue in particular, 310).

78. Alcestis not only replaces herself, but even fashions herself. Her preparations for death show her positioning herself as the subject of a tragic death (158–61). The diction (κόσμον. εὐπρεπῶς. ἠσκήσατο, 161) suggests an artisanal effort reminiscent of the creation of Pandora, the original mimetic female, an association heightened by the erotic and nuptial overtones of the passage (159,

161, 174). On the Pandora model as it bears on *Alcestis*, see Bassi 1989: 25; O'Higgins 1993.

79. There is a dangerous tendency to read *Alcestis* through Shakespeare's *A Winter's Tale*, which resembles it in many ways, but also differs significantly. There the rebirth of Hermione is represented literally by her statue coming to life; but Alcestis, unlike Hermione, was really dead (*pace* Verrall [1913]); and whereas Hermione's statue returns to speech and subject status, Alcestis's silent return to life makes her more like the statue (which is never actually built). Thus, though I am indebted to Adelman's (object-relations-oriented) reading of that play (1992), her specific interpretations are not directly applicable to *Alcestis*. For a comparison of *Alcestis* and *A Winter's Tale*, see Ketterer 1990.

80. Contra, see Segal 1993: 48–49, who places the grieving Admetus on the side of tragedy.

81. *Pace* Rosenmeyer (1963: 219–20) and Scully (1986: 137).

82. "The usual *Non tibi hoc soli*" (Dale 1954 ad 416–19). G. Smith (1982: 138–39) sees these lines rather as undermining the value of Alcestis's sacrifice.

83. Dale remarks that "the form of the Chorus's consolation here, a personal anecdote in place of the usual generalities (to which it returns in the antistrophe), is unusual and arresting" (1954 ad 903ff.).

84. Critics arguing along this line point to Heracles' traditional association with gluttony and excessive feasting; see Dale 1954: xxi and ad 754–55. Burnett (1971: 38) notes that by 438 B.C. Heracles had appeared onstage almost exclusively in comedy and satyr plays. Poole (1990: 112–13), analyzing the parallels between this episode of *Alcestis* and the seduction scene of *Cyclops* (519–607), argues for a strong homosexual subtext here; he suggests that Heracles is trying to seduce the slave. This would be in keeping not only with Heracles' mythic character, but also with the sympotic setting, and might be seen as a displacement of the eroticism inherent within male homosocial relations.

85. Scodel 1979: 62. Note, too, the urban setting of this scene, similar to those of sympotica but far from the rural wilderness of satyr plays.

86. Garner (1988: 66–71) argues persuasively for an association of Heracles with epinician, both in this speech and in his *agōnes* at the end of the play. The parallels between Heracles' speech and Bacchylides 3 are particularly compelling. I do not think these two generic allusions—epinician and sympotic poetry—are irreconcilable: both are *kōmoi*, originating in aristocratic male sociality, the former perhaps approaching that society from without and the latter from within. Furthermore, Kurke (1990) has argued for Pindar that there are generic borrowings within epinician from a sympotic genre of *hypothēkai*; she includes among these borrowings several of the passages cited by Garner as evidence of the "epinician" cast of Heracles' speech (including Bacch. 3.76–84), as well as the *Admētou logos* that links Admetus definitively with sympotic literature.

87. On this genre, see Kurke 1990: 90–94. For other attestations of the

Admētou logos, see Ar. *Vesp.* 1239; Ar. *Pelargoi* (fr. 430 Kock); Cratinus *Cheirōnes* (fr. 236 Kock); Phot. lex. p. 32 (Reitz); Suda a493 (Adler); Hesych. a1154, 1165 (Latte); Athenaeus *Deip.* 2.2 p. 159.12–13; Eust. *Il.* 326.38; Zenobius 1.18; Diogenes 2.68.

88. Scodel 1979: 51.

89. Praxilla 3 = *Carmina Convivalia* 897 (*PMG*). Scodel (1979: 51 n. 3) summarizes the scholarship on the connection between this song and *Alcestis*.

90. *Terpsis* is linked to the pleasure of the symposium throughout the Theognidean corpus (e.g., Theog. 567, 767, 778, 791, 984–88, 1042, 1047, 1066–68). As we shall see in the next chapter, the maternal cathexis also eliminates *erōs*; sexuality (*terpsis, erōs*) will return along with the symposium through the bond with Heracles.

91. Cf. Segal (1993: 70, 86), who reads Alcestis's silence as a reminder of death and thus a recursion of the tragic in the midst of this "comic" scene. Burnett (1971: 45), on the other hand, sees in this final scene the "full expression of the satyresque": "The disguise, the trick, the girl won at the games as a prize, the imputations of lustfulness to Admetus all come from satyr play and serve to convert this shortest of trilogies into a tetralogy."

92. Many critics—amazingly—do not even comment upon Alcestis's silence. Dale (1954 ad 1146) takes a functionalist approach that is echoed by many: Euripides was limited to two speaking actors. Others take Heracles at his word, and elaborate the ritual prohibition against her speaking (Rosenmeyer 1963: 245; Betts 1965: 181–82; Trammell 1968: 85–91). Verrall (1913: 73–74) thinks Euripides is parodying Aeschylus's notorious silences; Beye (1959) sees it as a sign of marital discord; Rehm (1994: 93), as a sign of Alcestis's power. Burnett (1983: 268 n. 24) takes it as proof that Alcestis has been dead (against Verrall's claim that she was not) and a symbol of the miracle of her resurrection, whereas Drew (1913: 310) believes that Alcestis is still dead at the end. Von Fritz (1962), Rabinowitz (1993: 84–99), and Segal (1993: 86) take a line closer to my own, arguing that Alcestis's silence undermines the play's ostensibly happy resolution. For a full discussion, see Riemer 1989: 93–103.

93. The attempts to explain this number have been various: see, for example, Trammell 1968: 89–91 on the rites of "trita," and Dale 1954 ad 1146 on the mystical significance of the number. Although three days is a common unit of time in a variety of rituals and festivals, that does not preclude a more specific reference here.

CHAPTER 9

1. Mauss [1950] 1990: 37, 39; cf. above, Chapter 4.
2. The phenomenon I am identifying, I believe, is the same as Burnett's "gra-

tuitous benefaction" (1983: 256–59), and like her I will oppose it to the calculated economy of Pheres and Thanatos; however, I emphasize more than she does the excess of such benefactions and the negative impact they have on the play's economy. An argument close to Burnett's is developed by Golden (1970–71: 117–18).

3. Her gift replicates Apollo's (and, indeed, enables his: his offer is meaningless unless someone will make the sacrifice for Admetus), and it thus is not the origin of the economic unbalance. However, within the play it is Alcestis's gift and not Apollo's that becomes the focus of the dramatic dilemma; hers and not the god's is the gift that Admetus must but cannot reciprocate. Hartigan's (1991) interpretation of the play centers on Apollo's ambiguous gift; cf. Bergson 1985.

4. Klein's understanding of the operation is different. For her, a positive object relation with the mother (and ultimate reparation of the mother as good internal object) lends the security necessary for future object relations. Her logic is additive rather than substitutive.

5. See Ar. *Thesm.* 383–432; *Ran.* 1043–56.

6. Critics have alternately condemned this lack of passion as cold and sterile (an indication of Alcestis's selfishness and Admetus's hypocrisy) or praised it as a sign of devotion unswayed by lust (adding to the glory of Alcestis's decision). See, for the former view, Beye 1959: 124 (who criticizes Alcestis's "obvious disregard for Admetus as well as his for her"); for the latter, Burnett 1983: 260 and n. 9. Dale expostulates: "Of course she loves Admetus—what else made her die for him?" (1954: xxvi). See the discussion in Michelini 1987: 326. Phaedrus in Plato's *Symposium* (179b4–d1) revises the myth so that it is *erōs* that drives Alcestis to her self-sacrifice. In his version, all the story's relations are realigned around *erōs*, and it is this *erōs* that inspires the gods to restore Alcestis to life. Euripides' version of the myth is closer to Socrates' (or Diotima's) use of the story as an example of spiritual, nonphysical love (208d2–3).

7. Rabinowitz (1993: 82) suggests that Alcestis takes on the role of the "phallic mother" who "threatens Admetos with 'castration' by denying him access to another woman."

8. Opinion on the statue has varied wildly: Beye (1959: 114 and n. 10) thinks it "either ludicrous in the extreme, or disgusting"; Burnett (1971: 36 [= 1983: 261]) finds it "positive, delicately stated, and filled with a powerful meaning"; Golden (1970–71: 121) sees it as Admetus's "genuine adoration of Alcestis"; Rosenmeyer (1963: 228) condemns it as "a fantasy which borders on the abnormal, not to raise the issue of good taste"; Rabinowitz (1993: 80–81) takes the statue as a form of fetishization, which contains the threat posed by Alcestis's demand that Admetus not remarry.

9. We can see the statue as a substitution rather than a sublimation (Vernant 1983a: 310; Bassi 1989: 24–25; O'Higgins 1993), or as a failure of metaphor; Admetus is unable either to transfer or to transform his libidinal cathexis (which

is the essence of sublimation), but can only reattach it to the lost object. The statue thus represents an encrypting of the lost object within the self, rather than a drive toward new object relations. Kristeva (1989: 12) describes this substitution: for those suffering depression, "sadness is really the sole object; more precisely it is a substitute object they become attached to, an object they tame and cherish for lack of another."

10. Rabinowitz (1993: 82) writes (facetiously?), "If that cold stiffens him, he will be a man with a man's power." Cf. O'Higgins 1993: 85. Drew (1913: 306) notes the extent to which this necrophiliac fantasy is fulfilled in Admetus's remarriage to the "dead" Alcestis at the end of the play.

11. For a discussion of the parallels between the economies of libido, commodities, and signification, see Goux 1990.

12. The failure of signification is a feature for Klein of a troubled depressive transition. For her, mental capacity and symbol formation grow out of the depressive position: the loss of the object, real or fantasied, is repaired by the subject's ability to represent it symbolically. See "The Importance of Symbol-Formation in the Development of the Ego" (Klein 1984, 1: 219–32). The end of mourning is thus not only a psychic accomplishment, but also a cognitive one.

13. Golden (1970–71: 120) considers this "the major conflict of the play," although he frames it in different terms than my own.

14. On Pheres' cynical attitude toward Alcestis's sacrifice, see G. Smith 1982: 134–37; she argues that Euripides uses Pheres to challenge the traditional story and to show that Alcestis's true heroism is her life, not her death.

15. Burnett 1971: 40: "The house, for him, was a complex of lands and flocks to be counted and consumed, not a complex of ideals to be preserved."

16. LSJ (s.v. πατρῷος) differentiates between πατρῷος and πάτριος: the former indicates patrimonial possession while the latter expresses hereditary manners, customs, institutions. Pheres also considers marriage a source of potential profit (627–28).

17. Apollo's economy is similar to Alcestis's: it is his impossible gift that creates the tragic situation, and his attitude is distinctly plutocratic, as Thanatos points out (57, 59). Thanatos, on the other hand, is concerned only to get the body he is owed (49, 63). On the connection of the *agōn* between Pheres and Admetus and the prologue's *agōn*, see Golden 1970–71: 118.

18. Cf. 720: μνήστευε πολλάς, ὡς θάνωσι πλείονες ("Woo many women, so that more can die!").

19. One could interpret in this way Admetus's promises to Alcestis (328–68), which many critics have seen as excessive to the point of hypocrisy (e.g. Hartigan 1991: 25–27; contra, Burnett 1971: 36–37). Rabinowitz (1993: 80–81) offers the interesting interpretation that Admetus's hyperbole is a form of fetishism, which contains the threat posed by Alcestis's excessive demands of him.

20. Heracles perceives Admetus's offer as an attack (ἀλλ' ἦ πέπονθα δειν'

ὑπὸ ξένων ἐμῶν, "But I have suffered terribly at the hands of my *xenoi*," 816) and condemns it (1017–18) as deceitful and coercive, even as he recognizes the generosity behind it. Cf. Michelini 1987: 327. I return to the coercion of this transaction in the final section of this chapter.

21. In the disenchanted economy of Pheres and Alcestis's excessive agalmatization, we can perhaps see two different economic strategies available to the liturgy class in fifth-century Athens. As an economic *agōn*, the exchange of lives resembles the Athenian procedure of *antidosis*. Admetus is called upon to pay a liturgy, as it were, on his life; he challenges all his *philoi*, and Alcestis accepts the challenge and pays in his stead (ἀντιδίδωμι is used twice to describe the exchange, at 340 and 956). According to some (see J. K. Davies 1971: xvii; 1981: 26; Finley 1973: 150–54; Whitehead 1983; Christ 1990: 150), liturgies were an honor, the loss of economic wealth compensated by a gain in symbolic wealth. This is the economic attitude behind Alcestis's gift; by giving all that she had, she bankrupted herself, but reaped an unequaled symbolic reward. She carries this logic to an extreme, however: the resultant stagnation of the play's economy moves us from a competitive aristocracy to a tyranny, where all wealth and prestige are concentrated in one person. In contrast to this symbolic economics was a more materialistic logic, according to which liturgies were not an opportunity to display one's prestige but rather an onerous and intrusive diminution of material resources (see Gabrielsen 1986; Christ 1990). Thus Pheres condemns Alcestis for her folly in taking on this burden (726–28); he gives what is required, and no more (686, 689), willingly trading symbolic wealth (*kleos*) for material (life). On the process, frequency, and manipulation of *antidosis*, see J. K. Davies 1967; Gabrielsen 1987; Christ 1990.

22. Of course, neither the economy of *xenia* nor the homosocial relations it implies are, in any real sense, "new." I use the word not to suggest a historical development, but to indicate a progression within the play.

23. This rejection is especially clear if we follow Purgold in reading κέρδιον (cognate with κέρδος, "material profit") for the codices' κύδιον.

24. Kristeva 1989: 23.

25. Ibid.: 28.

26. See W. D. Smith 1960: 134–36 on the importance of "good breeding" in the play.

27. Not only a queen on earth, she will also have the privilege of *prohedria* in the underworld: εἰ δέ τι κἀκεῖ / πλέον ἔστ' ἀγαθοῖς, τούτων μετέχουσ᾽ / Ἅιδου νύμφηι παρεδρεύοις. ("If there are prerogatives for the noble even there, you will have a share of them and will hold the seat of honor by Hades' bride," 744–46).

28. On the technical legal vocabulary of this *agōn*, see W. D. Smith 1960: 135.

29. This repetition is picked up by the chorus, which uses forms of *kakos* twice more in the following two lines.

30. For discussions of the issues involved in this *agōn* and the criteria—philosophical and legal—according to which we should judge it, see Thury 1988: 205–9; Lloyd 1992: 37–41.

31. On the actual legality of these claims, see Thury 1988: 199–202.

32. Compare Pheres' statement that he is no slave bought with money, ἀργυρώνητον, 676.

33. Disinheritance of a son by a father was apparently quite rare in classical Athens (see Harrison 1968: 75–76; Thury 1988: 201); the inversion here, then, is an extreme statement. Nonetheless, Thury argues that intergenerational strife was so prevalent in Greek society that "Admetus' attitude is clearly not shocking to the chorus and would not cause his condemnation by the audience" (201).

34. Dale (1954) writes on 209–12: "It is making too much of these lines to see in them an indication of Admetus' unpopularity with his disaffected subjects. Rather do they serve to characterize the Chorus." Cf. xxii–xxix and ad 326–27, 474, 565; see also her defense of Admetus's "sincere, heart-rending grief" at 365–66 (cf. xxvi).

35. See Dale 1954 ad 600ff. on the sense of *ekpheretai*.

36. Thus Dale (ibid.): "The Chorus are confident that this apparent excess is really good sense; Admetus has an instinct for the right which is denied to them, and they can but admire—and hope that virtue will again be rewarded."

37. The pronouns in this passage are masculine, but we have seen (above, Chapter 8, note 36) that Alcestis is often referred to in the masculine.

38. Segal (1993: 69) remarks upon the public and official nature of this greeting, which "has something of the dignity of a state visit." Note the negative version of this reciprocal hailing in the relationship between Pheres and Admetus (691). Their relationship, too, is mirroring: Pheres and Admetus do define one another as equal, but as equally base rather than equally noble.

39. See Dale (1954 ad loc.) on the connotations of τὸ λοιπόν in this line: the implication is not that Admetus has failed to be *dikaios* and *eusebēs* so far, but that he should continue to be in the future (contra, Verrall 1913: 43).

40. Cf. 15–17, 640. Scodel (1979: 58) likens this *elenkhos* to Theognis's *basanos*, the touchstone that proves a man a gentleman (e.g., Theogn. 1104–6).

41. Lacan 1977: 1–7; cf. above, Introduction.

42. Although Lacan does not spell out the precise relationship between the mirror stage and the Oedipal complex, it seems that the latter is the first instantiation of the laws contained in the former, a reenactment in the social sphere of the alienated identification of the mirror stage. See Lacan 1977: 5–6. Moreover, the triangular arrangement of the mirror scene (mother, child, and mirror image) is replicated in the Oedipal triangle, in which the identification between son and father is guaranteed (and its impossibilities erased) by the otherness of the mother.

43. Rabinowitz (1993: 80) also takes it as such, arguing that Admetus gets to marry his "mother" by metaphorically killing his father. She does not, however,

emphasize the Oedipal nature of the relationship with Heracles; thus my interpretation of *Alcestis* in some ways resembles more closely her reading of *Hippolytus* and *Ion*, which end, she argues, with the homosocial bond between father and son reinforced through the displacement of the mother (see, especially, 210–15).

44. Pheres does not, of course, either want or get to keep Alcestis for himself; the point is rather that by refusing to die, he deprives Admetus of her. The problem that in the Oedipal complex is temporal (i.e., the father denies the son in the present but will cede to him in the future) is here telescoped, so that the frustration is permanent.

45. The evidence for the veiling is circumstantial; it must be assumed in order to explain Admetus's failure to recognize his wife immediately. See Rabinowitz 1993: 87 and cf. the hypothesis: "Unveiling her, Heracles revealed the woman whom Admetus longed for."

46. See Foley 1985: 88; Halleran 1988: 124–28; Rabinowitz 1993: 90; Segal 1993: 80.

47. The only other occurrence is Eur. fr. 26.3 (N). Poole (1990: 113) argues that the context for these lines is homosexual *erōs*: desire for a woman, as Sedgwick (1985) shows, mediates between the homosocial and the homosexual.

48. This translation follows Diggle's (1987) and Dale's (1954) preferred reading (νέοι γάμοι πόθου) against the codices' νέου γάμου πόθοι.

49. Likewise, it is only in his relationship to Heracles that Admetus can assert his own paternal identity. Alcestis had claimed genealogical control over their children (325), thus herself becoming the *phytōr*. But after her death, in conversation with Heracles, Admetus reaffirms himself as *phytōr* (515).

50. O'Higgins (1993) also compares Alcestis to Pandora, but not as an object of exchange between gods and men.

51. On the parallels between the Apollo/Asclepius myth and the Admetus/Alcestis story, see D. M. Jones 1948: 51–52; Conacher 1967: 227–33; Golden 1970–71.

52. The same lines close *Andromache, Helen, Bacchae*, and (with a different opening line) *Medea*. Dale believes that the exodus "could well have been originally written for this play" (1954 ad 1159–63), but its connection to the play is still rather tenuous. Cf. Lefkowitz 1989: 81–82.

53. Cf. Rabinowitz 1993: 97: "The satisfaction Euripides grants Admetos must have been reassuring to males in the audience."

54. Cf. Aes. *Cho.* 831–37. Loraux (1986a) offers a reading of the matricide in *Choephoroe* similar to the interpretation of *Alcestis* offered here. Incorporating both Freud and Klein, she shows how the body of the mother (in this case Clytemnestra) is both nourishing and erotic; the decapitation of the gorgon, she suggests, is simultaneously a matricide and a penetration (91).

55. P. R. Slater 1968: 16–18, 318–20; Loraux 1986a; Vernant 1991: 111–

138, 141–50. Freud, in his article "Medusa's Head" (Freud [1922] 1955: 273–74), associates this icon with "the terrifying genitals of the mother." Cf. Ferenczi, "On the Symbolism of the Head of Medusa," in Ferenczi 1926. Rabinowitz (1993: 85) interprets this line similarly, pointing out that the sexual context (1051–56) adds to the association of the gorgon with genitalia. She sees the gorgon as representing both a fear of female sexuality and a fear of castration (the "phallic mother").

56. Kristeva 1989: 27–30. This final act provides a neat ring-composition with the origin of Admetus's problems according to one mythic tradition. Apollodorus (1.105–6) tells that Admetus forgot to sacrifice to Artemis at his wedding; when he opened the door to his wedding chamber, the room was filled with snakes (a portent of his death). If we take this story (with P. R. Slater 1968: 70 and Rabinowitz 1993: 69) as a metaphor for male fear of female sexuality, then the decapitation of the gorgon represents the elimination of this threat. But this is beyond the scope of the play, which offers no reason for Admetus's death beyond the basic fact of human mortality.

57. P. R. Slater 1968: 337–96. Heracles' relationship with Hera exemplifies the hostile and suffocating relationship between mother and son that Slater identifies throughout Greek mythology.

58. See above, Chapter 7, note 29.

59. Nielson 1976: 92.

60. Admetus as inherently deserving: Dale 1954; Burnett 1971, 1983; Lloyd 1985. Admetus as repentant: Grube 1941: 129–46; D. M. Jones 1948: 50; Webster 1967: 52; Conacher 1967: 336–39; Vellacott 1975: 105; Halleran 1982; Buxton 1985; Hartigan 1991; Golden 1970–71; Segal 1992: 147.

61. Verrall 1913; Beye 1959; W. D. Smith 1960; Von Fritz 1962; Nielson 1976.

62. J. Gregory (1979) takes as the starting point for her discussion of the play the relation between this ode and the last scene. Cf. Lloyd 1985: 124; J. Gregory 1991: 19–46, esp. 43–46; Segal 1993: 39–40.

63. J. Gregory (1991: 44–46) reaches the opposite conclusion: she argues that Alcestis's return implies Admetus's death, and therefore reconfirms the egalitarian philosophy of Thanatos.

64. The violence implicit within this exchange is explicit in the dialogue between Apollo and Thanatos. There is no *kharis* between the two gods (60), and any exchange between them will be predicated upon force, rather than mutual goodwill (70–71). The agonism behind the final exchange is also deflected onto the broken *xenia* relation between Heracles and Diomedes (484). This violent labor is closely linked to the friendly exchange of Alcestis: Admetus is to keep Alcestis while Heracles is performing this labor (1020–24), and the hospitality between Admetus and Heracles established by this exchange is deferred until after Heracles completes the labor (1149–50). The threat of hostile relations thus

underlies (and motivates) friendly relations, as Mauss notes: "To refuse to give, to fail to invite, just as to refuse to accept, is tantamount to declaring war" ([1950] 1990: 13). Cf. Bourdieu 1977: 14: "Every exchange contains a more or less dissimulated challenge."

65. Various interpretations have been put forward to explain Heracles' motives here. Drew (1913: 315) sees Heracles as just a "goodnatured, drunken simpleton . . . playing out an innocent, not a malevolent joke." Beye (1959: 117) and Fitzgerald (1991: 86–88), on the other hand, do find Heracles' deceit malevolent. Rehm (1994: 93) is not alone in viewing this as Heracles' revenge for Admetus's deceit. Rabinowitz (1993: 88–90) sees the joke as a form of male bonding that contains the threat posed by Alcestis's liminality.

66. The paradox that Admetus must betray Alcestis in order to win her back has been accepted or justified by scholars with amazing sanguinity. See, for example, W. D. Smith (1960: 144), who argues that by accepting Alcestis as a concubine (rather than a wife), Admetus does not violate his promise.

67. Not to mention the schism between the female character and the male actor, on which see O'Higgins 1993: 92. O'Higgins notes further that the actor who plays the mute Alcestis is not the same one who played Alcestis at the beginning: "Beneath the mask, the individual is doubly alien" (94).

68. See Rose in Lacan 1982: 43, 47.

69. Dyson (1988: 18) notes, too, the absence of the children in the final scene: thus an important source of Alcestis's authority in the play is eliminated.

70. Myers 1917: 218; Vellacott 1975: 228; Rehm 1994: 95. For other interpretations, see Chapter 8, note 92 above.

BIBLIOGRAPHY

A&A   Antike und Abendland
AC   L'Antiquité classique
AClass   Acta Classica
AJAH   American Journal of Ancient History
AJP   American Journal of Philology
BICS   Bulletin of the Institute of Classical Studies
BMCR   Bryn Mawr Classical Review
C&M   Classica et Mediaevalia
CA   Classical Antiquity
CJ   Classical Journal
CP   Classical Philology
CQ   Classical Quarterly
CR   Classical Review
G&R   Greece and Rome
GRBS   Greek, Roman, and Byzantine Studies
HSCP   Harvard Studies in Classical Philology
JHS   Journal of Hellenic Studies
PCPS   Proceedings of the Cambridge Philological Society
QUCC   Quaderni Urbinati di Cultura Classica
RFIC   Rivista di filologia e di instruzione classica
SAWW   Sitzungsberichte der Österreichischen Akademie der Wissenschaft
         in Wien
TAPA   Transactions of the American Philological Association
YCS   Yale Classical Studies

Adams, S. M. 1957. *Sophocles the Playwright. Phoenix*, suppl. 3. Toronto: University of Toronto Press.

Adelman, J. 1992. *Suffocating Mothers: Fantasies of Maternal Origin in Shakespeare's Plays*. New York: Routledge.

Adkins, A. W. H. 1960. *Merit and Responsibility*. Chicago: University of Chicago Press.

Alexiou, M. 1974. *The Ritual Lament in Greek Tradition*. Cambridge: Cambridge University Press.

Althusser, L. 1971. *Essays on Ideology*. Trans. B. Brewster. London: Verso.

Appadurai, A. 1986. "Introduction: Commodities and the Politics of Value." In *The Social Life of Things: Commodities in Cultural Perspective*. Cambridge: Cambridge University Press.

Armstrong, D., and A. E. Hanson. 1986. "Two Notes on Greek Tragedy." *BICS* 33: 97–103.

Armstrong, D., and E. Ratchford. 1985. "Aeschylus, *Agamemnon* 228–48." *BICS* 32: 1–11.

Arthur, M. 1982. "Cultural Strategies in Hesiod's *Theogony*: Law, Family, Society." *Arethusa* 15.1.2: 63–82.

———. 1983. "The Dream of a World without Women: Poetics and the Circles of Order in the *Theogony* Prooemium." *Arethusa* 16.1.2: 97–116.

Austin, M. M., and P. Vidal-Naquet. 1977. *Economic and Social History of Ancient Greece*. Berkeley: University of California Press.

Bamberger, J. 1974. "The Myth of Matriarchy: Why Men Rule in Primitive Society." In M. Rosaldo and L. Lamphere, eds., *Woman, Culture, and Society*. Stanford: Stanford University Press.

Barker, F. 1984. *The Tremulous Private Body: Essays on Subjection*. New York: Methuen.

Barlow, S. A. 1971. *The Imagery of Euripides*. London: Methuen.

Barnes, H. 1968. "Greek Tragicomedy." In J. R. Wilson, ed., *Twentieth Century Interpretations of Euripides' Alcestis*. Englewood Cliffs, N.J.: Prentice-Hall.

Barrett, M. 1988. *Women's Oppression Today: Problems in Marxist Feminist Analysis*. London: Verso.

Barrett, W. S., ed. 1964. *Euripides: Hippolytos*. Oxford: Clarendon.

Bassi, K. 1989. "The Actor as Actress in Euripides' *Alcestis*." In J. Redmond, ed., *Women in Theatre*. Cambridge: Cambridge University Press.

———. Forthcoming. *Acting Like Men: Gender and Performance in Ancient Greece*. Ann Arbor: University of Michigan Press.

Baudrillard, J. 1981. *For a Critique of the Political Economy of the Sign*. Trans. C. Levin. St. Louis: Telos.

Beauvoir, S. [1952] 1974. *The Second Sex*. Trans. and ed. H. M. Parshley. New York: Vintage.

Benveniste, E. 1969. *Le Vocabulaire des institutions indo-européennes.* Vol. 1. Paris: Les Éditions de minuit.

Bergren, A. 1983. "Language and the Female in Early Greek Thought." *Arethusa* 16.1.2: 69–95.

Bergson, L. 1985. "Randbemerkungen zur *Alkestis* des Euripides." *Eranos* 83: 7–22.

Betts, G. G. 1965. "The Silence of Alcestis." *Mnemosyne* 18.2: 181–82.

Beye, C. R. 1959. "Alcestis and Her Critics." *GRBS* 2.2: 109–27.

Blok, J. 1987. "Sexual Asymmetry: A Historiographical Essay." In J. Blok and P. Mason, eds., *Sexual Asymmetry: Studies in Ancient Society.* Amsterdam: J. C. Gieben.

Bohannan, P. 1959. "The Impact of Money on an African Subsistence Economy." *Journal of Economic History* 19.4: 491–503.

Bourdieu, P. 1977. *Outline of a Theory of Practice.* Trans. R. Nice. Cambridge: Cambridge University Press.

———. 1984. *Distinction: A Social Critique of the Judgement of Taste.* Trans. R. Nice. Cambridge, Mass.: Harvard University Press.

———. 1990a. *The Logic of Practice.* Trans. R. Nice. Stanford: Stanford University Press.

———. 1990b. "La Domination masculine." *Recherche en sciences sociales* 84: 2–31.

Bowie, A. M. 1993. "Religion and Politics in Aeschylus' *Oresteia.*" *CQ* 43.1: 10–31.

Bowra, C. M. 1944. *Sophoclean Tragedy.* Oxford: Clarendon.

Bradley, E. M. 1980. "Admetus and the Triumph of Failure in Euripides' *Alcestis.*" *Ramus* 9.2: 112–27.

Brulé, P. 1987. *La Fille d'Athènes.* Paris: Les Belles Lettres.

Burian, P. 1986. "Zeus Soter Tritos and Some Triads in Aeschylus' *Oresteia.*" *AJP* 107.3: 332–42.

Burkert, W. 1985. *Greek Religion.* Trans. J. Raffan. Cambridge, Mass.: Harvard University Press.

Burnett, A. P. 1971. *Catastrophe Survived: Euripides' Plays of Mixed Reversal.* Oxford: Clarendon.

———. 1983. "The Virtues of Admetus." In E. Segal, ed., *Oxford Readings in Greek Tragedy.* Oxford: Oxford University Press.

Burton, R. W. B. 1980. *The Chorus in Sophocles' Tragedies.* Oxford: Clarendon.

Butler, J. 1990. *Gender Trouble: Feminism and the Subversion of Identity.* New York: Routledge.

———. 1993. *Bodies That Matter: On the Discursive Limits of "Sex."* New York: Routledge.

Buxton, R. G. A. 1985. "Euripides' *Alcestis:* Five Aspects of an Interpretation." *Dodone:* 75–89.

Calame, C. 1977. *Les Choeurs de jeunes filles en Grèce archaïque*. Rome: Edizioni dell'Ateneo & Bizzarri.

Campbell, A. Y. 1958. "Sophocles' *Trachiniae:* Discussions of Some Textual Problems." *CQ* 8.1: 18–24.

Cantarella, E. 1985. "Dangling Virgins: Myth, Ritual, and the Place of Women in Ancient Greece." In S. R. Suleiman, ed., *The Female Body in Western Culture*. Cambridge, Mass.: Harvard University Press.

Carson, A. 1986. *Eros, The Bittersweet*. Princeton: Princeton University Press.

———. 1990. "Putting Her in Her Place: Woman, Dirt, and Desire." In D. Halperin, J. Winkler, and F. Zeitlin, eds. *Before Sexuality*. Princeton: Princeton University Press.

Cartledge, P. 1993. *The Greeks: A Portrait of Self and Others*. Oxford: Oxford University Press.

Castellani, V. 1979. "Notes on the Structure of Euripides' *Alcestis*." *AJP* 100.4: 487–96.

Chesler, P. 1973. *Women and Madness*. New York: Avon.

Chodorow, N. 1978. *The Reproduction of Mothering: Psychoanalysis and the Sociology of Gender*. Berkeley: University of California Press.

———. 1989. *Feminism and Psychoanalytic Theory*. New Haven, Conn.: Yale University Press.

Christ, M. 1990. "Liturgy Avoidance and *Antidosis* in Classical Athens." *TAPA* 120: 147–69.

Cixous, H. 1976. "The Laugh of the Medusa." *Signs* 1.4: 875–93.

Cixous, H., and C. Clément. 1986. *The Newly Born Woman*. Trans. B. Wing. Minneapolis: University of Minnesota Press.

Clover, C. 1992. *Men, Women, and Chain Saws: Gender in the Modern Horror Film*. Princeton: Princeton University Press.

Cohen, D. 1986. "The Theodicy of Aeschylus: Justice and Tyranny in the *Oresteia*." *G&R* 33.2: 129–40.

———. 1989. "Seclusion, Separation, and the Status of Women in Classical Athens." *G&R* 36: 3–15.

———. 1991. *Law, Sexuality, and Society*. Cambridge: Cambridge University Press.

Conacher, D. J. 1967. *Euripidean Drama: Myth, Theme and Structure*. Toronto: University of Toronto Press.

———. 1987. *Aeschylus' Oresteia: A Literary Commentary*. Toronto: University of Toronto Press.

Connor, W. R. 1971. *The New Politicians of Fifth-Century Athens*. Princeton: Princeton University Press.

Cowie, E. 1990. "Woman as Sign." In P. Adams and E. Cowie, eds., *The Woman in Question*. Cambridge, Mass.: MIT Press.

Crane, G. 1993. "The Politics of Consumption and Generosity in the Carpet Scene of the *Agamemnon*." *CP* 88.2: 117–36.

Cunningham, M. L. 1984. "Aeschylus, *Agamemnon* 231–247." *BICS* 31: 9–12.

Dale, A. M., ed. 1954. *Euripides' Alcestis*. Oxford: Clarendon.

Davies, J. K. 1967. "Demosthenes on Liturgies: A Note." *JHS* 87: 33–40.

———. 1971. *Athenian Propertied Families, 600–300 B.C.* Oxford: Clarendon.

———. 1981. *Wealth and the Power of Wealth in Classical Athens*. Salem, N.H.: Arno.

Davies, M., ed. 1991. *Sophocles' Trachiniae*. Oxford: Oxford University Press.

Dawe, R. 1963. "Inconsistency of Plot and Character in Aeschylus." *PCPS* 189.9: 21–61.

———. 1978. *Studies on the Text of Sophocles*. Vol. 2. Leiden: Brill.

Deleuze, G., and F. Guattari. 1983. *Anti-Oedipus: Capitalism and Schizophrenia*. Trans. R. Hurley, M. Seem, and H. R. Lane. Minneapolis: University of Minnesota Press.

Dellner, J. 1994. "Review Article: N. S. Rabinowitz *Anxiety Veiled: Euripides and the Traffic in Women*." *BMCR* 5.6: 540–44.

Denniston, J. D., and D. Page, eds. 1957. *Aeschylus Agamemnon*. Oxford: Clarendon.

de Ste. Croix, G. E. M. 1981. *The Class Struggle in the Ancient Greek World*. Ithaca, N.Y.: Cornell University Press.

Detienne, M. 1967. *Les Maîtres de vérité dans la Grèce archaïque*. Paris: François Maspero.

Detienne, M., and J.-P. Vernant. 1978. *Cunning Intelligence in Greek Culture and Society*. Trans. J. Lloyd. Atlantic Highlands, N.J.: Humanities Press.

Devereux, G. 1975. *Tragédie et poésie grecques*. Paris: Flammarion.

Diggle, J., ed. 1987. *Euripides Fabulae*. Vol. 1. Oxford: Oxford University Press.

Dodds, E. R. 1960. "Morals and Politics in the 'Oresteia.'" *PCPS* 186: 19–31.

Donlan, W. 1980. *The Aristocratic Ideal in Ancient Greece*. Lawrence, Kans.: Coronado.

———. 1981. "Scale, Value and Function in the Homeric Economy." *AJAH* 6: 101–17.

———. 1989. "The Unequal Exchange between Glaucus and Diomedes in Light of the Homeric Gift-Economy." *Phoenix* 43.1: 1–15.

Dover, K. J. 1973. "Some Neglected Aspects of Agamemnon's Dilemma." *JHS* 93: 58–69.

———. 1976. "ΗΛΙΟΣ ΚΗΡΥΞ." In J. M. Bremer, S. L. Radt, and C. J. Ruijgh, eds., *Miscellanea Tragica in Honorem J. C. Kamerbeek*. Amsterdam: A. Hakkert.

———. 1978. *Greek Homosexuality*. London: Duckworth.

———. 1987. "The Red Fabric in the *Agamemnon*." In *Greece and the Greeks*. Oxford: Basil Blackwell.

Dowden, K. 1989. *Death and the Maiden: Girls' Initiation Rites in Greek Mythology*. New York: Routledge.

Drew, D. L. 1913. "Euripides' *Alcestis*." *AJP* 52.4: 295–319.

duBois, P. 1979. "On Horse/Men, Amazons and Endogamy." *Arethusa* 12.1: 35–49.

———. 1982. *Centaurs and Amazons*. Ann Arbor: University of Michigan Press.

———. 1988. *Sowing the Body: Psychoanalysis and Ancient Representations of Women*. Chicago: University of Chicago Press.

Dupont-Roc, R., and A. le Boulluec. 1976. "Le Charme du récit." In *Écriture et theorie poétiques*. Paris: Presses de l'École Normale Superieure.

Dyson, M. 1988. "Alcestis' Children and the Character of Admetus." *JHS* 108: 13–23.

Earle, M. L. 1902. "Studies in Sophocles' *Trachinians*." *TAPA* 33: 5–21.

Earp, F. R. 1939. "The *Trachiniae*." *CR* 53.4: 113–15.

———. 1944. *The Style of Sophocles*. Cambridge: Cambridge University Press.

Easterling, P. E. 1968. "Sophocles' *Trachiniae*." *BICS* 15: 58–70.

———. 1973. "Presentation of Character in Aeschylus." *G&R* 20: 3–19.

———. 1977. "Character in Sophocles." *G&R* 24: 121–29.

———. 1981. "The End of the *Trachiniae*." *BICS* 6.1: 56–75.

———, ed. 1982. *Sophocles Trachiniae*. Cambridge: Cambridge University Press.

———. 1990. "Constructing Character in Greek Tragedy." In Pelling 1990.

Edgeworth, R. J. 1988. "'Saffron-Colored' Terms in Aeschylus." *Glotta* 66: 179–82.

Elferink, L. J. 1982. "The Beginning of Euripides' *Alcestis*." *AClass* 25: 43–50.

Elmsley, P., ed. 1825. *Scholia in Sophoclis Tragoedias Septem*. Oxford: Oxford University Press.

Errandonea, I. 1927. "Deianira vere ΔΗΙ-ΑΝΕΙΡΑ." *Mnemosyne* 55: 145–64.

Faber, M. D. 1970. *Suicide and Greek Tragedy*. New York: Sphinx.

Fagles, R., trans. 1966. *Aeschylus, the Oresteia*. New York: Viking Press.

Fantham, E., H. P. Foley, N. B. Kampen, S. B. Pomeroy, and H. A. Shapiro, eds. 1994. *Women in the Classical World*. Oxford: Oxford University Press.

Faraone, C. 1994. "Deianira's Mistake and the Demise of Heracles: Erotic Magic in Sophocles' *Trachiniae*." *Helios* 21.2: 115–36.

Faraone, C., and D. Obbink, eds. 1991. *Magika Hiera: Ancient Greek Magic and Religion*. Oxford: Oxford University Press.

Felman, S. 1975. "Women and Madness: The Critical Phallacy." *Diacritics* 5.4: 2–10.

Ferenczi, S. 1926. "On the Symbolism of the Head of Medusa." In *Further Contributions to the Theory and Technique of Psychoanalysis*. New York: Boni and Liveright.

Fineman, J. 1986. *Shakespeare's Perjured Eye: The Invention of Poetic Subjectivity in the Sonnets*. Berkeley: University of California Press.

Finley, J. H. 1966. "Politics and Early Attic Tragedy." *HSCP* 71: 1–15.

Finley, M. I. 1952. *Studies in Land and Credit in Ancient Athens, 500–200 B.C.* New Brunswick, N.J.: Rutgers University Press.

————. [1954] 1988. *The World of Odysseus*. London: Penguin.

————. 1955. "Marriage, Sale and Gift in the Homeric World." *Revue Internationale des Droits de l'Antiquité* 3.2: 167–94. [= 1981: 223–45.]

————. 1973. *The Ancient Economy*. Berkeley: University of California Press.

————. 1981. *Economy and Society in Ancient Greece*. London: Chatto and Windus.

Fitzgerald, G. J. 1991. "The Euripidean Heracles: An Intellectual and a Coward?" *Mnemosyne* 44: 85–95.

Flintoff, E. 1987. "The Treading of the Cloth." *QUCC* 25.1: 119–30.

Foley, H., ed. 1981a. *Reflections of Women in Antiquity*. London: Gordon and Breach Science Publishers.

————. 1981b. "The Conception of Women in Athenian Drama." In Foley 1981a.

————. 1982a. "Marriage and Sacrifice in Euripides' *Iphigeneia in Aulis*." *Arethusa* 15: 159–80.

————. 1982b. "The 'Female Intruder' Reconsidered: Women in Aristophanes' *Lysistrata* and *Ecclesiazusae*." *CP* 77.1: 1–21.

————. 1985. *Ritual Irony*. Ithaca, N.Y.: Cornell University Press.

————. 1993. "The Politics of Tragic Lamentation." In A. Sommerstein, S. Halliwell, J. Henderson, and B. Zimmerman, eds., *Tragedy, Comedy and the Polis*. Bari: Levante Editori.

————. 1995. "Review Article: N. S. Rabinowitz *Anxiety Veiled: Euripides and the Traffic in Women*." *CP* 90.1: 82–86.

Foucault, M. 1978. *The History of Sexuality*. Vol. 1. *An Introduction*. Trans. R. Hurley. New York: Vintage.

Fraenkel, E., ed. 1950. *Aeschylus Agamemnon*. Oxford: Clarendon.

Freud, S. [1922] 1955. *Beyond the Pleasure Principle and Other Works*. Trans. J. Strachey. London: Hogarth.

————. 1963. *General Psychological Theory*. New York: Macmillan.

Friis Johansen, H. 1986. "Heracles in Sophocles' *Trachiniae*." *C&M* 37: 47–61.

Fuqua, C. 1980. "Heroism, Heracles, and the 'Trachiniae'." *Traditio* 36: 1–81.

Gabrielsen, V. 1986. "Φανερά and Ἀφανὴς Οὐσία in Classical Athens." *C&M* 37: 99–114.

————. 1987. "The *Antidosis* Procedure in Classical Athens." *C&M* 38: 7–38.

Gagarin, M. 1976. *Aeschylean Drama*. Berkeley: University of California Press.

Gantz, T. 1983. "The Chorus of Aischylos' *Agamemnon*." *HSCP* 87: 65–86.

Gardiner, C. 1987. *The Sophoclean Chorus*. Iowa City: University of Iowa Press.

Garlan, Y. 1988. *Slavery in Ancient Greece*. Trans. J. Lloyd. Ithaca, N.Y.: Cornell University Press.

Garner, R. 1988. "Death and Victory in Euripides' *Alcestis*." *CA* 7.1: 58–71.

————. 1990. *From Homer to Tragedy: The Art of Allusion in Greek Poetry*. New York: Routledge.

Garvie, A. F., ed. 1986. *Aeschylus Choephori.* Oxford: Clarendon.

Gasti, H. 1993. "Sophocles' *Trachiniae:* A Social or Externalized Aspect of Deianeira's Morality." *A&A* 39: 20–28.

Gellie, G. H. 1972. *Sophocles: A Reading.* Melbourne: Melbourne University Press.

Gellrich, M. 1995. "Interpreting Greek Tragedy: History, Theory, and the New Philology." In B. Goff, ed., *History, Tragedy, Theory: Dialogues on Athenian Drama.* Austin: University of Texas Press.

Gernet, L. 1981a. "'Value' in Greek Myth." In R. L. Gordon, ed., *Myth, Religion, and Society.* Cambridge: Cambridge University Press.

———. 1981b. "The Nobility in Ancient Greece." In *The Anthropology of Ancient Greece,* trans. J. Hamilton and B. Nagy. Baltimore: The Johns Hopkins University Press.

———. 1981c. "Marriages of Tyrants." In *The Anthropology of Ancient Greece,* trans. J. Hamilton and B. Nagy. Baltimore: The Johns Hopkins University Press.

Gilbert, S., and S. Gubar. 1979. *The Madwoman in the Attic: The Woman Writer and the Nineteenth-Century Imagination.* New Haven, Conn.: Yale University Press.

Gill, C. 1990. "The Character-Personality Distinction." In Pelling 1990.

Girard, R. 1972. *Deceit, Desire and the Novel: Self and Other in Literary Structure.* Trans. Y. Freccero. Baltimore: The Johns Hopkins University Press.

Golden, L. 1970–71. "Euripides' *Alcestis:* Structure and Theme." *CJ* 66.1: 116–25.

Goldfarb, B. E. 1992. "The Conflict of Obligations in Euripides' *Alcestis.*" *GRBS* 33.2: 109–26.

Goldhill, S. 1984. *Language, Sexuality, Narrative: The Oresteia.* Cambridge: Cambridge University Press.

———. 1990a. "The Great Dionysia and Civic Ideology." In J. J. Winkler and F. I. Zeitlin, eds., *Nothing to Do with Dionysos?* Princeton: Princeton University Press.

———. 1990b. "Character and Action, Representation and Reading: Greek Tragedy and Its Critics." In Pelling 1990.

———. 1991. "Violence in Greek Tragedy." In J. Redmond, ed., *Violence in Drama. Themes in Drama* 13. Cambridge: Cambridge University Press.

———. 1994. "Representing Democracy: Women at the Great Dionysia." In R. Osborne and S. Hornblower, eds., *Ritual, Finance, Politics: Athenian Democratic Accounts Presented to David Lewis.* Oxford: Clarendon.

Gomme, A. W. 1925. "The Position of Women in Athens in the Fifth and Fourth Centuries." *CP* 20: 1–25.

Gould, J. 1978. "Dramatic Character and 'Human Intelligibility' in Greek Tragedy." *PCPS* 204: 43–67.

———. 1980. "Law, Custom, and Myth: Aspects of the Social Position of Women in Classical Athens." *JHS* 100: 38–59.

Gouldner, A. W. 1965. *Enter Plato: Classical Greece and the Origins of Social Theory.* New York: Basic Books.

Goux, J.-J. 1990. *Symbolic Economies: After Marx and Freud.* Ithaca, N.Y.: Cornell University Press.

Gramsci, A. 1971. *Selections from the Prison Notebooks.* Trans. and ed. Q. Hoare and G. N. Smith. New York: International Publishers.

Gregory, C. A. 1982. *Gifts and Commodities.* London: Academic.

Gregory, J. 1979. "Euripides' *Alcestis.*" *Hermes* 107: 259–69.

———. 1991. *Euripides and the Instruction of the Athenians.* Ann Arbor: University of Michigan Press.

Griffith, M. 1978. "Euripides' *Alkestis* 636–641." *HSCP* 82: 83–86.

———. 1995. "Brilliant Dynasts: Power and Politics in the *Oresteia.*" *CA* 14.1: 62–129.

Griffith, R. D. 1991. "Πῶς λιπόναυς γένωμαι . . . : (Aeschylus, *Agamemnon* 212)." *AJP* 112.2: 173–77.

Grube, G. M. A. 1941. *The Drama of Euripides.* London: Methuen.

Hajistephanou, C. E. 1975. *The Use of Physis and Its Cognates in Greek Tragedy with Special Reference to Character Drawing.* Cyprus: Zavallis.

Hall, E. 1989. *Inventing the Barbarian: Greek Self-Definition through Tragedy.* New York: Oxford University Press.

Halleran, M. R. 1982. "Alkestis Redux." *HSCP* 86: 51–54.

———. 1986. "Lichas' Lies and Sophoclean Innovation." *GRBS* 27.1: 239–49.

———. 1988. "Text and Ceremony at the Close of Euripides' *Alkestis.*" *Eranos* 86: 123–29.

Halliwell, S. 1990. "Traditional Greek Conceptions of Character." In Pelling 1990.

Halperin, D. M. 1990a. "The Democratic Body: Prostitution and Citizenship in Classical Athens." *differences* 2.1: 1–28.

———. 1990b. "Why Is Diotima a Woman? Platonic *Eros* and the Figuration of Gender." In D. Halperin, J. Winkler, and F. Zeitlin, eds., *Before Sexuality.* Princeton: Princeton University Press.

Hammond, N. G. L. 1961. "Land Tenure in Athens and Solon's Seisachtheia." *JHS* 81: 76–98.

———. 1965. "Personal Freedom and Its Limitations in the *Oresteia.*" *JHS* 85: 42–55.

Hanson, A. E. 1990. "The Medical Writers' Woman." In D. Halperin, J. Winkler, and F. Zeitlin, eds., *Before Sexuality.* Princeton: Princeton University Press.

Harrison, A. R. W. 1968. *The Law of Athens.* Oxford: Clarendon.

Hartigan, K. 1991. *Ambiguity and Self-Deception: The Apollo and Artemis Plays of Euripides.* New York: Peter Lang.

Hartsock, N. 1985. *Money, Sex, and Power: Toward a Feminist Historical Materialism.* Boston: Northeastern University Press.

Hasebroek, J. 1933. *Trade and Politics in Ancient Greece.* London: G. Bell and Sons.

Hayley, H. W., ed. 1898. *The Alcestis of Euripides.* Boston: Gunn and Co.

Headlam, W. G., and G. Thomson, eds. 1938. *The Oresteia of Aeschylus.* Cambridge: Cambridge University Press.

Heiden, B. 1981. "Lichas' Rhetoric of Justice in Sophocles' *Trachiniae*." *Hermes* 116: 13–23.

———. 1989. *Tragic Rhetoric: An Interpretation of Sophocles' Trachiniae.* New York: Peter Lang.

———. 1993. "Emotion, Acting, and the Athenian *ethos*." In A. Sommerstein, S. Halliwell, J. Henderson, and B. Zimmerman, eds., *Tragedy, Comedy and the Polis.* Bari: Levante Editori.

Henderson, J., ed. 1987. *Aristophanes Lysistrata.* Oxford: Clarendon.

———. 1991. "Women and the Athenian Dramatic Festivals." *TAPA* 121: 133–48.

Henrichs, A. 1980. "Human Sacrifice in Greek Religion: Three Case Studies." In *Le Sacrifice dans l'antiquité.* Geneva: Fondation Hardt.

Herman, G. 1987. *Ritualised Friendship and the Greek City.* Cambridge: Cambridge University Press.

Hester, D. A. 1980. "Deianeira's 'Deception Speech'." *Antichthon* 14: 1–8.

Hirschon, R., ed. 1984. *Woman and Property—Women as Property.* London: St. Martin's.

Hoey, T. F. 1970. "The *Trachiniae* and Unity of Hero." *Arethusa* 3.1: 1–22.

———. 1972. "Sun Symbolism in the Parodos of the *Trachiniae*." *Arethusa* 5.3: 133–54.

———. 1977. "Ambiguity in the Exodus of Sophocles' *Trachiniae*." *Arethusa* 10: 269–94.

Holoka, J. P. 1985. "The Point of the Simile in Aeschylus *Agamemnon* 241." *CP* 80: 228–29.

Holt, P. 1987. "Light in Sophokles' *Trachiniai*." *CA* 6.2: 205–17.

———. 1989. "The End of the *Trachiniai* and the Fate of Herakles." *JHS* 109: 69–80.

Hooker, J. T. 1977. "Sophocles, *Trachiniae* 112–121." *Eranos* 75.1: 71–72.

Humphreys, S. 1974. "The Nothoi of Kynosarges." *JHS* 94: 88–95.

———. 1978. *Anthropology and the Greeks.* London: Routledge.

Huston, N. 1986. "The Matrix of War: Mothers and Heroes." In S. R. Suleiman, ed., *The Female Body in Western Culture.* Cambridge, Mass.: Harvard University Press.

Irigaray, L. 1977. *This Sex Which Is Not One.* Trans. C. Porter. Ithaca, N.Y.: Cornell University Press.

Jakob, D. J. 1990. "Zu Euripides *Alkestis* 320–2." *Mnemosyne* 43: 432–34.

Jameson, F. 1981. *The Political Unconscious*. Ithaca, N.Y.: Cornell University Press.

Jebb, R. C., ed. 1892. *Sophocles, Part V: The Trachiniae*. Cambridge: Cambridge University Press.

Johnstone, S. 1994. "Virtuous Toil, Vicious Work: Xenophon on Aristocratic Style." *CP* 89.3: 219–40.

Jones, D. M. 1948. "Euripides' *Alcestis*." *CR* 62.2: 50–55.

Jones, J. [1962] 1980. *On Aristotle and Greek Tragedy*. Stanford: Stanford University Press.

Just, R. 1975. "Conceptions of Women in Classical Athens." *Journal of the Anthropological Society of Oxford* 6.1: 153–70.

———. 1989. *Women in Athenian Law and Life*. New York: Routledge.

Kamerbeek, J. C., ed. 1959. *The Plays of Sophocles*. Vol. 2. Leiden: E. J. Brill.

Kane, R. 1988. "The Structure of Sophocles' *Trachiniae*: 'Diptych' or 'Trilogy'?" *Phoenix* 43.4: 198–211.

Ketterer, R. C. 1990. "Machines for the Suppression of Time: Statues in *Suor Angelica*, *A Winter's Tale*, and *Alcestis*." *Comparative Drama* 24.1: 3–23.

Keuls, E. 1985. *The Reign of the Phallus: Sexual Politics in Ancient Athens*. New York: Harper & Row.

King, H. 1983. "Bound to Bleed: Artemis and Greek Women." In A. Cameron and A. Kuhrt, eds., *Images of Women in Antiquity*. London: Croom Helm.

Kirkwood, G. M. 1941. "The Dramatic Unity of Sophocles' *Trachiniae*." *TAPA* 72: 203–11.

———. 1954. "The Dramatic Role of the Chorus in Sophocles." *Phoenix* 8: 1–23.

Kitto, H. D. F. [1939] 1966a. *Greek Tragedy*. New York: Methuen.

———. 1966b. *Poesis: Structure and Thought*. Berkeley: University of California Press.

Klein, M. 1963. *Our Adult World and Other Essays*. New York: Basic Books.

———. 1984. *The Writings of Melanie Klein*. Vols. 1–4. New York: Free Press.

Knox, B. M. W. 1952. "The Lion in the House." *CP* 47: 17–25. [= 1979: 27–38.]

———. 1964. *The Heroic Temper*. Berkeley: University of California Press.

———. 1979. *Word and Action: Essays on the Ancient Theater*. Baltimore: The Johns Hopkins University Press.

Koniaris, G. L. 1980. "An Obscene Word in Aeschylus (I)." *AJP* 101.1: 42–44.

Konishi, H. 1989. "Agamemnon's Reasons for Yielding." *AJP* 110.2: 210–22.

Kott, J. 1973. *The Eating of the Gods*. Trans. B. Taborski. New York: Random House.

Kovacs, D. 1987. "The Way of a God with a Maid in Aeschylus' *Agamemnon*." *CP* 82.4: 326–33.

Kraay, C. M. 1964. "Hoards, Small Change and the Origin of Coinage." *JHS* 84: 76–91.

———. 1976. *Archaic and Classical Greek Coins*. Berkeley: University of California Press.

Kraay, C. M., M. Thompson, and O. Mørkholm, eds. 1973. *An Inventory of Greek Coin Hoards*. New York: American Numismatic Society.

Kraus, C. S. 1991. "λόγος μὲν ἔστ᾽ ἀρχαῖος: Stories and Story-Telling in Sophocles' *Trachiniae*." *TAPA* 121: 75–98.

Kristeva, J. 1980. "Motherhood according to Giovanni Bellini." In L. S. Roudiez, ed., *Desire in Language*, trans. T. Gora, A. Jardine, and L. Roudiez. New York: Columbia University Press.

———. 1982. *Powers of Horror: An Essay on Abjection*. Trans. L. Roudiez. New York: Columbia University Press.

———. 1989. *Black Sun: Depression and Melancholia*. Trans. L. Roudiez. New York: Columbia University Press.

Kuhn, A., and A. Wolpe. 1978. *Feminism and Materialism*. London: Routledge.

Kuhns, R. 1962. *The House, the City, and the Judge*. New York: Bobbs-Merrill.

Kurke, L. 1989. "Καπηλεία and Deceit: Theognis 59–60." *AJP* 110: 535–44.

———. 1990. "Pindar's Sixth *Pythian* and the Tradition of Advice Poetry." *TAPA* 120: 85–107.

———. 1991. *The Traffic in Praise: Pindar and the Poetics of Social Economy*. Ithaca, N.Y.: Cornell University Press.

———. 1992. "The Politics of ἁβροσύνη in Archaic Greece." *CA* 11.1: 91–120.

———. Forthcoming. "The Cultural Impact of (on) Democracy: Decentering Tragedy." In I. Morris and K. Raaflaub, eds., *Democracy 2500: Questions and Challenges*. Archaeological Institute of America Colloquium Series.

Lacan, J. 1977. *Écrits: A Selection*. Trans. A. Sheridan. New York: W. W. Norton.

———. 1982. *Feminine Sexuality*. Trans. and ed. J. Mitchell and J. Rose. New York: W. W. Norton.

———. 1988. *The Seminar of Jacques Lacan: Book II*. Ed. J.-A. Miller, trans. S. Tomaselli. New York: W. W. Norton.

Lacey, W. K. 1968. *The Family in Classical Greece*. Ithaca, N.Y.: Cornell University Press.

Laclau, E., and C. Mouffe. 1985. *Hegemony and Socialist Strategy: Towards a Radical Democratic Politics*. London: Verso.

Lawrence, S. E. 1976. "Artemis in the *Agamemnon*." *AJP* 97.2: 97–110.

———. 1978. "The Dramatic Epistemology of Sophocles' *Trachiniae*." *Phoenix* 32: 288–304.

Leacock, E. B. 1981. *Myths of Male Dominance: Collected Articles on Women Cross-Culturally*. New York: Monthly Review Press.

Lebeck, A. 1971. *The Oresteia: A Study in Language and Structure*. Washington, D.C.: The Center for Hellenic Studies.

Lefkowitz, M. 1989. "Impiety and Atheism in Euripides." *CP* 39.1: 70–82.

Lesky, A. 1925. "Alkestis: Der Mythos und das Drama." *SAWW* 203.2: 1–86.

———. 1966. "Decision and Responsibility in the Tragedy of Aeschylus." *JHS* 86: 78–85.

———. 1976. "Alkestis und Deianeira." In J. M. Bremer, S. L. Radt, C. J. Ruijgh, eds., *Miscellanea Tragica in Honorem J. C. Kamerbeek*. Amsterdam: A. Hakkert.

Lévi-Strauss, C. 1963. *Structural Anthropology*. Trans. C. Jacobsen and B. Grundfest Schoepf. New York: Basic Books.

———. 1969. *The Elementary Structures of Kinship*. Trans. J. H. Bell, J. R. von Sturmer, and R. Needham. Boston: Beacon.

Liviabella Furiani, P. 1990. "Le donne eschilee in guerra tra immaginario e realtà sociale." *Euphrosyne* 18: 9–22.

Lloyd, M. 1985. "Euripides' *Alcestis*." *G&R* 32.2: 119–31.

———. 1992. *The Agon in Euripides*. Oxford: Clarendon.

Lloyd-Jones, H. 1952. "The Robes of Iphigeneia." *CR* 2: 132–35.

———. 1962. "The Guilt of Agamemnon." *CQ*, n.s. 12: 187–99.

———. 1972. "Tycho Von Wilamowitz-Moellendorff on the Dramatic Technique of Sophocles." *CQ*, n.s. 22.2: 214–28.

———, trans. 1979. *Aeschylus: Oresteia, Agamemnon*. London: Duckworth.

———. 1983. "Artemis and Iphigeneia." *JHS* 103: 87–102.

Lloyd-Jones, H., and N. Wilson. 1990a. *Sophoclea: Studies on the Text of Sophocles*. Oxford: Oxford University Press.

———, eds. 1990b. *Sophoclis Fabulae*. Oxford: Clarendon.

Long, A. A. 1968. *Language and Thought in Sophocles*. London: Athlone.

Loraux, N. 1978. "Sur la race des femmes et quelqu'uns de ses tribus." *Arethusa* 11: 43–87. [= 1993: 72–110.]

———. 1981. "Le Lit, la guerre." *L'Homme* 21.1: 37–67. [= 1995: 23–42.]

———. 1984. "Le Fantôme de la sexualité." *La chose sexuelle, Nouvelle revue de psychanalyse* 29: 11–32. [= 1995: 194–210.]

———. 1986a. "Matrem Nudam: Quelques Versions Grecques." *Écrit du Temps* 11: 90–102.

———. 1986b. *The Invention of Athens: The Funeral Oration in the Classical City*. Trans. A. Sheridan. Cambridge, Mass.: Harvard University Press.

———. 1987. *Tragic Ways of Killing a Woman*. Trans. A. Forster. Cambridge, Mass.: Harvard University Press.

———. 1990. "Herakles: The Super-Male and the Feminine." In D. Halperin, J. Winkler, and F. Zeitlin, eds., *Before Sexuality*. Princeton: Princeton University Press. [= 1995: 116–39.]

———. 1993. *The Children of Athena*. Trans. C. Levine. Princeton: Princeton University Press.

———. 1995. *The Experiences of Tiresias: The Feminine and the Greek Man*. Trans. P. Wissing. Princeton: Princeton University Press.

Luschnig, C. A. E. 1992. "Interiors: Imaginary Spaces in *Alcestis* and *Medea*." *Mnemosyne* 45.1: 19–44.

McCall, M. 1972. "The *Trachiniae*: Structure, Focus, and Heracles." *AJP* 93: 142–63.

MacDowell, D. M. 1978. *The Law in Classical Athens*. London: Thames and Hudson.

MacKinnon, C. A. 1989. *Toward a Feminist Theory of the State*. Cambridge, Mass.: Harvard University Press.

MacKinnon, J. K. 1971. "Heracles' Intention in His Second Request of Hyllus: *Trachiniae* 1216–51." *CQ* 21: 33–41.

MacLaughlan, B. 1993. *The Age of Grace*. Princeton: Princeton University Press.

Maitland, J. 1992. "Dynasty and Family in the Athenian City State: A View from Attic Tragedy." *CQ* 42.1: 26–40.

March, J. 1990. "Euripides the Misogynist?" In A. Powell, ed., *Euripides, Women and Sexuality*. New York: Routledge.

Marcus, J. 1989. "The Asylums of Antaeus: Women, War, and Madness—Is There a Feminist Fetishism?" In H. A. Veeser, ed., *The New Historicism*. New York: Routledge.

Marx, K. 1906. *Capital*. Trans. S. Moore and E. Aveling. New York: Modern Library.

Mason, H. A. 1963. "The Women of Trachis." *Arion* 2: 59–81, 105–21.

Mastronarde, D. J. 1979. *Contact and Discontinuity*. Berkeley: UC Publications.

Maurizio, L. 1995. "Anthropology and Spirit Possession: A Reconsideration of the Pythia's Role at Delphi." *JHS* 115: 69–86.

Mauss, M. [1950] 1990. *The Gift*. Trans. W. D. Halls. New York: W. W. Norton.

Meridor, R. 1987. "*Agamemnon* 944–57: Why Does Agamemnon Give In?" *CP* 82: 38–43.

Michelini, A. 1987. *Euripides and the Tragic Tradition*. Madison: University of Wisconsin Press.

Mikalson, J. D. 1986. "Zeus the Father and Heracles the Son in Tragedy." *TAPA* 116: 89–98.

Mitchell, J. 1975. *Psychoanalysis and Feminism: Freud, Reich, Laing and Women*. New York: Vintage-Random House.

Moi, T. 1991. "Appropriating Bourdieu: Feminist Theory and Pierre Bourdieu's Sociology of Culture." *New Literary History* 22: 1017–49.

Moorhouse, A. C. 1982. *The Syntax of Sophocles*. *Mnemosyne*, Suppl. 75. Leiden: Brill.

Morris, I. 1986. "Gift and Commodity in Archaic Greece." *Man* 21.1: 1–17.

Mouffe, C. 1979. "Hegemony and Ideology in Gramsci." In *Gramsci and Marxist Theory*. London: Verso.

———. 1993. *The Return of the Political*. London: Verso.

Murnaghan, S. 1988. "How a Woman Can Be More like a Man: The Dialogue between Ischomachus and His Wife in Xenophon's *Oeconomicus*." *Helios* 15.1: 9–22.

Murray, G., ed. 1963. *Euripidis Fabulae*. Vol. 1. Oxford: Oxford University Press.

Murray, O., ed. 1990. *Sympotica: A Symposium on the Symposion*. Oxford: Clarendon.

Musurillo, H. 1967. *The Light and the Darkness: Studies in the Dramatic Poetry of Sophocles*. Leiden: Brill.

Myers, J. L. 1917. "The Plot of the *Alcestis*." *JHS* 37: 195–234.

Nagler, M. 1974. *Spontaneity and Tradition*. Berkeley: University of California Press.

Nagy, G. 1979. *The Best of the Achaeans*. Baltimore: The Johns Hopkins University Press.

Nappa, C. 1994. "*Agamemnon* 717–36: The Parable of the Lion Cub." *Mnemosyne* 47.1: 82–85.

Nielson, R. M. 1976. "Alcestis: A Paradox in Dying." *Ramus* 5.2: 92–102.

North, H. 1966. *Sophrosyne: Self-Knowledge and Self-Restraint in Greek Literature*. Ithaca, N.Y.: Cornell University Press.

Norwood, G. 1920. *Greek Tragedy*. London: Methuen.

Nussbaum, M. C. 1986. *The Fragility of Goodness*. Cambridge: Cambridge University Press.

O'Higgins, D. 1993. "Above Rubies: Admetus' Perfect Wife." *Arethusa* 26.1: 77–99.

Oakley, J. H., and R. Sinos. 1993. *The Wedding in Ancient Athens*. Madison: University of Wisconsin Press.

Ober, J. 1989. *Mass and Elite in Democratic Athens*. Princeton: Princeton University Press.

Ober, J., and B. Strauss. 1990. "Drama, Political Rhetoric, and the Discourse of Athenian Democracy." In J. J. Winkler and F. I. Zeitlin, eds., *Nothing to Do with Dionysos?* Princeton: Princeton University Press.

Ormand, K. 1993. "More Wedding Imagery: *Trachiniae* 1053ff." *Mnemosyne* 42.2: 224–27.

Padel, R. 1990. "Making Space Speak." In J. J. Winkler and F. I. Zeitlin, eds., *Nothing to Do with Dionysos?* Princeton: Princeton University Press.

———. 1992. *In and Out of the Mind: Greek Images of the Tragic Self*. Princeton: Princeton University Press.

Page, D. 1960. "J. C. Kamerbeek: The Plays of Sophocles (Review Article)." *Gnomon* 32.4: 317–19.

———, ed. 1972. *Aeschyli Septem Quae Supersunt Tragoedias*. Oxford: Clarendon.

Parker, P. 1987. *Literary Fat Ladies: Rhetoric, Gender, Property*. New York: Methuen.

Parry, H. 1986. "Aphrodite and the Furies in Sophocles' *Trachiniae*." In M.

Cropp, E. Fantham, and S. E. Scully, eds., *Greek Tragedy and Its Legacy: Essays Presented to D. J. Conacher.* Calgary: University of Calgary Press.

Patterson, C. 1986. "Hai Attikai: The Other Athenians." *Helios* 13: 49–68.

Pelling, C., ed. 1990. *Characterization and Individuality in Greek Literature.* Oxford: Clarendon.

Pembroke, S. 1967. "Women in Charge: The Functions of Alternatives in Early Greek Tradition and the Ancient Idea of Matriarchy." *Journal of the Warburg and Courtauld Institutes* 30: 1–35.

Peradotto, J. J. 1964. "Some Patterns of Nature Imagery in the *Oresteia*." *AJP* 85: 378–93.

———. 1969. "The Omen of the Eagles and the ΗΘΟΣ of Agamemnon." *Phoenix* 23.3: 237–63.

Perlman, P. 1989. "Acting the She-Bear for Artemis." *Arethusa* 22.2: 111–34.

Pickard-Cambridge, A. W. 1946. *The Theatre of Dionysus in Athens.* Oxford: Clarendon.

Podlecki, A. J. 1972. "The Aeschylean Chorus as Dramatic Persona." In *Studi Classici in honore di Quintino Cataudella*, vol. 1. Catania: Università di Catania.

———. 1986. "Polis and Monarch in Early Attic Tragedy." In P. Euben, ed., *Greek Tragedy and Political Theory.* Berkeley: University of California Press.

———. 1990. "Could Women Attend the Theater in Ancient Athens?" *Ancient World* 21.1–2: 45–63.

———. 1993. "Κατ' ἀρχῆς γὰρ φιλαίτιος λεώς: The Concept of Leadership in Aeschylus." In A. Sommerstein, S. Halliwell, J. Henderson, and B. Zimmerman, eds., *Tragedy, Comedy and the Polis.* Bari: Levante Editori.

Poe, E. A. 1967. *Selected Writings.* London: Penguin.

Polanyi, K. 1968. *Primitive, Archaic, and Modern Economies.* New York: Doubleday.

Poliakoff, M. 1980. "The Third Fall in the *Oresteia*." *AJP* 101.3: 251–59.

———. 1982. "Euripides' *Alkestis* 1029–1032." *Mnemosyne* 35: 141–43.

———. 1987. *Combat Sports in the Ancient World.* New Haven, Conn.: Yale University Press.

Pomeroy, S. B. 1975. *Goddesses, Whores, Wives and Slaves: Women in Classical Antiquity.* New York: Dorset.

———, ed. 1991. *Women's History and Ancient History.* Chapel Hill: University of North Carolina Press.

Poole, W. 1990. "Male Homosexuality in Euripides." In A. Powell, ed., *Euripides, Women and Sexuality.* New York: Routledge.

Pope, M. 1986. "The Democratic Character of Aeschylus' *Agamemnon*." In M. Cropp, E. Fantham, and S. E. Scully, eds., *Greek Tragedy and Its Legacy: Essays Presented to D. J. Conacher.* Calgary: University of Calgary Press.

Pozzi, D. 1994. "Deianeira's Robe: Diction in Sophocles' *Trachiniae*." *Mnemosyne* 47.5: 577–85.

Prag, A. J. N. W. 1985. *The Oresteia: Iconographic and Narrative Tradition*. Chicago: Bolchazy-Carducci.

Rabinowitz, N. S. 1981. "From Force to Persuasion: Aeschylus' *Oresteia* as Cosmogonic Myth." *Ramus* 10.2: 159–91.

———. 1986. "Aphrodite and the Audience: Engendering the Reader." *Arethusa* 19.2: 171–85.

———. 1992. "Tragedy and the Politics of Containment." In A. Richlin, ed., *Pornography and Representation in Greece and Rome*. Oxford: Oxford University Press.

———. 1993. *Anxiety Veiled: Euripides and the Traffic in Women*. Ithaca, N.Y.: Cornell University Press.

Redfield, J. M. 1975. *Nature and Culture in the Iliad*. Chicago: University of Chicago Press.

———. 1982. "Notes on the Greek Wedding." *Arethusa* 15.1.2: 181–201.

Rehm, R. 1994. *Marriage to Death*. Princeton: Princeton University Press.

Reinhardt, K. [1947] 1979. *Sophocles*. Trans. A. and D. Harvey. Oxford: Basil Blackwell.

Renehan, R. 1985. "Review Article: A New Commentary on Euripides." *CP* 80.2: 143–75.

Richlin, A. 1983. *The Garden of Priapus: Sexuality and Aggression in Roman Humor*. New Haven, Conn.: Yale University Press.

Richter, D. 1971. "The Position of Women in Classical Athens." *CJ* 67: 1–8.

Riemer, P. 1989. *Die Alkestis des Euripides*. Frankfurt: Athenäum.

Ronnet, G. 1969. *Sophocle: Poète Tragique*. Paris: Éditions E. de Boccard.

Rose, P. W. 1992. *Sons of the Gods, Children of Earth: Ideology and Literary Form in Ancient Greece*. Ithaca, N.Y.: Cornell University Press.

Rosenbloom, D. 1995. "Myth, History, and Hegemony in Aeschylus." In B. Goff, ed., *History, Tragedy, Theory: Dialogues on Athenian Drama*. Austin: University of Texas Press.

Rosenmeyer, T. G. 1963. *The Masks of Tragedy*. Austin: University of Texas Press.

———. 1982. *The Art of Aeschylus*. Berkeley: University of California Press.

Roth, P. 1993. "The Theme of Corrupted *Xenia* in Aeschylus' *Oresteia*." *Mnemosyne* 46.1: 1–17.

Rousseau, J.-J. 1960. *Politics and the Arts: Letter to M. D'Alembert on the Theatre*. Trans. A. Bloom. Glencoe, Ill.: Free Press.

Roussel, D. 1976. *Tribu et Cité*. Paris: Annales Littéraires de l'Université de Besançon.

Rubin, G. 1975. "The Traffic in Women: Notes on the 'Political Economy' of Sex." In R. Reiter, ed., *Toward an Anthropology of Women*. New York: Monthly Review.

Ryzman, M. 1991. "Deianeira's Moral Behaviour in the Context of the Natural Laws in Sophocles' 'Trachiniae'." *Hermes* 119.4: 385–98.

———. 1993. "Heracles' Destructive Impulses: A Transgression of Natural Laws." *Revue Belge de philologie et d'histoire*. 71.1: 69–79.

Schaps, D. M. 1979. *Economic Rights of Women in Ancient Greece*. Edinburgh: Edinburgh University Press.

Schein, S. 1982. "The Cassandra Scene in Aeschylus' *Agamemnon*." *G&R* 29: 11–16.

———. 1988. "Φιλία in Euripides' *Alcestis*." *Métis* 3: 179–206.

Schwinge, E. R. 1962. *Die Stellung des Trachinierinnen im Werk des Sophokles*. Göttigen: Vandenhoeck and Ruprecht.

Scodel, R. 1979. "'Αδμήτου λόγος and the *Alcestis*." *HSCP* 83: 51–62.

Scully, S. E. 1986. "Some Issues in the Second Episode of Euripides' *Alcestis*." In M. Cropp, E. Fantham, and S. E. Scully, eds., *Greek Tragedy and Its Legacy: Essays Presented to D. J. Conacher*. Calgary: University of Calgary Press.

Seaford, R. 1981. "Dionysiac Drama and Dionysiac Mysteries." *CQ* 31: 252–75.

———. 1986. "Wedding, Ritual, and Textual Criticism in Sophocles' 'Women of Trachis'." *Hermes* 114.1: 50–58.

———. 1987. "The Tragic Wedding." *JHS* 72: 106–30.

———. 1990. "The Structural Problems of Marriage in Euripides." In A. Powell, ed., *Euripides, Women and Sexuality*. New York: Routledge.

———. 1994. *Reciprocity and Ritual: Homer and Tragedy in the Developing City-State*. Oxford: Clarendon.

Seale, D. 1982. *Vision and Stagecraft in Sophocles*. London: Croom Helm.

Sealey, R. 1990. *Women and Law in Classical Greece*. Chapel Hill: University of North Carolina Press.

Sedgwick, E. K. 1985. *Between Men: English Literature and Male Homosocial Desire*. New York: Columbia University Press.

Segal, C. 1975. "Mariage et sacrifice dans les *Trachiniennes* de Sophocle." *AC* 44: 30–53.

———. 1977. "Sophocles' *Trachiniae*: Myth, Poetry and Heroic Values." *YCS* 25: 99–158.

———. 1981. *Tragedy and Civilization: An Interpretation of Sophocles*. Cambridge, Mass.: Harvard University Press.

———. 1982. *Dionysiac Poetics and Euripides' Bacchae*. Princeton: Princeton University Press.

———. 1986. *Interpreting Greek Tragedy*. Ithaca, N.Y.: Cornell University Press.

———. 1992. "Euripides' *Alcestis*: Female Death and Male Tears." *CA* 11.1: 142–58.

———. 1993. *Euripides and the Poetics of Sorrow*. Durham, N.C.: Duke University Press.

Seidensticker, B. 1995. "Women on the Tragic Stage." In B. Goff, ed., *History, Tragedy, Theory: Dialogues on Athenian Drama*. Austin: University of Texas Press.

Silverman, K. 1983. *The Subject of Semiotics*. Oxford: Oxford University Press.

———. 1988. *The Acoustic Mirror: The Female Voice in Psychoanalysis and Cinema*. Bloomington: Indiana University Press.

———. 1992. *Male Subjectivity at the Margins*. New York: Routledge.

Simpson, M. 1971. "Why Does Agamemnon Yield?" *La Parola del Passato* 26: 94–101.

Sissa, G. 1990a. "Maidenhood without Maidenhead: The Female Body in Ancient Greece." In D. Halperin, J. Winkler, and F. Zeitlin, eds., *Before Sexuality*. Princeton: Princeton University Press.

———. 1990b. *Greek Virginity*. Trans. A. Goldhammer. Cambridge, Mass.: Harvard University Press.

Skutch, O. 1987. "Helen: Her Name and Nature." *JHS* 107: 188–92.

Slater, K. F. 1976. "Some Suggestions for Staging the *Trachiniae*." *Arion* 3.1: 57–68.

Slater, P. R. 1968. *The Glory of Hera: Greek Mythology and the Greek Family*. Boston: Beacon.

Smith, G. 1982. "The *Alcestis* of Euripides: An Interpretation." *RFIC* 111: 129–44.

Smith, P. 1988. *Discerning the Subject*. Minneapolis: University of Minnesota Press.

Smith, P. M. 1980. *On the Hymn to Zeus in Aeschylus' Agamemnon*. APA American Classical Studies 5. Chico, Calif.: Scholars Press.

Smith, W. D. 1960. "The Ironic Structure in *Alcestis*." *Phoenix* 14.3: 127–45.

Snell, B. 1953. *The Discovery of the Mind*. Trans. T. G. Rosenmeyer. Oxford: Basil Blackwell.

Solmsen, F. 1985. "ἀλλ' εἰδέναι χρὴ δρῶσαν: The Meaning of Sophocles' *Trachiniai* 588–93." *AJP* 106.4: 490–96.

Sommerstein, A. 1980. "Artemis in *Agamemnon*: A Postscript." *AJP* 101.1: 165–70.

Sorum, C. E. 1978. "Monsters and the Family: The Exodos of Sophocles' *Trachiniae*." *GRBS* 19: 59–74.

Sourvinou, C. 1971. "Aristophanes' *Lysistrata* 645." *CQ* 21: 341.

Spivak, G. 1988. "Can the Subaltern Speak?" In C. Nelson and L. Grossberg, eds., *Marxism and the Interpretation of Culture*. Urbana: University of Illinois Press.

Stanton, G. R. 1990. "Φιλία and Ξενία in Euripides' *Alkestis*." *Hermes* 118.1: 42–54.

Starr, C. G. 1970. *Athenian Coinage*. Oxford: Clarendon.

Stinton, T. C. W. 1975. "*Hamartia* in Aristotle and Greek Tragedy." *CQ* 25: 221–54.

———. 1976. "Iphigeneia and the Bears of Brauron." *CQ* 26: 11.

Strathern, M. 1988. *The Gender of the Gift: Problems with Women and Problems with Society in Melanesia*. Berkeley: University of California Press.

Strauss, B. 1993. *Fathers and Sons in Athens: Ideology and Society in the Era of the Peloponnesian War*. Princeton: Princeton University Press.

Suzuki, M. 1989. *Metamorphoses of Helen: Authority, Difference, and the Epic*. Ithaca, N.Y.: Cornell University Press.

Taplin, O. 1972. "Aeschylean Silences and Silences in Aeschylus." *HSCP* 76: 57–98.

———. 1977. *The Stagecraft of Aeschylus*. Oxford: Clarendon.

Thalmann, W. G. 1985. "Speech and Silence in the *Oresteia* 2." *Phoenix* 39.3: 221–37.

———. 1993. "Euripides and Aeschylus: The Case of the *Hekabe*." *CA* 12.1: 126–59.

Thomson, G. 1966. *Aeschylus and Athens*. London: Lawrence and Wishart.

Thury, E. 1988. "Euripides' *Alcestis* and the Athenian Generation Gap." *Arethusa* 21.2: 197–214.

Trammell, E. 1968. "The Mute Alcestis." In J. R. Wilson, ed., *Twentieth-Century Interpretations of Euripides' Alcestis*. Englewood Cliffs, N.J.: Prentice-Hall.

Tyrrell, W. B. 1980. "An Obscene Word in Aeschylus (II)." *AJP* 101.1: 44–46.

Vellacott, P. 1975. *Ironic Drama*. Cambridge: Cambridge University Press.

Vermeule, E. 1979. *Aspects of Death in Early Greek Art and Poetry*. Berkeley: University of California Press.

Vernant, J.-P. 1980. *Myth and Society in Ancient Greece*. Trans. J. Lloyd. New York: Zone.

———. 1981. "The Myth of Prometheus in Hesiod." In R. L. Gordon, ed., *Myth, Religion, and Society*. Cambridge: Cambridge University Press.

———. 1982. *The Origins of Greek Thought*. Ithaca, N.Y.: Cornell University Press.

———. 1983a. "The Representation of the Invisible and the Psychological Category of the Double: The Colossos." In *Myth and Thought among the Greeks*. London: Routledge.

———. 1983b. "Hestia-Hermes: The Religious Expression of Space and Movement in Ancient Greece." In *Myth and Thought among the Greeks*. London: Routledge.

———. 1988. "The Tragic Subject: Historicity and Transhistoricity." In Vernant and Vidal-Naquet 1988.

———. 1991. *Mortals and Immortals*. Ed. F. I. Zeitlin. Princeton: Princeton University Press.

Vernant, J.-P., and P. Vidal-Naquet. 1988. *Myth and Tragedy in Ancient Greece*. Trans. J. Lloyd. New York: Zone.

Verrall, A. W. 1913. *Euripides the Rationalist*. Cambridge: Cambridge University Press.

Vickers, B. 1973. *Towards Greek Tragedy: Drama, Myth, Society*. London: Longman.

Vidal-Naquet, P. 1981. "Slavery and the Rule of Women in Tradition, Myth and

Utopia." In R. L. Gordon, ed., *Myth, Religion, and Society*. Cambridge: Cambridge University Press.

Von Fritz, K. 1962. "Euripides *Alkestis* und ihre modernen Nachahmer und Kritiker." In *Antike und moderne Tragödie, neun Abhandlungen*. Berlin: De Gruyter.

Wade-Gery, H. T. 1931. "Eupatridai, Archons and Areopagus." *CQ* 25: 1–11.

Waldock, A. J. A. 1966. *Sophocles the Dramatist*. Cambridge: Cambridge University Press.

Walters, K. R. 1983. "Perikles' Citizenship Law." *CA* 2.2: 314–36.

Webster, T. B. L. 1936a. *An Introduction to Sophocles*. Oxford: Clarendon.

———. 1936b. "Sophocles' *Trachiniae*." In C. Bailey, E. A. Barber, C. M. Bowra, J. D. Denniston, and D. L. Page, eds., *Greek Poetry and Life*. Oxford: Clarendon.

———. 1967. *The Tragedies of Euripides*. London: Methuen.

Weglage, M. 1991. "Leid und Erkenntnis: Zum Zeus-Hymnus im aischyleischen *Agamemnon*." *Hermes* 19.3: 265–81.

Weiner, A. B. 1976. *Women of Value, Men of Renown: New Perspectives in Trobriand Exchange*. Austin: University of Texas Press.

Wender, D. 1974. "The Will of the Beast: Sexual Imagery in the *Trachiniae*." *Ramus* 3.1: 1–17.

West, J. 1978. "Women, Sex and Class." In A. Kuhn and A. Wolpe, eds., *Feminism and Materialism*. London: Routledge.

West, M. L. 1981. "Sophoclis Tragoediae. Tom. 2. Ed. Dawe." *Gnomon* 53: 522–28.

———. 1990. *Studies in Aeschylus*. Stuttgart: Teubner.

Wet, B. X. de. 1983. "An Evaluation of the *Trachiniae* of Sophokles in the Light of Moral Values in Athens of the Fifth Century B.C." *Dionisio* 9: 213–26.

Whitehead, D. 1983. "Competitive Outlay and Community Profit: Φιλοτιμία in Democratic Athens." *C&M* 34: 55–74.

Whitman, C. H. 1951. *Sophocles: A Study in Heroic Humanism*. Cambridge, Mass.: Harvard University Press.

Wiersma, S. 1984. "Women in Sophocles." *Mnemosyne* 37: 25–55.

Wilamowitz, U. von. 1927. "Lesefrüchte." *Hermes* 62: 287–88.

Wilamowitz-Moellendorff, T. von. 1917. *Die Dramatische Technik des Sophokles*. *Philologische Untersuchungen* 22. Berlin: Weidmann.

Wilkins, J. 1990. "The State and the Individual: Euripides' Plays of Voluntary Self-Sacrifice." In A. Powell, ed., *Euripides, Women and Sexuality*. New York: Routledge.

Wilson, J. R., ed. 1968. *Twentieth-Century Interpretations of Euripides' Alcestis*. Englewood Cliffs, N.J.: Prentice-Hall.

Winkler, J. 1990a. "The Ephebes' Song: *Tragōidia* and *Polis*." In J. J. Winkler and F. I. Zeitlin, eds., *Nothing to Do with Dionysos?* Princeton: Princeton University Press.

——. 1990b. "Phallos Politikos: Representing the Body Politic in Athens." *differences* 2.1: 29–45.

——. 1990c. *The Constraints of Desire*. New York: Routledge.

Winnicott, D. W. 1971. *Playing and Reality*. New York: Routledge.

Winnington-Ingram, R. P. 1980. *Sophocles: An Interpretation*. Cambridge: Cambridge University Press.

——. 1983. *Studies in Aeschylus*. Cambridge: Cambridge University Press.

Wohl, V. J. 1993. "Standing by the *Stathmos*: Sexual Ideology in the *Odyssey*." *Arethusa* 26.1: 19–50.

——. 1996. "εὐσεβείας ἕνεκα καὶ φιλοτιμίας: Hegemony and Democracy at the Panathenaia." *C&M* 47: 25–88.

Young, K., C. Wolkowitz, and R. McCullagh, eds. 1981. *Of Marriage and the Market*. London: CSE Books.

Zeitlin, F. I. 1965. "The Motif of the Corrupted Sacrifice in Aeschylus' *Oresteia*." *TAPA* 96: 463–508.

——. 1981. "Travesties of Gender and Genre in Aristophanes' *Thesmophoriazousae*." In Foley 1981a. [= 1996: 375–416.]

——. 1982. "Cultic Models of the Female: Rites of Dionysus and Demeter." *Arethusa* 15: 129–58.

——. 1984. "The Dynamics of Misogyny: Myth and Mythmaking in the *Oresteia*." In J. Peradotto and J. P. Sullivan, eds., *Women in the Ancient World: The Arethusa Papers*. Albany: State University of New York Press. [= 1996: 87–119.]

——. 1985. "The Power of Aphrodite: Eros and the Boundaries of the Self in the *Hippolytus*." In P. Burian, ed., *Directions in Euripidean Criticism*. Durham, N.C.: Duke University Press. [= 1996: 219–84.]

——. 1990. "Playing the Other: Theater, Theatricality, and the Feminine in Greek Drama." In J. J. Winkler and F. I. Zeitlin, eds., *Nothing to Do with Dionysos?* Princeton: Princeton University Press. [= 1996: 341–74.]

——. 1994. "Review Article: N. S. Rabinowitz *Anxiety Veiled: Euripides and the Traffic in Women*." *BMCR* 5.6: 544–52.

——. 1996. *Playing the Other: Gender and Society in Classical Greek Literature*. Chicago: University of Chicago Press.

Zielinski, T. 1896. "Excurse zu den Trachinierinnen." *Philologus* 55: 491–540, 577–633.

Žižek, S. 1989. *The Sublime Object of Ideology*. New York: Verso.

Index

General Index

Specific works are given under the author's name; line numbers appear in italics. Passages from the three plays studied in the book are given in the *Index Locorum*, which follows.

Achelous, 6, 18, 19, 22, 32, 49, 54
Admētou logos, 149–150
Admetus, 121, 171–172; and Alcestis, 123–127, 128, 130, 138–144, 152–154, 168, 171, 174, 180; *anagnōrisis* of, 146, 157–158; and Apollo, 134–135, 157, 162; as aristocrat, 133, 159–163, 172–173; feminized, 139–141; and Heracles, 127–128, 157, 164–170, 173–174, 179, 261n.64; and Pheres, 135–136, 155–156, 160–161, 164, 167, 169, 170; as tragic hero, 146–150
Aegisthus, 103, 104, 116, 236n.12, 236n.13
Aeschylus, 68, 69, 70, 78, 85, 92, 103; *Eumenides 736–738*, 80; *Proteus*, 226n.117, 229n.4; *Septem 592*, 43
agalma, 25–27, 59, 61–63, 65–67, 69, 97; *agalma ploutou*, 86, 87,

90, 91, 155, 213n.7, 225n.113, 229n.5; Alcestis as, 156, 158; and aristocracy, 25, 61–63, 65, 81–82, 87–91, 104–105, 160; disenchantment of, 26–27, 86–89, 163; *domōn agalma*, 67, 68, 70, 71, 78, 81, 82, 86, 95; and gift exchange, 25, 61–62; Helen as, 83–85, 86, 95; Iphigeneia as, 67–68, 70–71, 78, 79, 81–82, 86; and *ploutos*, 83–84, 86–91, 96, 104–105, 111; women as, 25, 65–67
Agamemnon: as aristocrat, 86–90, 104–105; and Cassandra, 111–113, 114, 116; as commander, 70, 103–105; death of, 83, 97, 99, 107–110, 114; and Iphigeneia, 68, 74–82, 107
Agamemnon, xvi, 8, 25, 122, 133–134, 142, 146, 151, 171, 173; aristocracy in, 65, 81–82, 87–91, 104–105, 163, 235n.11; com-

Index Locorum

This index lists only passages from the three plays studied in the book. Line numbers appear in italics. References to other ancient texts are given in the general index under the author's name.

Printed and bound by CPI Group (UK) Ltd, Croydon, CR0 4YY

09/06/2025

14685838-0004